Diversity Education in the MENA Region

Hassan Abouabdelkader • Barry Tomalin
Editors

Diversity Education in the MENA Region

Bridging the Gaps in Language Learning

Editors
Hassan Abouabdelkader ⓘ
Ecole Nationales Supérieure d'Arts et Métiers
Moulay Ismail University
Meknes, Morocco

Barry Tomalin
Glasgow Caledonian University London
London, UK

ISBN 978-3-031-42692-6   ISBN 978-3-031-42693-3   (eBook)
https://doi.org/10.1007/978-3-031-42693-3

© The Editor(s) (if applicable) and The Author(s), under exclusive licence to Springer Nature Switzerland AG 2023
This work is subject to copyright. All rights are solely and exclusively licensed by the Publisher, whether the whole or part of the material is concerned, specifically the rights of translation, reprinting, reuse of illustrations, recitation, broadcasting, reproduction on microfilms or in any other physical way, and transmission or information storage and retrieval, electronic adaptation, computer software, or by similar or dissimilar methodology now known or hereafter developed.
The use of general descriptive names, registered names, trademarks, service marks, etc. in this publication does not imply, even in the absence of a specific statement, that such names are exempt from the relevant protective laws and regulations and therefore free for general use.
The publisher, the authors, and the editors are safe to assume that the advice and information in this book are believed to be true and accurate at the date of publication. Neither the publisher nor the authors or the editors give a warranty, expressed or implied, with respect to the material contained herein or for any errors or omissions that may have been made. The publisher remains neutral with regard to jurisdictional claims in published maps and institutional affiliations.

This Palgrave Macmillan imprint is published by the registered company Springer Nature Switzerland AG.
The registered company address is: Gewerbestrasse 11, 6330 Cham, Switzerland

Paper in this product is recyclable.

Foreword

The wrangle of seventy-two sects, establish excuse for all
When truth, they saw not, the door of fable they beat (Hafiz)

This couplet, specially its first hemstitch, from Hafiz, a renowned Iranian poet, implies that different cultures baselessly and futilely fight because they cannot fathom the truth that there are so many men, so many minds. This call for peace and tolerance has been a recurrent theme throughout the history among the thinkers in different cultures to the extent that different figures such as John Lennon's "Imagine" song yearned for it.

Apart from these utopian calls, education systems can basically encounter diversity in three different ways including nativism, assimilationism, and pluralism. Nativism xenophobically considers difference foreign or even hostile, and assimilationism does not tolerate collective difference, unless it is melted in dominant culture, but pluralism endeavors to respect difference as a necessary condition for equality and prosperity just as a salad bowl requires its different ingredients to taste delectable. Today neither the nativist nor the assimilationist philosophies can provide an answer for society and the education system because they are, by and large, inconsistent with human rights such as freedom and dignity, the volume of migration and demographic dynamics, and structural inclusion. They can also pose threats to cohesion, social capital, citizenship, science, and economy. Therefore, there is a need to move from assimilationism toward informed pluralism. The patchwork culture, marked with legitimization of specificity and its interaction (not integration) with other cultures, is generally a strength because, on the one hand, it can increase wellbeing, mental health, creative thinking, productivity, economic development, tolerance, understanding of one's culture of origin, and civility, and on the other hand, it can decrease social categorization, anxiety, conflict, polarization, and bias (Kim & Pierce, 2015; Montalvo & Reynal-Querol, 2014).

This need for pluralism incentivized many movements in educational research emerging in the form of fairness issues in argument-based approaches to validity, intercultural pragmatics, and culturally responsive pedagogy. However, the call for diversity and inclusion by any name, be it multicultural education or culturally responsive education, has not been sufficiently embraced yet by the stakeholders probably because humans are born ethnocentric, and education systems, which are responsible for developing humans, either were not concerned with diversity due to entrenched nativist or assimilationist philosophies or were scourged by a lack of support, determination, and evidence, if pluralistic. Banks' (2016, p. 3) argument that "multiculturalism could not have failed in Germany and the United Kingdom because it has never been effectively implemented in policy or practice" is a piece of evidence for the fact that diversity education has a precarious status even in the European countries.

When it comes to the Middle East and North Africa (MENA) and English language teaching, the situation gets even worse because they are largely imbued with infrastructural, political, ideological, and civil problems. No need to mention that the states in this region might not generally be considered true democracies in the western sense, and thus, it is apparent that democratic values including diversity education might not be as endorsed as they are in the western countries. This timely title not only showcases different interesting examples of negligence to multicultural education in the region but also troubleshoots the culprits in the light of factors including curriculum, learners, teachers, policy, ideology, and context.

As illustrated in this volume, English language education in the region is generally culture centric and politically motivated in different senses ranging from nativism to indifference. Educational policies in some countries, including Iran and Afghanistan, as conceived of in the light of essentialist renderings of Edward Said's orientalism, are ethnocentric, and thus unduly view English language teaching as "westoxification"—a Western cultural attack. However, as Barry Tomalin stated, quoting David Crystal, today English is no longer the language of the West because its non-native speakers outnumber the native ones. Some countries view it as a neutral transmissionist phenomenon, better called a "petri dish at the service of mechanical imparting of linguistic competence to students" (Salmani Nodoushan, 2023, p. 97), void of cultural shade, wherein learners are oppressed because they are viewed as passive containers. In fact, some countries and, in turn, teachers consider English language teaching Tyrannosaurus rex and some a lingua franca (Hyland, 2006). However, according to Salmani Nodoushan (2023), the language classroom, as a society in interaction with the macro society, should be a "free milieu, where both the teacher and the students bring their affordances, aspirations, and free will to bear on both language learning and social development" (p. 109). Most of the chapters in this title serve this cause and through empirical research shed light on the gamers involved, such as the top-down and bottom-up factors.

Effective implementation of multicultural education hinges upon top-down and bottom-up policies. In this title, it is shown, consistent to Banks (2016), that top-down transformations such as curricular redressing and bottom-up measures including teacher training are two wings of a bird. This title using empirical examples from the MENA region reifies Richard's (2017) conception that the organizational curriculum (i.e., developed by the authorities) and the enacted curriculum (customized by the teachers) can interplay and culminate in an emergent curriculum, where learning as a form of sociocultural development is shaped. The insights offered in this title overall suggest teachers are at the heart of any educational endeavor including diversity education, and their identity is manifold and complex. In this regard, this book can also contribute to the call of Barkhuizen (2017) for more research into language teacher identity.

This book in nicely put discussions introduces cooperative learning or its less structured counterpart, that is, collaborative learning, as an effective means for the implementation of diversity education. There is no need to mention that this book is among a few titles, if not the first one, which taps into the importance of cooperative learning for diversity education in English language teaching in the region. This book not only credibly reflects the current status of knowledge about the merits and functions of cooperative learning in peace building and culturally responsive pedagogy (See, Ferguson-Patrick, 2020, 2022; Hertz-Lazarowitz, 1999; Johnson & Johnson, 2014), but also is an admirable attempt to bridge the gap between theory and practice. This book has an advantage over some others because it draws upon the research evidence about the classroom use of cooperative learning (e.g., Tamimy et al., 2023) and honestly notes that the benefits of cooperative learning cannot be reaped unless they are effectively used. A word of caution is due here because cooperative learning, notwithstanding its suitability for diversity education, might not itself be by default consistent with the culture of some countries, specifically if they are considered too conservative and unassertive (see, Tamimy, 2019). Yet, it does not mean that eyes should be shut to its affordances; rather, it should be implemented with some modifications (Inns & Slavin, 2018).

Overall, the MENA region, despite its high cultural volatility arising due to the transition from traditionalism to modernism, not to mention post-modernism, and economic and political imperatives for global cooperation, is unfortunately still grappling with the rudimentary implementation of diversity education or even admitting the urgency for it, let alone its effective implementation. This is at odds with development visions many countries might have envisaged for themselves and democratic values such as peace and equality. This inattention will sooner or later show itself as social problems or even crises, which are better prevented than cured. This title, in accord with Banks (2016), depicts that the journey toward equity, diversity, and inclusion cannot be reduced to curriculum reforms, if reform at all, but also requires decent attention to intertwined players such as school culture, equitable pedagogy, prejudice reduction, and the knowledge construction process. Besides presenting the international reader with a less blurred image of the region, this book opens the black box of the complexity of English language teaching in this resource-rich part of the world so that researchers can find many interesting topics for their inquiries.

Shiraz University Mohammad Tamimy
Shiraz, Iran

References

Banks, J. A. (2016). *Cultural diversity and education: Foundations, curriculum, and teaching* (6th ed.). Routledge.

Barkhuizen, G. P. (2017). Language teacher identity research: An introduction. In G. P. Barkhuizen (Ed.), *Reflections on language teacher identity research* (pp. viii–278). Routledge.

Ferguson-Patrick, K. (2020). Cooperative learning in Swedish classrooms: Engagement and relationships as a focus for culturally diverse students. *Education Sciences, 10*(11), Article 312. https://doi.org/10.3390/educsci10110312

Ferguson-Patrick, K. (2022). Developing a democratic classroom and a democracy stance: Cooperative learning case studies from England and Sweden. *Education 3-13, 50*(3), 389–403. https://doi.org/10.1080/03004279.2020.1853195

Hertz-Lazarowitz, R. (1999). Cooperative learning in Israels Jewish and Arab schools: A community approach. *Theory Into Practice, 38*(2), 105–113. https://doi.org/10.1080/00405849909543840

Hyland, K. (2006). *English for academic purposes: An advanced resource book*. Routledge.

Inns, A. J., & Slavin, R. E. (2018). Cooperative learning: Theoretical foundations and relevance across cultures. In G. A. D. Liem & D. M. McInerney (Eds.), *Big theories revisited 2* (pp. 237–268). Information Age Publishing.

Johnson, D. W., & Johnson, R. T. (2014). Cooperative learning in 21st century. *Anales De Psicologia, 30*(3), 841–851. https://doi.org/10.6018/analesps.30.3.201241

Kim, K.-H., & Pierce, R. A. (2015). Cultural pluralism. In S. Thompson (Ed.), *Encyclopedia of diversity and social justice* (pp. 191–194). Rowman & Littlefield.

Montalvo, J. G., & Reynal-Querol, M. (2014). Cultural diversity, conflict, and economic development. In V. A. Ginsburgh & D. Throsby (Eds.), *Handbook of the economics of art and culture* (Vol. 2, pp. 485–506). Elsevier. https://doi.org/10.1016/B978-0-444-53776-8.00018-0

Richards, J. C. (2017). *Curriculum development in language teaching* (2nd ed.). Cambridge University Press.

Salmani Nodoushan, M. A. (2023). EFL classroom, petri dish, panopticon, and free world: How do they merge through action research? *International Journal of Language Studies, 17*(1), 97–116.

Tamimy, M. (2019). The cultural attitudes towards cooperative learning: What proverbs can offer. *Journal of Intercultural Communication Research, 48*(4), 416–434. https://doi.org/10.1080/17475759.2019.1639536

Tamimy, M., Rashidi, N., & Koh, J. H. L. (2023). The use of cooperative learning in English as foreign language classes: The prevalence, fidelity, and challenges. *Teaching and Teacher Education, 121*, Article 103915. https://doi.org/10.1016/j.tate.2022.103915

Contents

1 The Challenge of Diversity Education: Defending the Devil or Adjusting the Clock? 1
Hassan Abouabdelkader

Part I Diversity Management Education and Language Learning 11

2 Diversity in Tertiary Language Education 13
Barry Tomalin

3 Representation, Engagement, and Expression in Moroccan Higher Education Curricula: Focus on Reading Comprehension 27
Soufiane Abouabdelkader

4 Encouraging Diversity and Student Engagement in the Classroom 63
Deborah Swallow

Part II The Impact of Diversity Education, Equity, and
         Inclusion on Language Learning   75

5 Towards the Construction of a Diversity Education
   Landscape in Moroccan Higher Education Language
   Curricula   77
   Hassan Abouabdelkader

6 Sustainable Policies and Strategies in the MENA Region
   for Teaching English as a Foreign Language   99
   María Sagrario Salaberri-Ramiro and Abderrazak Zaafour

7 Diversity of ELT in Omani Higher Education   121
   Fawziya Al Zadjali and Sharita Viola Furtado

Part III Language Education Curricula, Inclusion, and
          Social Mobility in MENA   147

8 Linguistic Diversity in Education: The Case of Israel   149
   Anat Stavans

9 Students' and Teachers' Perceptions of Diversity
   Education in Moroccan Higher Education Language
   Curricula: A Case Study   179
   Soufiane Abouabdelkader and Mouhssine Ayouri

10 How Culturally Diverse Is the Virtual Space? Towards
    Inclusive Pedagogy: A Case Study at the Arab Open
    University   203
    Chahra Beloufa

Part IV Diversity Education and Intercultural Communication Issues in Language Learning in the MENA Region   229

11 The Mediatization of Education: Classroom Mediation as an Agent of Change in Middle Eastern Higher Education Systems   231
Hussein AlAhmad and Elias Kukali

12 When Inequalities Are Reversed: Algeria's Gender Inequity in Education   257
Wafaa Taleb

Part V Sustainability: Student Potential and Communication Ability in the Balance   291

13 Diversity and Inclusivity in Tertiary Language Education—The Case of Turkey—Turkiye   293
Ozlem Yuges

14 Understanding and Maximizing Diversity Education in the MENA Region   313
Mohamed Chtatou

15 Conclusion: The Way Forward   363
Hassan Abouabdelkader and Barry Tomalin

Index   371

Notes on Contributors

Hassan Abouabdelkader is Professor of Education, researcher, and educational consultant. He graduated from the faculty of Education, Mohammed V University, Rabat, Morocco and the Institute of Education, University of London, UK. His professional experience in librarianship and language teaching both, respectively, at the British Council, Rabat, and Moulay Ismail University, earned him large insights into the fields of research methods and Applied Linguistics.Abouabdelkader has also worked as teacher trainer for 20 years at the Ecole Normale Supérieure, Meknes, Morocco, before joining the ENSAM, Moulay Ismail University, where he worked as Professor of English and coordinator of the Communication Department. During this time, he supervised several doctoral dissertations and contributed to different educational reform commissions in Morocco.His academic works include his participation in several international conferences and seminars in the United States, Canada and several European countries. He has largely published in the field of education and English language teaching, EFL writing teaching and assessment. His major works include *Teaching EFL Writing in the 21st Century Arab World* (H. Abouabdelkader and Abdelhamid Ahmed, Edits, 2016), Palgrave Macmillan; *Assessing EFL Writing in the 21st Century Arab World* (Abdelhamid, A. and Abouabdelkader, H., Edits, 2018); *Teaching EFL Writing in the 21st Century Arab World: Realities and Challenges*, Macmillan Palgrave.

Soufiane Abouabdelkader, PhD, is an assistant lecturer at Chouaib Doukkali University, El Jadida, Morocco. His interests include research methods, statistics in the social sciences and assessment in English language teaching. He has participated in several national and international conferences and published several works. His major publications include a chapter in *Assessing Writing in English in the 21st Century Arab World* (Abouabdelkader and Abdelhamid, Eds., 2018), Macmillan Palgrave. He also co-published another chapter: Teachers' Feedback on EFL Students' Dissertation Writing in Morocco (Abdelhamid et al., Eds., 2020), Palgrave Macmillan. Soufiane is also a member of the research laboratories of the universities of Chouaib Doukkali and Ibn Tofail University in Kenitra.

Hussein AlAhmad is Assistant Professor of Strategic Communication, also in Teaching & Learning in Higher Education at the Faculty of Graduate Studies, Arab American University Ramallah, Palestine. Hussein is also an Associate Fellow of the British Higher Education Academy (Advanced HE) and Associate Fellow of ASPIRE (Accrediting Staff Professionalism in Research-Led Education). His ongoing research focuses on Arab media, educational communication, and strategic communication, with special emphasis on contemporary pan-Arab media and its impact on the political culture and democracy in Arab societies.

Fawziya Al Zadjali is an Omani educational consultant, certified trainer, presenter, writer, and researcher, who is known for her work in promoting English language teaching. She holds a PhD degree in Education specialized in Curriculum and Teacher Professional Development, from Leeds Becket University, UK, and a master's degree in TESOL specialized in "Teacher Education" from the University of Leeds, UK. Fawziya has a wealth of experience in the field of education in both the education and higher education sectors, where she worked as a teacher, supervisor, trainer, director, quality assurance senior manager and head of the Foundation Department. She has published several chapters and articles on education and English language teaching and learning. Fawziya is passionate about professional development and leadership. As a trainer, she developed and delivered various training courses and workshops related to teaching English, doing research, public speaking, presentation skills, interactive teaching methods and many more.

Mouhssine Ayouri is a highly experienced Moroccan public high school teacher of English language with a master's degree in Applied Language Studies. His main interests include EFL writing assessment, second language acquisition, and diversity education.

Chahra Beloufa is Assistant Professor of English at the Arab Open University, Dammam, Saudi Arabia. Beloufa graduated from the University of Paul Valery, France, in November 2017 She is a member of Applied Linguistics and Applied Teaching Association, founded by Zayed University. She is also a member of the French Society of Shakespeare and the American Society of Shakespeare. Her major fields of investigation are online pedagogies, virtual literacy, artificial intelligence in education, as well as the analysis of Shakespeare's discourses and plays. Chahra has been an active participant in various course studies in the Shakespeare Institute in Stratford-Upon-Avon: in 2014, "Reviewing Shakespeare" and "The Living Shakespeare" in May 2015. In 2017, Beloufa taught in *Oxford Partnership Colleges* in Sakaka, KSA, and in September 2018, she worked in *Laureate International Female college* in KSA. Chahra Beloufa is also a creative writer and an international poetess; her published anthology of poems is entitled *The Nightingale Whispers* (2012) and *Spiral* (2022). Other poems have been published in international anthologies such as *One Plus One, About Everything That Is Not Right*, with Hannie Rouweler and other poets.

Mohamed Chtatou is Professor of "Business Communication" at Université Internationale de Rabat (UIR) and of "Education" at Université Mohammed V in Rabat. He graduated from Mohammed V University in English Studies in 1976. In 1980 he got an MPhil from the School of Oriental and African Studies (SOAS) of the University of London in Amazigh Studies, and in 1982 a PhD in Amazigh Language and Anthropology. In 1987, he joined the Islamic Educational, Scientific and Cultural Organization (ISESCO), where he worked as a program specialist and later as a director of the Directorate of Education (worked on functional literacy, women empowerment, education planning, education of rural women and girls, special education, etc.), then director of the Directorate of Culture and director of the Directorate of External Relations and Cooperation. He is a political analyst with Moroccan, American, Gulf, French, Italian and British media on politics and culture in the Middle East, Islamism and religious terrorism.

Sharita Viola Furtado is a passionate, enthusiastic English language teacher with MA (English) and M.Ed. (Gold Medalist), teaching English in International college of Engineering and Management in the General Foundation Department. She has been providing quality education in Oman for 15+ years and believes in enhancing students' skills at various levels and encourages them to build a lifelong focused career. She's actively participated in many professional developmental activities and has shown keen interest in engaging in various constructive programs in society. She's passionate about actively participating in research-related activities, which will enhance her knowledge and facilitate efficient learning.

Elias Kukali is Assistant Professor of Communication, teaching in the Contemporary Public Relations program at the Faculty of Graduate Studies at Arab American University. Elias is the head of the Research Department at the Palestinian Center of Public Opinion (PCPO) and representative of WIN and Gallup International in Palestine. His research aims to uncover the complex interplay between leadership, public opinion, and communication theories, providing new insights into how people form and express their views on important social issues.

María Sagrario Salaberri Ramiro is a lecturer at the University of Almería (Spain) and teacher trainer with a PhD in TEFL. She has led a research project on Internationalisation in Higher Education and has participated in other research projects on bilingual education. Throughout her career, she has been active in fostering teacher professional development and the teaching of English as a foreign language in conferences, seminars and workshops delivered in different parts of the world. Author of many articles and books in the field, she has been involved in the development of EFL curriculum designs in Spain and curricular material for international publishers.

Anat Stavans, PhD, is Professor of Applied Linguistics in the English Department and former Director of the Research Authority at Beit Berl Academic College. Her research focuses on developmental and educational linguistics, trilingual acquisition and development, and cross-cultural and cross-linguistic literacy development. Stavans is the author of numerous articles on topics such as code switching, narrative input and development, immigrant bilingualism, educational language policy, parent-child interaction, and multiliteracy development. She co-edited a volume *Studies in Language and Language Education: Essays in Honor of Elite Olshtain* (with Irit Kupferberg, 2008, Magnes); she wrote *Linguistic and Developmental Analysis of Child-Directed Parental Narrative Input* (in Hebrew, NCJW) and co-authored *Multilingualism* (with Charlotte Hoffmann, CUP, 2015). In addition, she has developed and led several intervention projects concerning the fostering of early language and literacy development among educators and parents and served as consultant to several international agencies and institutions on multilingualism and multiliteracy. She has been appointed to the EU-COST Action N° IS1306, titled "New Speakers in a Multilingual Europe: Opportunities and Challenges", and to the EU-COST Action N° IS1401, titled "European Literacy Network", and serves as a member in ERASMUS + Higher Education Reform Expert (HERE) Forum. Stavans holds a grant from the Israel Science Foundation as the Principal Investigator in a research project on "Predictors of text quality in written expository texts: a developmental study". Currently, Stavans is involved in international collaborations on language and literacy development in early multilingualism.

Deborah Swallow, PhD, has a doctorate in Education and is a writer, trainer and university lecturer specialising in management and intercultural communication. She is a lecturer at Glasgow Caledonian University London, UK, and is the author of *Diversity Dashboard: A Manager's Guide to Navigating in Cross-cultural Turbulence*. She is a member of SIETAR, the Society for International Education, Training and Research, and director of the training company 4CInternational.

Wafaa Taleb holds a PhD in English and African Civilization from the University of Oran (Algeria). She works as a lecturer at Oran 2 Mohamed Ben Ahmed University (Algeria), where she teaches grammar, reading, writing and speaking to undergraduate students. She also teaches African, British, and American history and civilization to undergraduate and postgraduate students. She took part in several international conferences and published about methods of teaching English as a foreign language and also published widely on the subject of ethnic diversity and conflicts in Africa. Her main research focuses on Feminist movements in Africa and mainly in Algeria.Wafaa Taleb is also editor-in-chief of the interdisciplinary journal *Image, Iterculturalité et Didactique* (ISSN:1111-3936- EISSN:2661-7722), published by the University of Oran 2 Mohamed Ben Ahmed, Algeria.

Mohammad Tamimy is a doctorate candidate of Teaching English to the Speakers of Other Languages (TESOL) at the Department of Foreign Languages and Linguistics, Shiraz University, Shiraz, Iran. He is mainly interested in research on intercultural education and cooperative learning. He has published in a few national and international journals including the

Journal of Intercultural Communication Research, Teaching and Teacher Education, Qualitative Report, and *International Journal of Language Studies*. He has also served as a peer reviewer to international journals.

Barry Tomalin, MA, is a visiting lecturer at Glasgow Caledonian University, London, UK. He is Director of the Business Cultural Trainer's Certificate at International House, London, and Editor in Chief and Editorial Consultant of two international online academic journals, the *ICC-Language Journal,* and *Training, Language and Culture*. He has valued the opportunity to teach and address conferences in Algeria, Egypt, Saudi Arabia, Turkey and the UEA, and has worked in over 60 countries worldwide. He is the founder and facilitator of the Business Cultural Trainers Certificate. A published author in the language, intercultural and international communications fields, his major works include *Cultural Awareness* (Oxford University Press, 1995); *Key Business Skills* (Harper Collins 2012); *Cross-Cultural Communication, Theory and Practice* (Palgrave Macmillan 2013); *World Business Cultures-a Handbook* (Thorogood Publishing 2014), and numerous articles.

Ozlem Yuges is a PhD candidate in TESOL/Applied Linguistics at Westminster University, London. Of Turkish descent and British nationality, she has a CSc in Linguistics and has served as the ICC-Languages Coordinator and is an English language teacher and language and intercultural trainer at International House London Executive Centre. She has been working in education with various age groups including young adults and adult education since 2006 and has been involved in ongoing professional development and curriculum development in language education.

Abderrazak Zaafour is a teacher who holds a PhD in Applied Linguistics, Didactics, and Educational Innovation, specializing in teaching English as a Foreign Language (TEFL). He holds a PhD from the "International PhD School," University of Almeria, Spain, Faculty of Education Sciences, Department of English Philology. His research interests include didactics and educational innovation (Project-Based Learning [PBL], Cooperative Learning [CL], Intercultural Education [IE], New Technology [NT], and Motivation), focusing on investigating the most relevant, innovative, and recent methodologies for teaching and learning EFL. He is the author of many articles published in ranked international journals. Additionally, he has participated as a teacher in several intercultural exchange public programs (Moroccan and Spanish intercultural exchange) and in numerous workshops, conferences, and seminars delivered in different parts of the world.

Abbreviations

AOU	Academic Online University
APS	Algeria Press Service
BEM	Brevet d'Enseignement Moyen
CEFR	Common European Framework of Reference
CFL	Centre for Foreign Languages
CNES	Conseil National Economique, Social et Environnemental
CPBL	Cooperative Project-Based Learning
CSEFRS	Conseil Supérieur de l'Education, la CSEFRS Conseil Supérieure de l'Education, la Formation et de la Recherche Scientifique
DMIS	Developmental Model of Intercultural Sensitivity
DRT	Discourse Representation Theory
EFA	Education for All
EFL	English as a Foreign Language
HE	Higher Education
IRCAM	Institut Royal de la Culture Amazighe'
IT	Information Technology
LMD system	Licence (Bachelor), Master, Doctorate
MANCOVA	Multivariate Analysis of Covariance
MEN	Ministère de l'Education Nationale
MOOCs	Massive Open Online Courses
NCET	National Charter of Education, Training
NECL	The National E-Learning Center
NGO	Non Governmental organizations
OECD	Organisation for Economic Co-operation and Development
ONS	Office Nationale des Statistiques
PISA	Programme for International Student Assessment

RC	Reading Comprehension
REE	Representation, Engagement, and Expression
SDGs	Sustainable Development Goals
SMU	Singapore Management University
T&L	Teaching and Learning
UDL	Universal design for learning
UNESCO	The United Nations Educational, Scientific and Cultural Organization
UNHRC	United Nations Human Rights Council
UNICEF	The United Nations Children's Fund
WHO	World Health Organization

LIST OF CHARTS

Chart 12.1 Average repetition rate from 2000 to 2012. (Source: Calculation based on MEN data (UNICEF, 2014)) 266
Chart 12.2 Baccalaureate pass rate in 2015. (Source: Algeria Press Service (APS)) 267

List of Figures

Fig. 3.1	Materials and activities with guidance and support	44
Fig. 3.2	Materials with vocabulary-oriented activities	45
Fig. 3.3	Reading material that provides new content	46
Fig. 3.4	Language dealing with social and daily life situations	49
Fig. 3.5	Reading materials that provide cultural knowledge	50
Fig. 3.6	Texts that contain professional jargon vocabulary	52
Fig. 3.7	Materials that create discussions between groups	53
Fig. 7.1	Learners' English language proficiency level	130
Fig. 7.2	Cultural difference	132
Fig. 7.3	Use of L1 (first language)	133
Fig. 7.4	Students' educational background	135
Fig. 10.1	The process of inductive coding	221
Fig. 11.1	Key characteristics of the sample	241
Fig. 11.2	Mean scores on T&L dimension by school location	244
Fig. 12.1	(**a**) Success rate (%) for the Brevet d'études Fondamentales (BEF) and (**b**) success rate for the Baccalauréat Général (BAC) by Sex. Algeria, 1997–2015. (Source: 1997–2007 ONS, different publications; 2008–2009, CNES, unpublished document; 2014 Algerian press; 2015, MEN, in Ouadah-Bedidi (2018, 90))	263

List of Graphs

Graph 12.1	Dropout rate before the last year of middle school by gender in 2011. (Source: UNICEF (2014))	266
Graph 12.2	Primary repetition rate from 2000 to 2012. (Source: Calculation based on MEN data (UNICEF, 2014))	266
Graph 12.3	School enrollment rate by age of 6–15 years and by gender, ALGERIA, 2006. (Source: ONS (2008))	276

List of Tables

Table 3.1	Criteria for analysis	41
Table 3.2	Descriptive statistics related to 'accessibility'	43
Table 3.3	Descriptive statistics related to the 'usability' principle	47
Table 3.4	Statistics related to the principle of 'usability'	51
Table 7.1	Participant teachers	127
Table 7.2	Participant students: confidentiality and anonymity	128
Table 8.1	Background information on participants	170
Table 8.2	CanDo in English	170
Table 8.3	English use context (intimate and formal circle) and purpose (pleasure, business, sustainability)	171
Table 8.4	Rating (on a scale of 0–100) of the languages and their speech communities in society	172
Table 9.1	Descriptive statistics of curriculum philosophy and reform	185
Table 9.2	Descriptive statistics of content accessibility and transdisciplinary education	188
Table 9.3	Descriptive statistics of inclusive and equitable pedagogy	190
Table 9.4	Descriptive statistics of cultural understanding and community involvement	192
Table 9.5	Descriptive statistics of learning and assessment purposes	195
Table 10.1	Cultural considerations for course design	219
Table 10.2	Students' cultural awareness	220
Table 10.3	Students and philosophical concepts	221
Table 11.1	Distribution of universities across ownership type, campuses, and geographical locations	239
Table 11.2	Cluster selection of universities for research study	240
Table 11.3	Summary of indexes reliability estimates	242

Table 11.4	Pairwise comparison of schooling model across T&L dimensions	245
Table 11.5	Summary of T-Test results for the mean value of students answering "yes" to the media technique used	248
Table 12.1	Evolution of the number of Muslim boys and girls enrolled in public primary schools (6–13 years)	258
Table 12.2	Evolution of the participation rate of girls in the primary cycle from 1962/1963 to 2010/2011	261
Table 12.3	Number of female/male students in all cycles 2017/2022	262
Table 12.4	Evolution of the participation rate of girls from 1970/1971 to 2010/2011	262
Table 12.5	Proportion of girls enrolled in university and of students holding university degrees, by discipline, from 2004–2005 to 2010–2011	270
Table 12.6	The evolution of graduates: 2014/2015 to 2016/2017	271
Table 12.7	Teaching staff in secondary education by sex and discipline: 2015/2016 to 2017/2018	272
Table 12.8	Level of education of the population aged 10 and over, ALGERIA, 2006	275
Table 12.9	School enrollment rate of 6–15-year-olds	278

CHAPTER 1

The Challenge of Diversity Education: Defending the Devil or Adjusting the Clock?

Hassan Abouabdelkader

1   What Is Diversity Education? How Does It Relate to Language Learning, and What Aspects of Diversity Education Are Concerned? Is It a Real Issue in Language Pedagogy in MENA?

Based on the complexities inherent in the concept of diversity education itself, it is essential to put to the front the main claims of this volume by answering the above questions as they are reflected in the constituent chapters of the book. As it occurs in most fields of research, the issue of diversity in recent times has arisen to counter the discrimination and disparities between the sexes and races. As a result, several movements have upsurged to defend the rights of certain communities despite the still-existing controversies expressed by movements that seek to defend the identity of certain groups or fight the discrimination suffered by others, let alone the defenders of environmental legal rights, including biodiversity. All these discriminations are rooted in people's education and upbringing

H. Abouabdelkader (✉)
Ecole Nationales Supérieure d'Arts et Métiers, Moulay Ismail University, Meknes, Morocco

© The Author(s), under exclusive license to Springer Nature Switzerland AG 2023
H. Abouabdelkader, B. Tomalin (eds.), *Diversity Education in the MENA Region*, https://doi.org/10.1007/978-3-031-42693-3_1

and forged by educational patterns dictated by adult communities to serve some specific objectives. This book is not about all of these. It simply addresses meaningful aspects of diversity, equity, and inclusion that disallow the ills perpetrated in the language curricula and pedagogies and hamper learners of all ages, races, genders, and strata from development and growth.

The argument beneath this search is that using diversity, equity, and inclusion (DEI), as a buzzword that fits all, is unproductive unless it is given its real value and consideration. In the field of education, each of these entities drastically impacts the lives of whole generations. Their misuse in education impacts the social and psychological lives of millions of individuals. By associating the principles of diversity education with language learning, this book argues that language is closely related to people's thinking and actions and considers all the related concepts, such as equity and inclusion, as the main catalyst of human destiny, the trigger of students' engagement and interest in learning, and a manipulator of their drives and ambitions.

As it linguistically stands, diversity education refers to the extent to which an educational context or pedagogy offers equitable and inclusive opportunities for learners from diverse classes, genders, and races, as well as with diverse mental and physical abilities, on the one hand, and fights disparities, inequities, and inequalities among all learners, on the other. These challenges are taken into consideration in this volume both inside and outside the language classroom as a step toward promoting students' learning outcomes and well-being.

The 15 chapters of this book consider diversity issues as a propeller of learners' energy and enthusiasm for learning and a source of their success and learning outcomes. These chapters do not only address the way diversity education decisions in language education need to be considered from perspectives that promote students' learning, support what praises and encourages students, leverage their learning outcomes, and improve their universal understanding, but also warn against those features that impede their progress and generate inequalities among students.

Why write this book? Before engaging in this quest for solutions to the ills of learning in this emerging region, several questions came to mind. Some of these questions are: Why should education matters be investigated from dimensions that pertain to other fields of inquiry than classroom practices? Why should we scourge a noble enterprise with political buzzwords that are often used to propagandize unreachable and unsolvable issues?

On reflecting upon the historical developments of language teaching theories and approaches throughout the past four decades from my own experience as a language teacher, I realized that most trends of past research on language teaching methods have been unicentral on a trending issue. First, they were dedicated to the way languages need to be taught, focusing on teaching content and instructions and giving more attention to linguistic and metalinguistic issues such as themes, grammar, vocabulary variations, and language skills. The learning of any of these course components has always been proposed with no consideration at all for the human factor. Later, the shift to the way they can be learned with more focus on the teaching approaches that can best carry out the job surged as a key to language instruction. The shift to learner-motivational drives towards engaging learners in communicative activities and interaction (such as the teaching of standards, language skills, and strategies for learning) has now emerged as an influential trend in learner-centered approaches and pedagogies. Currently, the new generations of learners have changed, as have the social conditions, paving the way for new trends in research and suggesting new orientations in language learning methodologies. The diversity trend has come to raise issues that are socially, technologically, and timewise connected, putting learners at the forefront of language education needs. In this new orientation, pedagogical concern has moved to the restoration of what past pedagogies have damaged, which hampered learning and prevented many students from the previous generations from achieving their goals.

Because language plays a crucial role in the life of individuals, the functions and purposes of language learning are no longer concerned with learning the language per se. Any endeavor remains useless unless it integrates language education as a priority that promotes new means of adaptability and integration of all the conditions involved in learning. According to this perspective, the notions of 'language curriculum' and 'course contents and pedagogies' are no longer separate entities, with 'curriculum' being the property of educational policymakers who prescribe the ingredients of the recipe as a product, on the one hand, and 'course contents, pedagogies, and assessments', as a separate task the accomplishment of which is the responsibility of experts and practitioners who translate the 'good-looking parcel of thoughts and philosophies' into practical guidelines. Teamwork and collaboration between all the stakeholders are considered, in this book, as salient components of diversity education. The students and teachers have now joined the club and become determining agents in the design of what to teach and how to teach it.

Like most new paradigms, such as leadership, sustainability, constructivism, and collaborative learning, diversity education principles are issues that originate in political, economic, and other fields and reflect transdisciplinary knowledge. They have made the equation equal between teachers and learners in terms of appreciation and made teaching and learning two sides of the same coin. Language learning practices have nowadays urged teachers to go beyond the old boundaries and make more efforts to resolve the existing inequal and disruptive classrooms and pave the way for all students to be active contributors and benefactors of real-time conditions and resources (Claeys-Kulik et al., 2019) without denying the local languages, culture, and traditions of the people (Olssen & Peters, 2005, p. 330).

2 For Whom Does Diversity Education Bell Ring?

The relevance of diversity education as a theme of this book lies in its compelling and initiating forces that impact the issue of quality education assurance in the MENA countries. Theoretically, the issues of diversity, inclusion, and equity share common principles and insights; yet they are not conceived of in this book as interchangeable, and each of them has specific effects and implications. As complementary concepts, they are the concern of all the stakeholders in language education, and all of them lend themselves to the requirements of quality education assurance. As reflected in the chapters of the book, these subtle distinctions show that they are complementary and include the principles of motivation, collaboration, and quality education standards which leverage human rights, sustainability, and promotion of human ability. What makes this book distinctive is that it reconsiders the existing pedagogical trends in terms of the current social upheavals and with reference to the principles of development and progress needed in twenty-first-century education.

The main argument of this book is that international education in MENA is at the mercy of inappropriate and sometimes repressive educational policies that lead to inequitable learning outcomes and ignominious structural inequalities in higher education (Chap. 14). In many of these countries, educational policies are still using 'culture-centric approaches' to glorify old achievements and obscure learners' prospects, diverting students from reality. In addition to praising the positive aspects of these cultures, this book offers insights into the dysfunctions taking place and prompts new ways of cooperation within and between communities in the MENA region.

The chapters included in this volume put diversity education, equity, and inclusion in language learning at the forefront of the approaches to language instruction. The contributions examine matters related to educational policies and practices in the MENA region that impact students' learning. The works presented in the volume suggest that language learning is considered as a determining factor of human development in most countries investigated and reveal that educational policies and curricula in the whole region are a major concern in all its countries. The countries incorporated in this book include Morocco and Algeria from North Africa, Palestine, Israel, Saudi Arabia, Oman, and Iran from Asia. These works also reflect the concerns and worries of educationalists in the MENA region. They all portray the inequities and problems incurred by these communities and highlight their achievements, credentials, and expectations.

The first incentive underlying the choice of diversity education in this book is that teaching languages is not a matter of staffing learners with knowledge of the foreign language. Instead, it is much more a matter of how teaching and learning are perceived as indissociable catalysts that synergize the educational systems (Ahmed & Abouabdelkader, 2016) and resolve the existing inequities undermined by learners from the lower strata, the disabled, and others in the MENA countries.

The second incentive underlying this search as a potential source of inspiration that propelled our curiosity to probe the ills and credentials of learning languages in MENA countries is that there have been several attempts to improve learning pedagogies in this region both at the theoretical and practical levels. Unfortunately, achievement of these objectives is reported to be hampered by constraints and policies for which teachers are not responsible (See Chaps. 12 and 14). The researchers involved in this volume have succinctly highlighted the significance of curricular orientations, multicultural education contents, inappropriate pedagogies, and inequitable assessments, in teacher training programs, and re-evaluated language policies as key considerations in fostering a more inclusive educational environment (Bougroum & Ibourk, 2011; Ichou & Fathi, 2022; Imouri, 2021).

All the studies included in this volume attempt to explain the different factors involved in language learning in their respective region and amply describe how these factors are reflective of the internal and external learning drives and incentives that are conducive to students' learning outcomes. It is no wonder, then, that many English Language Teaching (ELT) researchers have shifted their interest to these socially grounded psychological phenomena in presenting themselves as education activists. Based on the current works of several researchers who have been extensively influential in the educational field, such as Rebecca Oxford, Michal Byram, Jack Richards, and Noam Chomsky, this repositioning of future academic research to redress the ills prompted by the social variables that directly impact learning and the human capital is part of the continuum.

According to this line of thinking, it must be admitted, several works reported in this book stress the undesirable effects of financial mishandling, administrative dysfunction, educators' egocentrism, and lack of consideration of learners' abilities, and assessment procedures and objectives as critical factors that need attention. Some chapters also express the mismatch between the theoretical claims of several curricula with the existing reality and the exigencies of the modern world. By actively addressing the challenges faced by language curriculum construction in terms of learning accommodations improvement and the management of learning outcomes, several chapters and case studies argue that the development of the countries of the MENA region needs to establish a more inclusive system that ensures equal opportunities for individuals from diverse backgrounds. This type of intervention empowers talented individuals, creates a love of learning, destroys the gaps between all the stakeholders, irrespective of their socio-economic status, their orientations, and encourages learners to pursue higher education and make meaningful contributions to the progress of society (Bougroum & Ibourk, 2011; see Chap. 11 this volume).

3   What Aspects of Diversity Education?

The points raised in this volume are also supportive of collaborative learning initiatives that build bonds between all the members of the community. Some of them are geared towards the infusion of diversity education in higher education curricula as a means of promoting students' knowledge and skills. Other chapters urge educational institutions to provide appropriate learning means and inclusive learning environments for students. These aspects of diversity education seek to demonstrate the various roles of language instructors in the provision and promotion of the learner to the forefront of the operation, the encouragement of their engagement and participation in their community, and the support of their academic and personal development within a societal framework. By equipping teachers to effectively address the diverse needs of students and promote cultural understanding, the groundwork is laid for an inclusive educational environment that values and celebrates different perspectives (see Chap. 6).

In a similar vein, most of the chapters included state that re-evaluating language policies is indispensable for creating an inclusive educational environment in their respective countries. Adopting language policies that consider the linguistic diversity of students and recognize the importance of both local and global languages fosters an environment where all students can effectively participate in the learning process. Such inclusive language policies enhance students' opportunities for academic success and prepare them for a globally interconnected world (Ichou & Fathi, 2022). By rethinking language as a medium of instruction, institutions acknowledge and value different linguistic backgrounds, promoting quality education, equality, and inclusion. To this end, this will likely lead to an inclusive higher education system that cultivates a diverse student background, fostering cross-cultural understanding and promoting a real sense of inclusion and equity.

By diversifying the scopes of the authors involved, this book attempts to research the variations in approaches, teaching pedagogies, and practices prevailing in the MENA region and analyzes ways that would contribute to a better educational shift and world vision, suggesting that diversity education is beneficial to language teaching and learning in all parts of the world, but in a different shape and manner.

As can be discovered in the different chapters of the book, one more crucial point is that diversity education is still an issue in the MENA countries, as many educational policies are still not in tune with the requirements of the twenty-first century, and many countries are still experiencing improper patterns of educational practice, using 'culture-centric approaches to glorify old achievements and obscure learners' prospects. Whether at the level of teaching materials or methodologies, one of the aims of this book is to delineate the current educational patterns in use in the MENA countries. These investigatory studies attempt to probe the various types of dysfunctions related to student and teacher behavior, assessment practices, and repercussions on students' learning outcomes and social mobility.

A distinctive asset of this book is that it includes several case studies that empirically explore the extent to which students and other entities of the social community in the MENA region may participate in the design and implementation of higher education language teaching curricula and pedagogical practices and promote the learning outcomes and social success of students. Similarly, the chapters presented in this volume explore the educational means and practices in search of new models and approaches that promote the required principles. Hence, particular attention is given to the issue of technology-empowered practices to identify new ways of fostering diversity-bound educational practices.

4 The Topics of the Book

The issues covered in this book offer insights into the state of diversity and inclusion in higher education as illustrated in the teaching approaches and the curricular orientations in several countries of the region. Theoretically, the existing research in the areas investigated in this book corroborates its findings. As reported by Abouabdelkader (2018), the values and behaviors in this region vary significantly both interculturally and philosophically, and the learning of languages makes additional demands on teachers, learners, and material writers in terms of diversity management and equity. The issues included in this volume incorporate topics related to different features of language education, including:

- Diversity education: Principles and practices.
- Diversity education, teacher education, and social change.
- Multicultural education and social change.
- Barriers to communication among language learners.
- Assessment and equity in a culturally diverse society.
- Class and gender and the challenges of diversity.
- Communication skills and leadership attainment.
- Diversity education and the new technologies.

By focusing on the curricular features and pedagogical practices used in the teaching of foreign languages in the MENA region from several perspectives, this book establishes the landscape of diversity education, equity, and inclusion as a major driver for change and a catalyst for development and growth.

Arguably, the value of the research included in this volume is multifaceted and highlights how some diversity education patterns affect societal changes in the world community. The chapters of the book depict inherent fallacies, repressive educational policies, inequitable learning opportunities, and structural inequalities that prevail in higher education in the MENA countries. By tracking off-beam educational decisions and practices, on the one hand, and panegyric and acclaimed practices and decisions, on the other, the book seeks to identify the ever-growing inequities that hamper the burgeoning of a thriving language learning culture.

5 Book Organization

The book is organized according to the logic of expository discourse that displays the various areas of the region at stake, diagnosing each of its constituent elements, their depiction and description, and finally their respective lessons. Hence, the chapters of the book—classified according to their related order—seek to portray the different specificities and variations of diversity, inclusion, and equity in this region and hopefully come up with pragmatic, useful, and pertinent solutions. All chapters are based on empirical research, ethical rules, and well-developed facts on diversity education in MENA. By including research related to several countries, this book provides a representative, valid, and reliable set of data that portray the different features of the issues under investigation.

The main orientation of all the chapters is not on prescriptive issues and assumptions. Instead, they all tap into the learners' and instructors' actions in real life and scrutinize the curriculum's roles in carrying out change. In a world where politics does not usually converge with the experience of the people, the purpose of the book is to provide bottom-up alternative actions that raise questions of critical analysis and fruitful debates on what can best remedy the ills of modern societies. To this end, each of the five parts of the book is introduced by a major chapter that addresses its scope and is followed by chapters that include case studies to illustrate the themes discussed in the main chapter.

Finally, this book is a diagnosis of some of the ills of the educational systems in MENA regarding the existing inequities and disparities between the different types of learners as portrayed in the current curricula and pedagogies adopted. It is aimed at supporting policy-makers, language practitioners, researchers, and curriculum designers whose concern is the improvement of classroom practices and learner-teacher relationships based on the notions of diversity, equity, and inclusion.

REFERENCES

Abouabdelkader, H. (2018). Conclusion and discussion. In A. Ahmed & H. Abouabdelkader (Eds.), *Assessing EFL writing in the 21st century Arab world: Revealing the unknown* (pp. 285–296). Springer International Publishing. https://doi.org/10.1007/978-3-319-64104-1_11

Ahmed, A., & Abouabdelkader, H. (2016). *Teaching EFL writing in the 21st century Arab world: Realities and challenges*. Palgrave Macmillan.

Bougroum, M., & Ibourk, A. (2011). Access and equity in financing higher education: The case of Morocco. *Prospects, 41*, 115–134.

Claeys-Kulik, A.-L., Jørgensen, T. E., & Stöber, H. (2019). Diversity, equity and inclusion in European higher education institutions. *Results from the INVITED Project*. Brussel: European University Association Asil, 51p.

Ichou, A., & Fathi, S. (2022). Promoting quality, equality and inclusion through rethinking mediums of instruction in Moroccan public schools. *International Journal of Language and Literary Studies, 4*(2), 296–320.

Imouri, E. M. (2021). Multicultural education integration in teacher training programs: Towards affirming diversity in Morocco. *American Journal of Qualitative Research, 5*(2 (In Progress)), 1–9. https://doi.org/10.29333/ajqr/11029

Olssen, M., & Peters, M. A. (2005). Neoliberalism, higher education and the knowledge economy: From the free market to knowledge capitalism. *Journal of Education Policy, 20*, 313–345.

PART I

Diversity Management Education and Language Learning

CHAPTER 2

Diversity in Tertiary Language Education

Barry Tomalin

1 INTRODUCTION

We live in a globalising world as the global economy brings ever more people from different parts of the world together through business and migration. Populations throughout the world are becoming more and more cosmopolitan as communities mix, especially in the world's largest cities. In tertiary education our classrooms may now contain students of many different nationalities working together to learn a foreign language, either as a subject in its own right or as a component module of other courses. In the case studies presented in this book, we have immigrant students studying in tertiary education in the MENA region and MENA students going to continue their studies and work abroad after graduation and completion of their first degrees. A major implication of this trend is the general acceptance of English as the lingua franca of international business and communication. Many tertiary-level courses are now taught in English in the MENA region partly because of the number of foreign

B. Tomalin (✉)
Glasgow Caledonian University London, London, UK
e-mail: barry.tomalin@gcu.ac.uk

© The Author(s), under exclusive license to Springer Nature Switzerland AG 2023
H. Abouabdelkader, B. Tomalin (eds.), *Diversity Education in the MENA Region*, https://doi.org/10.1007/978-3-031-42693-3_2

students and partly as a way of employing English as a medium of instruction to help prepare students for work in an international environment.

The key feature of this development during the last twenty years or so has been the importance of understanding the cultural background of those you are dealing with. So, the understanding of different culturally based beliefs and behaviour is becoming part of language teaching pedagogy. Unfortunately, as some of the case studies in this book show, foreign languages are taught as a linguistic system based on a study of grammar, basic vocabulary and pronunciation. What has been lacking is an insight into linguistic usage and how the language students have learned in the lectures or tutorials is actually used in 'real life', leaving many learners, when they go abroad or who emigrate, at something of a loss. As examples in the book show, some students feel a lack of enthusiasm for the language courses they are taking because of their inadequacy in helping them deal with real-life situations using a foreign language. That is why diversity and inclusion are becoming key features in language pedagogy and policy and need to become a key part of the language teaching and learning process at all levels of education. So, what do we mean by diversity and inclusion in language learning?

2   Diversity and Inclusion in Language Learning

Diversity and Inclusion, often referred to as D&I and as DEI (Diversity, Equity and Inclusion) has been of increasing importance in international business and education since the nineteenth century. As Rudenstine states, Presidents of Harvard University in the US stressed the importance of enrolling students from different nations, states, families, sects and living conditions to stimulate interaction between students of different nationalities and backgrounds (Rudenstine, 2001). In 1994 the United Nations UNESCO agency published *The Salamanca Statement and Framework for Action on Special Needs Education* (UNESCO, 1994). Its aim was to provide normative principles for inclusion and to recognise diversity as an asset. It was intended to support learning and also to meet individual learners' needs (Rapp & Corral-Granados, 2021). After some years of interim legislation in Britain, the Equality Act in 2010 outlawed discrimination based on race, religion, gender, age, disability and sexual orientation. The EU instituted an anti-racism plan 2020–2025 and individual EU members have agreed and published diversity policies.

2.1 Definition of Diversity, Equity and Inclusion

According to Özturgut, 2017 citing different experts, diversity, equity and inclusion can be defined a s follows:

Diversity: identifying and eliminating all forms of discrimination and encouraging the inclusion of people from different backgrounds with different beliefs and lifestyles (Avery & Thomas, 2004).
Equity: Equal access to higher education by ethnic minorities and low-income students (Bensimon & Polkingthorne, 2003).
Inclusion: Making sure all students feel welcome and that their learning styles are valued (Dougherty & Kienzl, 2006).

2.2 Diversity

Diversity applies to individuals both in the workplace and the education institution and refers to differences recognised in the community, principally, race, gender, age, ethnicity, religion, disability and neurodiversity (sexual orientation). Gender diversity refers to male and female members of the community and to non-binary gender, including LGBTQ+ (lesbian, gay, bisexual, transgender and questioning). As Nobel Prize Winner Richard Thaler noted in an interview with the international business consultancy, McKinsey, it's not just how different people are, it's how they think that matters (McKinsey, 2023). Recognising that diversity exists in the classroom, seeing its advantages, and incorporating its recognition in policy, curriculum, teaching materials, pedagogy and teacher training is an important development in second language education, especially at the tertiary level, both in undergraduate and postgraduate degrees and in vocational courses.

2.3 Equity

Equity means fair treatment for all our students from whatever background they come. Quite often foreign students feel ignored or undervalued because they sense that they are excluded from the academic community they have joined. It is important for educational organisations and, indeed, teachers and tutors, to check on their foreign students and help them feel part of the academic community, as it will help them in their studies. Evidence suggests that lack of a feeling of involvement in the academic community can have a negative effect on their studies and their ability to meet deadlines and produce assignments that achieve the results which will help them optimise their student careers and their access to the workplace.

2.4 *Inclusion*

Inclusion means how the university or college embraces all its students, especially those from overseas backgrounds, and helps them feel they can make a meaningful contribution both to their studies and also to the institution where they are studying. This may involve organisational roles such as becoming a student representative and helping staff recognise and deal with issues raised by students or being part of a student club or playing sports. Academically, it involves language teachers looking for opportunities for all students to relate what they are learning to their own interests and needs and creating activities that allow students to express their own experiences and ideas while using the grammar and some of the vocabulary they have learned.

3 HOW DIVERSITY CAN BENEFIT STUDENT SUCCESS

Diversity in tertiary second language education in universities, especially as more and more students are attending from diverse backgrounds, can have a deep effect not only on student life on and off campus but also on their academic studies and their future career. Why? Because studying with colleagues from different backgrounds challenges the beliefs and customs we take for granted and increases our awareness and acceptance of difference. It also leads to better collaboration and innovative ideas and techniques. In an article posted by Katie Brown on *Everfi.com*, she quotes the *Center for American Progress* as saying, "Research shows that the overall academic and social effects of increased racial diversity on campus are likely to be positive, ranging from higher levels of academic achievement to the improvement of near- and long-term intergroup relations" (Center for American Progress, posted May, 2020).

A second advantage of diversity in education is that in the classroom and outside, the students have the opportunity to interact with those from different backgrounds, and as a result, they learn to communicate effectively in different situations with those they are used to and improve both their thinking skills and critical awareness. A third advantage, according to

Katie Brown, is that the greater the stereotypes, the greater the challenge to stereotypes. These stereotypical views often develop in childhood and adolescence. A diverse classroom or campus can help see beyond the stereotypical image to the real person underneath and accept and come to value the difference. It's not just fellow students whose diversity affects students. Academic leaders, tutors and administrators from different backgrounds can have the same effect, especially where they represent cultures which are historically underrepresented in the academic community, according to Katie Brown. These lecturers, tutors and administrators can act as role models for students. This leads us to the next advantage of diversity on campus. It prepares students for life in the workplace. Katie Brown cites the American Council on Education as saying, "Education within a diverse setting prepares students to become good citizens in an increasingly complex, pluralistic society; it fosters mutual respect and teamwork, and it helps build communities whose members are judged by the quality of their character and their contributions" (American Council on Education, 2020).

4 Diversity and Decolonising the Curriculum

A leading research area in many university education departments is decolonising the curriculum. Many internationally spoken languages, such as English, French, Spanish, German, Italian and Portuguese are the result of colonisation at some point in their history by European powers, and the conventions of language usage and language teaching are still dominated by European language education. This means that many language learners, even at tertiary level, find themselves learning a foreign language based on Western rather than local values and lifestyle. This is the area that many European university education departments have been reviewing. In particular, they are examining language education policies, curricula, teaching materials, methodology used in the classroom, assessment and teacher training. The process of decolonising the curriculum involves investigating the origins and influence of colonisation and its effects on previously colonised cultures.

Inclusion leads to the concept of cooperative learning in language training educational policy, how it is expressed through the curriculum and what reforms might be needed to suit local requirements, what teaching materials are approved and recommended by the Ministry of Education, teaching methodology and how appropriate it is in working with a diverse language learning community, what assessment procedures are in place and where they originate and how policy, curriculum, materials, teaching methodology and assessment methods figure in the process of language teacher training. Subsequent chapters will explore many of these issues in the MENA region but let us examine the topics one by one.

4.1 Language Policy

Language policy is set by the government through the Ministry of Education which will decide what languages will be prioritised and will legislate on curricular policy, types of teaching materials, assessment, teachers and teacher training to meet the demands of society and the workplace as they see it. The job of the Ministry of Education is to set the standards and ensure conformity. But remember, conformity can be the enemy of diversity. So, the first task of any government education department is to explore the diversity of its population and how acknowledging its existence and promoting it can help education, particularly in this book, language education, to ensure universities' language training departments prosper. It will also prioritise the international languages that must be taught. As Professor David Crystal pointed out in 2004, English has the largest number of speakers globally, with about 1.5–2 billion speakers. Next comes Chinese with 1.1 billion speakers, then Hindi (India) with 602 million speakers, Spanish with 548 million speakers, French with 274.1 million speakers and, in sixth place, Arabic with 274 million speakers. What is most important is that native speakers of English are a minority at about 373 million, while over a billion non-native speakers use English as their primary official language and, according to David Crystal, a number that is continuing to increase (Crystal, 2004).

4.2 Curricular Policy

Curricular policy is decided by the Ministry, but it is also decided at a local level by universities and colleges. The problem with the language curriculum is that it is often based on life in the European communities rather than on the needs and lifestyles of local university learners. This means that the curriculum may specify grammatical concepts and vocabulary that are not recognised in the learning community. This is strengthened by the adoption of international syllabi such as the Council of Europe Framework of Reference (CEFR) which has been adopted by over 40 countries worldwide. CEFR supports language tests in Arabic and Turkish.

4.3 Materials

International publishers whose textbooks are used throughout the world are increasingly conscious of the need to recognise the cultural styles of the communities where the materials are being used and to adapt local and regional editions accordingly. There is also an increasing recognition of the importance of diversity and in the newest teaching materials, both online and in hard copy, it is important to adapt the dialogues and reading texts in language textbooks so that diversity is not ignored, and a more international approach taken.

The University of the Arts in London adopted a more international approach to the curriculum and teaching materials by adopting the following policies:

- *Examining* the impact of colonialism on disciplinary norms, aesthetics and representations of the 'other'
- *Exploring* the politics of cultural appropriation/representation as well as burdens of representation and the politics of production (sustainability)
- *Drawing* on the lived experience of students and centring on contemporary issues of relevance to students
- *Working* in partnership with students to develop curriculum content
- *Embedding* non-Western histories, perspectives and contributions to disciplines (University of the Arts London: 'Decolonising pedagogy and curriculum' The Exchange)

4.4 Assessment

When it comes to assessing language competence in relation to both university examining procedures and the requirements of language proficiency to work in international companies locally or overseas, assessment instruments developed in Europe or the US seem to dominate. If we take the example of English Language testing, much testing is dependent on Cambridge Examinations for different levels of English language proficiency focused on British English, IELTS (International English Language Testing System) a language test used to assess the ability to work in

English-speaking organisations in Australia and the UK and for American English, TOEFL (Test of English as a Foreign Language), developed in Princeton University, USA.

All of these examinations are considered essential qualifications for graduates intending to work or study abroad or for international organisations. All are considered commercially important, and all adopt a single universal test based on the CEFR described above in 1.3.2. All were developed in the 'global north' and applied internationally. That means that, in effect, the West defines the standards and this monolithic approach needs to be adapted to local requirements and standards. As Professor Michael Byram wrote, identity is crucial in communication and the more you ignore it, the more dangerous it is (Byram, 2023).

4.5 Pedagogy

How then should teaching methodology adapt, faced with multinational classes learning languages at degree level in national universities? The key is personalisation, engaging learners personally and encouraging them to apply the topic of the lesson to their own lives. The teacher can encourage the language learners to share their own thoughts in pairs or groups in the class. They can share their feelings, information about their lifestyle, their personal interests, their experience, their likes and dislikes and things they have done and would like to do in the future using the language they have learned. In 2021 Tanja Reiffenrath of the University of Göttingen in Germany suggested a number of strategies language teachers can use in the classroom to encourage the expression of diverse views and experience. First, it is important to get to know the group and use the diversity in the room as a resource by inviting students to contribute knowledge about local contexts and share their experiences. She stressed the value of having the students work in teams during a part of the course and design assignments in such a way that the diversity of the perspectives in the group contributes to the solution of the task, asking students to consider a question in their discipline from a comparative perspective and to get the students to join a simulation game that requires them to take on different roles and points of view. Using online resources for research and to organise personal presentations can also be very helpful.

There are, of course, problems. Teachers don't have time to complete the textbook lessons or to complete the curriculum and in many universities, classroom language teaching modules are being shortened, all allowing less time for student interaction and the expression of diverse experience and opinions. Teachers also feel they don't have the authority to challenge or adapt the curriculum to give more space to diverse beliefs and experiences. This can lead to a quite regimented teacher-dominant style in which the teacher talks and the students listen and do the tasks as required by the teaching materials. Maybe, to allow greater expression of diversity in the language classroom, the pedagogical approach may need an overhaul and the cooperative learning approach might provide the answer.

4.5.1 *Cooperative Learning*

Cooperative learning is about learning in small groups of four or five students, each group made up of students from diverse backgrounds and with diverse beliefs and experience. Its aim is to encourage the exchange of ideas between individuals from diverse backgrounds, help them feel 'part of the show' by including them in cooperative learning and group work and creating an atmosphere of interdependence. If correctly managed, it also creates an environment where higher-proficiency language students can help lower-proficiency students. Cooperative learning activities can be run in a hybrid environment, even though it is better face-to-face. As described by George Jacobs, Anita Lie and Siti Mina Tamah, cooperative learning involves setting tasks and splitting the class into groups to do the task (Jacobs et al., 2022). In her review of the book, Ozlem Yuges describes one of the techniques used in cooperative learning called 'Jigsaw', a reading and speaking activity which goes through four steps. In Step 1 each person in the group is given a number from 1–4 and studies part of a reading text in silence by themselves without telling any of their comrades. In Step 2 they join other groups as 'expert counsellors' comparing their text with others and answering their questions. In Step 3 they rejoin their original group, discuss the whole text and share what they have learned from the other group they worked with. Finally, in Step 4 they compile a test with open questions or maybe true/false questions on the text and try it out on the other groups in the class. In this way the students working in their groups work together to understand and discuss the text and develop a test to help fuller understanding. In doing so they demonstrate their diversity and build interdependence to get the best results. The origin of the 'Jigsaw' activity was in New York, where it was used to unite children from diverse backgrounds living in public housing in New York City and attending the same school (Yuges, 2023).

4.5.2 Teacher Training

It is clear that for teachers of languages, a level of fluency in the target language and knowledge about it are absolutely necessary. But teachers in training also need to understand much better how to manage a tutorial group to build interdependence, a feeling of community between students from diverse backgrounds and a greater appreciation of different beliefs, customs and behaviours within the group as well as the cultural background of the people whose language they are studying.

5 THE NEED FOR CHANGE

This section has explored some key issues faced by government and university authorities, as well as individual language teachers in how to manage diversity in language learning and teaching at tertiary level. In doing so it has examined policy, curriculum, materials, methodology and teacher training. Looking forward, change will be necessary and may take the form as listed below:

- *CURRICULUM*
  - Develop a new CEFR developed by international experts from the Global South as well as the Global North.
- *ASSESSMENT*

  - Review key assessment tools.
  - Examine how to localise and internationalise them.

- *MATERIALS*

  - Adapt to the local environment and recognise diversity.
  - Deal with broader international topics than European and American life.

- *PERSONALISATION*

  - Appeal to personal experience and background.

Connect the learners to their own experience.

- **TEACHER TRAINING**
    - Train teachers to be sensitive to the language used in the local context.
    - Train teachers to encourage the expression of diverse beliefs and experiences as part of practising the target language to build confidence and the feeling of belonging.

5.1 Recognising Cultural and Diversity Differences in the Classroom

One of the key developments in Europe and the US in the last decade has been the growth of what are called the 'Woke' pedagogy and 'Cancel culture'. 'Woke' pedagogy deals with removing blindness towards issues, principally regarding gender and race, and ensuring that teaching understands and involves students in discussions of issues that may arise. 'Cancel culture' is action taken to remove topics which offend the 'woke' culture in teaching materials and pedagogy and involving the class and seeking their views on issues that arise. 'Woke' pedagogy supports diversity in language learning by raising awareness and encouraging students to share their personal interests and concerns. However, in some universities, the work of the 'cancel culture' followers has been quite extreme in physically removing images of figures and symbols deemed to be inappropriate by the 'woke' movement and can be quite controversial. Altheria Caldera, a teacher at a university in Texas, USA, offers some helpful guidelines for teachers discussing 'woke' issues in the classroom (Caldera, 2018). The first is to facilitate conversations about injustice and inequity and to listen compassionately to student views and opinions. This demonstrates empathy and understanding and will have a big impact on students, especially where they can discuss their home lives in response to the topic under consideration and use the language they are learning or find new language to help them present their own opinions more fluently. As Caldera points out, students will feel that their lives matter (Caldera, 2018, ibid). Finding other teaching materials outside those especially produced for the classroom, such as posters, dramas, music or art and using digital media can be a positive source of learning stimuli using picture-based or sound-based authentic materials. By being involved in such discussions, the students can develop their critical thinking and awareness skills and their ability to evaluate issues, thereby producing ideas, not just consuming and practising the language in the situations in the textbook. Finally, being able to discuss diversity and 'woke' issues at whatever level will build skills and knowledge that they can apply to other courses they are involved in at tertiary level (Caldera, 2018, Ibid).

6 Conclusion

As Caldera states, the key foci of 'woke' pedagogy are race, gender, religion and sexual orientation, followed by disability and age. Wherever you are teaching, it's positive to recognise and respect differences in classroom behaviour and to encourage learners with different lifestyles and ways of contributing to classroom discussion to take a full part. Of course, individuals may differ in their willingness to respond due to personal character or their upbringing and social beliefs. I am familiar with students who don't respond out of respect for the seniority of the teacher or a wish to preserve 'dignified silence.' Sometimes students prefer not to enter into discussion or talk about their own experience or beliefs for fear of making a mistake by using the wrong language or going outside local accepted cultural norms. In addition, the opportunities to raise issues in these areas may be limited by political considerations, university regulations and maybe other factors but the basic principle is unchanged. The active involvement of students means they feel engaged and learn how to better express themselves and their personal lives and interests in the language they are learning, thus embodying the importance of diversity and inclusion in the classroom, as the following chapters will demonstrate.

References

American Council on Education. (2020). Access at: https://www.acenet.edu/Pages/default.aspx

Avery, D. R., & Thomas, K. M. (2004). Blending content and contact: The roles of diversity curriculum and campus heterogeneity in fostering diversity management competency. *Academy of Management Learning and Education, 3*(4), 383–386.

Bensimon, E., & Polkingthorne, D. (2003). *Why equity matters: Implications for a democracy.* Los Angeles Center for Urban Education, University of Southern California.

Brown, K. (2020). *The top 5 ways that diversity in education benefits students' success,* Available at: www.everfi.com

Byram, M. (2023). *Quality and equity in education.* Multilingual Matters.

Caldera, A. (2018). Woke Pedagogy: A framework for teaching and learning. *Diversity, Social Justice and the Educational Leader, 2*(3) Available at: https://scholarworks.uttyler.edu/dsjel/vol2/iss3/1

Center for American Progress. (2020). Accessible at www.americanprogress.org›departments›education

Crystal, D. (2004). *The language revolution.* Wiley.

Dougherty, K. J., & Kienzl, G. S. (2006). It's not enough to get through the open door: Inequalities by social background in transfer from community colleges to four-year colleges. *Teachers College Record, 108*(3), 452–487.

Equality Act. (2010). Accessible at www.equalityhumanrights.com/en/equality-act/equality-act-2010

Jacobs, G., Lie, A., & Tamah, S. M. (2022). *Cooperative learning through a reflective lens.* Equinox Publishing.

McKinsey. (2023). *Insights on diversity and inclusion.* Accessible at https://www.mckinsey.com/featured-insights/diversity

Özturgut, O. (2017). Internationalisation for diversity, equity and inclusion. *Journal of Higher Education and Practice, 17*(6), 83.

Rapp, A. C., & Corral-Granados, A. (2021). Understanding inclusive education – A theoretical contribution from system theory and the constructionist perspective. *International Journal of Inclusive Education, UK.* Taylor and Francis. Access the article at: https://doi.org/10.1080/13603116.2021.1946725

Rudenstine, N. L. (2001). *Student diversity and higher learning.* Available at: http://nrs.harvard.edu/urn-3:HUL.InstRepos:2643119. Former President of Harvard University and a leading diplomat.

UNESCO. (1994). *The Salamanca Statement and Framework for action on special needs education*: Adopted by the World Conference on Special Needs Education; Access and Quality. Salamanca, Spain, 7–10 June 1994. [Google Scholar].

University of the Arts. (2021). *Decolonising pedagogy and the Curriculum*, London, University of the Arts. Accessible at https://tle.myblog.arts.ac.uk/spotlight-on-decolonising-pedagogy-and-curriculum/

Yuges, O. (2023). Cooperative learning through a reflexive lens review. *Training Language and Culture, 7*(2) Accessible at: www.rudn.TLCjournal.org

CHAPTER 3

Representation, Engagement, and Expression in Moroccan Higher Education Curricula: Focus on Reading Comprehension

Soufiane Abouabdelkader

1 Introduction

In his famous poem, "My heart leaps up", Wordsworth (1802) says that "The Child is the father of the Man", suggesting that both the traumatic and joyful experiences young people go through in their early years may have drastic effects on their adulthood life. With modern views of education, this trend is coming full circle. Care for the learners' wellbeing, among factors of personal growth, is becoming an essential element in the making of effective curricula.

In many communities of the MENA region, learners are still considered second-class citizens and considered as passive recipients of knowledge. In these environments, learners even in higher education are obedient to their instructors and to their elders through a cultural heritage from their elders, which hardly gives young people the right of expression. Perceived

---

S. Abouabdelkader (✉)
Faculty of Letters, Chouaib Doukkali University, El Jadida, Morocco

as such, the curricula designed for these learners are still a replica of old practices.

Now, these practices have no more room in this changing world where higher education curriculum renewal is for language learning what car-checking is for a long-distance traveler. It is not the change of parts at random; instead, it is a process of (1) repairing what goes wrong which might impair the whole process and (2) attending to every aspect that contributes to the travelers' confidence and trust during their journey, and finally (3) ensuring that it will achieve its function in proportion to its objectives. The condition of its success, therefore, depends on how focused, relevant, and appropriate this renewal process is in terms of its pragmatic realization. This thoroughly applies to all subjects of study in higher education, which constantly face new challenges and paradigm shifts and need to be aligned with the needs of students and societal changes.

One of the focal issues of this chapter is the extent to which the English language curricular content and practice reflected in the reading comprehension (RC) modules fit within universal norms that promote sustainability education in Moroccan higher education. The rationale underneath this search is that many undergraduate EFL students undergo several learning difficulties (Bouziane, 2019). Some of these issues relate to (1) the inability to understand some reading materials, others to (2) a lack of motivation to carry out some comprehension tasks and assignments (Nadori, 2020b; Wigfield, 1997), and some others to (3) improper learning strategies and support accommodations. These problems are shared by most EFL learners (Bouziane, 1993; Nadori, 2020a).

According to the framework adopted in this case study, analyzing reading comprehension from these perspectives needs to be considered in terms of its curricular philosophies, practices, and advantages for all students. The question here is: What is the use of teaching subjects which do not cater to the motivation and the needs of its essential stakeholders? Such a question is crucial to the design and implementation of these curricula and their sustainability. In the 'reading comprehension' module, these pedagogical hardships are due to several reasons.

First, commonly used to refer to a subject of study or a pedagogical activity, the construct RC is a compound of two complex and widely researched issues, 'reading' and 'comprehension', both of which are complex and interweaving psychological constructs (Collins & Smith, 1980; Goodman, 1967; Grabe & Stoller, 2002).

Second, these handicaps are rooted in the socio-economic backgrounds of the students as well as the disadvantageous pedagogical practices incurred from the curricular orientations in use (Kintsch, 1988; Kintsch & van Dijk, 1978; Nathan & Stanovich, 1991; Putnam, 1975; Stanovich, 2009).

Thirdly, reading comprehension is made even more difficult as it adds up the variability of 'cultural' meaning of the foreign language to these levels of complexity (Fathi & Afzali, 2020; Grabe, 2010; Urquhart & Weir, 2014). This intricate combination of an individually and societally governed mental activity suggests that reading comprehension, particularly in English as a foreign language, needs to be researched from both a social-psychological and cognitive perspective, involving language and content knowledge, as well as a social-psychological dimension through which the activity is carried out (Rao & Meo, 2016).

The argument behind investigating reading comprehension instruction from a UDL perspective is that this theoretical framework makes the social and psychological accommodations that promote learners' literacy growth, inclusion, and flexibility among the multiple means of effective instruction (Edyburn, 2021). As reported by the proponents of this framework, reading comprehension needs to be guided by guidelines and checkpoints which create effective conditions of learning for all students without any discrimination. As such, probing the reading comprehension from a diversity education perspective that takes students' concerns into consideration is surely a novel track of upgrading its benefits to standards which make sustainability of the human capital a major concern (Evmenova, 2018; Gargiulo & Metcalf, 2022; Meo, 2008).

2   Reviewing the Landscape

Analyzing reading comprehension from a UDL perspective that gives prevalence to students' accommodations and wellbeing is a continuation of the developments reached in previous paradigm shifts. This type of research is not new; it is a prospection that has already been explored under other constructs and in several disciplines throughout the history of education. This study uses this framework of reference in the analysis of reading comprehension due to its emphasis on the language teaching and learning bond and its appreciation of the social psychological factors and advantages of providing multiple means of learning for learners to promote their own literacy levels.

Based on all that, it is essential to draw a picture of the existing trends in RC research and shed light on how this approach may accommodate the requirements of reading comprehension components in EFL contexts.

2.1 Reading Comprehension in Moroccan Higher Education

Within Moroccan higher education, very few changes have occurred in the continuous reforms in the reading comprehension courses since its implementation in the 1970s. However, RC has always been considered as a fundamental and crucial subject of literacy instruction in undergraduate education. The modular system in Moroccan higher education was introduced in the 2003 reform as part of the License-Master-Doctorate (LMD) system (Altihami, 2010), Ayad et al. (2020) say that:

> This law represents the legal embodiment of the National Charter of Education in its section dedicated to higher education. It gave rise to the famous reform, License-Master-Doctorate (LMD), from 2003 to 2004, to align with the Bologna Process in Europe and aims to harmonize Morocco's study patterns with those of its partner countries to facilitate the mobility of students and teachers and to develop interuniversity cooperation. (p. 97)

It is worth mentioning that Law 01.00 (Dahir, 2000) contains several milestones drawn from the National Charter which give each university several rights related to responsibility, engagement, and self-assessment. Unfortunately, most of these rights are loose and prone to interpretation, and higher education institutions, Ayad et al. (2020) argue that:

> are not subject to any evaluation of their internal and external performance, their curricula, the adequacy of these programs to the needs of the socio-professional environment, or the quality of the education they provide. For example, teachers are never asked about the feedback of their student, the consistency of their services, or the effectiveness of their interventions. Some of their scientific research is subject to evaluation only, and in relative terms, through procedures established in the context of the funding of research projects. (p. 98)

The changes brought by this law have become more inclusive of further dimensions, skills, and competencies, but most of them are theoretical and leave vent to several pedagogical options. As a result, RC has become the responsibility of the faculty practitioners, and most of the curricular improvements brought forth mirror the developments they have reached in applied linguistics research with diverse gateways.

Later, new changes were introduced in the Strategic Vision Reform 2015–2030. Its milestones focus on the provision of quality assurance education of all the curricula on the basis of their endogenous and exogenous determinants (S. Abouabdelkader, 2018; Larouz & Abouabdelkader, 2020). Of interest in these milestones is their recommendation to involve students' engagement in the curricula construction and implementation. What is not provided, however, is the mechanism through which these diversity, equity, and inclusion recommendations can be put into practice. This gap leaves the responsibility of providing the necessary support and accommodation to improve students' reading comprehension abilities to the mercy of the teachers' pedagogical orientations and expertise. Such guidelines are also recommended by the Conseil Supérieur de l'Education, de la Formation et de la Recherche Scientifique (CSEFRS, 2019) for the improvement of quality education. The question of interest to the present chapter is: How do these principles of equity, inclusion, and sustainability relate to the design and implementation of RC modules, and how can they promote students' comprehension skills?

2.2 Do the RC Module Components Serve DEI?

It is argued in this chapter that the provision for support of any kind to students may affect their learning abilities. Similarly, the provision of effective instruments and materials are prone to positively impact their comprehension skills and education in general. Quality assurance norms applied in education give support to learning that promotes the wellbeing of students (Beerkens, 2018) and not only that of teachers. The question addressed in this chapter is: What are students' conceptions regarding the 'reading comprehension' course? What pedagogies are used? And what measures are taken for its assessment? (Ahmed & Abouabdelkader, 2018).

As a key module for the development of literacy skills, 'reading comprehension' in Moroccan higher education seeks to develop several of the skills included in the module guidelines (see Module Description Sample, Index 1). In most of the universities investigated in this study, the choice of the content and pedagogy adopted is the responsibility of the instructors in charge of the course and with respect to its objectives.

As it stands in our current university curricula, the teaching of reading comprehension is a crucial module in the undergraduate program that purports to encourage all students to promote their learning skills. Its conception is supposedly based on the new advances reached in applied linguistics. Yet, its implementation is not, to the best of my knowledge, empirically supported. Like most module description guidelines produced throughout the country, the reading comprehension modules for the first and third semesters produced by Chouaib Doukali University—with the approbation of the Ministry of National Education—(see Appendix X) include many objectives and checkpoints that are too broad and lend themselves to various interpretations. To illustrate this state-of-the-art, it is fair to shed some light on the current RC modules portrayed in the objectives reported in the official guidelines and approved by the Ministry of Higher Education. These descriptors are interesting guidelines, but they are not sufficiently explained or detailed. They abound in concepts that look attractive but may present some difficulties at the implementation level:

1. The targeted skills of the module are broad categories; the skills reported in these guidelines are not cut down to the targeted benchmarks and competencies that can be identified by all learners.
2. The denomination of literacy gains and attributes is not described in terms of accessible, doable, and usable criteria, and their conceptualization is not easy for teachers to implement in the assessments.
3. The skills involved are not accompanied by 'how-to activities and pedagogical practices, and the selected texts are left for teachers to find.
4. Different classes at the same level of instruction may be exposed to materials that have different orientations at several levels.

Pedagogically speaking, these difficulties are usually handled by the teachers in charge of these modules in the absence of a well-structured national curriculum core that clearly identifies the pedagogical frame of activities and grading scale of rubrics that take into consideration the concepts of equity and inclusion. Regarding learning, the provision of such milestones would offer better learning opportunities to all students.

2.3 Which Research Insights Matter?

Does the local literature on reading comprehension address DEI? The state of reading research in Moroccan higher education has been examined in several studies. In a seminal meta-analysis on reading comprehension instruction in Morocco, Bouziane (2019), reports that most of the existing local research attempts to describe the reading habits and strategies of Moroccan students of English and focuses on the processes of reading and strategies through which they are carried out. As some of these teachers suggest, students' reading comprehension abilities need to be dealt with on a larger scale (Oublal & El Fatwaki, 1994). Oublal (1996) argues that:

> a developing and an insecure reader who is still feeling his way along the difficult path of reading and whose advances, sometimes daring, others timid, are impeded by language thresholds, inefficient reading habits and faulty strategic behaviours. (p. 143)

Unfortunately, there have not been any developmental studies that analyze the transfer of these deficiencies across levels of education. Theoretically speaking, the teaching of reading comprehension in Moroccan higher education is generally achieved through interactive social-psychological tasks and comprehension questions that seek to develop students' higher-thinking reading processes (Anderson, 1999; Rumelhart, 2017; Zimmerman & Schunk, 2006), and its goals aim at promoting effective learning strategies (Hock & Mellard, 2005; Oxford & Burry-Stock, 1995) and literacy skills (Falk-Ross, 2001). The concerns reported in these meta-analyses attribute these gains to students' needs.

In practice, the pedagogy suggested for this course aims to provide opportunities for all the students to interact with texts based on their background knowledge, cultural knowledge, and perceptions of the reading material. Students' engagement and motivational drives are not always treated as essential interactions in the RC course. In all these studies, no report has been made regarding students' encouragement and support, nor has there been any indication of students' consideration in the construction and implementation of these modules. The tradition is that these values are an integral part of teachers' roles and duties. Injection of strategies and learning tips are usually implicit in the teachers' interventions and sporadically provided during classroom reading activities.

In fact, this task of considering students' needs, social conditions, and personal abilities is usually carried out by teachers who care for their students out of their cultural beliefs and personal professional development. What the learner gets from the RC module pedagogy matters more than what the reading materials offer. This equation equally applies to students who are responsible for their own understanding of and interaction with the reading materials of the module, as directed and propelled by the contextual clues and facilitated by the teachers' instructions and interactions.

Due to overcrowded classrooms, these drives and energies are not always issued through hands-on learning tasks; nor are they ignited through welcoming social accommodations. This chapter contends that for the development of EFL students' reading comprehension abilities, it is essential to provide students with better learning opportunities and conditions, on the one hand, and encourage teachers to focus more on pragmatic pedagogies that provide students with better accommodations and means for learning to read and reflecting upon their own learning, on the other.

2.4   How Does UDL Fit in Reading Comprehension?

UDL is a practical approach that provides tangible directions for the teachers to motivate learners, create useful contents, and engage learners in learning. It refers to a theory of learning and teaching that aims to cater to the needs of all students to help them develop and progress equitably and sustainably (King-Sears, 2009). In a succinct definition of the term UDL, Burgstahler (2009) argues that the validity of the concept to fit within educational theories of learning is that it has moved from a philosophical trend in 1998 to a scientifically proven construct in 2008. According to him, the assets of this scientifically valid framework for guiding educational practice aim to (a) provide flexible modes of information and (b) sort out the ways students engage in learning to respond or demonstrate knowledge and skills, in addition to (c) facilitate providing accommodations and opportunities for all learners, including students with disabilities and students who are limited English proficient (Burgstahler, 2009).

Based on these views, UDL is not limited to language development; it assumes that both language and content have a social functional interface that controls meaning and significance of a text for the learners. By stressing the importance of providing multiple means of representation, engagement, and expression, UDL paves the way toward a learning and teaching framework that makes reading comprehension enjoyable and rewarding. As used in the present study, these features of the reading comprehension module are assessed against the criteria of 'accessibility, doability, and usefulness'. Within UDL, these three key components of learning:

representation, engagement, and expression provide guidelines for creating inclusive learning environments for all learners (Cumming & Rose, 2022). As used in the study, these components address the following concerns for reading comprehension modules:

1. **Representation**: The concept of 'representation' refers to how information is presented in the reading materials. The question raised at this level is whether information is presented in a variety of formats (e.g., visual, auditory, tactile) to serve the diverse learning needs of students. For example, providing images and diagrams to support understanding for students with different learning styles or learning disabilities.
2. **Engagement**: This concept refers to students' engagement in learning. The question addressed here is whether instruction taps learners' interests, passions, and goals (e.g., providing choice in learning activities and incorporating real-life experiences and scenarios and other tools to promote engagement.
3. **Expression**: This concept analyzes how learners demonstrate their understanding and mastery of content. The question here is finding out the extent to which learners are provided with the appropriate skills and means to demonstrate their understanding, such as writing, speaking, journal writing, portfolios, or IT-assisted projects.

For each of the above principles, a set of checkpoints have been provided (Courey et al., 2013), which guide the teachers to recognize students' needs (Robinson & Wizer, 2016). These checkpoints address all the factors affecting language instruction.

2.5 Is UDL Compatible with RC Models in Moroccan Higher Education?

The guidelines and checkpoints of UDL suggest that the change in language education can come from the teachers. Many of the paradigms introduced in modern language learning and teaching theories are just reformulations of old ones. Some others are additive to the values of the existing ones. UDL is one of these paradigms; it brings to the forefront new dimensions that are essential for education in emerging countries.

The investigation of these dimensions in the current models of the 'reading comprehension' modules adopted in Moroccan universities aims to uncover the state of the art of English language teaching in higher education and its implementation of diversity education principles. This chapter discusses these issues as they have been gleaned from the data collected from both students and teachers.

One of the features of UDL is that it advocates for the provision of means that promote cognitive processes and stimulate actual generating forces, as indicated in modern theories of learning. The multitude of possibilities offered by UDL leave teachers to browse across a multitude of checkpoints and choose what suits the needs of their learners and the specificities of their contexts (Banks, 2004; Robinson, 2016). Discourse approaches to reading interaction and construction analysts like Van Dijk and Kintsch are not excluded from this line of thinking (S. Abouabdelkader, 2019; Alghonaim, 2018). In the context of reading in a foreign language, the provision of these textual representations is part of what the model recommends in the teaching and learning of reading; these knowledge states can guide the students toward developing a sense of awareness of the discourse structures and facilitate the comprehension and construction of texts (H. Abouabdelkader, 1999).

Within this tradition, Discourse Representation Theory (DRT) (Liu et al., 2018) offers multiple layers for representing the meaning of sentences and discourse, including anaphora, presuppositions, and temporal expressions. This theory of meaning representation integrates various levels of meaning representation for discourse comprehension and production.

Unlike the traditional models, whose concern is getting the correct message from a text (Gilakjani & Ahmadi, 2011), the merits of UDL in reading comprehension are that it incorporates the subjective self of the readers and their orientations in the processes of reading. From the 2020s onward, such pedagogies have been common in most reading comprehension teaching courses. The gains from that model are that it attends to the psychological aspects of the learners rather than just the components of the course. As can be seen in the guidelines of the reading comprehension modules in Moroccan universities, the promotion of students' cognitive abilities to accommodate their needs with the requirements of academic education is short of the dimensions given to these representations in the UDL framework. In parallel with Kintsch's views, Van Dijk's (1982) approach to discourse processes provides clues for recommendations regarding the teaching of reading comprehension. According to him:

Not only knowledge but also opinions and attitudes play an important role in the comprehension and cognitive representation of discourse. To model this 'subjective understanding' we need a format for the representation of opinions and attitudes in semantic memory and strategies for their use in comprehension. (p. 35)

Research on learning styles and strategies (Mokhtari & Reichard, 2004; Oxford, 2011) is concomitant with the claims made so far. Its delineation of the incurring strategies in reading comprehension in a foreign language has also been reported to be affected by the learners' prior trajectories, among the other factors which determine the quality of reading outcomes. The importance of learners' perceptions and attitudes in the reading comprehension process is considerable and requires the development of efficacious strategies through training and instruction. As reported in the literature, opinions and attitudes have a determining effect on learners' motivation and learning outcomes.

A major advantage of this type of research is that it offers useful strategy assessment scales (Oxford & Burry-Stock, 1995) that reflect the type of processing used in learning languages and suggests that the success of learning to read highly depends on the efficacy of support and guidance provided to learners (R. Oxford, Personal communication, 2022).

With the insurgence of several reading comprehension models, UDL constitutes a diversity education trend which seems to gear toward universal categories of reading components which lead towards the construction of homogeneity within diversion in educational contexts. As described by Grabe (2009), reading comprehension is handled through several models of instruction that reflect the trending theories of their time.

Importantly, the claims of UDL about reading comprehension do not diverge from the existing theories of reading comprehension. Though originally known since Kant (Carrell, 1984), Schema theory, for instance, gained a lot of impetus in the 1980s and still gets a lot of advocacies among current researchers, its impetus is rooted in principles that make the learner in the center of the process itself. As a paradigm shift from the top-down approaches whose concern at that time was centered on language (the product) as the carrier of meaning, An (2013) and Rumelhart (2017) applied schema theory to reading research to give importance to the learning environment. The added value of schema theory to this theoretical perspective is provided by Kintsch's (1988) 'construction-integration' text model that derives its power from psychological research.

Its importance for the current theoretical framework lies in providing useful checkpoints for students to form strong bonds between the linguistic and psychological features of reading comprehension (Grabe, 2009). The advantage of UDL to reading comprehension in the Moroccan context is that it identifies the right checkpoints for teachers to pay attention to in the module at the levels of representation, engagement, and expression.

In alignment with these studies, it is necessary for the context to contribute to the development of students' reading abilities and drives. Time is over for practices and approaches that are top-down and that ignore the disparities between learners or consider them second-class citizens. If the purpose of education is to promote literacy skills among students, it is essential to build up bonds that foster students' learning and tear down the borderlines that may hamper their engagement in learning. Issues of accessibility, inclusion, and equity in learning in higher education are crucial components of these requirements. The success of a curriculum depends on how much it fits the clients of that curriculum.

One of the main concerns of this study is that in addition to the language burden EFL students struggle with, many social, psychological, and cognitive factors have become a major concern for educators in their attempts to upgrade the reading comprehension course content and pedagogy to high levels of expectations (Acim, 2018).

The developments reached in the UDL assign to the reading process its social psychological dimension and make reading comprehension a combination of literacy skills (Grabe, 2009; Grabe & Stoller, 2002), learning strategies (Oxford, 2011), knowledge management and empowerment, and attitudes towards the reading materials and pedagogies (Anderson, 1999; Zimmerman & Schunk, 2006), as well as a socio-economic issue, as stated in a succinct report on the MENA region's literacy rate (Maamouri, 1998).

By combining the three principles of UDL, namely the provision of multiple means of representation, engagement, and expression, the approach to reading comprehension in a foreign language research advocated in this study considers the development of communication skills and strategies (Fathi & Afzali, 2020; Laufer, 1992) within an effective set of contents and pedagogical practices that are aligned with students' learning experience as important factors for the design and implementation of effective learning outcomes and literacy achievement (Mokhtari & Reichard, 2004; Nouri & Zerhouni, 2016).

2.6 Where Should We Go from Here?

To give reading comprehension in a foreign language its pragmatic due, examination of learners' needs and expectations, the use of UDL as a theoretical framework serves the purpose of isolating the features required in the design of a reading comprehension course that fits all. It probes the reading materials and pedagogical practices in terms of their viability to provide opportunities for learners to access the reading materials, engage in the reading process, and express their understanding of all aspects of the RC material through various means of communication. Finally, it compares the teachers' perceptions of reading comprehension materials in terms of these three criteria.

As reported in the literature, the adoption of UDL as a safeguard principle is not alien to reading comprehension research; it is an integral part of the educational principles of the national curriculum as well as the current educational trends. This means that promoting students' potential is a matter of making principle-based curricula. What are, then, the benefits of such a design in the construction of a reading comprehension course?

It is argued in this chapter that the linguistic and cognitive content of a reading comprehension course cannot be attended to separately and that the features of the RC module need to be investigated in terms of the way they are formulated, the pedagogy through which they are transmitted, and the assessments by which they are evaluated. To this end, the present study utilizes the principles of UDL as potential factors for investigation.

3 Case Study Summary

Here is a brief overview of the research methodology adopted in this study.

3.1 The Method

To give reading comprehension in a foreign language its pragmatic due, this study examines some of the learners' conceptions, needs, and expectations of the RC module, using the UDL as a theoretical framework.

3.2 Research Design

The research design is quantitative and uses the Universal Design for Learning as a theoretical framework. The objective of the study is to isolate the extent to which the RC module provides multiple means of representation, engagement, and expression in terms of their accessibility, doability, and expression for students. Its main objective is to draw some empirical evidence on the features required in the design and implementation of a reading comprehension course. In particular, this case study probes the reading comprehension (RC) materials and activities in terms of their viability with UDL principles. Finally, it compares the teachers' perceptions of reading comprehension materials in terms of these three criteria.

3.3 Sample and Instrument

This research study features 174 undergraduate students from two Moroccan universities (Chouaib Doukali, El Jadida; and Moulay Ismail University, Meknes, Morocco). All the students have Reading Comprehension (RC) as a major module. The data collected consists of a 44-item questionnaire (15 related to accessibility, 14 to doability, and 15 to usability) to investigate students' perceptions of the means of Representation, Engagement, and Expression (REE) used in the RC modules. The distribution of the three principles of REE, as described in the UDL framework, has been assessed in terms of three of their constituent criteria: 'Accessibility, Doability, and Usability' (ADU). The factors involved in the instruments are spread on an equal basis and disposed of in Table 3.1. Regarding the convergent validity of the questionnaire, the scales' reliability was also calculated by Cronbach's alpha coefficients. The values ranged between 0.613 and 0.716 for each of the three principles (ADU), which were above the minimum acceptable value of 0.5.

3.4 Research Questions

For this chapter, two major research questions were raised to probe the value of UDL principles in the RC course. These are:

1. How do students rate Representation, Engagement, and Expression in the RC module?
2. What are some of the most important dimensions of REE reported in the study?

Table 3.1 Criteria for analysis

UDL principles	Reading comprehension content, pedagogy, and assessment features
Means ofrepresentation *Accessibility*	Content formats: Linear/non-linear texts; tables and diagrams & text transcript); PowerPoint presentations. Readings format: Handouts; digital texts; captions; interactive websites Reading genres: Fiction; argumentative; expository; plays, non-linear texts; etc.
Means ofengagement *Doability*	Feedback to students; teachers' responses to students' queries; choice of activities team and group work. Support provision; using real classroom for final project. Clarity of module instructions; encouragement of projects; follow-up activities.
Means ofexpression *Usability*	Flexibility of activities, assignments, and assessments. Creation of opportunities and discussions Encouragement of learning communities. Encouragement of peer feedback on the reading contents.

UDL principles incorporated in reading comprehension modules

Central to these two questions is the search for the significance of the factors selected for students regarding reading comprehension materials and activities. The three principles examined in this study examine the extent to which the RC module offers multiple means of representation, engagement, and expression and are assessed in terms of their accessibility, doability, and usability by the students. These criteria of evaluation are sufficient checkpoints to draw a clear picture of the state of the art of teaching and learning reading comprehension as manifested in the modules taught to undergraduates. As indicated in Table 3.1 below, these criteria relate to a set of features of the course.

The focus of the chosen features is the extent to which the reading comprehension modules provide multiple means of representation (e.g., content variety and format, such as genres, digital, and other types of resources), multiple means of engagement (e.g., modes of completing tasks, types of activities, e.g., personalized, collaborative activities, and other), and multiple means of expression (thinking and critical skills involved, e.g., assignments, discussions, reports, projects). These learning means have been evaluated in terms of their personal and societal credentials, namely, namely, accessibility, doability, and usefulness.

Central to these two research questions is the search for significance of the principles adopted in the theoretical framework of the study and the extent to which the RC course facilitates students' access to and engagement in course content, pedagogy, and assessment practices. It is assumed in the study that these research questions will lead us to the establishment of some of the features to be taken in reading comprehension materials and activities designed for EFL students. Data analysis procedures utilized descriptive statistics for all the variables included in the research instrument. These analyses are reported through their related figures for each research question and with reference to the questions addressed in the study.

4 Results of the Case Study

The results reveal variability between the three factors investigated is not significant as the obtained results display similar levels of importance for all the principles with regard to the variables investigated.

The findings related to RQ1 *(How do students rate Representation, Engagement, and Expression in the RC module?)* report the cumulative effect of three principles investigated. The obtained analyses indicate that all the three principles *(Accessibility: 9/15 items are important, Usability: 8/15 items are important, and Doability: 10/14 items are important though with a relatively varying degree)*. All of them have proved to be significant and consonant with students' perceptions of reading comprehension materials and activities. As these findings amply show, reading comprehension in English as a foreign language is likely to earn students' engagement if consideration is given to these factors in the design and implementation of reading materials and activities, and therefore, support the claims made by the proponents of this approach.

4.1 The Means of REE in the Balance

The results report that students' reactions towards the provision of multiple means of Representation, Engagement, and Expression are consistent with students' conceptions and expectations in terms of their accessibility, engagement, and expression force are viewed by undergraduates in the RC modules adopted in some Moroccan universities. The observations gleaned on each of the guidelines reflect in many ways the realities revealed in the state-of-the-art section regarding the content,

Table 3.2 Descriptive statistics related to 'accessibility'

Accessibility	N	Min	Max	Mean	Std. Deviation
Acc_i1 electronic_copies	174	1.00	5.00	3.4540	1.06204
Acc_i2 internet_access	174	1.00	5.00	2.9713	1.12988
Acc_i3 hard_copies_or_in_a_textbook	174	1.00	5.00	3.3678	1.08180
Acc_i4 focused_instructions	174	1.00	5.00	3.7816	1.01918
Acc_i5 tips_and_sample_answers	174	1.00	5.00	3.8908	1.01698
Acc_i6 require_sufficient_background_knowledge	174	1.00	5.00	3.6552	1.01807
Acc_i7 literary_text_with_images	174	1.00	5.00	3.5977	1.23025
Acc_i8 materials&activities_w_guidance_and_explanations	174	1.00	5.00	4.2241	.86103
Acc_i9 different_format_cards_pictures_and_tables	174	1.00	5.00	3.7471	1.08823
Acc_i10 texts_with_multiple_choice_questions	174	1.00	5.00	3.5287	1.21016
Acc_i11 texts_that_are_descriptive	174	1.00	5.00	3.3391	1.11478
Acc_i12 vocabulary_oriented_activities	174	1.00	5.00	3.8161	1.05927
Acc_i13 new_content	174	1.00	5.00	3.9943	.97659
Acc_i14 use_of_dictionaries	174	1.00	5.00	3.6494	1.14199
Acc_i15 internet_resources	174	1.00	5.00	3.4310	1.19892

pedagogy, and assessment practices adopted in the reading comprehension module offered in the first and the third semesters of university studies. Details of the results related to the means of representation and accessibility are reported in Table 3.2.

The findings (see Table 3.2) indicate the value of providing multiple means of representation that make 'reading comprehension' module accessible, doable, and useful for all students.

The variability between the three factors investigated is not significant, as the obtained results display similar levels of importance of all the principles regarding the variables of accessibility, doability, and usefulness. The value of the figures reported in these tables lies in that they display the importance of providing reading materials that are easily accessed by all learners. It also suggests that teachers do their best to provide diverse means for learning for all students.

4.2 Means of Representation and Accessibility

Within the context under investigation, accessibility measures that have been under study are crucial for the effective completion of the RC texts.

These measures comprise the type of information provided and the ways it is shaped. As for the findings related to RQ2 concerning accessibility (What are some of the most important dimensions of REE reported in the study?), 9 out of 15 of the items included in the questionnaire are of paramount importance for the respondents, indicating the relevance of having materials that are easily accessible and that offer the opportunity for interaction, while at the same time match their potential abilities. These opportunities are highly proclaimed in the research bulk related to making teaching materials equitably accessible to learners. As Edyburn (2010), "Accessibility describes an environment where access is equitably provided to everyone at the same time." (p. 34). Details of the results related to Means of Representation and Accessibility are presented below:

It is noteworthy that among the categories examined, three items emerge from the lot, namely 8, 12, and 13. As shown in Table 3.1 and described in Fig. 3.1, item N.8 stresses the importance of the pedagogical feature of the reading comprehension activity. It puts emphasis on the role played by the teacher in the reading activity and makes it of paramount importance in students' engagement. This finding is supported in the

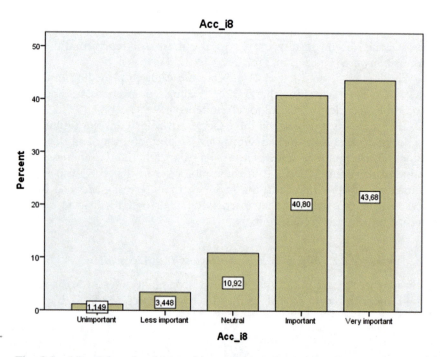

Fig. 3.1 Materials and activities with guidance and support

focus-group interviews, as most students highly appreciate the efforts made by the faculty in helping students access the materials to be studied.

Similarly, items number 12 and 13 (see Figs.3.2 and 3.3) emphasize two different features of the reading content and suggest learners' interest in vocabulary and new content knowledge that is accessible and consonant with their level of instruction, paving the road to the developmental milestone of the reading comprehension module (King-Sears, 2009).

These findings, as shown in Figs. 3.2 and 3.3, confirm the necessity to offer students materials and activities that empower their communicative abilities while stressing the viability of accessibility at the language selection level as a determining factor in the construction of a reading comprehension course in the EFL context. The results displayed in these figures also indicate that the provision of content knowledge that promotes students' literacy skills is equally significant for these learners. Based on the fact that vocabulary knowledge and content knowledge empower

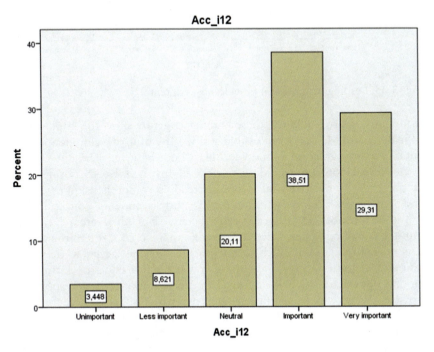

Fig. 3.2 Materials with vocabulary-oriented activities

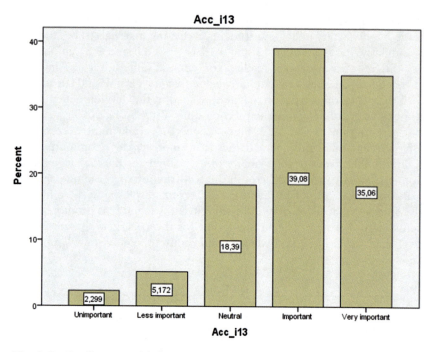

Fig. 3.3 Reading material that provides new content

students' cognitive abilities, these findings cogently show the importance of making the RC course accessible and worthy of its developmental orientations through content and vocabulary knowledge enrichment.

As a final note on attending to accessibility, it is worth noting that among the least positively rated items in reading comprehension materials and activities, but more significant for the study is students' conception of using the technologies to access reading materials. Unlike research carried out in the United States, where learning is empowered through the provision of multiple means which aid the learning process, access to the technologies in the context of the study is a breach of equal opportunities among these learners. This finding is an expression of students' appreciation for having scaffolding opportunities that would support them through their zone of proximal development (ZPD), although most of them lack access to the new technologies. If the end of the RC module is to foster students' learning, the means is no less important for its achievement.

4.3 Means of Engagement and Doability

As a means of engagement, 'doability' assesses how learners are motivated and engaged in the learning process. This process involves determining the extent to which the teaching materials and pedagogies are doable, motivating students' motivation to get involved in the RC activities, and suitable to their level of interaction with the reading materials offered by the module. In the UDL framework, this 'doability' component is about providing multiple means of engagement. The factors investigated assesses how instruction taps into learners' interests, passions, and goals. Examples included in this rubric comprise whether the choice in learning activities incorporates real-world examples and scenarios and whether it uses other interactive tools to promote engagement.

The results of the 'doability variable reveal its congruence with the learners' perceptions of reading materials and activities and fully support the claims of UDL. Its asset, as revealed in the findings reported (see Table 3.3, below), is that it stands for what learners aim for in their

Table 3.3 Descriptive statistics related to the 'usability' principle

Usability	N	Min	Max	Mean	Std. Deviation
Usa_i1 entertaining_narrative_texts	174	1.00	5.00	2.7241	1.20394
Usa_i2 dealing_w_social_&_daily_life_situations	174	1.00	5.00	4.2356	.96571
Usa_i3 texts_about_scientific_and_technological_issues	174	1.00	5.00	3.3391	1.23764
Usa_i4 texts_and_materials_about_arts	174	1.00	5.00	3.6207	1.14034
Usa_i5 language - rich_reading_materials	174	1.00	5.00	3.2011	1.13270
Usa_i6 texts_about_philosophical_issues	174	1.00	5.00	3.7471	.99384
Usa_i7 long_texts_that_provide_a_lot_of_information	174	1.00	5.00	3.3851	.99479
Usa_i8 research_analytic_texts	174	1.00	5.00	3.3563	1.14778
Usa_i9 materials_that_provide_cultural_knowledge	174	1.00	5.00	4.0977	1.10527
Usa_i10 contain_figures_and_digits	174	1.00	5.00	4.2184	1.12178
Usa_i11 reading_materials_to_summarize	174	1.00	5.00	3.9540	1.17693
Usa_i12 demands_analyzing_and_evaluating	174	1.00	5.00	3.3046	1.11960
Usa_i13 materials _that_call_for_Ss_reasoning	174	1.00	5.00	3.5402	.99484
Usa_i14 materials_and_activities_to_comment_on	174	1.00	5.00	3.3851	1.07843
Usa_i15 materials_with_the_target_language_jargon	174	1.00	5.00	3.6724	1.18353

vocational activities. In fact, it is a major finding in the present study to claim that, of the three UDL principles examined in relation to students' conceptions of reading comprehension at the university level, the principle of 'doability' is the most important, suggesting that learners' success depends on how much the tasks, the materials, and the methods are appealing to them.

As the results indicate (see Table 3.3), 12 out of 16 items have been reported to highly rate the 'doability' feature of reading materials and activities. The distribution reported in the above table is the most significant feature revealed in the analyses. Its constituents relate to learners' high interest and concern with the acquisition of knowledge related to (i2) social and daily life situations, (i9) materials that provide cultural knowledge, and texts that contain evidence through figures and digits (i10).

A closely related factor relates to *Language Dealing with Social and Daily Life Situations*. Hence, the results (see Fig. 3.4) show that language ability to develop communication skills is also found to be a significant factor in reading comprehension. This finding complies with the claims made by King-Sears (2014) that pairing new vocabulary terms with vocabulary with which students are familiar, such as pairing *use* and *utilize*, can increase students' vocabulary skills while reducing unnecessary complexity for students who are still learning synonyms. (p. 199). The doability feature of vocabulary, i.e., the extent to which it encourages them to engage in learning, is therefore a key factor in learning.

As can be seen in all the items displayed in Table 3.3 and Fig. 3.5, one of the controversial issues that professionals keep raising regarding the reading materials used in the RC module is the extent to which they effectively handle cultural information. Issues addressed concern authentic materials which address sensible issues and religious extremist movements. These cases, for example, are usually avoided and conceived of as exceptions rather than rules. What matters for students is what converges with their interests and needs.

Finally, Fig. 3.5 emphasizes one of the key components of UDL, namely that of promoting diversity and tolerance as a means of promoting internationalization and cultural understanding among the members of twenty-first-century communities, suggesting that learners' perception of literacy as provided by the RC module needs to be taken into consideration in the

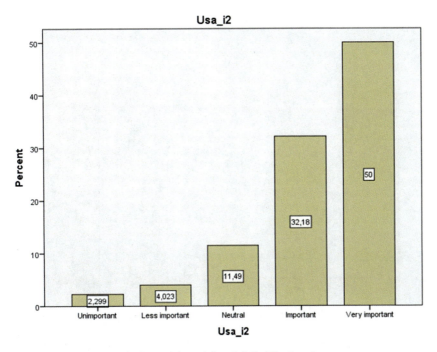

Fig. 3.4 Language dealing with social and daily life situations

selection, design, and implementation of reading comprehension materials and activities.

4.4 The Means of Expression and 'Usability' in the Balance

The multiple means of expression through which reading comprehension is conveyed in the RC module are limited in the means by which learners can express themselves. These means are usually confined within the reading classroom to question-answer practices and discussions. Little resort is made to other means of expression, such as writing, presenting, and outside class assignments. These means of expression refer to how learners demonstrate their understanding and mastery of linear and non-linear discourse. In the UDL framework, usability is about providing multiple means of expression for the teaching materials and practices. This relates to the means through which students can express their understanding of

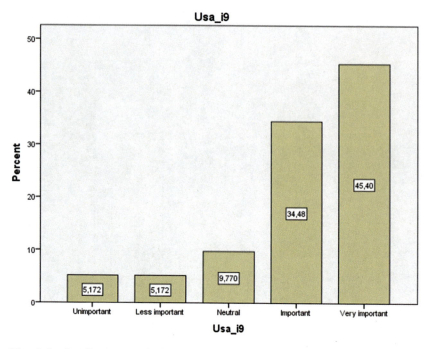

Fig. 3.5 Reading materials that provide cultural knowledge

reading materials, including both linear and non-linear discourse. This examines whether the module provides learners with various ways to demonstrate their understanding, such as writing, speaking, or creating multimedia projects. In the writing research, this refers to the extent to which learners have access to tools and resources that support their expression, such as assistive technology or scaffolding activities to support their writing (A. Ahmed & H. Abouabdelkader, 2016).

The findings related to 'usability' (see Table 3.4) reflect the importance of cognitive development and cooperative learning, as advocated in the UDL research models. Seven items are reported to fully reflect students' perceptions of reading materials and activities that address their cognitive and linguistic abilities.

The findings of the study indicate that professional jargon vocabulary (see Fig. 3.6) is a major focal issue in reading in a foreign language and, therefore, support the view that language is of vital importance and

Table 3.4 Statistics related to the principle of 'usability'

Doability	N	Min	Max	Mean	Std. Deviation
Doa_i1 long_texts_that_require_attention	174	1.00	5.00	3.8218	1.11603
Doa_i2 texts_with_challenging_language	174	1.00	5.00	3.6494	1.15207
Doa_i3 texts_that_contain_rich_vocabulary	174	1.00	5.00	3.6092	1.17149
Doa_i4 texts_professional_jargon_vocabulary	174	1.00	5.00	3.8678	1.01992
Doa_i5 short_texts_that_require_little_time_to_do	174	1.00	5.00	2.9770	1.45035
Doa_i6 do_not_exceed_a_quarter_or_half_a_page	174	1.00	5.00	3.5345	1.28866
Doa_i7 activities_that_rely_on_personal_abilities	174	1.00	5.00	3.3276	1.14883
Doa_i8 activities_that_demand_immediate_action	174	1.00	5.00	3.8218	1.07380
Doa_i9 questions_that_demand_a_lot_of_reflection	174	1.00	5.00	3.2069	1.15441
Doa_i10 activities_that_involve_interaction_btw_Ss	174	1.00	5.00	3.5632	1.09334
Doa_i11 activities_that_create_discussions_btw_groups	174	1.00	5.00	3.6207	1.03400
Doa_i12 activities_that_can_be_done_in_groups	174	1.00	5.00	3.7356	1.03644
Doa_i13 activities_that_include_charts_and_diagrams	174	1.00	5.00	3.6494	1.09020
Doa_i14 tasks_that_assess_ability_to_locate_inf._in text	174	1.00	5.00	3.4138	1.15355

constitutes an essential instrument that allows learners to operate in the foreign language with pragmatic reasons.

Similarly, the claims made in the present study, interaction between learners (see Fig. 3.6) needs to be a crucial component in the design and implementation of reading comprehension EC materials in higher education.

As a pedagogical activity, the value of the reading comprehension is shown to be in its support for collaborative work, suggesting that the provision of reading material is closely tied up with its related pedagogy. Teaching reading comprehension, accordingly, can be much more beneficial to learners when it is done with a social purpose that puts learners in situations where they test their understanding and use of the foreign language with their peers. As shown in Fig. 3.7, creating opportunities for

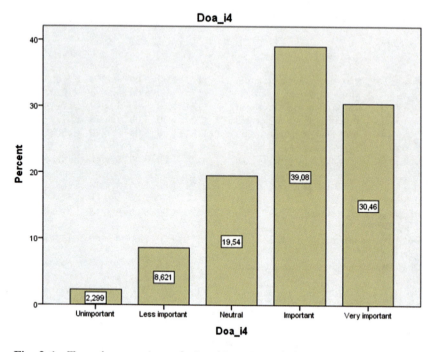

Fig. 3.6 Texts that contain professional jargon vocabulary

group discussions through meaningful debates and discussions is highly beneficial for learners.

Altogether, the findings related to most of the variables included under the 'usability' paradigm suggest that the more a reading material is bound to create social interaction between students, the more it is bound to create opportunities for learning. We do not learn something we are not going to use. This finding reflects students' interest in the provision of multiple means whereby collaborative activities that involve learners in group discussions, supporting the claims of UDL advocates (Connell & Sanford, 1999), 1997).

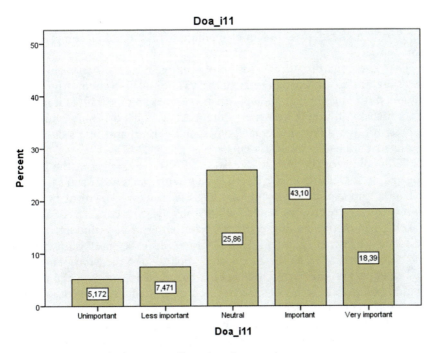

Fig. 3.7 Materials that create discussions between groups

5 General Conclusions and Discussion

The results obtained from the case study and the research findings reported in this chapter amply support the relevance of UDL principles in the construction of a viable RC module for university students. These findings suggest that the construction and implementation of RC modules can be more promising for students if teachers offer effective means of representation, multiple opportunities for students' engagement in the reading contents, and accessible means to materials that serve their concerns and needs.

By the same token, the findings reported in the study disclose the dissatisfaction expressed by students regarding some features of the RC modules. They suggest that many components of the RC course still require review at the level of content, pedagogy, and assessment. To leverage students' learning outcomes and expectations to maximum advantage, it is argued in this chapter that students' perceptions of the learning contents and pedagogies are crucial in the identification of the factors that can be improved in the design and implementation of a reading comprehension course.

The views regarding the provision of multiple means of representation also suggest that the current state of the RC module's content can better students' reading abilities and appreciation of reading itself if (1) it places more focus on multiple means of content accessibility, doability, and usefulness through different formats, types, and genres, and offers different means that are useful to all students.

The findings of the case study also call for some changes at the pedagogical level. Despite all the efforts made by the faculty, moving from a stellar cast approach in which every single instructor is in front of their own vision to a teamwork framework that involves the concerns of all the stakeholders of the reading comprehension enterprise, including course designers, instructors, and students. This would make the vision global and comprehensive of all the checkpoints applicable to the Moroccan EFL higher education context. This suggests the need to improve the pedagogical practices in terms of student-oriented guidelines, as advocated by UDL guidelines and checkpoints.

A third recommendation that can be gleaned from the obtained findings concerns the assessments in use, which needs to be attended to meticulously in order to make assessments more formative and more equitable for all learners. As mentioned in the introduction to this chapter, curricular changes need to address the needs of students in real-time, rather than referring to best practices of a particular time or community. Until now the assessments of the RC module are not based on a national set of rubrics and standards that can attribute a consistent level of competence, nor are they consonant with the multiple means of representation, engagement, and expression suggested by the UDL framework. At the same time, they succinctly reveal that the actual pedagogies are still discriminating between students and do not always cater to the needs of all students with learning disabilities in terms of feedback and support. The same drawbacks are also reported for assessment practices at the level of multiple means of expression, as most students are assessed using the same means and using the same tools. RC modules are assessed through an end-of-module exam, with reference to no other types of performance.

Based on all these analyses, it is highly recommended that further research be conducted from a UDL perspective in order to make the current pedagogies address the social and psychological features of the learners within their own environment.

Appendix

Questionnaire

This questionnaire aims at identifying the necessary features of a Reading Comprehension Module. The purpose is to examine some of the teachers' motivational drives and needs. If you agree with the above purpose, please fill in the questionnaire as requested. Your collaboration is highly appreciated.

How do you value the importance of the following features in a reading comprehension course? Unimportant (1); less important (2); somewhat important (3); important (4); very important (5).

For each of the items below, tick a box to show how important it is for you when (you are presented with):

	Statement	Unimportant	Less important	Somewhat important	Important	Very important
1.	Texts are accessible in electronic copies.					
2.	Texts that require internet access.					
3.	Texts are accessible as hard copies or in a textbook.					
4.	Texts are accompanied with focused instructions.					
5	Texts are provided with tips and sample answers.					
6.	Resources that require sufficient background knowledge.					
7.	Literary text with images.					

(*continued*)

(continued)

Statement	Unimportant	Less important	Somewhat important	Important	Very important
8. Materials and activities with guidance and explanations.					
9. Materials in different format, such as cards, pictures, and table.					
10. Texts with multiple-choice questions.					
11. Texts that are descriptive.					
12. Materials with vocabulary-oriented activities.					
13. Reading material that provides new content.					
14. Texts and activities that allow for the use of dictionaries.					
15. Texts and activities that allow for the use of internet resources.					
16. Texts representing the foreign language culture.					
17. Texts and activities dealing with social and daily life situations.					
18. Texts about scientific and technological issues.					
19. Texts and materials about arts.					
20. Language-rich reading materials					

(continued)

(continued)

Statement	Unimportant	Less important	Somewhat important	Important	Very important
21. Texts about philosophical issues.					
22. Long texts that provide a lot of information.					
23. Research analytic texts.					
24. Reading materials that provide cultural knowledge.					
25. Texts that contain figures and digits.					
26. Reading materials to summarize.					
27. Materials that demand analyzing and evaluating.					
28. Materials and activities that call for students' reasoning					
29. Materials and activities to comment on.					
30. Materials and activities with the target language jargon.					
31. Long texts that require attention.					
32. Texts with challenging language.					
33. Texts that contain rich vocabulary.					
34. Materials that use jargon vocabulary used by professionals.					
35. Short texts that require little time to do.					

(continued)

(continued)

Statement	Unimportant	Less important	Somewhat important	Important	Very important
36. Texts that do not exceed a quarter or half a page.					
37. Texts and activities that rely on personal abilities.					
38. Texts and activities that demand immediate action.					
39. Text questions that demand a lot of reflection.					
40. Materials and activities that involve interaction between students.					
41. Materials and activities that create discussions between groups.					
42. Materials and activities that can be done in groups.					
43. Activities that include charts and diagrams.					
44. Tasks that assess one's ability to locate information in the text.					

Thank you for your time & feedback!

References

Abouabdelkader, H. (1999). *Metacognitive strategies used by Moroccan University EFL student-writers: A process-oriented discourse analysis of argumentative composition writing*. Unpublished Ph. D. Thesis, Faculty of Education.

Abouabdelkader, S. (2018). Moroccan EFL university students' composing skills in the balance: Assessment procedures and outcomes. In A. M. Ahmed & H. Abouabdelkader (Eds.), *Assessing EFL writing in the 21st century Arab world: Revealing the unknown* (pp. 79–109). Palgrave Macmillan. https://doi.org/10.1007/978-3-319-64104-1_4

Abouabdelkader, S. (2019). *The effect of functional vocabulary on engineering students' proficiency in English: Aligning curricula with employability standards.* [Unpublished Doctoral thesis]. Ibn Tofail.

Acim, R. (2018). The Socratic method of instruction: An experience with a reading comprehension course. *Journal of Educational Research and Practice, 8*(1), 4.

Ahmed, A., & Abouabdelkader, H. (2016). *Teaching EFL writing in the 21st century Arab world: Realities and challenges.* Palgrave Macmillan.

Ahmed, A., & Abouabdelkader, H. (2018). *Assessing EFL writing in the 21st century Arab world: Revealing the unknown.* Springer.

Alghonaim, A. S. (2018). Explicit ESL/EFL reading-writing connection: An issue to explore in ESL/EFL settings. *Theory and Practice in Language Studies, 8*(4), 385–392.

Altihami, D. (2010). Implementing the LMD system: Experience of the philosophy department in the Cadi Ayyad University in Marakkech. *Towards an Arab Higher Education Space: International Challenges and Societal Responsibilities: Proceedings of the Arab Regional Conference on Higher Education,* 201–211.

An, S. (2013). Schema theory in reading. *Theory & Practice in Language Studies, 3*(1).

Anderson, N. J. (1999). Improving reading speed: Activities for the classroom. *Forum, 37*(2), n2.

Ayad, K., Bennani, K. D., & Elhachloufi, M. (2020). Evolution of university governance in Morocco: What is the impact? *International Journal of Higher Education, 9*(5), 94–104.

Banks, J. A. (2004). Multicultural education: Historical development, dimensions, and practice. In J. A. Banks & C. A. M. Banks (Eds.), *Handbook of research on multicultural education* (2nd ed., pp. 3–29). San Francisco: Jossey-Bass.

Beerkens, M. (2018). Evidence-based policy and higher education quality assurance: Progress, pitfalls and promise. *European Journal of Higher Education, 8*(3), 272–287.

Bouziane, A. (1993). *Towards an effective use of reading texts: An investigation* (pp. 83–97). Proceedings of the XIIIth MATE Annual Conference.

Bouziane, A. (2019). *ELT issues in Morocco: A research-based perspective.* Moroccan Association of Teachers of English.

Burgstahler, S. (2009). *Universal design: Process, principles, and applications.* DO-IT.

Carrell, P. L. (1984). Schema theory and ESL reading: Classroom implications and applications. *The Modern Language Journal, 68*(4), 332–343.

Collins, A., & Smith, E. E. (1980). *Teaching the process of reading comprehension.* BBN Report; No. 4393.

Connell, B. R., & Sanford, J. A. (1999). *Research implications of universal design* (pp. 35–57). Enabling Environments: Measuring the Impact of Environment on Disability and Rehabilitation.

Courey, S. J., Tappe, P., Siker, J., & LePage, P. (2013). Improved lesson planning with Universal Design for Learning (UDL). *Teacher Education and Special Education: The Journal of the Teacher Education Division of the Council for Exceptional Children, 36*(1), 7–27. https://doi.org/10.1177/0888406412446178

CSEFRS. (2019). *Réforme de l'enseignement supérieur-perspectives stratégique.* https://www.csefrs.ma/wp-content/uploads/2019/07/enseignement-supe%CC%81rieur-fr.pdf

Cumming, T. M., & Rose, M. C. (2022). Exploring universal design for learning as an accessibility tool in higher education: A review of the current literature. *The Australian Educational Researcher, 49*(5), 1025–1043.

Dahir n° 1-00-199 du 15 safar 1421 (19 mai 2000) portant promulgation de la loi n° 01-00 portant organisation de l'enseignement supérieur.

Edyburn, D. L. (2010). Would you recognize universal design for learning if you saw it? Ten propositions for new directions for the second decade of UDL. *Learning Disability Quarterly, 33*(1), 33–41.

Edyburn, D. L. (2021). Universal usability and universal design for learning. *Intervention in School and Clinic, 56*(5), 310–315.

Evmenova, A. (2018). Preparing teachers to use universal design for learning to support diverse learners. *Journal of Online Learning Research, 4*(2), 147–171.

Falk-Ross, F. C. (2001). Toward the new literacy: Changes in college students' reading comprehension strategies following reading/writing projects. *Journal of Adolescent & Adult Literacy, 45*(4), 278–288.

Fathi, J., & Afzali, M. (2020). The effect of second language Reading strategy instruction on young Iranian EFL learners' reading comprehension. *International Journal of Instruction, 13*(1), 475–488.

Gargiulo, R. M., & Metcalf, D. (2022). *Teaching in today's inclusive classrooms: A universal design for learning approach.* Cengage Learning.

Gilakjani, A. P., & Ahmadi, M. R. (2011). A study of factors affecting EFL learners' English listening comprehension and the strategies for improvement.

Goodman, K. S. (1967). Reading: A psycholinguistic guessing game. *Journal of the Reading Specialist, 6*(4), 126–135. https://doi.org/10.1080/19388076709556976

Grabe, W. (2009). 24 teaching and testing Reading. *The Handbook of Language Teaching, 441.*

Grabe, W. (2010). Fluency in reading—Thirty-five years later. *Special Issue: In Honor of Paul Nation, 22*(1), 71–83.

Grabe, W., & Stoller, F. L. (2002). *Teaching reading.* Pearson Education.

Hock, M., & Mellard, D. (2005). Reading comprehension strategies for adult literacy outcomes. *Journal of Adolescent & Adult Literacy, 49*(3), 192–200.

King-Sears, M. (2009). Universal design for learning: Technology and pedagogy. *Learning Disability Quarterly, 32,* 199–201. https://doi.org/10.2307/27740372

King-Sears, P. (2014). Introduction to learning disability quarterly special series on universal design for learning: Part one of two. *Learning Disability Quarterly, 37*(2), 68–70.

Kintsch, W. (1988). The role of knowledge in discourse comprehension: A construction-integration model. *Psychological Review, 95*(2), 163.

Kintsch, W., & van Dijk, T. A. (1978). Toward a model of text comprehension and production. *Psychological Review, 85*(5), 363–394.

Larouz, M., & Abouabdelkader, S. (2020). Teachers' feedback on EFL students' dissertation writing in Morocco. In A. M. Ahmed, S. Troudi, & S. Riley (Eds.), *Feedback in L2 English writing in the Arab world: Inside the black box* (pp. 201–232). Palgrave Macmillan. https://doi.org/10.1007/978-3-030-25830-6_8

Laufer, B. (1992). Reading in a foreign language: How does L2 lexical knowledge interact with the reader's general academic ability'. *Journal of Research in Reading, 15*(2), 95–103.

Liu, J., Cohen, S. B., & Lapata, M. (2018). *Discourse representation structure parsing* (pp. 429–439). Proceedings of the 56th Annual Meeting of the Association for Computational Linguistics (Volume 1: Long Papers). https://doi.org/10.18653/v1/P18-1040

Maamouri, M. (1998). *Language education and human development: Arabic diglossia and its impact on the quality of education in the Arab region.* The Mediterranean Development Forum.

Meo, G. (2008). Curriculum planning for all learners: Applying universal design for learning (UDL) to a high school reading comprehension program. *Preventing School Failure: Alternative Education for Children and Youth, 52*(2), 21–30.

Mokhtari, K., & Reichard, C. (2004). Investigating the strategic reading processes of first and second language readers in two different cultural contexts. *System, 32*(3), 379–394.

Nadori, N. (2020a). An ecological perspective on Reading development: A theoretical framework to guide empirical research. *Journal of English Language Teaching and Linguistics, 5*(2), Article 2. https://doi.org/10.21462/jeltl.v5i2.397

Nadori, N. (2020b). The predictive effects of reading motivation constructs and reading practice on Moroccan fourth graders reading comprehension achievement: An analysis of PIRLS 2011 study. *European Journal of Teaching and Education, 2*(2), 138–151.

Nathan, R. G., & Stanovich, K. E. (1991). The causes and consequences of differences in reading fluency. *Theory Into Practice, 30*(3), 176–184.

Nouri, N., & Zerhouni, B. (2016). The relationship between vocabulary knowledge and reading comprehension among Moroccan EFL learners. *Journal of Humanities and Social Science, 21*(10), 19–26.

Oublal, F. (1996). *Reading in English as a foreign language: The effects of training Moroccan learners in the use of inferencing strategies.* [Unpublished D.E.S. Dissertation]. Faculty of Education.

Oublal, F., & El Fatwaki, L. H. (1994). *Can we make our learners more interested in reading in the foreign language?* pp. 76–87.

Oxford, R. L. (2011). Strategies for learning a second or foreign language. *Language Teaching, 44*(2), 167–180.

Oxford, R. L., & Burry-Stock, J. A. (1995). Assessing the use of language learning strategies worldwide with the ESL/EFL version of the strategy inventory for language learning (SILL). *System, 23*(1), 1–23.

Putnam, H. (1975). The Meaning of "Meaning." Language, Mind, and Knowledge, 7(13), 131–193.

Rao, K., & Meo, G. (2016). Using universal design for learning to design standards-based lessons. *SAGE Open, 6*(4), 2158244016680688.

Robinson, D. E., & Wizer, D. R. (2016). Universal design for learning and the quality matters guidelines for the design and implementation of online learning events. *International Journal of Technology in Teaching and Learning, 12*(1), 17–32.

Rumelhart, D. E. (2017). Schemata: The building blocks of cognition. In *Theoretical issues in reading comprehension* (pp. 33–58). Routledge.

Stanovich, K. E. (2009). Matthew effects in reading: Some consequences of individual differences in the acquisition of literacy. *Journal of Education, 189*(1–2), 23–55.

Urquhart, A. H., & Weir, C. J. (2014). *Reading in a second language: Process, product and practice.* Routledge.

Van Dijk, T. A. (1982). Opinions and attitudes in discourse comprehension. In *Advances in psychology* (Vol. 9, pp. 35–51). Elsevier.

Wigfield, A. (1997). Reading motivation: A domain-specific approach to motivation. *Educational Psychologist, 32*(2), 59–68.

Wordsworth, W. (1802). *My heart leaps up when I behold.* Poem.

Zimmerman, B., & Schunk, D. (2006). Competence and control beliefs: Distinguishing the means and ends. *Handbook of Educational Psychology, 2*, 349–367.

CHAPTER 4

Encouraging Diversity and Student Engagement in the Classroom

Deborah Swallow

1 Introduction: What Is Culture?

Two of the key features in foreign language learning at tertiary level are the background and training of the teacher and the background of the students. Additional to this is the fact that many students studying a second language (L2) may be studying or working abroad on completion of their degrees in their own country. What do these students face and how can language teachers at tertiary level help them? For language teachers, the understanding of how culture works, how to involve students more effectively in the learning process and how to equip them for the next steps in their student or work careers overseas are all crucial teaching skills and are at the root of diversity and inclusion in education. Helping students understand the cultural background of the L2 they are learning and how it relates to their own background and interests is fundamental in building student personal engagement and student engagement is central

D. Swallow (✉)
Glasgow Caledonian University London, London, UK
e-mail: deborah.swallow@gcu.ac.uk

© The Author(s), under exclusive license to Springer Nature Switzerland AG 2023
H. Abouabdelkader, B. Tomalin (eds.), *Diversity Education in the MENA Region*, https://doi.org/10.1007/978-3-031-42693-3_4

to diversity and inclusion in language education. It is a skill that teachers trained as linguists and taught to teach the L2 grammatical structure, core vocabulary and pronunciation without preparing students for the background context where they might encounter differences is a recurring theme in this book.

So, what is culture? One of the world's leading cultural theorists and trainers, Richard Lewis, defines it as follows:

> Cultural behaviour is the end product of collected wisdom, filtered and passed down through hundreds of generations and translated into hardened, undiscussable core beliefs, values, notions, and persistent action patterns. (Lewis, 2022)

Culture, as Lewis notes, involves not just beliefs and behaviour but the use of language. For many travellers abroad, the foreign language they have learned at home may sound very different in a foreign environment.

2 Foreign Language Teaching and Learning Abroad

A key way of consolidating a foreign language learned in tertiary education at home is to take the opportunity to use it where it is a national language. For many MENA graduates continuing their studies in other parts of the world, the use of the language they have learned can be a real challenge in the country where it is spoken as a national language. This is the same for students from all over the world; pronunciation, accent, vocabulary and even grammar, in some instances, can seem very different to what they have learned at university and at home.

The reason is that in their own country, they have learned a foreign language as a linguistic system. They have not learned how the language is actually used internationally and how it has been adapted to the needs of particular communities. Language idiom and language usage are either absent in their university courses or very limited.

The question this chapter explores is how university-educated language students adapt or fail to adapt to new environments where the language they have learned is spoken.

For many students, an overseas study period is an adventure and often a defining positive experience in their lives. However, for others, it can be a period of intense loneliness and dislocation, which can affect their studies. Interviews carried out among students at a university in London, the capital of the UK, identified seven areas of disidentification and dissatisfaction with their new overseas environment (Swallow & Tomalin, 2022).

1. Distance: The first one was distance. Many students pursuing postgraduate studies in universities abroad were living some distance from where they were studying and therefore students often went straight back 'home' to their lodgings after lectures and missed out on social events in the university. This meant that their opportunity to socialise, build relationships and make friends at the university was much more difficult.
2. Loneliness: The second area of difficulty was because of the inaccessibility of the family they were living with or the lodgings, maybe a hall of residence, where they were accommodated. Quite often they found they had a room where they felt very isolated, either from the family they were living with or from the hall where they were lodged. This led to intense loneliness and discomfort. The absence of a social relationship could leave them very lonely, especially at weekends.
3. Isolation: The third area, partly a result of the first two, was that as a result of their experience, the students concerned failed to mix easily, leaving them feeling isolated and excluded. This meant that instead of practising the language they had learned at their own universities, they were denying themselves the opportunity to do so in the international environment and note and discuss the differences they found in conversations, social sight signs, publicity and domestic TV.
4. Understanding: The fourth area was in the classroom or lecture hall. They couldn't understand their teacher. There are several possible reasons for this. The accent they were used to may be very different as teachers came from different regions in the country and, most commonly, spoke far too fast for foreign learners to easily understand them. The other factor was the language used. Foreign students were often bemused by the idioms and acronyms used by lecturers, which they never explained and didn't pause long enough to allow the meaning to sink in. Students wanted to ask for explanations but didn't dare interrupt and ask the meaning because they didn't want to reveal their lack of fluency. Hence the use of mobile

phones in the lecture hall as students searched for the meaning online.
5. Nationalism: A fifth area was nationalism. Most students mixed with others of their own national or regional background and some students could feel very isolated and out of place. This would also occur in the classroom or lecture hall, where students of the same national group would sit together as a group. Once again, this inhibited cross-cultural exchange and left many feeling isolated and out of touch.
6. Burnout: These factors can place huge pressures on some foreign students who succumb to burnout. They no longer feel able to work and reject rather than adopt and adapt to all the experiences their new environment can offer.
7. Culture shock: Adapting to the different lifestyle of the new country is often experienced as culture shock, which affects the quality of students' academic work. This is discussed later on in this chapter.

What can teachers and fellow students do about it to support those continuing their studies overseas? First, we can take a personal interest and encourage foreign students to share their experiences and the difficulties they face. The use of group work in class and breakout rooms in online tutoring can encourage foreign students to make friends. Also, keeping in touch with the student representative, if there is one, can alert teachers to possible individual problems. Also, if necessary, a student's issues regarding travel and accommodation can be referred to administration and even, if appropriate, pastoral care can be very effective. The key issue for teachers is to develop sensitivity so that they can be aware of possible student problems and be able to direct them to where they can get help. Just showing personal interest and empathy can help resolve difficulties.

One very good teaching technique is to get students to examine their experience inthe host country by using the MBI process. MBI stands for Map, Bridge and Integrateand it works like this. First, invite your students to share with you or the classincidents that they have found difficult to deal with in the host country, what we callcritical incidents. Ask them to describe the critical incident in three stages. The first isMap. What did they experience that was different and how would it be different for them at home in their own countries? Stage 2 is Bridge. Ask why people were behaving differently. This is the vital process of showing empathy with the host population. Stage 3 is Integrate.

Decide what needs to change in order to fit in with the society. And, finally, ask what people have learned about the new culture they are in as a result of applying the MBI process. A ten-minute session devoted to MBI from time to time in class can really help students resolve problems and develop empathy with their new environment and those they deal with (DiStefano & Maznevski, 2003).

So, a few tips for teachers and administrators: first, slow down and make sure the important points are clear. Try to get to know your class a bit so you can identify possible difficulties. If necessary, get the support of the student care body or even pastoral care (regardless of religious denomination). Keep in contact with the student representative to be aware of possible problems. Most importantly, just by showing interest, you build student engagement and involvement.

3   Dealing with Culture Shock

If you've lived abroad or had to live and work in a different environment, you've probably all had this experience. One day you wake up and you feel depressed but you don't know why. You are missing friends and family, and you ask yourself, 'Why am I here?' You feel loneliness and anxiety which often lead to depression. You may be overworking or underperforming, and you may suffer burnout.

What's going on? It's not the student. It's culture shock. Culture shock is the shock of being away from family, friends and daily routines. One day they wake up and they feel depressed but they don't know why. They are missing friends and family and asking themselves, 'Why am I here?' Culture shock usually emerges about four to six weeks after arriving in the new national environment and can last for up to four months. Students can expect a short period of culture shock followed by a series of mini-shocks as they integrate.

Are they going to go through three months of misery, settling into a new environment? According to the originator of the Culture Shock theory, Kaverlo Oberg, culture shock is represented as a U curve, manifesting through four stages (Oberg, 1960).

Stage 1 is the thrill or the shock of being in a new environment.
Stage 2 is the point where things may go wrong because of your difficulty in adapting to the new environment. This is the culture shock.

Stage 3 is the one where you gradually recover and get used to where and how you are living and working, culminating in:
Stage 4 where you integrate with the new environment.

Barbara Marx adapted the culture shock U curve into a W curve. While accepting the four stages proposed by Oberg, she said that culture shock re-occurred at various points during a period in a foreign country on the way to integration with the new society, as shown in the chart below (Marx, 2001).

Barbara Marx
(the W curve – shocks recur)

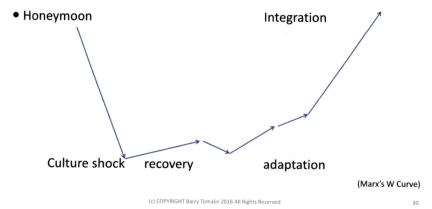

(Marx's W Curve)

Perhaps the most influential theory of how culture shock works is Milton Bennett's DMIS model. DMIS stands for Developmental Model of Intercultural Sensitivity, and Bennett divided the understanding of culture shock into two areas; ethnocentrism (relating primarily to your own ethnographic background) and ethnorelativism (relating your ethnic background to the new environment you are in) (Bennett, 2013). He described the process of moving between the two stages in six steps, summarised as follows.

Ethnocentric Stage

1. Denial: 'I act like I'm at home.'
2. Defence: 'This place is terrible!' Or 'My place sucks!'
3. Minimisation: 'We're all the same.'

Ethnorelative Stage

4. Acceptance: 'I recognise we're different.'
5. Adaptation: 'I adapt.'
6. Integration: 'I feel like I belong.'

The DMIS model is now universally recognised as a key factor in students settling into a new environment overseas or foreign students coming to study or live in the MENA region. Teaching a second language to foreign visitors is just not enough. Teachers need to understand and empathise with the adaptation problems their students might be going through and find time and ways of advising them. The same is important for hosts if the students are staying with a family and, to some extent, with registrars and other officials. But teachers are in the frontline, and they will be the first to notice if their students are experiencing problems, as it is likely to affect their studies and may even lead to absence.

So, what can educational authorities, teachers and residential hosts do to help learners studying abroad or likely to go abroad? Spending part of a class period explaining culture shock and how to cope with it is a major although often disregarded contribution to student success. What can teachers suggest?

First of all, people abroad should expect culture shock to occur to some degree, caused by something going wrong, probably with their studies or their surroundings. When culture shock occurs, sufferers should just treat it like the flu. They can take a bit of time off and go to bed and try and relax, but there are a number of comfort strategies seasoned travellers recommend. Learn about it.

1. Expect it – it will happen in some form or other.
2. Don't get too busy too quickly.
3. Leave time to settle in.
4. Keep in contact – with friends and family at home.
5. If you need help, ask and see a doctor if you need to.

For students intending to continue their studies abroad, there are other strategies for settling in more easily that teachers can suggest.

- Take comfort things – not just photos, films and music, but also a duvet, a cushion, a favourite mug.
- Find comfort places – find a place similar to where they feel comfortable at home. (A park, a place of religious worship and a hotel lounge are just three examples).
- Don't let people's sports or exercise routines slip. If they are used to regular exercise and decide to leave it till they've settled in, they'll feel sluggish.
- Advise them to use Webcam, WhatsApp, and Zoom and schedule virtual communication with friends and family at home during coffee breaks or mealtimes.
- Get them to think about creating a regular blog or diary about what they have learned abroad. Lots of students study/travel abroad and would value following them online. They might also use the Web to find out more about the country they are in and what makes it special.

All these are things that teachers can teach in the second language and which students will find valuable. Taking the time for students to talk about their own interests and how they can follow them in their new environment is an important part of recognising diversity and getting students more engaged with the class and the language they are learning. In addition, there is something else they should know, it's worse going home!

4   Coming Home

Research suggests that most students and teachers going home after living abroad find repatriation more difficult than relocation. Therefore, as part of recognising diversity, in order to preserve student engagement, it is important to support students and colleagues in the difficulties they may experience on coming home after a period studying or teaching abroad. How is it that people back home in their own country experience problems? One is that inevitably they have changed while being abroad and have gradually gotten used to another country's lifestyle and beliefs and customs. In short, they are not the same. However, people coming home often expect that everything will be the same as when they left. It often isn't and people at home change as well. A common problem is that people at home often don't show particular interest in returnees' adventures overseas. Inviting returnees to share their experiences of being abroad and discussing in class what they have learned can be an important part of raising student engagement.

Culture shock is not pleasant but, as we have suggested, there are things you and your students can do to lessen the impact. However, as seasoned travellers and overseas workers will tell you, it's worse coming home! Why?

You've changed. You expect everything at home to be the same but that's changed too and people may not be interested in your extraordinary adventures abroad. The food tastes different to what you're used to. Your university or school is not the same, things you expected have changed or gone altogether and prices have probably gone up. Most of all, things you enjoyed in your new environment are not available at home. So, how do you deal with it?

For students and teaching staff returning home from being abroad for some time and helping them to settle in, experts suggest four stages. The first stage occurs even before students or colleagues return home.

Stage 1: Leave-taking and departure
Stage 2: The honeymoon stage
Stage 3: Reverse culture shock
Stage 4: Adjustment

Let us explore each stage in turn.

1. Leave-taking and departure: Say goodbye to friends and colleagues and teachers in the country the student is leaving. Make sure the school entry back home is organised. Make sure the student has made contact with friends and family before leaving to ensure a good reception.
2. The honeymoon stage: This is the honeymoon period. It is so nice to be home. Craig Storti describes it as 'vacationland home' (Storti, 2011). Of course, the returnee will notice changes, but the important thing is not to judge them and to be aware that she or he has changed too.
3. Reverse culture shock: Students should be warned to expect a reverse culture shock period when she or he may feel taken for granted by people with no interest in their experience of living

abroad. Returnees often feel marginalised, and it can be both alienating and even frightening.
4. Adjustment: Of course, this uncomfortable period won't last as the student achieves balance, re-establishes routines or gets used to new routines. In doing so, the student experiences less anxiety and doubt and is better able to judge objectively any negative experiences in returning home and settling in.

Once again there are a number of steps the teacher can advise their students intending to go to the country whose language they have been learning to take. The role of the foreign language teacher is fundamental in helping students who have been abroad to re-establish themselves in the educational process and continue their studies. Asking students to share their foreign experiences in class can really help the students concerned feel engaged with the learning process. Also, the teacher may act as a mentor, where personal conversations can take place in tutorial sessions. In some cases, the teacher may even recommend access to pastoral or medical support where appropriate. There are a number of things you can do.

1. Think ahead: What are you going to do when you get home? Will there be things you've learned overseas that you want to use at home? How? Look for ways to validate the overseas experience. (Meet the diaspora of the country you've been in, listen to music, read books about it, tell your friends and other students about it, have a class discussion about where you've been and what it was like.) If you feel depressed or need support, talk to friends you trust, and arrange with your school or college for mentoring or counselling.
2. At university / work: Find out how things have changed at home and don't get upset. Maybe have a 'coming home' party to catch up with everyone. Keep in touch with overseas friends via social media. Identify a personal mentor you can rely on. Talk to others who've studied abroad. What was it like for them? How did they adapt? Above all, don't jump to conclusions. See what lessons you can learn and apply them.

As teachers, if you can offer a class about culture shock in the first month of the course, allowing debate and discussion, it will be really helpful. Also, in the last month or so, offer a class on Coming Home to help your students prepare to deal with possible issues that might arise when they go back to their own countries and give them strategies they can use to overcome difficulties. Above all, remember that showing interest in your students can really make a difference to how they feel about their time in your country and help them to adapt and study successfully. Some teachers will undoubtedly say they haven't got time and that it's not part of their job. The aim of this chapter is to demonstrate that the teacher's awareness and preparedness to support the process of re-integration by getting the students to share their experience of being abroad and coming home is an important way of getting returning students to re-engage with their studies, resulting in better results in examinations and projects they undertake. Therefore, the argument is that incorporating culture shock and reverse culture shock as topics in the foreign language and other classes for even just a few minutes can really matter.

5 Conclusion and Recommendations

Diversity and inclusion, as described in Chap. 1, are not automatic. When students from the MENA region or other areas travel overseas to the countries whose language they have studied in their own countries, they often feel profoundly discouraged by the experience. The solution for their teachers and colleagues is to provide support, both in their own country and where they are studying or working abroad. Also important is to get students to discuss their experience of travelling abroad to the country whose language they are learning at home. This will be an important part of student support and a way of increasing students' engagement in the learning process.

Note This chapter is partly based on a presentation given in 2022 to HEURO – The Association of UK Higher Education European Officers.

References

Bennett, M. (2013). *Basic concepts of intercultural communication (Second edition): Paradigms, principles and practices.* Intercultural Press.

DiStefano, J. J., & Maznevski, M. L. (2003). Developing global managers: Integrating theory, behavior, data and performance. In W. Mobley & P. Dorfman (Eds.), *Advances in global leadership* (Vol. 3, pp. 341–371). JAI Press.

Lewis, R. D. (2022). *When cultures collide* (4th ed.). NB Books.

Marx, B. (2001). *Breaking through culture shock*. NB Books.
Oberg, K. (1960). Cultural shock: Adjustment to new cultural environments. *Practical Anthropology, 7*, 177–182.
Storti, C. (2011). *The art of coming home*. John Murray, Hachette UK.
Swallow, D., & Tomalin, B. (2022). *HEURO Conference presentation*, Delivered at HEURO Conference, UK, Leicester University.

PART II

The Impact of Diversity Education, Equity, and Inclusion on Language Learning

CHAPTER 5

Towards the Construction of a Diversity Education Landscape in Moroccan Higher Education Language Curricula

Hassan Abouabdelkader

1 Introduction

If it needs more than 200 years for our planet to reach Civilisation Type I, which is millions of years behind Civilisation Type II, from which our planet has received some signals, say scientists, it means that our education needs to harness its rhythm and speed to align its progress with the requirements of future generations. This means that educational progress depends on the efficacy of alignment selected for our communities. The argument is that today's power lies in how much we work together to construct a shared future. Though highly debated and contravened (Qin et al., 2014), diversity, equity, and inclusion are considered in this chapter as the tools whereby we can achieve this objective and bridge the existing gaps in language education. If properly attended to in most MENA countries, these ailing conditions are likely to serve as an open window for

H. Abouabdelkader (✉)
Ecole Nationales Supérieure d'Arts et Métiers, Moulay Ismail University, Meknes, Morocco

students' growth and development and a means to overcome the existing inequities and provide new accommodations for all students in the region.

Like in most developing countries, Morocco expends a lot of efforts to promote its educational system and remedy deficiencies, but most of these efforts cannot solve the learning problems crisis. Among the key factors responsible for the misalignment of curricula, the World Bank established four criteria among the causes of the dysfunctioning of education in many countries. Of all these causes identified (World Bank, 2020), the present chapter propels Cause 4, which gives more impetus to citizens—teachers and learners are the determinant factors of accountability for their educational conditions—to the forefront of these priorities. As potential carriers of change, teachers enjoy several auspicious privileges; they benefit from the respect of all social strata. They can carry out research, make observations of what happens in their classes and curricula, supplement solutions, and build up educational projects.

In practice, teachers are the direct partners of learners; they have a large spectrum of activity in the achievement of change. Their work includes a lot of interaction that may harness the powers of learners and promote their development and growth. Reports from the HCI 2020 indicate that the increase of the human capital ratio in Morocco obtained at the level of learning outcomes from data collected in 2010 was 6% more significant due to the improvements achieved, but that "important challenges persist related to the quality of education, equity, and management of the sector" (World Bank, 2020). Despite the efforts pursued in the Education Act in 2019 (2015–2030), the World Bank issued a set of recommendations which urge the country to adopt new approaches and search for new partnerships to overcome the prevailing learning crisis. These critical interventions are reported by researchers and international organisations to rest on the country's continuing efforts to invest in human capital, one of the components of diversity education targets.

This chapter seeks to examine the state of diversity education principles as perceived and practised in English language courses in Moroccan higher education. Its search is oriented towards understanding the mechanisms of diversity education through the philosophies and principles underlying the curricula, the pedagogies, and the assessment practices. The major dimension under examination is how both teachers and students can tweak learning accommodations of the theories, conceptions and practices, as reflected in the content of the English curricula, the pedagogies and activities in use, and finally the assessment types and practices.

The argument is that the achievements done so far do not fit the learners of the current generation. Officially, there is agreement among international institutions that equity between the sexes is in harmony with the claims of the Constitution and the National Charter of Education (NCET, 1999). According to the Education for All National Report (EFA, 2015):

> The constitution has set the right to vocational training in article 31 that stipulates that the public authorities work to mobilize all the available means to ease the equitable access of the female and male citizens to the conditions that allow them to benefit from the right to vocational training and physical and artistic education. (p. 92)

Furthermore, the National Education and Training Charter (NCET) states, in the basic principles, the education and training system aim at the materialization of the principle of equality of citizens and the equal chances that are presented to them and the right of all girls and boys to education be it in rural or urban areas according to the Moroccan constitution (NCET, 1999).

Though conceived and shaped by the country's policymakers, these three dimensions of the curriculum are being reviewed and reconsidered on a continuous basis. In fact, the English curricula have gone through several reforms and shifts during the last two decades through a series of educational reforms (Ben Haman, 2021). The inception of the concept of diversity education in the curricula, as it applies to the profile of learners, has evolved hand in hand with societal changes. As can be gleaned from current research and the analyses provided in this chapter, it has brought hopes that all learners will have equal opportunities for learning, but it has also raised worries within the community of researchers and academics as well as among other stakeholders. Consultation of the existing literature on the concept itself abounds in controversies and polemics concerning some of its constituents (Hessick, 2014). Local conceptions of freedom of speech are tied up with national religious and political beliefs that are rooted in turn in the notion of citizenship and belonging. In Moroccan HE language curricula, avoidance strategy is the winner, as such crises might cause threats to national unity. Extremist views of this kind are liable to make the concept of diversity imbued with cultural and political dimensions that are detrimental to the noble enterprise of education.

2 Diversity Education and Language Learning

The concept of diversity education is used in this chapter as an approach that combines the principles of equity and inclusion together within a single paradigm. As amply explained by Tomalin (this volume), it refers to the provision of opportunities, incentives and accommodations that leverage learning for all students and makes learning a pleasurable task rather than a burden for students. The question that arises at this stage is: What aspects of diversity education are implemented and how do they impact the existing curricula?

As a pedagogy that strives toward quality education, diversity education prioritises the growth and development of the student and "recognizes the complex interplay between the cognitive and affective dimensions of learning and calls on faculty to address 'the whole student'" (Eynon and Iuzzini, 2020, p. 2) rather than being limited to the mere delivery of the curricular contents. In this chapter, the establishment of viable language learning contents, pedagogies, and assessments that make the learner at the core of the mediation process of learning is a question of engaging all the stakeholders in bridging the gap between learners, teachers, and their environment. It aims to make them partners who negotiate these contents, pedagogies and assessments to improve them. There is nothing worse than having a partner who does not care for you. It is, therefore, essential to see it as a process that promotes success of diverse and heterogeneous student collaboration and contributes to the learners' development and growth in compliance with students' involvement in societal projects and cooperation (Arce-Trigatti & Anderson, 2020; Watkins & Ebersold, 2016).

The descriptive components of a diversity-bound language curriculum are clearly and openly stated in appropriate principles, standards, guidelines and consonant assessment orientations and practices. These constituents are made accessible, serviceable, and amenable to effective learning outcomes (Watkins & Ebersold, 2016). In practice, its efficacy depends on the importance teachers give to the social-psychological aspects of learning that leverage students' motivation, collaboration, and engagement in learning. Finally and equally important is that diversity education in language learning addresses issues that hamper fair treatment and equitable assessments of learning outcomes by suggesting practical ways of making language learning an enterprise where learners from different cultural backgrounds, different learning disabilities and different gender and race receive equal accommodations. In these words, diversity education is an educational approach that seeks to create a more inclusive society where students can work together and with mutual respect.

2.1 Diversity Education Reforms in Moroccan Higher Education

The developments and practices of diversity education principles in use in Moroccan Higher Education and their agreement with sustainability and education quality assurance are amply reported in the literature (Morchid, 2020).

Most reforms of higher education in Morocco are a reaction to what is being done in developed countries. Focal issues of most of these reforms has often been on what can improve sustainability issues (Fahim et al., 2021) and promote students' abilities in terms of skills and learning outcome (Ben Ajiba & Zerhouni, 2019; Zepke & Leach, 2010).

Within the National Charter of Education and Training (NCET, 1999), the language policy of Morocco is based on a set of values and principles that address main world changes and theoretical shifts in education. It is closely related to the developments reached and aims at an establishment of harmonious practices that integrate the Moroccan learners within universal objectives. Its concern with the choice of a trending educational paradigm is oriented towards the selection of principles that promote literacy standards among citizens while using updated paradigms and trends. Hence, language education in the resulting curricula seeks to make language learning (1) a means of promoting literacy skills, 2) a communication tool—or instrument—for promoting growth and development and freeing the learners' 'social character' (Rassool, 2007, p. 1) from the disrupted dynamic inherited from colonial habitus (Bourdieu, 1991). These shifts are usually accompanied by buzzwords such as 'sustainability', 'governance', 'employability' and 'accountability', the translation of which is usually done by teachers at the content, pedagogy and assessment of the language curricula.

To overcome these challenges, these objectives of the language curricula encourage the incorporation of diversity issues as a key component that fosters cultural understanding by commending values and principles such as tolerance, equity, and understanding. Based on the existing literature, these goals are, however, confined within the boundaries of citizenship and quality education assurance principles as reported by the Higher

Council for Education, Training, and Scientific Research (CSEFRS) (Morchid, 2020) in several reports (CSEFRS, 2014, 2018, 2019). Due to problems of policy implementation difficulties, conflicting views regarding the details of certain issues persist, and their applicability remains in the hands of teachers and students. For example, the notion of 'freedom of speech' among students and faculty is geared towards enabling students to debate issues from their own perspectives, but it is often tied up with the notions mentioned above and governed by national religious and political beliefs. This approach is not detrimental to any group or community. In fact, the concept itself abounds in controversies and polemics concerning some of its constituents (Hessick, 2014). To counterattack these threats to the cultural identity and stability of the country in Moroccan HE language curricula, avoidance strategy of conflicting issues is the winner, as extremist views of this kind are liable to make the concept of diversity imbued with sensitive political dimensions that are detrimental to the noble enterprise of education.

Compared with the state of the curricula of the 1970s till 1990s, nevertheless, recent outcomes of these reforms indicate a clear educational policy and practice regarding the issue of diversity, equity and inclusion. World Bank reports (2020) indicate that the increase of the human capital ratio in Morocco obtained at the level of learning outcomes was significant due to the improvements achieved, but that "important challenges persist related to the quality of education, equity, and management of the sector" (World Bank, 2020), and several efforts were pursued in the Education Act in 2019 (2015–2030) to align curricula with the new exigencies and cross the drivers of quality education. To reduce the inequalities inherent in the curricula, the World Bank issued a set of recommendations which urge the country to adopt new approaches and search for new partnerships to overcome the prevailing learning crisis. These critical interventions are reported by researchers and international organisations to rest on the country's continuing efforts to invest in human capital and the implementation of inclusive and equitable means of education (Fahim et al., 2021; Morchid, 2020).

The reform series is not then to be interrupted. With the introduction of the LMD system in higher education curriculum evaluation in 2003 (Altihami, 2010), application of these measures has, therefore, been allotted to national commissions that capitalise on system alignment with diversity education principles and literacy standards as potential requirements for module accreditation. From a personal experience in these commissions, the application of conceptions and practices offered in the curriculum guidelines provided by the Ministry of Higher Education, and their impact on students' growth and their concerns for students' prospective careers are key considerations in these commissions. Though conceived and shaped by the country's policymakers (CSEFRS, 2014), these dimensions of the curriculum have been reviewed and reconsidered on a continuous basis. As a result, English curricula in the last two decades have gone through several shifts in a process that aims at improving quality education for all.

3   Research Trends and Diversity Education

Analysis of the principles and guidelines of diversity education included in Moroccan education reforms reports the government's support for an efficacious curriculum through the introduction of criteria for equality, relevance and sustainability to leverage students' motivation, collaboration and engagement in learning.

In a synthetic analysis of the reforms between 1999 and 2019, Morchid (2020) states that substantial efforts have been made by Morocco towards achieving the imperatives of quality education and says that "the gender parity indices give evidence of efficient accommodation of equality and equity in education. On the other hand, adult basic literacy is still a goal area in need of repair". (p. 54). Another study using the SWAT-AHP analysis method by Fahim et al. (2021) in which strength (S), weakness (W), opportunity (O), and threat (T) are the four analytical parameters, succinctly investigated a set of social-related factors. Their study acknowledges that big strides towards democratisation and sustainability of education have been made in higher education, but that there is still much to do. It is argued in this chapter that what needs to be done relates to the practical features of social behaviour that usually impact students' empowerment, engagement, and development.

Other researches of the reforms of higher education and their related laws in Morocco from 1999 to 2022 reveal that the improvements introduced are a reaction to what is being done in developed countries. Focal issues of most of these reforms have often been on what can improve sustainability issues and quality education assurance (Fahim et al., 2021) to promote students' abilities in terms of skills and learning outcomes (Ben Ajiba & Zerhouni, 2019; Zepke & Leach, 2010). Based on that, Moroccan educational policy is, to a large extent, up to date at the theoretical level.

As echoed in the CSEFRS reports (NCET, 1999; CSEFRS, 2014; World Bank, 2020), the laws and updates inherent in these reforms recommend to all the stakeholders to promote awareness of and respect for diversity and inclusion in the construction and implementation of educational curricula and pedagogies.

According to the existing research done by several individual and institutional bodies, the attractiveness of diversity education in the Moroccan context is highlighted by the country's desire to keep up its educational system with the evolving world priorities and challenges. In the same vein, it is harnessed by its surface assets, which attend to the human factor as a crucial component of development and growth in twenty-first-century education. The drive underneath its manifestation in the language curricula is the promotion of at the core of several new approaches to learning in general, such as Universal Design for Learning (Dalton et al., 2019) and learning communities (Otto et al., 2015; Zhao & Kuh, 2004). Most researchers uphold the features of these instructional designs for their consonance with the new theories of learning and with the concerns of the new generations. In the Moroccan context, these features are recommended in the NCET (1999) and approved by the faculty. Nonetheless, some of these aspects are alien to the Moroccan culture due to their susceptibility to disrupt the inclinations of the community.

4 Diversity Principles and Sustainable Education

With the rise of globalisation, Moroccan higher education institutions have displayed deep concern with pedagogical decisions that address the issue of sustainability as a key factor of growth. As a result, English language teaching (ELT) curricula have gone through several shifts across many reforms (Elfatihi, 2019; Errihani, 2017). Though improved, in some respects, the inherent traditions in these curricula are still imbued with traditional views of education which grant power and authority to instructors and administration within a limited sphere of action. Students' major function in the curriculum is limited to a passive role of resilience (Kohstall, 2015). To overcome these disparities, Morocco has taken significant strides in advancing inclusive education through its endorsement of international agreements and implementation of legislation and reforms (Watkins & Ebersold, 2016; World Bank 2020).

An instance of this is demonstrated by the country's commitment to the UN Convention, ratified in 2009, which ensures that individuals with disabilities are given the opportunity to engage in regular education settings and receive the necessary assistance (Aabi & Bracken, 2023). Important matters related to decision-making remain the concern of the ministry, the administration, and ultimately the faculty and their respective superiors, as mere executors. Like in most subjects taught in higher education, the teaching contents of English language curricula, as well as the pedagogies through which they are carried out, are based on official guidelines used by accreditation commissions supervised by faculty members in the evaluation and approval of all the modules proposed for instruction.

The contents of the reforms, however, do not hint at the inclusion or exclusion of any controversial issue, nor do they advertise for or warn against any phenomenon in the language curricula. Instead, they all make amendments that redress the ills of the preceding practices to improve them. In 2008, a seminal report by the World Bank recommends the promotion of teachers to a central role in the promotion of education and qualifies this option as 'the road not taken' as a means of involving them in the country's development and growth. This strategic path in support of the human factor as a carrier of change is also voiced by the (CSEFRS, 2014).

The struggle towards implementing diversity education in HE language curricula is fraught with numerous pragmatic steps to promote learning and encourage the faculty to remain in the race of the new pedagogical advances (CSEFRS, 2019). It must be noted, however, that the state of the art of language assessment in Moroccan higher education is an artefact at a boiling point, and several issues need checking and refurbishing at the level of diversity education, as stipulated by the modern approaches to language instruction. Despite the positive reports of the World Bank related to the state of assessment in Moroccan education, this cumbersome component of language education has several limitations at the level of diversity education principles. It is a burden for the faculty and its reconstruction cannot be dissociated from the introduction of new guidelines and orientations (S. Abouabdelkader, 2018). The analyses reported in this chapter equally suggest that a lot of efforts are being made by the Moroccan government in the field of language assessment (World Bank, 2020), but that more work remains at the level of certain aspects of diversity education.

This study seeks to examine the features of diversity education that affect English language students' learning outcomes as reflected in the curricula, pedagogies, and assessments. Three questions are raised to this end:

(a) What diversity, inclusion, and equity principles and practices are inherent in HE language curricula and pedagogical practices? And how do they impact the learners?
(b) How are these issues attended to pedagogically?
(c) What measures are being taken that impact language learning outcomes?

By examining Equity and inclusion issues in both studies, this chapter seeks to draw a landscape of language learning in Moroccan higher education through (1) analysing the extent to which the teaching curricula and teaching materials take into consideration the needs of the learners, their orientations, and concerns. On the other hand, the search aims (2) to diagnose the language learning pedagogic structure in terms of opportunities and accommodations that are offered to students to promote their learning and personal growth.

Questions of interest regarding whether university students receive the same treatment inside the classroom and equal opportunities for learning outside campus are answered in the case study carried out for the purpose of this chapter.

5 Summary of the Case Study

This case study analyses the current curricula in Moroccan universities, focusing on the diversity, equity and inclusion issues that characterise the ongoing language learning curricula and what needs repairing.

In this study, the points raised in the background review of the state of the art of diversity education in Moroccan university language curricula have been researched from perspectives that match its scope and objectives. First, all the participants are teachers, administrators, and students. Second, all its components relate to the features investigated in the chapter, as shown in the research question addressed in the study:

RQ: How do students and teachers rate the implementation of diversity, equity, and inclusion principles in Moroccan higher education language curricula and pedagogical practices?

5.1 Method: Qualitative

- Three focus group interviews with university administrators
- Sample: University staff, including the two vice-presidents, three Deans, fifteen teachers from four institutions: ENSAM, Faculty of Letters and Humanities, Ecole Supérieure de Téchnologie, and Faculty of Science; Moulay Ismail University.
- Three focus group interviews with eight, nine and ten students respectively (twenty-seven students in total).

5.2 Results and Applications

The findings reported from this study in the higher education institutions investigated reflect stances of two different positions: administration policies and planning and teachers' philosophies and practices, on the one hand, and the way they are perceived by students, on the other.

They indicate that diversity education is positively rated by the first category of respondents in terms of theories, conceptions and general policies, but there persist several issues to be resolved. The results obtained disclose some curricular assets related to the promotion of intercultural communication but also several drawbacks related to dropout and repletion of a large proportion of students. As expected, however, administrative staff have been reported to acclaim the government's decisions and actions achieved regarding the issue of diversity, equity and inclusion policies adopted in their respective universities. Students, on their turn, express satisfaction with certain features of the curricula but have reservations about the disconnections between training and work opportunities in the faculties of arts, among other issues, while teachers have been more reserved and more concerned with pedagogical attributes of diversity education as experienced in their courses.

5.3 Curricular Assets and Drawbacks

The main gain of the results reported in this section is that they describe the state of diversity education in language learning in Moroccan HE through tangible facts from administrators', teachers' and students' stances. Unsurprisingly, the views reported by administrators panegyrize the state of diversity education in the English programmes as the best elaborated one in the university. They attribute this achievement to the way the English departments are run and the measures taken to solve the conflicts between the faculty members and with students. These respondents reveal that there is unanimous consensus that language curricula have always been considered as a tool for transmitting issues that carry civic education values and reflect the needs and intentions of the ruling majority and, to some extent, those of the academic community. The nature of these values is reported to be comprehensive of ethical issues related to the appreciation of the student, as a major factor of development.

The administration staff also report that a lot of efforts are made to encourage teachers to provide curricula that reflect the objectives sought in the ministerial guidelines in terms of inclusion and equity. They commend the work done by their 'Communication Departments' for providing updates and news in educational research and scientific meetings. Such initiative has not been highly rated by teachers who believe that these services are redundant and a waste of time and money. Administrative staff's counterargument is that these services are not useless and that their function is to facilitate the trajectories of research and promotion for all teachers and students alike. For instance, they serve to give notice of unfolded funds for colloquia and conference participation based on the principle of information access to all.

The staff respondents also report that English language teaching is highly valued in the national curriculum and that it serves as a tool for the promotion of research and that curricular changes have gone hand in hand with government and trending changes (Henry et al., 2013). They confirm the facts reported earlier: that the faculty are the translators of the ministerial guidelines into tangible contents and practices. Regarding the contribution of the university to diversity education principles, this category of respondents proclaims their efforts to support students' engagement in the development of the country, and that they do their best to establish partnerships that open opportunities of growth for all the stakeholders, by offering equal opportunities to all. This suggests that it is possible to improve higher education quality through investing in less costly programmes in which the human factor is the major agent of change (Gontareva et al., 2019).

The results also reveal that the work done in the English Studies departments all over the country is academic and professional and that the number of students enrolled in these departments nationally outweighs that of all other departments. Among the decisions by the universities to improve language teaching in engineering schools, more English teaching staff have been recruited in recent years, making the number of teachers double since 2019. These decisions constitute an important step towards offering students better conditions for learning.

More funds have also been pumped into education to sort out the problems incurred by the COVID-19 pandemic, on the one hand, and the exigencies of globalisation, on the other, which enabled universities to improve their technology facilities. These efforts have served Moroccan universities to provide access opportunities for all students in the English curricula. In a succinct study on the effects of promoting e-learning in Moroccan higher education on students' learning, El Firdoussi et al. (2020) report that:

> Online learning means education that uses Internet technology [3]. It has changed the concept of traditional education within the last few years, by creating education flexibility without being limited by distance, space, and time. In online learning, the latest technology needs to be used to enhance the learning process and interactions between professors, students, and technicians. It may be identified as a significant factor that can either encourage or hinder student and professor usage of e-learning. Online learning also reduces cost without reducing the quality of learning. For these reasons, professors are expected to be more facilitators, collaborators, mentors, trainers, directors, and study partners and provide choices and greater accountability for students to learn. (p. 12)

Unfortunately, such opportunities have not been proportional due to social inequities and unstructured prevision of students' concerns, as not all students could afford to buy computers to keep up with those who can, and not all of them together were prepared to use the technologies to follow their course both synchronously and asynchronously.

A further proof of this development, as reported by the administration staff, is the establishment of international partnerships to facilitate students' mobility and facilitating opportunities to achieve their academic dreams, supporting the claims made in the related research that globalisation has made us live in a big village (Graddol, 2006). In engineering schools, for instance, English language instruction, usually referred to as English for Specific purposes (ESP) is viewed as a key to employability and inclusion of all learners in and outside the country, and a key to development and growth (Irudayasamy et al., 2020). These factors endorse the earlier arguments that diversity education is entrenched in the educational decisions implemented in a curriculum for the purpose of providing better opportunities of learning for all students (Ben Haman, 2021).

5.4 Teachers' Contribution

The staff and faculty respondents report that English language teaching is highly valued in the national curriculum and that it serves as a tool for the promotion of research and that curricular changes have gone hand in hand with government and trending changes (Henry et al., 2013). Since its inception in the national curriculum, standards-based education has been implemented in Moroccan university curricula as stipulated in the National Charter (1999) as the main driver for development and change. In fact, the teaching curricula in use are imbued with newer approaches, such as collaborative learning, personalised instruction, and often using "what works" approaches in which teachers are considered as coaches and counsellors to learners. As revealed in the case study, teachers' concern is oriented towards encouraging them to use their expertise and experience in providing contents and pedagogies that favour the learners' inclinations and the national guidelines, by offering equal opportunities to all learners and improving students' literacy skills and providing contents and pedagogies that favour the learners' inclinations and the national guidelines. The teachers involved in the study also report that they fully contribute to the construction and implementation of the English language teaching curricula and pedagogies and that they make every effort to include several elements that contribute to inclusive and equitable opportunities. As stated in a study on the teaching of reading comprehension in Moroccan universities (Abouabdelkader, n.d.), this type of proceeding could be more beneficial to all universities if these contents were handled systematically on a consensual basis among all the faculty based on clear guidelines and checkpoints (Kenen, 2007). The focus group results related to the ups and downs of these language curricula and the way they are implemented in terms of their consideration of diversity education issues have revealed two main paths: one is that the concern of the university staff and faculty is to encourage the development of students' communication strategies through contents that fit the vocational orientations of students and the provision of pedagogies that are congruous with the needs of the students and that promote their literacy skills. This attitude is also shared by the students. The second is that teachers also support this line of thinking and confirm that they now implement pedagogies that are inclusive of all students and activities that involve students in collaborative and teamwork projects. For all of them, this objective is carried out by means of materials that are up to date and reflect the concerns of the students, and their focus is always on "what works" which would develop their students' engagement in real-life situations and would help them reflect, analyse, and understand people and facts from all nations.

Regarding the teaching of literacy skills used in the Moroccan language learning curricula, students report that teachers focus on language skills, including reading, writing, listening, and speaking. Students also report that equity and inclusion issues are made through topical selection and relevance, and its pragmatic realisation is gauged in terms of their social benefits, universal values, and personal growth. These reports indicate that full engagement of both males and females is not achieved, as students from rural areas and poor families are at its earliest stages. Both teachers and students support the relevance of the courses for providing students with knowledge and thinking skills. This new orientation is also supported in the existing research studies (Beniche et al., 2021; Smare & Elfatihi, 2022).

Other issues dealt with in this chapter involve the pedagogical decisions taken by teachers in the teaching of literacy skills. According to the results of the survey, providing access to literacy resources is one of the priorities of all university institutions. The results reveal that language curriculum budgeting policy has had a lot of impact on the improvements achieved. For instance, the budget allotted to HE institutions has more than doubled, especially in providing teaching and learning information technologies to enable students to have easy access to language development resources, such as books, documents and websites. Besides, the recruitment of teaching staff has also been considerable. These accomplishments have been pursued for the purpose of eradicating the disparities between students and providing opportunities for literacy skill attainment for all.

To the question of whether there are differences between students from different social classes or genders in language learning, the participants refute the idea of unequal treatment between students in terms of support and opportunities to develop and improve their literacy skills. Both administrators and teachers, on the one hand, and students, on the other, agree that the university has become more aware of this issue and that they are advancing towards securing better accommodations for all students. "It is important to check the extent to which the teaching and learning materials are comprehensible or difficult for students and developing students' literacy skills". In another statement: "63% of our students, declares one of these administrators, come from public schools and all of them enjoy the same learning opportunities". This statement also applies to students from the ENSAM, Meknes, an internationally highly esteemed engineering school. In engineering schools, there is full consensus between faculty and students on the provision of effective learning accommodations, materials, and services regarding the different types of accommodations offered on equal basis to both girls and boys. It is no wonder, then, that the level of students' English proficiency is above average, as reported in the study results.

5.5   Assessments in the English Curricula

Both the results of the study and the existing research report that assessment in language course is still an issue for students, and a thorny business for teachers. These results confirm the statement reported earlier and reported in the literature that the state of language assessment in Moroccan higher education displays several positive measures related to diversity education (Abouabdelkader, 2018; Bouziane, 2017; Larouz & Abouabdelkader, 2020) and that several of its features need fixing.

Examination of students' reactions to language assessments, as gleaned from the findings of the case study, reveals students' dissatisfaction with diversity education aspects of assessment. All of them report several deficiencies at the level of the categories investigated. There is considerable discrepancy between teachers' claims and students' views. While learning assessments have been reported by the administrative staff and faculty to be satisfactory in terms of their consistent results and relevance, they were expectedly reported by the students to be deficient in terms of fairness, disregard for disparities, and means of expression. These results reveal that 89% of the students interviewed refer to lack of fair assessment and inadequacy of the means and procedures adopted to assess learning outcomes. The warnings raised by these drawbacks might be among the factors that negatively impact students' learning outcomes and sometimes lead to failure for many students. Discrimination in terms of linguistic disabilities have been reported in students' claims include: "some test provided at the different levels do not take into consideration students' level of literacy or the contents of the courses". Issues related to cultural understanding have also been revealed to be significant factors of assessment dissonance with students' satisfaction: "some tests do not take into account students' cultural backgrounds and biased against students with little exposure to the Anglophone culture".

This state is comprehensible. First, inability to match learning outcomes through standardised tests is costly and not affordable for universities due to the large numbers of students. Second, absence of bodies in charge of designing valid and reliable grading rubrics that are congruent with learning outcomes. Third, neither the Ministry of Education nor the universities, themselves, have well-structured assessment departments. In view of these structural gaps, the faculty are to be commended for their efforts to sustain acceptable norms of equity among students. Finding solutions to the inherent challenges of 'language assessments' in content courses and vocational training constitutes a big challenge for Moroccan universities. In art schools (faculties of letters), the challenge is that of establishing common core standards at each of the three years of instruction on a consensual national or regional framework. In the vocational training institutions and faculties of science or medicine, for example, the instauration of standardised tests is still debatable since all of them have diverse vocational contents and develop different skills. Regarding the learning-assessment bond, all of these HE institutions, the curricula adopted are not based on a particular framework.

The discriminatory assessment problems associated with the end-of-term exams are attributed to the wrong choice of students' linguistic and cognitive abilities. As reported by some students: "Some tests provided at the different levels do not take into consideration students' level of literacy, instruction, as well as the contents of the courses". Issues related to cultural understanding have also been revealed to be significant factors of assessment dissonance with students' satisfaction: "some tests do not take into account students' cultural backgrounds and biased against students with little exposure to the Anglophone culture".

6 Conclusions and Implications

This chapter argues that diversity principles are crucial to the promotion of learning among students and that their impact can be decisive in students' engagement and development. It also argues that consideration of these principles is crucial to the development of students' cultural understanding and improvement of their learning outcomes.

The different aspects of diversity education attended to in the Moroccan HE English language curricula reported and examined in this chapter suggest that lots of efforts have been made to improve students' learning outcomes and that these efforts involve both the infrastructure of the universities themselves, by providing access to information technology assistance, learning opportunities, and learning accommodations for all. These results also suggest that there persist several challenges for both administrators and faculty to overcome, especially in establishing teaching and learning, and learning and assessment. The aspects of diversity investigated suggest that there still exist certain teacher behaviours that need to be aligned with the new generations of learners. As argued throughout this chapter:

- The recurrent updating of the curricula through a contingent of reforms has also been reported to have created a dynamic of improvement and a sense of responsibility among the faculty.
- It also illustrates the worries and concerns of the government to improve the different aspects of higher education curricula and improve its standards.
- In their turn, teachers are reported to constructively contribute to the change brought forth by the world economy and policy developments and their impact on new teaching approaches and practices. Finally, the chapter raises the issue of combining language learning objectives and assessment practices to fulfill the objectives of the curriculum as a key feature of diversity education in Moroccan higher education.

These different aspects of diversity education amply describe the state of the art of English language learning and teaching in Moroccan higher education, as described in the work done in the consecutive reforms in Moroccan higher education and expressed in the worries and concerns of researchers and practitioners to improve the different aspects of higher education curricula.

To conclude, the chapter supports the use of diversity principles and checkpoints for attaining higher levels of quality education and establishing strong bonds between teaching, learning, and the different types of assessment.

References

Aabi, M., & Bracken, S. (2023). 5.2 Drawing from the global to act local: How Universal Design for Learning lends itself to facilitating inclusion in Moroccan higher education. *Making Inclusive Higher Education a Reality: Creating a University for All.*

Abouabdelkader, S. (2018). Moroccan EFL university students' composing skills in the balance: Assessment procedures and outcomes. In A. M. Ahmed & H. Abouabdelkader (Eds.), *Assessing EFL writing in the 21st century Arab world: Revealing the unknown* (pp. 79–109). Palgrave Macmillan. https://doi.org/10.1007/978-3-319-64104-1_4

Abouabdelkader, S. (n.d.). Assessing the principles of diversity education in the Moroccan higher education curricula: Focus on reading comprehension. In H. Abouabdelkader & B. Tomalin (Eds.), *Diversity education in the MENA region: Bridging the gaps in language learning.* Palgrave Macmillan.

Altihami, D. (2010). Implementing the LMD system: Experience of the philosophy department in the Cadi Ayyad University in Marakkech. *Towards an Arab Higher Education Space: International Challenges and Societal Responsibilities: Proceedings of the Arab Regional Conference on Higher Education,* 201–211.

Arce-Trigatti, A., & Anderson, A. (2020). Defining diversity: A critical discourse analysis of public educational texts. *Discourse: Studies in the Cultural Politics of Education, 41*(1), 3–20. https://doi.org/10.1080/01596306.2018.1462575

Ben Ajiba, I., & Zerhouni, B. (2019). Student engagement for quality enhancement and responding to student needs in the Moroccan university: The case of the English studies track. *Arab World English Journal, 10*(3), 165–177. https://doi.org/10.24093/awej/vol10no3.11

Ben Haman, O. (2021). The Moroccan education system, dilemma of language and think-tanks: The challenges of social development for the North African country. *The Journal of North African Studies, 26*(4), 709–732.

Beniche, M., Larouz, M., & Anasse, K. (2021). Examining the relationship between critical thinking skills and argumentative writing skills in Moroccan Preparatory Classes of Higher Engineering Schools (CPGE). *International Journal of Linguistics, Literature and Translation, 4*(9), 194–201.

Bourdieu, P. (1991). *Language and symbolic power.* Harvard University Press.

Bouziane, A. (2017). Why should the assessment of literacy in Morocco be revisited? *Evaluation in Foreign Language Education in the Middle East and North Africa,* 305–314.

CSEFRS. (2014). La mise en œuvre de la charte nationale d'éducation et de formation 2000–2013, acquis, déficits et défis. *Rapport Analytique.* goo.gl/JGAAXH.

CSEFRS. (2018). *L'enseignement supérieur au Maroc – Efficacité, efficience et défis du système à accès ouvert.* https://www.csefrs.ma/publications/lenseignement-superieur-au-maroc/?lang=fr

CSEFRS. (2019). *Réforme de l'enseignement supérieur-perspectives stratégique.* https://www.csefrs.ma/wp-content/uploads/2019/07/enseignement-supe%CC%81rieur-fr.pdf

Dalton, E. M., Lyner-Cleophas, M., Ferguson, B. T., & McKenzie, J. (2019). Inclusion, universal design and universal design for learning in higher education: South Africa and the United States. *African Journal of Disability, 8.* https://doi.org/10.4102/ajod.v8i0.519

EFA. (2015). Education for all 2015 National Review Report: Morocco. *National Report.* https://unesdoc.unesco.org/ark:/48223/pf0000231799

El Firdoussi, S., Lachgar, M., Kabaili, H., Rochdi, A., Goujdami, D., & El Firdoussi, L. (2020). Assessing distance learning in higher education during the COVID-19 pandemic. *Education Research International, 2020,* 1–13.

Elfatihi, M. (2019). ELT in Morocco: Past, present and future. *Research in Humanities and Social Sciences (Laboratory of Values, Society and Development), 3,* 6–15.

Errihani, M. (2017). English education policy and practice in Morocco. *English Language Education Policy in the Middle East and North Africa,* 115–131.

Eynon, B., & Iuzzini, J. (2020). Teaching & Learning Toolkit: A research-based guide to building a culture of Teaching & Learning Excellence. *Achieving the Dream.*

Fahim, A., Tan, Q., Naz, B., ul Ain, Q. U., & Bazai, S. U. (2021). Sustainable higher education reform quality assessment using SWOT analysis with integration of AHP and entropy models: A case study of Morocco. *Sustainability, 13*(8), 4312. https://doi.org/10.3390/su13084312

Gontareva, I., Borovyk, M., Babenko, V., Perevozova, I., & Mokhnenko, A. (2019). Identification of efficiency factors for control over information and communication provision of sustainable development in higher education institutions.

Graddol, D. (2006). *English next* (Vol. 62). British Council London.

Henry, M., Lingard, B., Rizvi, F., & Taylor, S. (2013). *Educational policy and the politics of change.* Routledge.

Hessick, F. A. (2014). Cases, controversies, and diversity. *Northwestern University Law Review, 109,* 57.

Irudayasamy, J., Souidi, N. M., & Hankins, C. (2020). Impact of an ESP course on English language proficiency of undergraduate engineering students: A case study at Dhofar University. *International Journal of Higher Education, 9*(2), 309–320.

Kenen, P. B. (2007). *Reform of the International Monetary Fund.* Council on Foreign Relations New York.

Kohstall, F. (2015). From reform to resistance: Universities and student mobilisation in Egypt and Morocco before and after the Arab uprisings. *British Journal of Middle Eastern Studies, 42*(1), 59–73.

Larouz, M., & Abouabdelkader, S. (2020). Teachers' feedback on EFL students' dissertation writing in Morocco. In A. M. Ahmed, S. Troudi, & S. Riley (Eds.), *Feedback in L2 English writing in the Arab world: Inside the black box* (pp. 201–232). Palgrave Macmillan. https://doi.org/10.1007/978-3-030-25830-6_8

Morchid, N. (2020). Investigating quality education in moroccan educational reforms from 1999 to 2019. *Journal of Research & Method in Education, 10*(1), 54–61.

NCET. (1999). *Charte Nationale d'Education et de Formation.* Commission Spécial Education Formation (p. 157). www.dfc.gov.ma

Otto, S., Evins, M. A., Boyer-Pennington, M., & Brinthaupt, T. M. (2015). Learning communities in higher education: Best practices. *Journal of Student Success and Retention, 2*(1).

Qin, J., Muenjohn, N., & Chhetri, P. (2014). *A review of diversity conceptualizations: Variety, trends, and a framework.* Accessible at: https://www.researchgate.net/publication/278402546_A_Review_of_Diversity_Conceptualizations_Variety_Trends_and_a_Framework

Rassool, N. (2007). Global issues in language, education and development. In *Global issues in language, education and development.* Multilingual Matters.

Smare, Z., & Elfatihi, M. (2022). Developing creative thinking skills in EFL classes in Morocco. *International Journal of Language and Literary Studies, 4*(3), 221–246.

Watkins, A., & Ebersold, S. (2016). Efficiency, effectiveness and equity within inclusive education systems. In *Implementing inclusive education: Issues in bridging the policy-practice gap* (Vol. 8, pp. 229–253). Emerald Group Publishing Limited.

World Bank. (2020). Feature Story. Morocco: A case for building a stronger education system in the post Covid-19 era. https://www.worldbank.org/en/news/feature/2020/10/27/a-case-for-building-a-stronger-education-system-in-the-post-covid-19-era

Zepke, N., & Leach, L. (2010). Improving student engagement: Ten proposals for action. *Active Learning in Higher Education, 11*(3), 167–177.

Zhao, C.-M., & Kuh, G. D. (2004). Adding value: Learning communities and student engagement. *Research in Higher Education, 45*(2), 115–138. https://doi.org/10.1023/B:RIHE.0000015692.88534.de

CHAPTER 6

Sustainable Policies and Strategies in the MENA Region for Teaching English as a Foreign Language

María Sagrario Salaberri-Ramiro ⓘ
and Abderrazak Zaafour ⓘ

1 Introduction

One central goal in this chapter is to reflect on policies and strategies implemented in the MENA region to promote the teaching and learning of English as a foreign language in order to analyse the sustainability of these policies and to what degree they promote (or not) inequality for different reasons. Teaching and learning English is both an opportunity and a challenge nowadays: a means to enhance the quality of teaching and learning but also a means of reinforcing global inequalities as the teaching of foreign languages (mainly English) has been considered a requirement for the internationalisation of education.

M. S. Salaberri-Ramiro (✉) • A. Zaafour
University of Almería, Almería, Spain
e-mail: sagrario@ual.es; zaafourabderrazak@gmail.com

© The Author(s), under exclusive license to Springer Nature Switzerland AG 2023
H. Abouabdelkader, B. Tomalin (eds.), *Diversity Education in the MENA Region*, https://doi.org/10.1007/978-3-031-42693-3_6

However, it is relevant to take into account that the dominant role of English in internationalisation can be a threat to cultural identities and even languages and can even contribute to the maintenance of inequalities in education. In the same line, the overwhelming use of English in education may contribute to undermining other languages and cultures and undervaluing the knowledge generated through them to the extent of ignoring it. In this context, the teaching and learning of English as a foreign language or/ and as a means of instruction (bilingual programmes) should not be regarded as a goal in itself but rather as an effective instrument to achieve other goals like, among others:

- To be aware of the fact that teaching in a language that is not the group's mainstream language can limit the development of pedagogical approaches and the quality of education.
- Be critical towards the acceptance of imported curricula that affect cultural identity.
- Reflect on the effects of monolingualism and multilingualism.
- Consider the role of local languages and cultures and give them visibility.
- Prepare students and staff for intercultural and globally-oriented environments.
- Enhance the quality of education and research in varied languages and cultural contexts.
- Provide students with tools for life and work in an intercultural and globalising world.
- Deliver service to society and community social engagement, etc.

In this chapter, there is a focus on the geographical, historical and cultural context of the MENA region; aspects of globalisation in the region; implementation of language policies and policies addressed to guarantee the achievement of Sustainable Development Goals (SDGs). A close view of the case of Morocco is provided as well as a proposal of samples of indicators to analyse diversity and inequality in the MENA region as a tool for self-awareness.

2 Geographical, Historical, and Cultural Contexts of the MENA Region

In the following subsections, the countries that make up part of the region have been described briefly emphasising the relevance of their location, the historical features as well as the cultural context.

2.1 Geographical Context

The Middle East and North Africa (MENA) is a geographically, historically, and culturally rich, diverse, and vast region. It stretches from the Atlantic coast of Morocco in the west all the way through the Mediterranean ports of North Africa and the Levant into the Red Sea inlets of the Arabian Peninsula and further into the Persian Gulf, located on the two continents of Asia and Africa (Britannica, 2023). The term commonly includes 21 countries (Chen, 2023) or territories that constitute the region: the North African Countries of Morocco, Algeria, Tunisia, Libya, Egypt, and the Asian countries of Bahrain, Cyprus, Kuwait, Oman, Qatar, Saudi Arabia, Iran, Iraq, Israel, Palestine, Jordan, Lebanon, Yemen, Syria, Turkey and the United Arab Emirates. Iran has the largest area (636,000-mile^2), followed by Egypt (384,000-mile^2), Turkey (297,000-mile^2) and Morocco (172,000-mile^2). Israel (7900-mile^2), Kuwait (7000-mile^2) and Qatar (4000-mile^2) are smaller countries in the MENA region. The most populous country is Egypt (80.3 million), followed by Iran (76.9 million), Turkey (76.8 million) and Morocco (34.9 million), while Qatar is considered one of the least populous countries with (1.4 million), followed by Kuwait (3.5 million) and Israel (7.59 million) (Kabasakal et al., 2012).

Led to considerable geographical challenges, the region's countries benefit from an advantageous geographical position at the crossroads of Europe, Africa, and Asia, in addition to the existence of a young and progressively educated population and significant potential in growing areas, especially renewable energies, tourism, industrial production, attracting foreign investments and business development services (Chen, 2023). These facts, to some extent, have broadened economic openness, diversification and private sector enhancement, but there still exist problems that have not been addressed adequately, especially regarding economic and social issues. Therefore, more extensive reforms are needed to adopt inclusive, diverse, and sustainable development models that provide equal chances for everyone, particularly for the younger generation and women.

Undoubtedly, this can only be accomplished through the approach of equitable and sustainable educational policies that guarantees openness to the world through learning foreign languages and diverse cultures and, at the same time, ensure the preservation of indigenous languages and cultures and the cultural heritage of peoples without posing any threat to them (El-Aswad, 2019).

2.2   Historical Context

Two different and complementary aspects are approached here, including human civilization as well as education and the European colonisation in the region.

2.2.1   Human Civilisation in the MENA Region

The region has a very rich historical context that spans several millennia, and it is considered one of the earliest civilisations in human history which has witnessed significant cultural, political and economic development (Dipak & Mustapha, 2003). Ancient Egypt, with its pharaohs, pyramids, and Nile River came into existence around 3100 BCE (Al Abbasi, 2017). Mesopotamia, which is located in Iraq, witnessed the rise of powerful empires like the Sumerians, Babylonians, and Assyrians. The Persian Empire, centred in modern-day Iran, ruled over wide swaths of the region, while the Phoenicians, who were situated in what is now Lebanon, were widely recognised traders and marines in addition to conflicts and interactions with other parts of the world. The emergence of Islam during the seventh century CE brought about significant transformations in both the MENA region and the world. The early Islamic caliphates, particularly the Umayyad and Abbasi, facilitated a remarkable era of intellectual, scientific, and cultural progress commonly referred to as the Islamic Golden Age. Scholars hailing from diverse backgrounds made remarkable contributions across a wide range of fields including mathematics, astronomy, medicine, and philosophy. This era witnessed the rise of renowned centres of learning and innovation in cities such as Baghdad, Cairo, and Cordoba. These vibrant intellectual hubs became beacons of knowledge, attracting scholars from different parts of the world and fostering an atmosphere of intellectual exchange.

2.2.2 Education and European Colonisation in the Region

Education and European colonisation in the region are intricately linked, as the advent of the colonial powers had a profound impact on the educational system in the region. During the nineteenth and first half of the twentieth centuries, most of the region was colonised by the Europeans, mainly French, Spanish, and British, who instituted compulsory modern education and implemented policies aimed at exerting control and influencing the local population (Ponnuchamy, 2017). The European colonisers introduced their own educational models, curriculum, and languages, often displacing or marginalising indigenous educational traditions in the MENA region. As a result, European languages, cultures, and values were widely disseminated, while local languages and cultural practices were marginalised.

Additionally, native access to formal schooling was restricted for two principal reasons: first, colonial powers did not want indigenous people to be equipped with the knowledge and skills to challenge their dominance. Hence, limiting modern instruction, particularly European language education, to a small number of scholars would boost colonial administration while weakening the nationalist outlook. Second, the existence of Koranic schools, which represent the original educational system at that time, competed with the colonial one, firstly because of its religious references and secondly because it opposed Western cultural dominion.

During the colonisation era, education inequality forms took place by offering access to education to those with high social status and ethnicity, the ruling elites, and privileged groups, while the majority of the population had limited access to quality education or were entirely excluded from formal schooling (Or, 2017). However, it is important to acknowledge that resistance to colonial education and cultural assimilation emerged within the region. Local populations, intellectuals, and nationalist movements began advocating for decolonisation, cultural preservation, and the development of education systems that would empower the local populace. In the wake of the mid-twentieth-century decolonisation wave, many MENA countries embarked on educational reforms to regain control over their curricula, languages, and cultural heritage. This period witnessed the establishment of national education institutions and renewed emphasis on promoting local languages, history, and traditions. Today, the legacy of European colonisation in the MENA region is still evident in various aspects of education. Foreign languages continue to dominate as mediums of instruction, particularly, French, English, and sometimes other languages like Spanish, Italian, and German, especially in higher education, both in international and private schools. Regarding higher education, it is relevant to analyse the increased privatisation happening at that stage in order to rethink the current socio-economic development models in the region (Akkari, 2021) as well as the role of Arabic in relation to national identity and pragmatism (Badry & Willoughby, 2015).

It should be mentioned that North African countries like Morocco, Algeria, Tunisia, Libya, and Egypt have historically been more open to learning foreign languages due to their geographical proximity as well as historical and cultural interactions with Europe. In contrast, Persian Gulf countries, including Saudi Arabia, Qatar, United Arab Emirates, Bahrain, Kuwait, and Oman put a stronger emphasis on Arabic as the primary language and as a reflection of their identity, while English is frequently taught in schools as a foreign language and used as a language of business.

Choosing a language of instruction in schools or universities of the MENA region can depend on a variety of aspects, including historical, political, cultural, and economic considerations. Western educational models continue to influence the system through the adoption of their curricula, principally in subjects like mathematics, sciences, and languages. This stems from the objective of aligning the local educational systems with the global ones to prepare students for international education abroad. However, the main ongoing challenge remains in reconciling knowledge with local cultural contexts and values to create a more culturally relevant and inclusive education.

During the second half of the twentieth century, education was viewed as a human capital investment, which certainly has long-term benefits for both individuals as well as the broader public. When colonisation was over, many countries from the region struggled to liberate themselves from the curricula, textbooks, and ideals of their former colonial past. Educational researchers (Agbaria et al., 2015; Bardy & Willoughby, 2015; Benmamoun et al., 2013) and many others, since independence, have been regularly discussing the quality and sustainability of their education according to their context (local languages and cultures). Recently, the regional context is characterised by the move of a number of countries in the Maghrib region towards the adoption of English in education (e.g., Morocco, Algeria, Tunisia).

3 Cultural Context

Many common themes emerge from the historical and cultural experiences in the region. Firstly, Islam as the principal religion plays a significant role in the cultural context as the wide majority of the population identifies as Muslims, with social norms, family structures, and everyday living frequently influenced by Islamic ideals and practises (Bayat & Herrera, 2010). Religious rituals like prayers and fasting during Ramadan are significant cultural observances, and Islamic traditions are extensively embraced. Traditional values and customs, family values, hospitality, care, and respect for elders as well as a sense of community are generally highly regarded. Arabic is the most widely spoken language in the region and it serves as a common cultural thread in the formation of the region's identity along with other languages such as Amazigh, Kurdish, Persian, and Turkish which reflect the linguistic richness and cultural diversity of the MENA region (Kabasakal et al., 2012).

Despite the fact that the countries of the region share many societal norms, some cultural, geographical, ethnic, and socioeconomic differences do exist. Educational policy developers need to be sensitive to these differences when adopting language curricula. Most of the time, the context, which includes religion, history, language, laws, political systems and ethnic subcultures, decides the most successful manner to design teaching programmes. Although the educational past and present of each country are markedly different, several considerable resemblances exist. These similarities provide a starting point for a country-to-country comparison and a better understanding of some of the problems that need to be solved if the educational systems are to be structurally improved.

4 Aspects of Globalisation in the Region

Globalisation is an inevitable factor in people's life, it has made the world increasingly open and enhanced the demand for more integrated systems in all facets of human life. Teaching English in the Arab world is one of the factors that has been influenced by globalisation over the last two decades (Alhawary, 2017; Grin, 2005). Nowadays, there is an increased demand for English proficiency, as it has become a global language of business and communication.

Countries of the region are deeply engaged in global trade, tourism, hospitality, and international collaboration, which cannot succeed without fluent participative individuals or institutions. Undoubtedly, proficiency in English opens up opportunities for national as well as international employment to individuals in the region. However, globalisation and the emphasis on English language proficiency have created linguistic and socioeconomic disparities since access to quality English language education differs between urban and rural zones. Efforts are needed now more than ever to urgently rethink models of social and economic development and fundamental reforms to promote upward social mobility of youth and provide education to marginalised populations and enhance educational opportunities for girls and women.

Learning English has become a necessity linked to conditions of cultural globalisation as well as the scientific and technological revolution that has encompassed the whole world. One of the main reasons for adopting a clear trend towards teaching English at different educational levels in the MENA region is that it is a leading means of global communication as well as scientific and cultural knowledge (Marsh, 2006). The globalisation of English in these countries has created a development in its education and, in general, schools and universities in non-anglophone contexts are part of this tendency, offering courses and programmes in English that are growing at an unprecedented rate (Macaro et al., 2015). Universities around the region have become internationalised in recent years, and this has been a focus for higher education institutes (HEI) to strengthen their global competitiveness, which is considered a 'pandemic in proportion' (Chapple, 2015: 1). Overall, globalisation has had a substantial influence on the MENA region, carrying economic opportunities, technological advancement, and cultural exchange. However, it has also posed challenges and inequalities that need to be addressed for more inclusive and sustainable development in the region.

What has been described above can take us to pose some questions regarding the dominant role of English in internationalisation, as it can be a threat to cultural identities and even languages and can contribute to the maintenance of inequalities in education. In fact, the overwhelming use of English in education may contribute to undermining other languages and cultures and undervaluing the knowledge generated through them to the extent of ignoring it. In this context, it is relevant to consider the concept of "Englishization" which has been defined recently (Wilkinson & Gabriëls, 2021: 14) as "the process in which the English language is increasingly gaining ground in domains where another language was previously used". This is the case when English is used as a medium of instruction at different educational levels and mainly in higher education in many European countries, but with dispersion in non-Anglophone contexts, like the MENA region.

5 Implementation of Language Policies

Language Education policies in the Middle East and North Africa vary across countries which reflect the diverse linguistic landscape as well as the historical, cultural, and political contexts, together with the complex set of principles, beliefs, and practices that are ingrained in the region's past. Regardless of the general uniformity, there exist some differences in terms of culture, religion, and minority languages as well as a variety of Arabic dialects spoken as vernacular languages in different parts of the region. For a sustainable and diverse language education, the implemented policies in the region should take into account all these variables.

Children and youth of today are leaders and workforce of tomorrow who need to be offered learning opportunities that are relevant, lifelong, and capable of arming them with knowledge and skills that prepare them for the future. It is paramount that teaching language policies reach all learners, regardless of gender, race, ability, or background. The use of the most modern instructional practices along with effective technological tools that have untapped potential in education and can leverage to deliver, support, measure and manage language learning.

The theory of language policy proposed by Spolsky (2004, 2007, 2021, among others) has been constructed for more than two decades since his first publication on language policy (1996). He makes a distinction between language practices (what people do), language beliefs or ideologies (what they think they should do) and language management (the planning of how the selected language policy can be enacted and practiced, that is, when someone tries to change the practices or beliefs of others). Among other matters, Spolsky (2021) raises relevant issues regarding language policy that are closely related to the context of the MENA region like environmental conditions (geography, demographic forces, etc.); public institutions for communication, culture, religion, etc.; economic pressure and neoliberalism; certain languages and language varieties that lack economic value are being lost and their speakers are forced to shift to a larger and apparently more powerful variety; the conflict between two frequent opposing goals: the desire to choose a language with maximum economic advantage and the desire to choose the national heritage-identifying language, etc. We describe below policies addressed to guarantee the achievement of SDGs and samples of pedagogical policies to support that attainment.

(a) *Policies Addressed to Guarantee the Achievement of Sustainable Development Goals (SDGs)*

The Sustainable Development Goals (SDGs) are a set of 17 goals adopted by all United Nations Member States in 2015. These goals serve as a collective framework for achieving peace and prosperity for both people and the planet and offer outlines that guide us towards a sustainable future, addressing various educational, environmental, and economic challenges that we face today and will continue to face in the coming years (United Nations, 2015). Among the 17 SDGs is Goal 4 which has been established to guarantee quality, equitable, and inclusive education and promote lifelong learning opportunities for all children and adults. Integrating SDGs should be implemented from early childhood through secondary up to higher education, providing learners with knowledge, skills, values, and attitudes to understand and address the social, economic, and environmental challenges. This should be done by permeating sustainable development concepts into various subjects to promote critical thinking, participatory learning, and to build a sense of responsibility and engagement among learners to create a more sustainable future.

Since each nation in the Middle East and North Africa gained independence, free and publicly funded education has been a fundamental tenet of the social contract. Governments in the post-independence era substantially widened their educational institutions as a result of a rapid increase in young populations, the attempt to establish nationalism, and the need to construct democratic and political legitimacy along with general advances for new regimes by making education a fundamental right of citizenship. Providing basic education at that time was a real challenge because of the rapid growth of the population which is considered among the highest in the world. However, with a few exceptions, education systems in the region today provide basic education to most children, education is compulsory in primary grades all over the region's countries and, in some others, through lower secondary grades. When it comes to completion rates, the Middle East and

North Africa have one of the highest among the developing countries. Almost 93% of all children who start primary school complete the cycle and progress to secondary school, compared to less than 70% in Sub-Saharan Africa and Latin America (UNESCO, 1998).

Arabic and other local languages in the MENA countries are frequently regarded as rigid perspective standards and it is critical to investigate how language policy can become more democratic and inclusive, and how this is already happening, if not on the national, official level, in other domains such as school, classrooms, family, or social media. Additionally, language policies in the region cannot be understood without taking into account the legacy of resisted colonialism and outside interference (Al-Wer, 2013; Bassiounney, 2009; Suleiman, 2013; Versteegh, 2014). One of the challenges would be for policymakers to look beyond the region's history and consider the goals and ideals the population hopes to achieve (Shohamy, 2014). Achieving enduring and inclusive foreign language education requires the implementation of structural reforms, improvement and modernisation of existing programmes, investigation of emerging policies and initiatives, assessing them, and providing improved information to policymakers to ensure the creation of equal opportunities and equitable distribution of knowledge.

(b) *Pedagogical Policies*

To ensure the promotion and integration of the SDGs into English language teaching in the MENA region, several policies can be implemented to promote and integrate the principles of SDGs into English language education, below are some examples:

1. *Curriculum design*: Ensure that the SDGs are clearly represented in the English language curricula by incorporating contents and activities connected to the SDGs to foster a sense of global citizenship and sustainability and to reduce socio-economic disparity through English language programmes.
2. *Teacher training*: By providing professional development opportunities through workshops, seminars and online courses, English language teachers can enhance their knowledge and equip themselves with pedagogical approaches

that integrate sustainable concepts (Kwee, 2021). It is also relevant to foster partnerships between schools, universities, English language institutions, and other organisations and offer opportunities for teachers to share their experiences and best practices, empowering them to take up responsibilities and make decisions related to incorporating SDGs into their English teaching. Teachers need to stay updated on research, resources and best practices for teaching English as a foreign language in the MENA region.

3. *Cooperative Project-Based Learning (CPBL)*: Encourage the incorporation of CPBL approaches in English language classrooms that allow students to work cooperatively and engage in authentic real-world issues to address local or global challenges related to sustainable development which enhance their critical thinking, problem-solving, action and creativity (Zaafour & Salaberri-Ramiro, 2022).

4. *Resources and Materials*: It is important to take into consideration authenticity while developing English language teaching resources and materials that incorporate themes which are related to SDGs and show respect for the local cultural norms, traditions values, and heritage of the specific country or the region, avoiding topics that may be considered controversial or offensive in the local context. Incorporating elements of local cultures and examples from daily lives makes English learning more relatable and helps learners develop a sense of global citizenship and appreciation for diverse cultures. A critical focus should be put on the use of "imported" textbooks which do not integrate local life and environment of the MENA region, instead, the use of locally produced instructional materials like videos, integrated stories, folklore, and historical narratives that reflect the local cultures and context can boost the learners' language proficiency and enhance their motivation (Lasekan & Godoy, 2020). Paying attention to these aspects helps students share their own cultural experiences and perspectives, and create a rich and diverse learning environment which fosters a sense of pride and connection to their own traditions while learning English.

5. *Assessment and Evaluation*: Integrate sustainability-related competencies and indicators in English language assessment to measure the effectiveness of integrating SDGs in English language education and provide clear feedback on students' learning.

The efficient implementation of these policies can contribute to the achievement of the SDGs by fostering a generation of English language learners who are knowledgeable, critical thinkers, and active participators in sustainable development in the MENA region, supporting the preservation of local identities, strengthening connections, and enriching the overall educational experience of learners.

6 THE CASE OF MOROCCO: A CLOSE VIEW

Shedding light on the current Moroccan educational policies regarding the teaching of foreign languages, which is considered an important part of the educational system, the debate over which language is best suited to serve as Morocco's first foreign language and language of education is heating up. Indeed, the Moroccan linguistic state is known for its complexity and multilingual nature, and due to the variety of local spoken languages, students benefit from instruction through the country's official language 'Arabic' and the dominant language which is 'French' in most cases. This language remains an important part of the Moroccan curriculum and has historically been taught as a second language in schools for many years, and is still broadly used in government business, and higher education. Besides, other foreign languages came to exist for historical, economical, and social reasons, being English and Spanish at the forefront and taught from the middle school level. In this vein, French is still considered the country's first official foreign language although it faces a continuous spread of English which has been gaining more prominence in recent years supported by globalisation and internationalisation of education. The Moroccan government has recognised the important position of English as a global language and has made great efforts to improve the quality of its education at schools.

Many language institutes and centres exist in Morocco that offer language courses for both Moroccans and foreigners. These language training courses are in French or English and also in other languages with a focus on general language proficiency levels as well as specialised language skills for general or specific purposes. Among the most famous English language centres, the British Council Morocco and the American Language Centre (ALC) can be highlighted. Regarding the French language centres, the most relevant are the French Institute of Morocco and the Alliance Française Morocco. These are just some examples, however, there are many other public universities as well as private centres throughout the country which provide comprehensive courses covering oral communication skills, grammar, vocabulary, and pronunciation.

6.1 The Shift from French to English

The shift from French to English in Morocco has been gaining ground during the past few decades. Even though French has historically been the dominant foreign language in Morocco (Or, 2017), English has recently gained increasing interest and emphasis as it is regarded a language of globalisation and the lingua-franca of the world, which is obviously spreading in Morocco as an adaption to the shift of contemporary life. Noticeably, more and more families are increasingly keen to enrol their children in English language learning centres at an early age believing that this language opens wider horizons in the academic and professional path (Errihani, 2017). At the beginning of each school season, there are growing societal demands for the adoption of English as the first foreign language in schools instead of French, and these demands were accompanied in September 2022 by the launch of a petition signed by thousands of Moroccans.

Furthermore, the petition called for the abolition of the teaching of scientific subjects in French in schools and the discontinuation of the use of this language in official institutions. The Ministry of National Education reacted to the petition and has recently announced a shift towards teaching gradually science subjects in English instead of French (Ben Hammou & Kesbi, 2021). The current education system adopts the teaching of English from the third year of secondary education and the last three years of high school education, which means that students in public schools learn English for only four years. In contrast, most private schools teach English from the first year of primary school, which creates a disparity between the achievements of public and private students in this language, which perpetuates an aspect of inequality that should be reconsidered sooner rather than later.

Responding to the growing demands, and through progressive government plans, the Ministry of Education (2015), through its "Strategic

Vision of education reform 2015–2030", is now reacting by moving towards the adoption of English in the teaching of scientific subjects at all secondary school levels by 2030. Starting next year, the Ministry of National Education will get ready for the workshops of teaching scientific subjects in English. However, what is new for the academic year 2023–2024 is the generalisation of English language teaching in the first and the second years of preparatory secondary education, provided that the teaching of the English language will be integrated into different levels in descending order down to the fourth primary grade. On the other hand, the Ministry of Higher Education and Scientific Research has launched a plan to internationalise the University of Morocco by opening new English pathways.

In the academic year 2022–2023, 10 new Bachelor's degrees, 7 master's degrees and Doctor of Medicine degrees have been accredited in English. As well as the accreditation of 21 English diplomas at private and partner universities, as stated in a presentation of the Minister of Higher Education in the Parliament during his presentation of the draft budget for 2023. According to the same source, more than 12.000 students will study modules in English as part of their courses during this University season. The period 2022–2024 is considered a stage of preparation for the implementation of this plan through training and qualifying teachers, preparing curricula, and renewing textbooks for secondary levels to keep up with this reform and change. The Curriculum Director indicated that there is intensive coordination with the Ministry of Higher Education in order to open more classes in English in universities, whether in medicine, engineering or others so that baccalaureate graduates do not find themselves after years of studying English in front of a class taught in French or facing a dead end.

The government plans are linked to the growing interests of Moroccan society, especially the youth, in learning English since the scientific production in this language is higher than in French, which has been displaced and will continue for a period of 5 to 10 years. A report made by the British Council has suggested that 74% of young Moroccans believe that English will replace French in the next five years. This stems from the fact that 40% of those 1200 young Moroccans between 15 and 25 years who were surveyed have recognised the value and importance of English in today's world, considering it as an important language to learn while only 10% preferred French. Furthermore, the report outlined that this young generation has been provided with opportunities to improve their

English language abilities through online social interaction, movies, and educational platforms due to the Covid-19 pandemia.

A study by Khadija Abdous (2020) speculates on possible future trends of English education in Morocco and outlines the probable challenges which might result from the tension between the internationalisation and domestication of English uncovered in two rival sectors, i.e., the private and public education systems which have led to inequality and segregation. More precisely, the inequality lies in the fact that private institutes suits exclusively to those who can pay, whereas more than 80% of the students are enrolled in public schools which in most cases lack some basic teaching materials and infrastructure. In addition, the government's cost-cutting drive resulted in several ongoing programmes in which experienced and qualified public-school teachers were encouraged to leave the profession or retire early. Additionally, Abdous points out that the increase in the number of private schools does not correlate with improved learning outcomes for students and one of the main reasons behind this is the low quality of teacher training. Undeniably, this reinforces inequality in education and runs counter to the stated goal of the "Ministry's Strategic Vision" of achieving a school of quality and equitable opportunities.

6.2 Challenges Faced by Teachers in Adapting to Teaching Science Subjects in English

Switching to teaching scientific subjects in English might be a challenge for teachers in the region. These challenges include the lack of sufficient English language proficiency to effectively explain complex scientific concepts which may contribute to the misunderstanding of these contents on the part of the learners and lead to a potential achievement gap among students. English proficiency levels certainly vary from one country to another among teachers as well as students since English is taught as the first foreign language in some countries, while in others it is considered a second or foreign language, which can negatively affect the quality of instruction.

Additionally, teachers often encounter a shortage of resources, such as textbooks and reference materials that can inhibit their ability to plan and perform stimulating lessons that effectively convey scientific knowledge (Boakye & Ampiah, 2017). Thus, teachers need to develop effective pedagogical strategies and instructional approaches to facilitate student understanding, motivate active engagement and promote scientific curiosity while ensuring language acquisition which might be very challenging for both teachers and students. Furthermore, teaching science in English may run against cultural and societal norms in the MENA region as students and their families attach a higher value to learn Arabic which leads to disengagement and resistance to the use of English as a medium of instruction. Another challenge may arise while designing appropriate assessments to measure students' comprehension of scientific concepts in English; this requires great attention from teachers to the language barriers that learners may face.

According to a study conducted in Morocco, science and technology teachers hold positive attitudes towards changes in language of instruction, however, they do not agree with the way this initiative is being implemented, since neither teachers nor students have been prepared to cope with a foreign language as a medium of instruction. Teachers suggest that the shift to English should start as the first foreign language at the early stages of primary Education (Ben Hammou & Kesbi, 2021).

To overcome these challenges, it is important to provide instructors with the technical and pedagogical support, materials and tools they need in addition to promote professional development and training opportunities to enhance their linguistic skills (Cañada et al., 2022). It is also important to seek initiatives to eliminate the socioeconomic disparity, establishing a balance between protecting cultural heritage, ensuring inclusivity and transparency, promoting national identity, and guaranteeing the acquisition of needed skills that students require to succeed in a globalised world where English is leading the scientific communication. Indeed, cooperation between educators, language experts, decision-makers, educational institutions and other interested parties can assist to solve these issues regarding successful science instruction and create inclusive and efficient language policies.

7 Samples of Indicators to Diversity and Inequality in the MENA Region and the Impact of Languages on Sustainable Development Goals

First of all, it is important to state that indicators are not understood in this context as a means to set rankings to compare educational institutions or countries, but as means to provide a tool for self-awareness, to allow for profiling and self-assessment and to help develop a broad set of relevant indicators. Some questions for reflexion have been added to help the reader think about relevant issues tackled in the chapter.

As an example of *Indicators*, the following are suggested:

(a) Those addressed to build, sustain, and guarantee language policies after a process of awareness:

- Analyse language policy of a country, public institutions, or companies as a certain type of policy can protect varied languages and cultures or not.
- Publish agreed norms and legal texts to assure the implementation of policies throughout time but also to revise them systematically.
- Fix budgets to cope with set objectives.
- Establish evaluation strategies that take to possible improvements.

(b) Those addressed to guarantee the achievement of Sustainable Development Goals (SDGs):

- Value local languages and cultures and integration of content and language to approach varied situations like:
    - Role of local languages and cultures.
    - Existence of heritage language minorities.
    - Overcoming situations of forced linguistic and cultural assimilation eluding the social and cultural capital present in the classrooms.

- Identify domains where dominant languages and cultures are displacing other languages:
    - Presence in classrooms of vulnerable groups (race/gender), refugees, migrants, and other language minority groups either permanently or temporarily.
    - International dissemination of quality research .
    - Place of multilingual and multicultural practices in the classroom.

As regards *Questions for reflexion*, these are some examples:

(a) Is English ...

- Harming and limiting the dissemination and quality of research and education?
- Helping both personal and collective identity to become multilingual rather than monolingual?
- An added barrier for students who struggle to find the opportunity to study higher education in their L1?
- A top-down or a bottom-up choice/ decision?

And last but not least:

(a) How can the teaching of English as a foreign language contribute to "leave no one behind"?

8   Conclusions and Implications

Policies and strategies implemented in the MENA region regarding English language teaching have undergone a significant process of development and evolution. The importance given to the English language reflects its value as a global language which can be used in different aspects of people's lives. This recognition aligns with the need to empower individuals with the essential skills to be effective participators in our globalised world. Aiming to develop language proficiency is considered one of the main reasons why most countries in the region adopt bilingual education (Arabic and English). To fulfil this objective, efforts have been made to empower language instruction with new innovative tools, e.g., digital platforms, online resources, and computer-assisted language learning, which have positively motivated learners to participate in interactive activities.

However, more and deeper reflections are required to critically evaluate the policies and strategies implemented in the MENA region concerning English language teaching for two main reasons. First, to fight against the overshadowed value of linguistic diversity in the region and the potential marginalisation of local languages, in addition to the erosion of linguistic diversity in the region which has been shaped by the growing emphasis and dominance of English. Second, to keep a balance between teaching English as a universal language and conserving the cultural identity of the region as a whole. The integration of culturally relevant content that promotes local literature and heritage can help to maintain the linguistic and cultural richness as well as diversity that characterise the region. Thus, policymakers should address the resource gap by investing in infrastructure and continuous professional development, ensuring that the teaching of English provides equitable opportunities and leaves 'no one behind' regardless of their social rank.

We hope this chapter may call the attention of language policy makers, researchers in the fields of applied linguistics, educational sciences, and sociolinguistics with reference to the teaching and learning of English as a foreign language in the context of the MENA region.

References

Abdous, K. (2020). Privatisation of education in Morocco–A multi-speed education system and a polarised society. *Education International Research, 6*(2).

Agbaria, A. K., Mustafa, M., & Jabareen, Y. T. (2015). 'In your face' democracy: Education for belonging and its challenges in Israel. *British Educational Research Journal, 41*(1), 143–175.

Akkari, A. (2021). Higher education in the Arab region: Globalization, privatization and prospects. In J. Zajda (Ed.), *Third international handbook of globalisation, education and policy research*. Springer. https://doi.org/10.1007/978-3-030-66003-1_14

Al Abbasi, M. (2017). Local politics in the MENA region comes with many challenges. *The Arab Weekly*. https://thearabweekly.com/local-politics-mena-region-comes-many-challenges

Alhawary, M. T. (2017). Empirical directions in the future of Arabic second language acquisition research and second language pedagogy. In K. M. Wahba, Z. A. Taha, & L. England (Eds.), *Handbook for Arabic language teaching professionals in the 21st century II* (pp. 408–421). Routledge.

Al-Wer, E. (2013). Sociolinguistics. In J. Owens (Ed.), *The Oxford handbook of Arabic linguistics* (pp. 241–263). Oxford University Press.

Badry, F., & Willoughby, J. (2015). Arabic in Higher Education: Questions of national identity and pragmatism. In *Higher education revolutions in the Gulf* (pp. 179–203). Routledge.

Bassiouney, R. (2009). *Arabic sociolinguistics*. Edinburgh University Press.

Bayat, A., & Herrera, L. (Eds.). (2010). *Being young and Muslim. New cultural politics in the Global South and North*. Oxford University Press. https://doi.org/10.1093/acprof:oso/9780195369212.001.000

Ben Hammou, S., & Kesbi, A. (2021). The teaching of science subjects through foreign languages in Moroccan Secondary Schools: Science teachers' perceptions and experiences. *RELC Journal*. https://doi.org/10.1177/00336882211035832

Benmamoun, E., Montrul, S., & Polinsky, M. (2013). Heritage languages and their speakers: Opportunities and challenges for linguistics. *Theoretical Linguistics, 39*(3–4), 129–181. https://doi.org/10.1515/tl-2013-0009

Boakye, C., & Ampiah, J. G. (2017). Challenges and solutions: The experiences of newly qualified science teachers. *SAGE Open*. https://doi.org/10.1177/2158244017706710

Britannica, The Editors of Encyclopaedia. (2023, May 31). Middle East. *Encyclopedia Britannica*. https://www.britannica.com/place/Middle-East. Accessed 6 June 2023.

Cañada, E., Postrero, L. S., Perez, C., Gargar, L., Gaan, D., & Tantog, A. J. (2022). Challenges and coping strategies of English teachers in teaching English subjects in the new normal. *International Journal of Academic Multidisciplinary Research, 6*(12), 243–253.

Chapple, J. (2015). Teaching in English is not necessarily the teaching of English. *International Education Studies, 8*(3), 1–13. Available online at: https://doi.org/10.5539/ies.v8n3p1

Chen, J. (2023). Middle East and North Africa (MENA): Countries and economy. *Investopedia*. Retrieved from https://www.investopedia.com/terms/m/middle-east-and-north-africa-mena.asp

Dipak, D., & Mustapha Kamel, N. (2003). *Trade, investment, and development in the Middle East and North Africa*. documents1.worldbank.org. World Bank. Archived from the original on 22 January 2021. Retrieved 18 April 2023.

El-Aswad, E. S. (2019). *The quality of life and policy issues among the Middle East and North African countries*. Springer.

Errihani, M. (2017). English education policy and practice in Morocco. In R. Kirkpatrick (Ed.), *English language education policy in the Middle East and North Africa* (Language policy) (Vol. 13). Springer. https://doi.org/10.1007/978-3-319-46778-88

Grin, F. (2005). Linguistic human rights as a source of policy guidelines: A critical assessment. *Journal of SocioLinguistics, 9*(3), 448–460.

Kabasakal, H., Dastmalchian, A., Karacay, G., & Bayraktar, S. (2012). Leadership and culture in the MENA region: An analysis of the GLOBE project. *Journal of World Business, 47*(4), 519–529.

Kwee, C. T. T. (2021). I want to teach sustainable development in my English classroom: A case study of incorporating sustainable development goals in English teaching. *Sustainability, 13*(8), 4195.

Lasekan, O., & Godoy, M. (2020). Towards a sustainable local development of instructional material: An impact assessment of locally produced videos on EFL learners' skills and individual difference factors. *Frontiers in Psychology, 11*, 2075.

Macaro, E., Graham, S., & Woore, R. (2015). *Improving foreign language teaching: Towards a research-based curriculum and pedagogy*. Routledge.

Marsh, D. (2006, March). English as medium of instruction in the new global linguistic order: Global characteristics, local consequences. In *Second Annual Conference for Middle East Teachers of Science, Mathematics and Computing*, METSMaC 2006.

Ministry of National Education. (2015). Strategic Vision (2015–2030). Retrieved from https://www.csefrs.ma/publications

Or, I. G. (2017). Language policy and education in the Middle East and North Africa. In T. L. McCarty & S. May (Eds.), *Language policy and political issues in education* (3rd ed.). Springer.

Ponnuchamy, G. (2017). History of English-as-a-second-language teaching in the Middle East and the current scenario in Bahrain. *Arab World English Journal (AWEJ), 8*.

Shohamy, E. (2014). The weight of English in global perspective: The role of English in Israel. *Review of Research in Education, 38*, 273–289.

Spolsky, B. (1996). Prolegomena to an Israeli language policy. In T. Hickey & J. Williams (Eds.), *Language, education and society in a changing world* (pp. 45–53). IRAAL/Multilingual Matters Ltd.

Spolsky, B. (2004). *Language policy*. Cambridge University Press.

Spolsky, B. (2007). Towards a theory of language policy. *Working Papers in Educational Linguistics, 22*(1), 1–14.

Spolsky, B. (2021). *Rethinking language policy*. Edinburgh University Press. http://www.jstor.org/stable/10.3366/j.ctv1ns7n6q

Suleiman, Y. (2013). *Arabic in the fray: Language ideology and cultural politics*. Edinburgh University Press.

UNESCO. (1998). *Rapport mondial sur l'éducation*. UNESCO.

United Nations General Assembly. (2015). *Transforming our world: The 2030 agenda for sustainable development*. United Nations.

Versteegh, K. (2014). *The Arabic language* (2nd ed.). Edinburgh University Press.

Wilkinson, R., & Gabriels, R. (Eds.). (2021). *The Englishization of higher education in Europe*. Amsterdam University Press. https://doi.org/10.5117/9789463727358

Zaafour, A., & Salaberri-Ramiro, M. S. (2022). Incorporating cooperative project-based learning in the teaching of English as a foreign language: Teachers' perspectives. *Education Sciences, 12*(6), 388.

CHAPTER 7

Diversity of ELT in Omani Higher Education

Fawziya Al Zadjali and Sharita Viola Furtado

1 Introduction

In general, the term "Diversity" refers to dissimilarity and distinction between members of a group. This distinction includes noticeable differences in cultures, ethnicity, gender, and language (Banks et al., 2005; Musawi et al., 2022). Diversity in English language teaching (ELT) manifests itself as learners derive from different backgrounds and ethnic groups. These differences in ELT classrooms have begun to gain attention by scholars in the field of ELT. However, there is less focused attention on diversity in ELT in HE, particularly in the MENA region.

Accordingly, this chapter sets to explore the concept of diversity in Omani HE institutions by exploring the perceptions of both teachers and students on the concept of diversity in ELT. The data collected for the purpose of writing this chapter is based on small-scale research data.

F. Al Zadjali (✉)
Freelancer Educational Consultant, Muscat, Sultanate of Oman

Muscat, Oman

S. V. Furtado
International College of Engineering and Management, Seeb, Sultanate of Oman

© The Author(s), under exclusive license to Springer Nature Switzerland AG 2023
H. Abouabdelkader, B. Tomalin (eds.), *Diversity Education in the MENA Region*, https://doi.org/10.1007/978-3-031-42693-3_7

The significance of this chapter comes from being specifically concentrating on learner diversity in ELT in Omani Higher education institutions. Learner diversity is one of the essential categories of diversity according to Banks et al. (2005). This research is considered a significant addition to the field of ELT, by both scholars and professionals.

This chapter begins by introducing the contextual background for this research by shedding light on ELT in HE in Oman and the status of diversity in the Omani HE institutions. Then, it presents some relevant literature on diversity in ELT. Data collection and analysis methods are presented followed by the findings from this small-scale research. Finally, this chapter concludes by stating some recommendations for policymakers, researchers, and practitioners in the field of ELT in HE contexts.

2 Contextual Background

Oman has experienced rapid growth since the rise of 1 July 1970 dawn to cover Oman with various developments in all sectors including Education under the leadership of his Majesty Sultan Qaboos bin Said, may his soul rest in peace. Since the 1970s, the educational sector has experienced ongoing improvements in the number of schools, Higher Education institutions, developments of principles, curriculum, and teacher education to name a few. English language teaching in Higher Education has also got its share from the development cycle that has covered the country.

2.1 *English Language Teaching in HE in Oman*

English is considered the official second language in Oman and has become the medium of instruction for many HE institutions, except for majors that specialize in Arabic. In Omani Higher Education Institutions, English is a compulsory module for the Foundation or pre-university level. This is the year before specialization in all majors in HE. Furthermore, English is taught as a module on its own to year one university/college students for majors that require the use of English such as medicine and engineering. The students who enroll in Omani HE institutions are both Omani's and international students. It is fair to say that Omani HE institutions have begun to attract international students from both Arab and non-Arab countries. This has added to Oman's diverse nature.

2.2 Diversity Status in Omani HE Education Institutions

Oman is a diverse country in all aspects. Diversity is reflected in Oman's different cultures across regions and governorates, in the different tribes of Omanis' such as Zadjali and Balushi that descend from Asia as well as Swahili that descends from Africa. This diversity has imposed some culture and language differences between Omani's themselves, not to mention the expatriates who live in Oman, who brought their own cultures and languages too.

Diversity in Higher Education is represented by the type of education that is offered to students, which eliminates the differences of gender, religion, race, first language, ethnic group, and cultural background.

3   Literature Review

English language teaching in Oman is deeply rooted in the recent development reported in current literature globally and locally. It has progressed across the years alongside the well-known learning theories, starting with the behaviorism up to date with the communicative theory and others. Since diversity in education was accepted a long time ago (Banks et al., 2005; Sunthonkanokpong & Murphy, 2020; Musawi et al., 2022), ELT pedagogy has developed accordingly and embraced diversity.

As a relatively new concept, diversity in education has received considerable attention since the last decade due to social changes, like migration, that impacted educational institutions and resulted in a mixture of cultures and ethnic backgrounds (Sunthonkanokpong & Murphy, 2020). Accordingly, diversity in education has drastically affected ELT and manifested itself due to the kind of students who join English language classrooms either in schools or higher education institutions. According to Banks et al. (2005), there are 12 principles for diversity in education that need to be considered. These principles have been grouped into five categories. The categories relate to *teacher learning, student learning, intergroup relations, school governance, organization* and *equity* and *assessment*.

Although all five categories can be considered as a challenge for English language teachers, *learner diversity* can mount as the highest challenge that face teachers. This is because learners descend from various *cultural backgrounds* with *different first languages*, derive from *different ethnic groups*, have *different educational backgrounds*, and differ in their *English language proficiency levels*.

Although diversity in education has received considerable attention from research, the examination of learner diversity in ELT has not reached saturation yet. Accordingly, this chapter considers learner diversity in ELT by considering the views of ELT professionals and students in HE institutions in Oman.

The research conducted by Greenup et al. (2020) has examined ESL teachers' principles and practices in relation to learner diversity in one of the important English language training programs for adult migrants and refugees in Australia. The findings from this qualitative research indicated that teachers' practice was not associated with any specific teaching method; however, their practice was driven by their classes teaching context. In addition, the findings demonstrated that diversity of English language proficiency level was common for teachers; however ethnic background, educational background, and L1 experiences were less common amongst the participating teachers. Another similar research that focused on learner diversity was conducted in Oman by Musawi et al. (2022). This research examined learner beliefs and experiences in diverse classrooms. The study focused on different subjects including the English language. The 283 students (11th and 12th grades), who participated in this study, were from five different international schools in Muscat, the capital city of Oman. The findings demonstrated that non-Arab learners rated their teachers highly in terms of teaching methods, curriculum design, and assessment when compared with Omani and Arab learners. The significance of both studies is that they both focus on learner diversity in ELT classrooms in relation to various areas ranging from their first language, English language proficiency level, and educational background to learners' views of their teachers' teaching methods and curriculum design.

Another study conducted by Al-Obaydi (2019) in Iraq particularly in Diyala governorate that is diverse in its ethic, religion, and languages, which set to measure students' perceptions and attitudes towards teaching cultures in Iraq and their interaction with that. The study involved 50 students from the University of Diyala. The findings from this study revealed that students were satisfied and positive about studying foreign and different cultures as the one in their course books. The study also discovered that the students who come from different cultures themselves appreciate other and foreign cultures more. A similar study was conducted by Chinh (2013) to explore the attitudes towards diverse culture integration into ELT in Vietnam. The participants were ten fresh graduates whose age was between 23 and 25 years. This qualitative study that used reflective journals to collect the views and attitudes of the participants towards diverse culture education in ELT discovered that all participants welcome the inclusion of diverse cultures into ELT. The significance of both studies above is that there is an awareness amongst HE learners about the importance of addressing and referral to other cultures in ELT contexts.

The current chapter examines the perceptions of both teachers and learners towards learner diversity in ELT utilizing the four principles explored by Greenup et al. (2020) in Australia that explored the teachers' views. The current study exploits the student diversity principles and involves students' views into the research in the Omani context. From a sociocultural perspective, this research explored the perceptions of both teachers and students towards learner diversity in HE ELT contexts. The questions raised in this research are:

1. What are the perceptions of Higher Education teachers on the implementation of learner diversity in ELT classrooms?
2. What are the perceptions of Higher Education students on the implementation of learner diversity in ELT classrooms?

Both research questions have been explored in relation to the following learner diversity areas:

1. Students' English language proficiency levels
2. Culture difference
3. Use of students' L1 (First language)
4. Students' previous educational background

4 THEORETICAL FRAMEWORK

Theory frames teaching and learning and acts like a pillar for research and practice. This research utilizes the "sociocultural theory" by Vygotsky (1962) as its theoretical framework. The sociocultural theory is very relevant to diversity and cultures as it simply means that student learning can only happen within a social and cultural context as learners are social in nature. Thus, the sociocultural underpinned the research questions, data collection methods, and findings, as well as the researchers' position.

5   Data Collection Methods

This chapter is based on small-scale mixed data collection methods. The methods used are surveys and focus group interviews. The mixed method type of research enables the collection of both vast numbers of data together with precise insights into the topics being investigated or explored (Creswell & Creswell, 2018).

This study utilized a custom designed questionnaire on a Likert Scale (close ended questions) format to gain more insights on the four areas under investigation. These are (1) learners' English language proficiency level, (2) culture difference, (3) use of L1, and (4) Educational background.

Surveys and *questionnaires* are generally utilized to assess attitudes, opinions, and behaviors of individuals relating to a particular issue (Rose et al., 2014). Additionally, surveys are implemented in a systematic process of gathering data pertaining to a particular topic (Thayer-Hart et al., 2010).

Since questionnaires are considered as quantitative data collection methods, *focus group interviews* are highly recommended as qualitative data collection methods that aim to gain the perceptions of participants on shared or common knowledge. Thus, focus groups are ideal for understanding cultures (Savin-Baden & Major, 2013).

In this study, the questionnaire collected data from HE ELT teachers from different colleges and universities, and the focus group interview was conducted with some HE students in the Sultanate of Oman.

5.1   *The Questionnaire*

The questionnaire utilized includes two main parts. The first part collects information about teachers' background like gender, qualification, title, nationality, and years of experience. The second part of the questionnaire relates to learners and focuses on the four areas being explored through this research.

The questionnaire has been sent as a soft copy using google forms. All of the questions are in English. The purpose and aims of the research were made clear to the participants on the same questionnaire. Additionally, it was made clear that their responses would be treated confidentially, and their identity would remain anonymous and will be utilized for research purposes only.

For the study, a questionnaire was prepared using Google forms and distributed via social media channels like WhatsApp to English language teachers teaching in Higher education institutions in Oman depending on both researchers' network. Twenty-one teachers responded to the questionnaire out of which 52.4% teachers were male and 47.6% teachers were female.

Out of the 21 teachers who responded, 95.2% teachers were teaching English in HE institutions in Oman and just 4.8% teachers were teaching subjects other than English. As for their qualification, 52.4% teachers had Bachelor degree, whereas 33.3% teachers had Master degree and 14.3% teachers had PhD. Most of the teachers who participated in the survey were Omanis (71.4%) and only 28.6% of them were from other nationalities teaching in HE institutions in Oman. Currently, 61.9% of the teachers who participated are teaching at the college level whereas 38.1% are teaching at the university level. Table 7.1 provides the basic information about the participant teachers, who filled in the questionnaire.

In addition to the questionnaire administered to the teachers, a focus group interview has been conducted with some of the HE students to validate and confirm the findings reached from the teachers' views and to explore the same areas from the students' point of view.

Table 7.1 Participant teachers

No of participants	*21 participants*
Gender	10 male
	11 female
Title	20 English teachers
	1 other (not specified)
Qualification	11 Bachelor
	7 Masters
	3 PhD
Years of experience	9 teachers – 16+ above years of experience
	2 teachers – 11–15 years
	4 teachers – 6–10 years
	6 teachers – 0–5 years
Nationality	15 Omani
	6 non-Omani
Institution type	13 teach in colleges
	8 teach in universities

5.2 Focus Group Interview

Four female students participated in a focus group discussion, who met with the main researcher in a quiet corner in one of the cafes in Muscat as per the students' request. The meeting went smoothly, and notes were taken by the researcher. The focus group meeting explored the same questions from the questionnaire with the students. The students belong to the same HE institution. Three of them were in their first year of study and one was in her second year. The students were a mixture of those who studied in government/state schools and those who went to private institutions. One of the participants experienced life abroad during her schooling time due to the nature of her father's work. The students were fluent in English and requested the interview to run in English. The participant students come from diverse cultures in Oman, and most of them spoke another language besides Arabic in their homes. Table 7.2 below, in turn, provides the details of the participating students and their names. All names used for the students are pseudonyms to ensure confidentiality.

As part of the ethical measures taken, all participants have been informed about the research aims, process, ethics, and assured anonymity and confidentiality (Savin-Baden & Major, 2013) and that their views would only be used for research purposes without any referral to their identity. This assurance has been written on the survey form and on separate consent forms which the focus group participants read and signed.

The data collected has been analyzed using the Qualitative Content Analysis approach by Krueger and Casey (2009) through coding and categorizing of key areas related to the research questions.

Table 7.2 Participant students: confidentiality and anonymity

No	Name	Year of study	Languages spoken at home	Previous educational background
1.	Raneem	First	Arabic	Government school in Oman
2.	Malak	First	Arabic and English	Private international school in Oman and abroad
3.	Rawan	Second	Arabic and Balushi[a]	Government school in Oman
4.	Salwa	First	Arabic and Balushi	Government school in Oman

[a]Balushi is one of the local and most common languages in Oman that belongs to the Balushi tribe

6 The Findings

The data from both the questionnaire and the focus groups was analyzed qualitatively through certain stages. The use of Google forms made life easier as it provided summaries and graphs for each question with the responses gained. The analysis involved a three-stage process according to Miles and Huberman (1994) and King and Horrocks (2010), which were (1) the descriptive coding, (2) the interpretive coding, and finally defining of (3) the overarching codes.

The first stage was the "descriptive coding", where the data was managed. This stage involved the familiarization stage (Spencer et al., 2013), where raw data (transcripts/notes) was read and interesting and relevant topics or areas were identified, without any attempt to interpret. The next stage was the interpretive stage, where the data was interpreted, and meaning was made out of it. This stage involved grouping similar points/topics without any influence of any theory the researchers could be influenced by. Finally, at the overarching codes stage, the categories from the interpretive codes were grouped based on similarity, and themes/concepts were drawn out of them.

Responses from both teachers and students will be presented according to the areas explored in both the questionnaire and the focus group interview. These are (1) learners English language proficiency level, (2) culture difference, (3) use of L1, and (4) Educational background.

Part One: Learners' English Language Proficiency Level The research literature review edited by Galloway (2020) explained that students' language proficiency levels play a role in their success in HE. One of the practices in ELT classrooms that considers learner diversity is to teach in mixed-level or mixed-ability classrooms. To get the teachers views on the relationship between teaching in mixed-ability or mixed-level classrooms and students' English language proficiency levels, the following statements have been explored:

- Students learn better in mixed English level classrooms
- Students' confidence increases in mixed English language level classrooms
- Students with low English language proficiency levels can benefit from using only English for teaching

- Mixed English level classrooms help to enrich students' vocabulary levels
- Placement tests are effective for measuring students' English language levels

The graph in Fig. 7.1 provides a clear picture about the percentage of the teachers who agreed with the statements.

According to the graph above, more than half of the 21 participating teachers supported teaching in mixed ability classrooms for ELT. The benefits for students as stated by the teachers include improvements in students' learning abilities, increase in their confidence levels, development of their vocabulary levels, and approval of placement tests as being a proper measure of students' English language proficiency levels. The only point that teachers do not appear to support is using only English for teaching, as less than half of the teachers (45.5%) thought that in mixed-level classrooms, using only English does not necessarily impact positively on students with low English language proficiency levels.

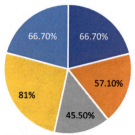

Teaching mixed English level classrooms

- Students learn better in mixed English level classrooms
- Students' confidence increases in mixed English language level classrooms
- Students with low English language proficiency levels can benefit from using only English for teaching
- Mixed English level classrooms help to enrich students' vocabulary levels
- Placement tests are effective for measuring students' English language levels

Fig. 7.1 Learners' English language proficiency level

As for the students, most of them agreed that students learn better in mixed-level classrooms. The students mentioned that these types of mixed classes can enrich students' vocabulary levels and would help the lower-level students or the shy ones. However, one of the students was neutral in her response and thought that mixed-level classes might have a negative effect if the difference is high between the students such as being extremely high and exceptionally low. Although most of the teachers thought that students' confidence develops in this type of class, three out of four students were neutral about it and only one agreed. They thought that students' confidence might increase highly to the level where they can become overconfident towards their peers. As for the increase in the vocabulary levels, all students agreed and thought that students' vocabulary levels would improve, especially for low-level students. However, the students thought that this statement might not necessarily be true for high-level students as their vocabulary level might remain the same. In addition, all students thought that placement tests are effective for measuring students' language proficiency levels.

Although, the students agreed with the teachers over all of the statements related to the improvements gained from teaching in mixed-ability classrooms, their response contradicted the teachers' response on using only English language in the classroom. While the teachers did not fully support this statement, the students supported it highly and explained that using only English would expose students to more English in the classroom, and this would result in improving their English language proficiency levels. Based on our experiences in teaching at the Foundation level (pre-university), we noticed that students' welcome lessons to be taught in English; however, the low-level students would request some terms to be translated into Arabic to them. This is due to most of the students being state school leavers, where English is taught as one subject for 40 minutes a day. This lack of exposure to English becomes a challenge in HE. Accordingly, teaching in mixed-level classrooms would support those students English language proficiency level and help to improve it.

Part Two: Cultural Difference As can be seen in Fig. 7.2, many teachers supported referral to students' cultures both in the teaching materials and while teaching and thought that this impacts positively on students and supports their learning of English as more that 90% of the teachers supported the latter point.

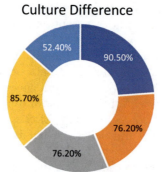

- Addressing students' culture supports their learning of English language
- English language teaching materials must address different cultures
- referring to students' culture builds their confidence level
- referring to students' culture helps in developing a good relationship between teachers and students
- referring to students' culture in classroom could cause embarrassment to the students

Fig. 7.2 Cultural difference

The graph of Fig. 7.2 shows that teachers believe that culture has a big impact in learning English language. Unlike the teachers, the responses of the students varied over this statement. Surprisingly, some of them could not see any relationship between addressing their cultures, and the role culture can play in supporting their learning of the English language. However, through the discussion, they explained that by teachers addressing their cultures, they can feel included and real-life examples would enhance their learning skills.

Whether referral to students' cultures can build their confidence and help to develop a good relationship with the teacher or not, the teachers supported these two points as it is clear from the graph. Similarly, all students approved this and explained that when teachers address their cultures, this would raise awareness towards other cultures and teachers can become close to students and understand them. In addition, the students highlighted the point of inclusion that would result from addressing different cultures in ELT classrooms and explained that they would feel comfortable with their teachers if they referred to their culture. For example, when teachers get students to describe different occasions procedures in

Use of L1 (First language)

■ using students L1 to explain a concept or lesson supports their learning of English language
■ using students L1 to explain a topic, or a concept supports their understanding of the course content
■ using learners L1 builds students confidence levels
■ using learners L1 develops a good relationship between the teachers and the students
■ using learners L1 in develops their academic skills, such as summarizing, problem solving and note taking

Fig. 7.3 Use of L1 (first language)

their cultures, such as Eid[1] celebrations or weddings. This can make students feel included and proud of themselves and of the cultures they belong to.

Figure 7.3 shows that the only point that had the least consensus from the teachers relates to the negative impact of referring to student cultures. It has been found that 52.40% of the teachers agreed that referral to students' cultures might embarrass them. Unlike the teachers, all students did not agree that referral to students' culture could embarrass them and explained that this depends on the teacher and the kind of relationship they have with their students. They also explained that mentioning students' cultures would embarrass the students if the teacher's way was insulting and offensive.

Part Three: Use of L1 (First Language) Whether "using students L1 to explain a concept or lesson supports their learning of English language," 57.10% of the teachers supported the use of students L1 in HE institutions (see Fig. 7.3). This is quite bizarre for two reasons. The first reason being that Arabic is not necessarily the first language for all students. Second, English is supposed to be the medium of instruction in ELT

---

[1] Eid is an Islamic occasion that Muslims celebrate twice a year.

classrooms. Unlike the teachers, students did not welcome the idea of using L1 to support their learning of English. They claimed that using English would be better than using Arabic as L1 because for many students' Arabic is not necessarily their L1.

As for using students L1 to explain a topic or a concept and the role this can play to support their understanding or comprehension of course content, both teachers and students supported this. However, students preferred to keep the use of L1/Arabic at a vocabulary level.

Regarding the role of using students L1 to raise students' confidence level, Fig. 7.3 also shows that 52.4% of the teachers agreed that using learners L1 builds their confidence levels. However, most of the students disagreed with this statement and thought that confidence increases when students understand English more and can participate and use it. This indicates that students' confidence does not necessarily link to using their L1 in the classroom.

Whether using learners L1 develops a good relationship between the teachers and the learners, 66.70% of the teachers supported that the relationship between students and teachers will become good if teachers use students' L1. The students' responses varied over this; however, they explained that there would be more appreciation for the teacher if she/he knows the students' L1 and are aware of it as this can raise the students' confidence and might result in having fun classes. From our experience, using some Arabic words to enhance students understanding of a concept, such as "drought" puts the students at ease and lifts the burden of being lost and not knowing the meaning. This, therefore, impacts on their confidence, as they feel included in the lesson flow.

Finally, there were varied views over the point related to the relationship between using learners L1 and the improvement of their academic skills, such as summarizing, problem solving, and note taking. Although more than half of the teachers supported this point, the participating students did not see any link between the development of their academic skills and the use of L1 in the classroom. They hesitantly said that if there is any benefit, that would be for the lower-level students and not for all.

Part Four: Students Educational Background/Previous Education
When asked about the role of students' educational background/previous education in supporting students' learning of English language,

interestingly, 100% of teachers agreed that students educational background/previous education supports their learning of English language in HE.

On the contrary, Fig. 7.4 shows that the students did not agree with the statement and explained that acquisition and learning of English does not necessarily come from the previous educational background. They explained that they have developed and taught themselves English through social media, such as YouTube, listening to English songs, watching movies, reading books, etc.

Concerning the question of "whether academic skills such as note taking are a result of students' educational background," 66.7% of teachers agreed that academic skills are a result of students' educational background while 28.6% disagreed and a small percent of 4.8% were neutral (see Fig. 7.4). The students agreed that their academic skills are a result of their educational background, but they added the private tutor's[2] role as well in this regard.

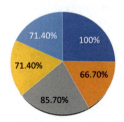

- Students educational background/ previous education supports their learning of the English language
- Academic skills such as note taking are a result oof students' educational background
- Students' educational background play a vital role in their confidence level
- Having rich knowledge and skills related to learning English are a result of strong educational background
- Students' motivation and interest in learning English relate to their educational background

Fig. 7.4 Students' educational background

[2] Private tutors is a common practice in the Arab world. This means that parents or students themselves hire a private tutor to teach them some modules after formal college or school time.

In relation to the link between students' educational background and their confidence levels, the reposes of the participants differed. Although most of the teachers agreed with this statement as it is clear from the graph above, all students were neutral in this regard. They explained that there are other aspects or reasons behind one's confidence other than their educational background.

According to Fig. 7.4, 71.4% of the teachers believed that students' rich knowledge and skills related to learning English are a result of a strong educational background. However, the students' views were quite different and thought that previous education can help, but there are other sources that can play a role in enriching students' knowledge and skills of English.

Similar to the point above, 71.4% of the teachers believed that students' motivation and interest in learning English relates to their educational background. Conversely, the students' opinions varied over this statement, and they explained that their motivation and interest can be linked to other reasons, such as a personal interest. This finding relates to the work by Dörnyei (2009) on the theory of L2 Motivational Self System. Dörnyei found that there are three sources for learner motivation, which relate to (1) how learners see themselves, (2) learner desires, and the satisfaction and (3) positive learning experiences of English/another language (Hadfield & Dörnyei, 2013). The third source supports the teachers' views that students' motivation and interest in learning English relates to their previous educational background and to the students' views of other sources being the reason behind their motivation and interest.

To conclude, the analysis of the data from this research showed that teachers and students are aware of the concept "learner diversity" and have positive perceptions regarding its implementation in ELT contexts. The next section will present the findings reached from the analysis.

7 Discussion of Findings

The findings from this research can be grouped into three areas. This research discovered that implementing diversity in ELT is beneficial and supports not only students' learning of the English language; rather it develops their confidence and inclusion and can impact positively on their relationship with each other and with their teachers.

7.1 Knowledge of English Language

Considering diversity of students' *cultures* while teaching and in textbooks, the students *different English language proficiency levels*, and *teaching English in mixed level classrooms*, impacts positively on enriching students' knowledge of the English language. For example, being in mixed-level classes can impact positively on student learning of English, and their vocabulary level would increase based on their exposure to different English language levels, based on the kind of discussions related to addressing their cultures and languages, and based the textbooks that cater for different cultures. This finding supports the finding reached by Al-Subaiei (2017), who conducted quantitative research on 30 English language teachers at King Abdulaziz University in Saudi Arabia. All teachers in this study taught in mixed level classrooms. The study found that differentiation strategies and classroom management are effective for student success. Thus, student success in learning can possibly be gained in mixed-level classroom if teachers are equipped with the necessary skills and are ready for such teaching mixed-ability groups.

Having discussed the benefits of diversity on improving students' knowledge of the English language, the data demonstrated that *using L1* to explain areas related to learning English is not necessarily beneficial and that students can benefit more from using only English in the ELT classroom. This is because their opportunity to be exposed to English would increase, and they would experience different accents and ways to express oneself in English from their teachers and peers. This finding supports the finding reached from the research literature review edited by Galloway (2020) that demonstrated lecturers and students' positive attitudes towards the use of L1 for content comprehension. The disagreement between teachers and students over the use of L1 in the English language classroom indicates that each party views it from their own point of view. For teachers who supported the use of L1 to explain some concepts and terms, their views were based on their keenness to ensure student understanding of lesson content. In contrary, the students thought that using L1 would hinder their exposure to English, and they rejected it, particularly for explaining grammar as L1 can worsen rather than support understanding in this regard. This finding is supported by the same review mentioned earlier by Galloway (2020), as it reached another contradicting finding regarding the use of L1 from content lecturers,[3] which views L1 as a hinder because it excludes international students and is considered a violation of official policies and documents of the institution.

Furthermore, the data demonstrated that using L1 does not necessarily help to develop student's academic skills, such as summarizing, problem solving, and note taking. The exposure to English from other sources impacts positively on the students learning of the academic skills, not using L1 while teaching English.

Although teaching in mixed-level classes, considering student cultures and their English language proficiency levels, is found to impact positively on student knowledge and learning of English, *previous educational background* does not necessarily do the same. The data demonstrated a mismatch between teachers and students' perceptions over the impact of previous education on learning English. While 100% of the teachers agreed that previous education supports student learning of the English language, the students' views were quite different, and they explained that they can learn English from other sources, such as YouTube, social media, movies, and songs, and explained that their English language level and knowledge of English is not a result of their previous schooling time only.

In sum, this research discovered that learner diversity is achieved by considering students' cultures, their proficiency levels, and teaching in mixed-level classes. Therefore, this learner diversity consideration impacts positively on student learning of English in HE contexts. This research also discovered that using L1 in English lessons and student previous educational background do not necessarily support their learning of English as there are other factors that can play a role too.

7.2 Student Confidence and Inclusion

The findings from this research supported the idea that the implementation of learner diversity in ELT can raise students' confidence level and help develop their personality. This research discovered that considering students' cultures in the teaching context can raise their confidence levels and get the students to feel included.

The other finding reached over the relationship between teaching in mixed-level classes and student confidence was that it can either raise or lower students' confidence as not all students are competent, and the

---

[3] Content lecturers teach modules other than English.

low-level ones might see these types of classes as a challenge for them, while the bright students might become overconfident in this case.

In addition to the benefit of teaching English in mixed-level classes on students' confidence, the data demonstrated that referring to students' cultures while teaching can raise their confidence level as they would feel included and feel the sense of belonging. The same fact applies to having textbooks that consider diversity of cultures in them. This means that students' awareness of the different cultures would raise, and teachers would become closer to students.

Although considering students' cultures in ELT is found to be beneficial for raising students' confidence level, using L1 to teach English is not linked with raising students' confidence levels. The students explained their views and said, "*once they understand more, they would participate more and their confidence would increase*" and they added that by not using L1 students will get more exposed to English, something that can raise their confidence level too.

Furthermore, students' educational background is not found to play a key role in raising students' confidence level as they would compare themselves to others in relation to their economic status, etc. Although more than half of the teachers agreed that students' educational background plays a role in their confidence level, the students responses varied over this. According to the students, this is not necessarily true as explained by them "*other aspects affect your confidence than your educational background*". This finding contradicts with the finding reached by Hill (2017), who found a strong correlation between students' previous educational experiences and their academic confidence.

To conclude, this research discovered that student confidence level increases whenever their cultures or different cultures are considered in ELT contexts. This means that diversity of student cultures impacts positively on students' confidence levels and accordingly builds their personality. However, this research found that student confidence is not directly linked to being in a mixed level class, nor to the use of their L1 or their educational background. The findings demonstrated that there are other aspects and reasons that play a role in raising students' confidence and that mentioning different cultures is one of them.

7.3 Relationships with the Teacher and Peers

The findings from this research demonstrated that the relationship between students and teachers improves and develops when student cultures are referred to by the teachers. When cultures are considered, the students would feel more comfortable with the teachers. Although referring to student culture is found to be useful, this referral to cultures can embarrass some students if this referral was expressed negatively by the teacher or peer students.

In addition to culture referral, this research found that using learners L1 can or might help to enhance the relationship between teachers and learners. Even though there was not any consensus between teachers' and learners' responses over the relationship between the use of L1 and the development of a good relationship between teachers and students, the responses leaned towards its approval. The students explained that by using students L1, teachers would be appreciated more by the students and classes can become fun.

To sum up, it is not only referring to cultures that can boost the relationship between teachers and students, rather it is the way these cultures are referred to and mentioned in the teaching and learning contexts. In addition, some use of students L1 by the teachers can enhance the relationship between them and the students.

Having discussed the findings from this research, the next section will conclude this research and draw on some implications for the way forward.

8 Conclusion and Implications

This research aims to explore the perceptions of ELT teachers and college/university students on the implementation of four diversity principles in the Omani HE context. The principles explored are (1) learners English language proficiency level, (2) culture difference, (3) use of L1, and (4) Educational background. This mixed-method research implemented questionnaires and focus group interviews for its data collection. The data was analyzed using qualitative content analysis approach with coding and categorizing.

The findings from this research support previous research findings in relation to the role of diversity in enhancing student education and awareness in ELT contexts (Chinh, 2013; Musawi et al., 2022). This research discovered that referring to student cultures in textbooks and while teaching, teaching in mixed-level classes and considering student English language proficiency levels can all contribute to the improvement of student learning of English. The other finding discovered from this research is that HE students' confidence levels increase when their cultures are considered in teaching and learning contexts. In addition, this research found that referring to students' cultures positively in the classroom can enhance the relationship between teachers and students together with some use of students L1. However, this research discovered that using L1 and students' educational background does not necessarily support their learning of English nor boost their confidence levels. Finally, this research discovered that student educational background and previous schooling experiences can play a role in their English language proficiency levels. However, it does not necessarily shape the student proficiency levels bearing in mind the other sources that students benefit from, such as social media, songs, and movies.

The significance of this research is that it is conducted in a non-native speaking context in HE where there is not much research conducted on diversity in ELT. In addition to the nature of this research, the findings discovered would be a valued addition to the field of research in this regard.

8.1 Implications

Several implications can be drawn from the findings of the study.

8.1.1 Inclusion of Diversity Principles in Teacher Preparation and In-Service Training

According to the findings from this research, it appears that teachers and students are aware of student diversity, particularly the culture difference among learners and its value in supporting student learning in ELT. However, how sensitive teachers are towards the concept of culture difference and how to utilize and communicate it with learners in HE settings is something that is yet to be explored. Accordingly, it becomes unmistakable that pre-service teacher education and in-service training must include student and culture diversity and train teachers on how to utilize diversity in the classroom to support student learning of the English language. As stated by the students, it is not enough to refer to students "cultures and L1, rather the way this referral is made counts as well." As per the call by Pineda and Mishra (2023) that the term "diversity" needs to go global and universal, we recommend that Omani and other HE institutions that oversee teacher education to consider this recommendation for its significance.

Teacher – apprenticeship of observation – the term coined by Lortie back in 1975 has widely been acknowledged and realized by educators. The "apprenticeship of observation" refers to the teachers' previous experiences about teaching and learning that are rooted in their schooling and pre-service education (Richards, 2010). According to Beijaard et al. (2004), Flores and Day (2006), Nias (1989), Al Zadjali et al. (2016) both early and in-service teachers' beliefs play a key role in determining their actions and performances. The study conducted by Al Zadjali (2017) supported the role of teacher beliefs, values, attitudes, culture, and religion in forming teacher professional identity. Through teacher education and training programs, teacher professional identity must be unpacked, their beliefs, values, and self-image must be explored to understand the hidden beliefs of the teachers (Al Zadjali et al., 2016). By focusing on teachers' beliefs and values and training them on the inclusion of diversity in their teaching, this would impact positively on students. Accordingly, teachers and students would appreciate diversity more.

8.1.2   Inclusion of Diversity Principles in ELT Curriculum
It is the role of decision makers in HE institutions to ensure that the ELT curriculum utilized in their institutions contains diversity elements, such as referral to different cultures and different abilities, through texts, pictures, tasks, etc. This would help learners appreciate other cultures and welcome the diversity as discovered in the research conducted by Al-Obaydi (2019). For example, many coursebooks used in Omani institutions for the teaching of English use pictures portraying people from different races and colors to describe and serve diversity principles.

8.1.3   Language Teaching and Motivation in Mixed-Ability Classes
In addition to raising teachers' awareness on student and culture diversity, teacher education programs need to focus on educating and training teachers on how to teach in mixed-ability classrooms and when and how to use either the countries standard language like Arabic or refer to student's first language (L1). For example, L1 in Oman can be different languages, like Swahili, Balushi, and Jaballi.

Teaching in mixed-ability classes is one of the challenges that English teachers face as learners differ in their abilities, motivation, attitudes, and interests (Lightbown & Spada, 2006). Accordingly, it is paramount that

English language teachers must be equipped with the necessary skills and knowledge related to teaching in mixed-ability classes (Ansari, 2013; Al-Subaiei, 2017).

9 Further Research

There are some limitations with this research that need to be addressed in this chapter. First, this research would have benefited from triangulation of the data collection methods. However, as time has become a constraint to the process of conducting this research, both researchers validated the findings and related them to their own experiences. This is not to say that this research is biased and based on the researchers' beliefs; this is to state that both researchers are educators and possess experiences and knowledge about the area. Thus, both researchers adopted a reflexive view to this research by adopting Cousin's (2010) call for bringing in the "researcher self" into their research and the support for avoiding total objectivity.

The other limitation of this research is that the focus group was conducted with only female students. This research would have benefited from male students' views too. For further research, it is advisable to include both genders in the data collection methods as the case with the teachers in our research.

References

Al Zadjali, F. (2017). *The impact of curriculum prescription on English teacher professional identity in Oman* (Doctoral thesis, Leeds Beckett University). Link to Leeds Beckett Repository record https://eprints.leedsbeckett.ac.uk/id/eprint/4499

Al Zadjali, F., Sutcliffe, N., & Bligh, C. (2016). Inspiring teachers, inspiring learners: Impact of teacher professional identity on learner motivation in EFL classrooms. *Journal of Asia TEFL, 13*(4), 363.

Al-Obaydi, L. H. (2019). Cultural diversity, awareness and teaching: A study in an EFL context. *Journal of Asia TEFL, 16*(3), 987.

Al-Subaiei, M. S. (2017). Challenges in mixed ability classes and strategies utilized by ELI teachers to cope with them. *English Language Teaching, 10*(6), 182–189.

Ansari, M. S. (2013). Coping with the problems of mixed ability classes: A study in the context of teaching English as SL/FL. *International Journal of English: Literature, Language & Skills, 2*(1), 110–118.

Banks, J. A., Cookson, P., Gay, G., Hawley, W. D., Irvine, J. J., Nieto, S., et al. (2005). Education and diversity. *Social Education, 69*(1), 36–41.

Beijaard, D., Meijer, P. C., & Verloop, N. (2004). Reconsidering research on teachers' professional identity. *Teaching and Teacher Education, 20*(2), 107–128.

Chinh, N. D. (2013). Cultural diversity in English language teaching: Learners' voices. *English Language Teaching, 6*(4), 1–7.

Cousin, G. (2010). Positioning positionality. The reflexive turn. In M. Savin-Baden & C. H. Major (Eds.), *New approaches to qualitative research: Wisdom and uncertainty*. Routledge.

Creswell, J. W., & Creswell, J. D. (2018). *Research design: Qualitative, quantitative, and mixed methods approaches* (5th ed.). SAGE Publications, Inc.

Dörnyei, Z. (2009). The L2 motivational self system. In Z. Dörnyei, E. Ushioda, & Z. D'Ornyei (Eds.), *Motivation, language identity and the L2 self* (pp. 9–42). Multilingual Matters.

Flores, M. A., & Day, C. (2006). Contexts which shape and reshape new teachers' identities: A multi-perspective study. *Teaching and Teacher Education, 22*(2), 219–232.

Galloway, N. (2020). *English in higher education – English medium. Part 1: Literature review*. Accessed on 4th May 2023 from https://www.teachingenglish.org.uk/sites/teacheng/files/L020_English_HE_lit_review_FINAL.pdf

Greenup, C., Stracke, E., & Petraki, E. (2020). Learner diversity in the adult ESL classroom: Teachers' principles and practices. *English Australia Journal, 36*(1), 4–25.

Hadfield, J., & Dörnyei, Z. (2013). *Motivating learning: Research and resources in language teaching*. Pearson College Division.

Hill, K. (2017). *Food for thought: An exploration of the relationship of academic confidence to academic sustenance in Australian undergraduate students* (Durham theses, Durham University). Available at Durham E-Theses Online http://etheses.dur.ac.uk/11969/

King, N., & Horrocks, C. (2010). *Interviews in qualitative research*. SAGE.

Krueger, R. A., & Casey, M. A. (2009). *Focus groups: A practical guide for applied research* (4th ed.). Sage Publications.

Lightbown, P., & Spada, N. M. (2006). *How languages are learned*. Oxford University Press.

Miles, M., & Huberman, A. (1994). *Qualitative data analysis: An expanded source book*. SAGE Publication.

Musawi, A., Al-Ani, W., Amoozegar, A., & Al-Abri, K. (2022). Strategies for attention to diverse education in Omani society: Perceptions of secondary school students. *Education in Science, 12*, 398. https://doi.org/10.3390/educsci12060398

Nias, J. (1989). *Primary teachers talking: A study of teaching as work*. Routledge.

Pineda, P., & Mishra, S. (2023). The semantics of diversity in higher education: Differences between the Global North and Global South. *Higher Education, 85*, 865–886. https://doi.org/10.1007/s10734-022-00870-4

Richards, J. C. (2010). Competence and performance in language teaching. *RELC Journal, 41*(2), 101–122.

Rose, S., Spinks, L., & Canhoto, A. (2014). *Management research: Applying the principles.* Routledge.

Savin-Baden, M., & Major, C. H. (2013). *Qualitative research: The essential guide to theory and practice.* Routledge.

Spencer, L., Ritchie, J., O'Connor, W., Morrell, G., & Ormston, R. (2013). Analysis: In practice. In J. Ritchie (Ed.), *Qualitative research practice: A guide for social science students and researchers* (2nd ed., pp. 295–345). SAGE Publications Ltd.

Sunthonkanokpong, W., & Murphy, E. (2020). Pre-service teachers' concerns about diversity. *Journal of Applied Research in Higher Education, 13*, 1097–1109. Taylor & Francis.

Thayer-Hart, N., Dykema, J., Elver, K., Schaeffer, N. C., & Stevenson, J. (2010). *Survey fundamentals: A guide to designing and implementing surveys.* University of Wisconsin.

Vygotsky, L. (1962). *Thought and language.* MIT Press.

PART III

Language Education Curricula, Inclusion, and Social Mobility in MENA

CHAPTER 8

Linguistic Diversity in Education: The Case of Israel

Anat Stavans

1 Introduction

This volume has the objective to profile linguistic diversity in education in the Middle East and North Africa (MENA) region and its repercussions on learners' abilities and outcomes, as well as individual and societal prospects in a globalized world. Three major tiers were established to frame linguistic diversity in education: at the macro level are the national language policies (LP) within which language education policies (LEP) are parked; at the mezzo level are the institutional agents that are commissioned to ensure the enhancement of such linguistic diversity starting with the schools and culminating with the higher education; and lastly, at the micro level where we encounter the individual who is the carrier and executor of such language diversity.

This chapter, therefore, is an ambitious attempt to address these objectives as they are manifested in Israel, a plurilingual and pluricultural

A. Stavans (✉)
Beit Berl College, Kfar Saba, Israel

University of Pannonia, Veszprem, Hungary

country, that has been a living "ethno-linguistic laboratory" for nearly eight decades. Though the chapter will not address diversity, inclusion, and equity in a direct manner, the description of the macro, mezzo, and micro levels where linguistic diversity in education is established, conducted, and owned by different agents will be reflected upon.

2   The Macro-level: Languages of Israel

2.1   *The Language Diversity of Israel*

Modern Israel has been multilingual, multicultural, and multiethnic since its foundation. When the British took over the Mandate for Palestine in 1920 after the collapse of the Ottoman Empire, Hebrew, Arabic, and English were declared the official languages of the nation-state. English was dropped as one of the official languages once the British mandate ended, and the State of Israel was declared. Throughout the history of the State of Israel, Hebrew gained the status of the dominant language as part of Zionist ideology and as the symbol of the creation of a new collective identity (Halperin, 2015; Nahir, 1998; Or, 2017; Safran, 2005). It serves as a medium of instruction in Jewish schools and as a compulsory second language for all minorities. In addition, various languages, such as Arabic or French, have been offered to Hebrew speakers as foreign languages over the years (Spolsky & Shohamy, 1999).

Based on the 2021 Social Survey on Languages by the Central Bureau of Statistics of Israel, nearly 5.9 out of 9.2 million surveyed adults over 20 years of age were asked about their knowledge and use of languages in the languages of Israel. The survey stated that the mother tongue of the surveyed was: 68% Hebrew; 20% Arabic; 13% Russian; 2.1% English; 1.7% French; 1.1%; Spanish; 1.3% Yiddish; 0.9% Amharic; and 5.5% other languages. Concomitantly, 66% of the surveyed stated that they use Hebrew at home, and in particular, among the Arab sector, 4.2% use Hebrew as an additional language at home. At work, a total of 86% of the employed surveyed speak Hebrew of those 93% are in the Jewish sector and 47% are in the Arab sector. Among the Arab sector, 52% of the employed surveyed report speaking in Arabic at work while 30% of them report using Arabic in addition to Hebrew. While these numbers paint the picture of the prominent languages of Israel, Arabic has a unique characteristic of the language of a large minority in Israel; it is the language of all the countries surrounding Israel in the Middle East; and it is the heritage language of a large number of Israeli Jews, who immigrated from Arab-speaking countries. The linguistic repertoire of Israel includes Hebrew, Arabic, English, Russian, French, Spanish, Amharic, Tigrinya, Yiddish, Tagalog, Nepali, Hai, and Mandarin, among many other languages (Ben-Rafael et al., 2006; Or & Shohamy, 2016; Spolsky & Shohamy, 1999; Stavans, 2012).

A wide variety of languages contribute to Israel's linguistic mosaic as a result of (1) the existence of an autochthonous Arabic-speaking population; (2) massive waves of Jewish immigration from numerous countries; (3) the standardization and proliferation of Hebrew as the national language; and (4) the recent arrival of migrant workers, asylum seekers, and refugees, mainly from Africa and East Asia.

Arabic and Hebrew, two politically charged languages, shared the official language status. In 2018 when the controversial Nation-State Law was passed stripping Arabic as a co-official language of Israel and granting it "a special status in the state" and stipulates that the de facto status enjoyed by the language before the bill was passed must not be disturbed. The law, however, does not explain what the "special status" means and how this unique status will be implemented. With or without this bill, the reality is stronger than the law, and in fact, both Arabic and Hebrew play important roles in Israeli society.

Hebrew remains, nonetheless, the most widely used language in Israel in virtually all domains. It is used not only in administrative affairs, across the whole educational system, and in daily interpersonal communication but also in the written and audiovisual media, cinema, theatre, music, the book industry, and popular culture. This is not to say that Israel is a monolingual society. Arabic is the everyday language of the Arab community, but the clear communitarian gap makes Arabic a rather distant language for many Jews. There are scarce Arabic-speaking employees in the public and private sectors, where customer service and aid are provided, such as in the mobile phone companies and the medical services.

In contrast, English occupies a pivotal position as the country's major language of wider communication with the rest of the world, both virtually and face-to-face. English is the major second/foreign language learned by Israelis. Many other languages, from Russian to Circassian and from Yiddish to French, are also used to a major or lesser degree, mostly (though not always) among the older immigrant generations. Although it is a revived language and concern voiced by some Hebrew-ists as to the deterioration by means of an anglicization of the language, the Hebrew language system does not seem to be at risk.

English is a dominant language in the professional, economic, and political arenas, especially as it is the link with the world outside Israel. In fact, for a small country enclave with most of the Arab-speaking population in conflict, the only bridge to the outer world is through English, especially in cyberspace where most communication occurs in English. The status of English is uncontested in the area of "imported" entertainment or commerce. Television is not dubbed into any language, and subtitles are mainly provided in Hebrew and sometimes in Arabic. In emergencies or wartime, all public announcements are made in 10 to 15 languages. Public companies for services, such as electricity and telephone, have a call routing system that starts by allowing people to choose the language they want to use. The list usually includes English, Arabic, and Russian and, less frequently, Amharic, Spanish, and French. The main newscasts of the day (the longest one at 8 p.m. on national TV) often have a sign language interpreter.

Internal diversity has been managed and perceived either as a threat, a nuisance, or an asset by the various linguistic minorities and the veteran Israeli majority. Diversity is not only linguistic but ethnic, ideological, and political, all of which influence the identity and power individuals have in relation to themselves and others. The unfolding of the linguistic diversity inevitably shapes the identity of speakers in the way a minority perceives and manages itself in relation to the majority, other minorities, and in response to the majority's perception and management of the minority.

2.2   National Language Policy

Though Hebrew was used by the Jewish population in the region from the late nineteenth century onward, it was left to the different communities to determine their education and language policies. Eventually, many language policies aimed to replace immigrant and heritage languages (such as Yiddish, Ladino, and others) with Hebrew, presumably in the belief that this would promote the building of the nation. Today, Israel does not have a written Israeli constitution or a law that lays down language policy. The situation is somewhat unclear, as it leaves 'a confusion of possibilities' (Spolsky & Shohamy, 1999: 26). Stavans and Narkiss (2004) discuss Israeli language policy in relation to the language policies outlined by Lambert (1995), in which three main categories are established from a national rather than a minority group perspective: the 'homogeneous' category comprises states that have a main, majority language (e.g., the

USA); the 'dyadic' category characterizes countries with two or three main linguistic groups (e.g., Canada); and the 'mosaic' category includes countries that have various ethnic groups linguistically catered for by the language policy. Israel does not fall into any of these categories, as it is a mixture of all three: there is Hebrew hegemony although both Arabic and Hebrew have – albeit slightly unequal – official status; English enjoys de facto recognition in the public sphere; and the education system makes allowances for immigrant languages.

The language policy of Israel is defined in two official statements, establishing two official languages, Hebrew and Arabic, a mandatory requirement of one foreign language (usually English) and optional languages (mainly heritage languages). The language policy of the region prior to the creation of Israel stated:

All ordinances, official notices, and official forms of the Government and all official notices of local authorities and municipalities in areas to be prescribed by order of the High Commissioner shall be published in English, Arabic, and Hebrew.

The 82nd paragraph of the Palestine Order in Council issued on 14 August 1922 for the British Mandate of Palestine.

After the establishment of the State of Israel in 1948, the following amendment was introduced:

Any order in the law which requires the use of the English language is hereby abolished.

Adopted and amended by the State of Israel, 19 May 1948.

Essentially, Israel's covert language policy considers some of the languages of Israel today: Hebrew is regarded as the main official language that is spoken by most of its citizens; Arabic is the second official language, the medium of instruction in the Arabic sector of public schools and the heritage language of Jews from Arabic countries; English is the main foreign language; Yiddish, Ladino, Judeo-Arabic, Juhuri, and Judeo-Berber are endangered Jewish languages brought by the first waves of immigration; Russian, Polish, Hungarian, Spanish, French, Amharic, and Tigrinya are some of the community languages of later immigrants; French, German, and Japanese are some of the foreign languages taught in high schools and universities; and Armenian, Assyrian (Aramaic), and Circassian are some of the community languages of non-Jewish Israelis.

Within this diverse reality, the Jewish population generally uses Hebrew, and Jewish immigrants learn Hebrew in order to get integrated into mainstream Israeli society. Second-generation immigrants often become native speakers of Hebrew. Hebrew is also an important language for Palestinian Arabs in Israel since it is the main language of communication, government, commerce, and higher education, and a key to social mobility. Hebrew is a compulsory subject in all Arab schools, and knowledge of Hebrew is required for higher education, the job market, and dealing with the authorities or with business organizations.

In contrast to Hebrew, Arabic is used by the Arab population, which makes up about a fifth of Israel's population. Many Arabs in Israel identify themselves as Palestinians, although they vary by religion (Muslim, Christian, and Druze) as well as by origin, local identity, and political aspirations. Concomitantly, Arabic is also the heritage language of many of the Jewish immigrants from Arabic-speaking countries and their descendants, as well as the native language or lingua franca of some of the African refugees and asylum seekers. However, the fact that Arabic is shared by several groups in Israel does not add to its prestige or sociolinguistic "currency," both because all these groups are significantly marginalized and because the colloquial varieties of Arabic they use are typically regarded with low esteem even by Arabic speakers. Despite its relatively low prestige, Arabic is a language with high vitality in Arab towns and villages as in some neighborhoods and 'mixed' towns such as Jafa, Akko, and Ramleh.

English has an overall high status among the population as a prestigious and important language, one that provides opportunities in the world and guarantees a prosperous future. Other than that, Hebrew is the most dominant language in the public space, though this dominance has been jeopardized over the past 15 years and an increasing number of "Hebrew-ists"

(purists) resent this trend as the deterioration of not only the quality but the presence, use, and dominance of Hebrew in people's lives and in the public space. This issue is widely discussed in public by lay people and academics from different gender, age groups, ethnic origins, and sectors. This dispute is likely to continue.

2.3 Language Education Policy

In the absence of a constitution and very general provisions in the Basic (quasi-constitutional) Laws of Israel based on the individual liberties that were outlined in the Israeli Declaration of Independence, specific national language policies do not exist. Yet, in the past two decades, multilingual policies have become a major research and implementation trend in educational language policy (Donitsa-Schmidt et al., 2004; Yitzhaki, 2010, 2013; Spolsky & Shohamy, 1999; Amara et al., 2016), mostly as counter-reactions to monolingual ideologies prevailing in the school system (Amara, 2007; Amara & Mar'i, 2002; Shohamy, 2006, 2009). This does not mean that a single language was taught in schools, but rather that only one dominant language was the medium of instruction, and other languages were taught additionally often treating them in the curriculum and schedule of the school as yet another disciplinary course much like geography, physics, and history. Unlike the formal education systems' provisions for multilingualism, the reference to multilingual policies expanded the environments where linguistic diversity was encouraged and legitimized beyond the formal education to different local, home, and global languages. This shift is anchored in a growing awareness of immigrant and indigenous groups, who emphasize the value of heritage and world languages in a global world.

It was not until 1996 that a formal language education policy (LEP) was established commissioned by the Ministry of Education as a result of major sociopolitical developments (e.g., massive immigration wave from the former Soviet Union, influx of refugees, and foreign workers and the Israeli-Palestinian Peace talks) rather than explicit advocacy acts (Tannenbaum et al., 2022). The policy published and explained by the Ministry of Education in a Director-General's Circular on 1 June 1995, revised on 15 April 1996, and implemented by schools and teachers as of September 1996 (Ministry of Education, 1995, 1996), addressed a language education policy in terms of *mother tongue* teaching and *second and foreign language* education (Spolsky & Shohamy, 1999). The foreign languages, except for English, had their own language inspectorate and curriculum and were optional on a national level.

This first comprehensive education language policy – also known as the '3 plus' policy – highlighted the pivotal role of home and immigrant languages as a propelling force for the country both at the individual and national level. At the core of the LEP there was the requirement that every student learn three languages and at least one additional language (community, heritage, or world language). One of the three languages is the student/pupil *mother tongue* – either Hebrew or Arabic – to be learned in accordance with the cannons of literacy (in Hebrew and Arabic) as the mother tongues for the two sectors: Jewish and Arab; and for immigrants or ex-pats with other mother tongues, language maintenance provisions are made (e.g., in Russian, French, and Amharic), such as the possibility to take the school-leaving examination in a language of their choice. The *second language* in this LEP refers to Hebrew or Arabic for non-speakers of these languages. Hebrew as a second languages should be taught to: (a) the immigrants during one year after arrival with the purpose of gaining literacy; and (b) the Arabs from the second grade until the twelfth grade. Arabic as a second language: (a) is compulsory for Hebrew speakers from 7th to 10th grades; (b) is optional in 5th and 6th as well as 11th and 12th grades, where the second language graduation requirement can be in other languages, typically French; (c) for new immigrants, there is no Arabic requirement.

Despite the requirement for second language education for the Jewish and the Arab sector, Hebrew is compulsory as a second language for the Arab sector throughout most of the schooling years, whereas Arabic is optional as a second language for the Jewish sector and is limited in years. The leading and first *foreign language* in the education system is English implemented in both the Jewish and Arab sectors. EFL is compulsory from 3rd grade (2 hours a week) to 12th grade (at least 4 hours a week), and it is optional in the 1st and 2nd grade within the regular school schedule (often in affluent areas in Israel as parents incur additional payment for these classes despite the Israeli free education system). In the Jewish sector, French is a second foreign language availed as an option; it is rarely preferred over English, and as it is the community language of a sizable body of Francophone immigrants, it is offered as optional (or as an alternative to the required Arabic in high school). Russian is also an optional language for new immigrants (as an alternative to Arabic or French) as is Spanish (which drew on the popular Spanish-language soap operas in the early 1990s) instead of French and Arabic. The policy encourages students to study another foreign language, but this is not mandatory. There are Yiddish courses (which is also used as the language of instruction and taught in independent ultra-orthodox schools), Ladino, Spanish, and German, and recently we have seen the presence (again in affluent areas and through parent initiatives and financing) of other languages such as Japanese, Chinese, and Israeli Sign Language.

Since in Israel there are separate educational systems (coordinated by a single ministry) for Arabs and Jews, both Arabic and Hebrew serve as mediums of instruction, each within its own community. Additionally, the first official policy advocated that each of the communities was expected to learn the language of the other (Ministry of Education 1996). While the process of making an education language policy was rapid and efficient, several years after its introduction, it was clear that it had a modest impact (Stavans & Narkiss, 2004). There were not many attempts to spread the guiding principles in meaningful ways, no real financial support was allocated to its introduction nor was there any special training for teachers or principals in implementing the new policy. The change of guards at the Ministry after the following elections resulted in a neglect of the implementation of the LEP but resulted in a significant growth in Jewish students enrolling in Arabic language courses, both spoken and Modern Standard Arabic as part of their studies (Donitsa-Schmidt et al., 2004; Tannenbaum & Tahar, 2008; Tannenbaum et al., 2020).

3 The Mezzo-Level: Institutional Educational Agencies

From the national (macro) perspective on the place and policies related to the languages of Israel (Slosky & Shohamy, 1999), we zoom into the mezzo level which constitutes the institutional educational agents that operationalize in tandem the national policies, realities, and practices. First, we will survey the higher education agents which include all post-scholastic obligatory education institutions such as universities and colleges (Donitsa-Schmidt et al., 2022; Mizel, 2021; Shohamy, 2012); then we will conclude with the compulsory schooling institutions on the path to the individuals (micro) perspective in charge of educating children to become productive and engaged citizens.

3.1 The Languages of Higher Education (HE): ENGLISH or €NG£I$H? The Thrust of a Start-Up Nation

The dynamics of science and language development are not independent from the global economic power of the countries they represent and the emergence of global empires. They are closely related to the general industrial and cultural development of a country or group of countries, although complex relations arise between general factors of development and the specific function languages adopt within specialized domains. Furthermore, science, technology, and language constitute strategic components of a community's cognitive capital in a present and future society of knowledge. To approach the topic of planning an international scientific communication (ISC) a series of provisions are needed. In the first place we should ask ourselves: who plans what and for whom? Who are the actors behind a scene that tends to blow a big smokescreen over a series of mechanisms, policy decisions, and the power relations implicated in language planning? As Baldauf and Kaplan (2003) convincingly point out, the identification of the actors, the interested parties, the stakeholders, and the decision-makers seems crucial for language policy and planning issues (Stavans & Lindgren, 2021). So far, the shift from a model of limited multilingualism for scientific communication at the beginning of the twentieth century to the present hegemony of English (Ammon, 1998) has rarely been analyzed from the perspective of overt or hidden agency or power relations. Rather, the process commonly appears as a naturalistic course of action along the lines of Crystal's (1997) well-known formula about the advent of English as the global language: English is 'a language which has repeatedly found itself in the right place at the right time' (1997: 110).

If we take language communities both as actors and targets of language policy decisions, we will usually encounter divergent perspectives and interests at stake. The relationship between the common and specialized scientific languages, for instance, has been a matter of debate and controversial strategies since the Renaissance (Kheimets & Epstein, 2005). The international sphere of science is often identified as an independent unit that supposedly regulates its own field of action. To a large extent, however, the allegedly 'independent' market represents the interest and expresses the power of the English-speaking scientific community and its publishing industry who are vividly interested in extending their market and reducing competition. Moreover, big multinational corporations have considerably influenced the development of science and technology, especially in fields directly related to their production, and are commonly inclined to support a drive to English monopoly when they expect advantages from such centralization (e.g., the scientific and commercial bond in the times of the Covid pandemic is such an example).

The central sociolinguistic question is whether the present-day hegemony of one language in the multilingual field of science – be it Hebrew or Arabic in Israel – will give way to an English monolingual monopoly, possibly with irreversible consequences for other languages and their communities; or whether the international scientific development will be able to advance from an orientation of multilingualism as a problem, to an enrichment perspective of plurilingualism in academia. The advantages of scientific communication in one language, closely connected to the expansion of electronic communication, have usually been taken for granted and are widely promoted by most actors. Possible disadvantages for many scientific communities and for the advancement of science itself seem less evident and are often dismissed as provincial backwardness in an era of globalization.

In sum, higher education in Israel is linguistically driven by instrumentality rather than ideology when the dominant language is concerned. The sustainability of science and economy in the particular Israeli geopolitical context dictates that the use and choice of English is paramount in the academic arena making ENGLISH synonymous to €NG£I$H. Neither perspectives of "all or nothing" reflecting extreme universalistic beliefs that language does not matter in science nor that science is best expressed in English contribute to both social and individual advancement. The scientific outcomes that translate into economic propellers primarily cultivated in higher education institutions must also be determined by the cultural diversity of the population and enriched by a plurality of languages. Language is neither neutral nor detached; it materializes in discourse structures and forms part of specific cultural models of how to conceive the world by each society. The reduction of scientific advancement to one language would probably limit scientific creativity itself and increase existing asymmetries in access to international scientific production and the diffusion of local scientific production.

Considering gains and losses in fostering ENGLISH for €NG£I$H in the interface between academia, scientific development, and economic growth in Israel, it is probably not to the advantage of any linguistic community to homogenize and polarize scientific growth at the price of fossilization and loss of spearheading a domain. Efforts to maintain and revitalize plurilingualism in all areas of science (hard and soft), even if existing asymmetries will probably not disappear altogether. A pluralistic language policy could sustain the development of terminology, data banks, and publications in a local language(s) such as Hebrew and Arabic and facilitate better access to English and other languages to enhance the development of a pluralistic international society of knowledge, to balance job opportunities for all minorities, and to benefit not only from linguistic and cultural diversity but also from diversity of thought and creativity. Do higher education institutions – universities and colleges – provide for such plurilingual policy?

3.2 Languages at Universities and Colleges

While compulsory and higher education are under the governance of the same Ministry and follow the same national and social agendas, they are closely related as they feed each other in terms of policies, plannings, management, and priorities. Moreover, they are both designed to render the social and economic engine of the nation.

The compulsory education (K-12) system is fully governed and budgeted by the Ministry of Education (ME) which in turn is responsible for overseeing and regulating education in the country. In Israel, the education system is divided into four stream clusters, each with its own unique characteristics and curriculum: (a) public secular state education; (b) public religious state education; (c) Ultra-Orthodox education (funded by the government but autonomous and self-governed); (d) Arab education (in Arabic and tailored to the Arab community); and (e) Druze education (in cooperation with the Druze community, carried out in Arabic and follows a Druze community tailored-curriculum).

Unlike the compulsory education (discussed in the next section), the post-scholastic education (Higher Education, aka HE) in Israel is governed by the Council for Higher Education (CHE) in Israel and determines policy for the higher education system. Concomitantly and in tandem, the Planning and Budgeting Committee (PBC) is responsible for funding the higher education Israeli system and define the budget allocation for the academic institutions in accordance with social and national needs and priorities. The CHE is subordinated to the Ministry of Education and has close ties with the ministry of science and technology. The CHE oversees the academic and budgetary activities of 9 public universities and research institutes and nearly 58 general, technological, and educational colleges (some funded by the PBC).

It has long been argued throughout history that the cradle of social and intellectual changes has been in academia. Donitsa-Schmidt, Amara, and Mar'i (2022) argue for the centrality of academia in education that:

[a]cademia is acknowledged as playing a significant role in shaping society, directly and indirectly. Higher education institutions are central sources of knowledge and discourse design (Etzkowitz & Viale, 2010); they are a symbol of ethics and values (Bok & Bok, 2009); a place that cultivates economic, social, and political leaders (Astin & Astin, 2000); and the scene of social and political activism. Furthermore, formal education is known to influence social engagement and foster critical thinking. Over the years, the world has witnessed the involvement of academics and students who have protested regime injustices and reacted to social inequality, violent conflicts, and neglect of democratic values (pp. 77).

As such, academia provides the conditions not only to set national priorities and guidelines but also enable and promote individual growth that translates into long-term national capital. Academia is a hub for diverse skills, it is ready to develop new ideas, comment on society and its challenges, and engage in bold experimentation in sustainable living. The role of HE institutions is to train professionals who develop, lead, manage, teach, educate, work in, and influence society's infrastructure. Higher education is privileged with having unique academic freedom. Though HE in most colleges and universities are subsidized by the government, they are relatively accessible to most of the adult population in Israel in terms of financial access but not always in terms of linguistic accessibility (Amara et al., 2016; Or & Shohamy, 2016).

The hegemony of Hebrew in HE institutions (not schools) has been documented and discussed historically and currently by Spolsky and Shohamy (2001) in terms of: (a) the level of studies (undergraduate and graduate); (b) the subjects of study (social sciences, humanities, and STEM); (c) access to information/knowledge sources; (d) national and social ideologies; and (e) economic and political caveats. The Hebrew University was the first to establish the Hebrew hegemony policy which was followed by most of the younger universities and colleges and with the time has seen changes to give way to English. These newer universities are more tolerant of English and more ready to accept the writing of theses and dissertations in scientific subjects in English in order to speed up the process of international publication and or capacitate its graduates to compete in the international scientific and laboral platforms. To date, with the exception of the Weizmann Institute of Science, almost all university courses are taught in Hebrew with obvious exceptions such as the departments of English Language and Literature (who teach in English) and non-Hebrew literature departments (such as French, Spanish, and Yiddish). There are parallel/duplicated programs in the fields of medicine and economics that attract foreign students and faculty and are conducted in English. But as a whole, the language of the lecture rooms, the seminar, and the laboratories, as well as of the corridors and cafeterias, is predominantly spoken Hebrew. We will return to the prominence of English in current academia.

The marginalization of the languages of large linguistic minorities such as Russian immigrants and the Arab sector in Israel from academia is clear. Of the 63 higher education institutions, in only three Arabic is the medium of instruction. The presence of Arabic in the majority of the HE institutions: (a) there is a lack of Arabic in public spaces despite the large number of Arab students studying in them (Shohamy & Ghazaleh-Mahajneh, 2012); (b) there are no provisions catering to Arab students' linguistic and cultural needs (despite the guidelines by Israel's Council for Higher Education) such as in the institutional website, signage, keyboard letters in computing centers, campus services, and cultural activities (Abu-Ras & Maayan, 2014); (c) there is limited use of Arabic in Arab language department (Amara et al., 2016); and (d) there are ambivalent opinions about the status and place of the Arabic language in Israel by Jewish lecturers and students though they recognize the importance of Arabic (albeit with low instrumental value).

The hegemony of the majority official language of Israel – Hebrew – in HE institutions while motivated initially in the earlier stages of the establishment of the nation-state by ideology, on one hand has remained, and on the other hand, it has not been impermeable to change. Such hegemony, not necessarily particular to Israel but prevalent in many Western countries, inevitably creates a disadvantage for those who are not speakers of the majority language or the main language of Instruction in the public HE institutions. This may not be the case for private HE institutions. While Hebrew is the main language of instruction in academia in the undergraduate and post graduate studies, English has a central role as Spolsky and Shohamy (2001) state that while.

> [c]ontrol over language choice in written theses and dissertations is clearly easiest to enforce, as all pass through central university committees. It is in reading requirements that the penetration of English has been most effective and even accepted [because there is a substantial amount of information in] scientific and technical written sources in English which it is impractical

to translate into Hebrew and the need for written and oral communication in a world language with non-Hebrew speaking academics. (p. 171)

With the advance of technology and the instant access to information, the basal need for reading ability and comprehension in English is obvious. All HE institutions require an English Reading Comprehension level which is provided by special EAP courses depending on the student's placement in a psychometric entrance exam. Students must complete the "exemption" requirement either by successfully completing the courses or by scoring at an exemption level in the exam.

The assumption that most course material is published in English (with the exception of some disciplines like bible and Hebrew) and most of the disciplinary terminology is in English, this requirement is overarching in all HE institutions and constitutes a major part of the course's bibliography. Yet, students often find ways to get around the readings in English as most lecturers tend to repeat in Hebrew in the lecture the material from the reading in a guided, focused, and succinct way. Sometimes, students will bypass the required reading by purchasing a translation or by dividing the reading amongst them and generating summaries in Hebrew to be shared. This is typical for undergraduates but among advanced levels, and particularly in scientific fields, a student who cannot read English easily is likely to be severely handicapped as they are expected to publish and present their work in international arenas. Moreover, Israeli academics in all but a handful of Hebrew-bound subjects (Jewish studies, for instance) are expected to publish internationally, which means publishing in English or another world language.

The centrality of English for academic success begins its grooming already in the years of schooling. Some of the drawbacks in the achievements of the scholastic teaching of English becomes apparent at university level.

3.3 *Language in Schools*

Though the process of making an education language policy was rapid and efficient, several years after its introduction, it was clear it had a very marginal impact (Stavans & Narkiss, 2004). The guiding principles were not properly disseminated, financial resources for implementation and sustainability were not allocated, no update in teacher-training and no curricular or material amendments in its spirit were carried out. This was exacerbated by changes in the Ministry of Education following the recurrent elections and the resignation of top Ministry officials (i.e., the Director General, the person in charge of educational policy, and the Minister of Education). New governments in the years to follow did not place education at the top of their political agenda and even when it was at the higher level of priorities, the language education policy did not get any attention with the exception of promoting the L1 language and literacy capacity of children as these were motivated by international exams such as TIMMS and PISA.

Notwithstanding, time had its course, and by 2016 international and national socio- and geo-political changes had led to the recognition of the need for a multilingual policy that will generate the technological, economic, and glocalization currency. In this context, the realization is such that mastering English is not enough because there are contexts where other languages are more instrumental in enhancing social and economic mobility, especially for speakers of marginal languages (De Mejía, 2012; García & Lin, 2017; Piller, 2016). Few changes have occurred in regard to teaching Hebrew to Arabs and Arabic to Jews (Tannenbaum et al., 2022) and advocacy initiatives consisting of an expert consortium and culminating in a draft proposal for a multilingual education policy put forth by 'advocacy coalition framework' (Pierce et al., 2020; Sabatier, 1988).

As mentioned in previous sections, all schools in the Arab sector: (a) use Arabic as their language of instruction, (b) teach Hebrew as a second language, and (c) offer English as a foreign language. In Jewish state schools: (a) Hebrew is the language of instruction, (b) all pupils learn English (many schools start English classes before the official 3rd grade), (c) nearly 50% of pupils learn Arabic for four years and a significant number of students opt to learn French, Russian and, more recently, Spanish and Chinese. A curriculum is drawn up by the chief inspector for each language, with the advice of a national professional committee. The curriculum must be approved by the Ministry and is driven by the requirements for the school-leaving examinations (Bagrut) and the entrance examination to university. Though the Ministry states the optional and required teaching hours for each language, hours may be supplemented by local educational districts and by schools through their own resources (often in extracurricular programs financed by parents, philanthropic organizations, and aid in less affluent areas). At elementary and secondary school level, English is a mandatory language that is studied by all students. All students must continue with English at high school, and a large proportion also studies Arabic (about 50%), French (about 10%), or

Russian (2–3%). The mandatory language subjects in school-leaving examinations are Hebrew and English for all students from all sectors of the population.

The curriculum and material for <u>Hebrew</u> are structured in a standard way and include Hebrew grammar, language, and cultural and ideological aspects of both Hebrew and world literatures. Hebrew is often separated into language and grammar courses and literature courses. The disciplines are well established in university departments and formal examinations. In the past seven to ten years, there has been an increased interest in teaching literacy, especially in the last year of kindergarten and mainly in elementary schools, with provisions made by teacher training colleges to train specialized teachers. The teaching of Arabic in the Jewish sector is hampered by the difficulty of dealing with diglossia and the Palestinian local variety of spoken Arabic, which is highly influenced by dialects from neighboring Arab-speaking countries and Hebrew. While some programs focus on the spoken variety, most classes are taught in Hebrew and concentrate on the grammar and literature of the Modern Standard (Literary) language (Ministry of Education, 1996). Much of the instructional material for Arabic as a native language comes from abroad, especially from the big book fair that takes place annually in Cairo. One could argue that there is good reason to focus on the "standard" Arabic that is found mostly in written language, as this is the Arabic that unites the entire Arab-speaking world and thus provides a more "global" variety for the Jewish sector. However, the issue underlying this argument is that such Arabic is not learned for communication within Israel (between the Jewish and Arab populations), but for purposes of wider communication and particularly for written communication with the Arab world (Hallel & Spolsky, 1993).

By contrast, the Arab educational system in Israel has been, and continues to be, governed by political criteria which Palestinian Arabs have no say in formulating (Al-Haj, 1996; Mar'i, 1978; Swirski, 1999). From the first law regarding education in 1953, the Arab sector did not share the same premises of identity and values as the Jewish sector, nor there was a full autonomy for their education system to determine its aims, goals, and curricula. Though the Arab school system has a separate curriculum designed and supervised by the Ministry of Education – as does the religious sector – only in the past five years we have witnessed few Arab educators or administrators with decision-making powers who begun to claim their language education policy separate from the state's secular Jewish school system and similar to the religious sector that maintains autonomous control over its educational policy, aims and goals (Adalah, 2003; Mar'i, 1978; Swirski, 1999). In the early 1990s, an incipient move towards resolving this situation as stated by Amara and Mar'i (2002):

> The Ministry of Education and Culture set up a committee under the pedagogical secretariat and the inspectorate to deal with teaching Arabic in the Arab schools, and its function was to prepare a curriculum for teaching Arabic and its literature from 1st to 12th grades. This committee was subdivided into subcommittees to deal with the levels of study: a committee for the high schools, one for the junior high schools, one for the elementary schools, and one for general literature for the high schools.5 Each subcommittee had to formulate goals, write a curriculum, and prepare readers and a teacher's guide. (p. 69)

In the 1995–96 special circular, the principles, and objectives of the Ministry of Education language policy in Israel were formulated in rudimentary guidelines. These principles stated that the objectives of Arabic instruction at all scholastic levels where Arabic will be: (a) treated as a mother (L1) tongue where students had to achieve the highest levels of linguistic and literacy abilities in contextualized manner to comply with various communicative styles and registers; (b) allotted suitable teaching time in the schedule in elementary, middle, and high school but excluded as formal teaching in the kindergarten; (c) rigorously structured with greater emphasis on literacy especially stressing the written language and catering to the uniqueness of diglossia in the Arabic language.

Though the new and recently revised LEP for the Arabic school system has made some substantial changes over the past five decades, there is still a long way to go. As one of the two large minorities in the country, the LEP needs to surpass the basic concept of teaching a language as a "tool" of communication and sustainability and move to perceive language as an "instrument" and an "agent" of change. This move must view language and literacy in context as the "currency" used for and "investment" in the form of change recognizing the identity of this large minority which will also render "dividends" in the form of economic, scientific, and technological growth.

The centrality of English in the school curriculum is due to globalization and the needs established by the high-tech and scientific developments in Israel. Inevitably, there has been a change in emphasis in English teaching. In the period before the 1960s, the focus was on literature, grammar, and culture rather than on English as an international language of communication. Waves of immigration of English speakers from the UK and the USA provided a corpus of native speakers, who contributed greatly to teaching English, particularly in high schools. As most of the teachers were native English speakers and few had been trained to teach, there was great emphasis on oral language until two years after the language policy was launched. In re-thinking the language policy and the new needs of pupils, a curriculum was created to parallel that of Hebrew teaching, which involves literacy in early childhood and new world trends of greater communication, reading, and writing skills. This has had an impact on teaching materials, the structure of graduation examinations, university admission, and higher education graduation requirements. There is a large industry in English textbooks and computer-assisted language material that is highly sensitive to changes in the curriculum and examinations. Competition in this sector has led to relatively high-quality materials, some of which are exported to other countries.

The driving force behind the implementation and success of the language education policy is evaluation. At the end of high school, the Bagrut (school-graduation) examination serves both for graduation and university entrance purposes and sets the guidelines for the curriculum, materials, and teaching in the schools. The examinations are fairly traditional, and the marking is objective. However, the diploma mark from the Bagrut and a school mark provide a final grade that is not uniformly reliable. Consequently, higher education institutions such as colleges and universities also require a psychometric examination, which includes sections on verbal and analytic ability as well as proficiency in mainly literacy in Hebrew as a first or second language and English reading comprehension. Other assessments during the school years are carried out at local or district levels. From time to time, there are national proficiency assessments, especially in Arabic and English, and there are literacy assessments at the national level in second grade for Hebrew and fourth grade for Hebrew and English. Concomitantly, Israel has participated in the international PISA and TIMM exams, all of which have an English language component.

4 The Micro-level: Language Teachers as a Bridge Between "Ideal and Real"

Officially, teacher training colleges have the mandate to train kindergarten, elementary, middle school, and special education teachers (for kindergarten to 10th grade), while high school teachers (10th to 12th grades) are trained at the universities. While this is stipulated by the Ministry of Education, the scarcity of teachers, especially in the field of languages, means that teachers who were trained at teacher training colleges also teach at the high school level. Unlike in the universities, college teacher training involves disciplinary, pedagogical, and pre-service training for four years. At the universities, degrees (B.A. and B.Sc., among others) are completed in three years, and there is an additional teacher training year. The supply of trained teachers varies by subject.

As the teaching profession has been devalued worldwide in the past three decades, fewer people opt to be trained as teachers. They see teaching as a vocation rather than a profession. There is a shortage of English teachers so that in addition to the existing programs, the Ministry is conducting a program to recruit native English speakers with university degrees and offers them training in Hebrew and in the methodology of teaching English as a Foreign Language in accelerated programs with advantageous financial benefits especially in English and Math. The training of Arabic teachers for Hebrew speakers is also supported by the Israeli Defense Force, which conducts joint programs with teachers' colleges for elementary and middle school teachers and with the universities for high school teachers. As most Arabic teachers in the Hebrew sector only work part-time, there is ample opportunity to expand these programs. However, few of the qualified teachers are fluent enough to teach in Arabic. Often, if not always, they are not from the Arab sector.

Language teachers are supported by the Ministry of Education and by local education inspectors and advisers. Each language has its own support and in-service training. For example, there is a support unit especially for the teaching of Arabic to Hebrew speakers. In addition, there is professional support by associations such as the English Teachers' Association (ETNI) and academic organizations, such as the Language and Literacy Association (SCRIPT) or the Israeli Applied Linguistic Association (ILASH), and smaller and newer teachers' groups for other languages.

Teacher training is a pivotal amalgamating element that brings together different aspects of the LEP of the educational system. School teachers are a central agent in carrying out the LEP in a bottom-up manner from the early years of schooling (including early childhood education) onwards to higher education. Teachers are the constructors (Stavans & Lindgren, 2021) of the recently proposed multilingual education policy (Tannenbaum et al., 2022).

4.1 LEP Agency of English Language Teacher Trainees for the Arab and Jewish Sector: An Illustrative Case of Multilingual Self-Perception Towards the Implementation of a Multilingual LEP

Focusing on teacher trainees' perception of their own multilingualism in the limelight of their training to become English teachers allows for an unaccounted understanding of how their experiences with their own language education in the schooling years, their identity, and outlook on their future role in the education system, and the established LEP come together. To access this information, students from the Arab and Jewish sectors training to become English teachers in either sector were asked to write a language autobiography and complete a questionnaire as an assignment for a course on multilingualism. The choice of teacher trainees in the English language was based on a practical reason of accessibility to this group and on the premise that English teaching has more universal and less conflictual common grounds across the sector ideologies.

What transpires from these language autobiographies and the questionnaires sheds light on: (a) the similarities and differences between the two sectors in terms of their background information, subjective assessment of their English proficiency, and the patterns of English language use in terms of context and purpose; (b) their perception of the ethnolinguistic vitality of the three languages (Hebrew, Arabic, and English); and (c) the trajectory of their exposure to English.

(a) Background, proficiency in English, context, and purpose of use of English

Information about teacher trainees from the Jewish and Arab sector.

Table 8.1 shows that the Jewish trainees are older and often have previous academic degrees (not necessarily in language, literature, or education) and have a later start into higher education due to compulsory army service. Forty percent of the participants have more than the Hebrew

Table 8.1 Background information on participants

		Arab	Jewish
Age (in years)		24	41
Home language	More than L1	60%	40%
	English at home	20%	40%

Table 8.2 CanDo in English

Skills	Arab	Jewish
Speaking	97.6%	93.6%
Listening	92.8%	89.6%
Reading and writing	84%	87.2%

language used at home, and the "other" language is English also among the Jewish trainees. Arab trainees are younger and often have no previous higher education academic studies. Sixty percent stated that they use more than Arabic (L1) at home (mainly Hebrew), but twenty percent declared that they also use English at home.

Subjective English language assessment (CANDO).

The subjective English language proficiency as evaluated in the CanDo questionnaire (Table 8.2) indicates that when asked to assess their ability in one of these canonic skills of English language proficiency, on average, the Arab participant assesses their spoken abilities (speaking and listening) higher than their Jewish cohorts. In contrast, the Jewish participants tend to evaluate their written language ability (in reading and writing) higher than their Arab cohorts. The differences can be explained by expectations, experiences with the language in the local and global context, the language trajectory each sector does on the road to the English language and age.

The context and purpose of the English language use.

Table 8.3 shows that the context where English and the L1 (Arabic for the Arab sector and Hebrew for the Jewish sector) is no different in both groups. However, the purposes of using English in each sector are different. English for *pleasure* purposes such as entertainment, travel, sports, and religious activities is used equally to Arabic in the Arab sector, but it is used less than Hebrew in the Jewish sector. This may be explained by the

Table 8.3 English use context (intimate and formal circle) and purpose (pleasure, business, sustainability)

English used	Arab	Jewish
Context:		
Informal (family and friends)	L1 only	L1 only
Formal (work and neighbors)	L1 more than English	L1 more than English
Purpose:		
Pleasure	English and L1 equally	L1 more than English
(entertainment, travel, sports, religion)	English and L1 equally	English more than L1
Business	L1 more than English	English and L1 equally
(work and transactions)		
Sustainability		
(shopping, health, banks, government)		

need for the L1 in each group as constrained to the presence of the L1 in a majority versus a minority group.

Hence, while Hebrew is the majority language, there is more supply of leisure activities in Hebrew, and the need for English is a default. Concomitantly, in the Arab sector, albeit a large minority, the supply of leisure activities and their variability in the Arabic language are more limited and constraining and thus English is a supplementary alternative channel. In what concerns *business* activities such as work and transactions, the Arab sector uses both English and Arabic equally, but the Jewish sector uses more English than Hebrew. This may be explained by the use of the Internet and cyberspace interactions where for Hebrew speakers the use of Hebrew is limited and restricted to Hebrew speakers outside Israel who are very few. The Arab sector has a broader platform for the use of Arabic especially on the internet, as the Arab speaking world is wider and larger and that interaction relays on the written form of Arabic shared by all.

The use of English for *sustainability* – daily life acts such as shopping, bank, government offices, and health services – in the Arab sector L1 is used mostly as all sustainability activities occur within the community, village, or city, and English is used mainly for online shopping. In the Jewish sector, both Hebrew and English are used apar as most of the sustainability acts are carried out to a larger extent locally and globally.

(b) Perception of the ethnolinguistic vitality of the three languages (Hebrew, Arabic, and English) by Arab and Jewish teacher trainees

The perception of each sector as to the *prestige* of the three dominant languages in Israel varies within each sector in comparison to the three languages and across the sectors in regard to each language (described in Table 8.4). In the Arab sector, Hebrew is perceived as the most prestigious, followed by English, and then Arabic while in the Jewish sector, English is perceived as most prestigious followed by Hebrew and Arabic. This perception does not come as a surprise as the Arab sector's perception is grounded in a pragmatic reality viewed by a linguistic minority placing Hebrew and English as the dominant languages in their life and livelihood while Arabic is restricted to a more in-group community utilitarian and identity aspect of the language. By contrast, when comparing the prestige perspective between the sectors, the Arab sector's perspective seems to be motivated by a more local vision of the dominance and functionality of Hebrew and Arabic while the Jewish perspective is motivated by a more global and international context. For both sectors, English is perceived as quite important.

The perception of the use and presence of the three languages in *institutional* frameworks, such as government offices, post offices, hospitals, and banks, both sectors perceive Hebrew as dominant followed by Arabic and last English. The degrees of the ranking between the sectors' perception are most pronounced with regard to the Arabic and English languages as the former is perceived as more present by the Arab sector in comparison to the Jewish sector. This is explained by the fact that many

Table 8.4 Rating (on a scale of 0–100) of the languages and their speech communities in society

	Languages	*Arab*	*Jewish*
Prestige of the language	Hebrew	94	56
	Arabic	76	30
	English	80	86
Institutional use	Hebrew	100	94
	Arabic	88	68
	English	78	64
Taught in school	Hebrew	100	84
	Arabic	82	40
	English	96	94
Status of speech community	Hebrew	62	90
	Arabic	68	38
	English	56	86

institutional services that exist in the Arab villages and cities are more present as compared to Jewish cities and villages and also by the fact that in some of the institutional frameworks such as the health services (hospitals and pharmacies throughout the country) there is a large number of employees from the Arab sectors and Arabic is present.

The perception of the three languages as present within the *school* system, in the Arab sector, Hebrew stands out as dominant, and this is clearly backed by the language education policy described above both for school level and higher education; whereas the perception of the Jewish schooling is lower as Hebrew instruction is seen as the language of instruction in all disciplines. As for the perception of Arabic, we observe that the Arab sector regards Arabic similar to the way the Jewish sector regards Hebrew instruction – as the language of instruction whereas in the Jewish sector, Arabic is perceived as marginal only to Arabic language classes (compulsory and optional) throughout a limited number of schooling years and weekly hours. English by contrast is treated as the language that is of central importance (albeit not the language of instruction) for its duration throughout the school years and the allotted time in the schedule.

Last but not least is the perception of each sector in regard to the *speech-community* of each language in Israel. Each sector differs in their perception as to the status of the three languages' speakers. The Arab sector seems to regard all three speech communities as having quite similar suggestion and egalitarian indifference, whereas the Jewish sector regards highest the Hebrew and English speech community and lowest the Arabic speech community. This can be explained by geopolitical, ideological, and cultural reasons as well as by the fact that these two communities are predominant in the cities from where the Jewish participants come from and the frequent daily contact with these speech communities (i.e., large Anglo-Saxon immigrant concentrations).

(c) Linguistic autobiographies tracing their trajectory towards their linguistic repertoire

Much of what both Jewish and Arab teacher trainees relate in their autobiographies supports on one hand what the Macro and Mezzo levels of the languages of Israel and the diversity in its population has been discussed in the previous sections. The thematic thread in all autobiographies attests to: (a) a bi or trilingual (in few cases more than three languages) individual repertoire, (b) beyond L1, additional languages were mostly learned formally in school; (c) the languages in the repertoire are used frequently but differentially in intimate and more formal setting depending on the context and instrumentality; (d) there is satisfaction and even pride in a rich linguistic repertoire; (e) language preference; and (f) language mixing.

The divergence between the Arab and Jewish teacher trainees is how each theme is weighted in one or more languages. While both groups claim to be at least bilingual if not trilingual or more (see above a), they differ in their explanation of how and what the languages do for them. The Jewish sector that their bi/trilingualism is a global outlook as a result of a life trajectory that involved travel, immigration, and mobility; whereas the Arab sector was grounded in a more local outlook driven by curiosity and trendiness through access and consumption of music and television. Both groups state that the main source of their language learning (see above b) was the formal school system, but each sector seemed to supplement their learning informally. The Jewish sector reports that much of their additional language learning is a result of travel or friendships/socialization with foreigners through work and acquaintances whereas the Arab sector supplements the formal learning through seeking out fashionable and accessible cybernetic consumption of cultural experiences such as movies, games, music, and social media. As for the language use patterns (see above c), there are also marked differences between the groups. Among the Jewish sector, nearly all trainees report they are Hebrew-English bilinguals, using mostly Hebrew and occasionally English for instrumental purposes of work, pleasure (travel), and sustainability in the form of online shopping. The Arab sector, reports to be trilingual in Arabic (which is the most used language), Hebrew (used primarily at work outside of their community and for sustainability in the form of shopping or services), and English (used the least for pleasure in online – surfing, shopping, social media, and gaming). While the Jewish sector justifies their pride and satisfaction (see above d) of commanding a rich linguistic repertoire, they are critical and practical about their need and command of each language in their repertoire as a "currency of value for money"; whereas the Arab sector find pride and satisfaction in their language repertoire in a more romantic and naïve way as an outstanding virtue of a "currency of social standing and personal prestige." As far as each sector's preference for the languages in their repertoire (see e above), both prefer their L1 but the Arab sector also prefers English over Hebrew; yet, when reporting on whether they tend to mix the languages (see above f), the

Jewish sector claims to do very little mixing between L1 (Hebrew) and L2 (English), but the Arab sector states that the mix frequently between their L2 (Hebrew) and L1 (Arabic) even if Hebrew is the un-preferred language in their repertoire.

The picture that emerges through the linguistic repertoire reinforces the national and educational language policy in which these teacher trainees have been raised, educated, and developed their linguistic identity and ideology.

5 Concluding Remarks

The linguistic diversity in education in Israel as a case of multilingualism in the Middle East and North Africa (MENA) region has strong roots in the history, geopolitical situation, ideologies, interests, and identity of the nation. These in turn have been steadfastly sedimented in a dynamic language education policy in regard to the three dominant languages – Hebrew, Arabic, and English. Inevitably both national and educational policies have had repercussions on learners' abilities and outcomes, as well as individual and societal prospects in a globalized world as discussed through three explanatory tiers: at the macro level – the national language policies (LP) within which language education policies (LEP) are rooted and adjusted; the mezzo level – the institutional agents that are commissioned to ensure the enhancement of such linguistic diversity from formal compulsory schooling to optional higher education; and the micro level – the individual who is the carrier and executor of such language diversity.

This chapter addressed the central issues as they are manifested in Israel, a plurilingual and pluricultural country, that has been a living "ethno-linguistic laboratory" for nearly eight decades. Throughout the chapter allusions to diversity, inclusion, and equity are made by means of an in-depth description of the macro, mezzo, and micro levels where linguistic diversity in education is established, conducted, and owned by different agents will be reflected upon. Clearly, the Arab society of Israel juggles the languages as a reflection of their local (community and family), glocal (global and local in the context of a large minority in a nation in which Arabic has a semi-official status), and global (internationally but more specifically with an outlook to the Arabic-speaking world) ideology and identity. In tandem, the Jewish society – a geopolitical enclave in the region – relates to the languages instrumentally and prioritizes their centrality with practical and ideological outlook that is local (national) and global (internationally).

References

Abu Ras, T., & Maayan, Y. (2014). *Arabic and Arab culture on Israeli campuses: An updated look*. Dirasat, The Van Leer Jerusalem Institute and Sikkuy. [in Hebrew].

Adalah Legal Center for Arab Minority Rights in Israel. (2003). *Education rights—Palestinian citizens of Israel (report)*. Ismael Abu-Saad.

Al-Haj, M. (1996). *Education among the Arabs in Israel – Control and Social Change*. Magnes Press, Hebrew University. (Hebrew).

Amara, M. (2007). Teaching Hebrew to Palestinian pupils in Israel. *Current Issues in Language Planning, 8*(2), 243–254.

Amara, M., & Mar'i, A. A.-R. (2002). *Language education policy: The Arab minority in Israel*. Kluwer Academic Publishing.

Amara, M., Donitsa-Schmidt, S., & Mar'i, A. A. (2016). *Arabic in academia in Israel: Historical absence, present challenges, chances for the future*. [In Hebrew] Jerusalem: Van Leer Institute. https://www.researchgate.net/publication/312219327_Arabic_in_the_Israeli_Academy_Historical_absence_current_challenges_and_future_possibilities

Ammon, U. (1998). Ist Deutsch noch internationale Wissenschaftssprache?: Englisch auch für die Lehre an den deutschsprachigen Hochschulen, Berlin, New York: De Gruyter. https://doi.org/10.1515/9783110802689

Astin, A. W., & Astin, H. S. (2000). *Leadership reconsidered: Engaging higher education in social change*. W. K. Kellogg Foundation.

Baldauf, R. B., Jr., & Kaplan, R. B. (2003). Language policy decisions and power: Who are the actors? In P. M. Ryan & R. Terborg (Eds.), *Language: Issues of inequality* (pp. 19–37). Universidad Nacional Autonama de Mexico.

Ben-Rafael, E., Shohamy, E., Amara, M. H., & Trumper-Hecht, N. (2006). Linguistic landscape as symbolic construction of the public space: He case of Israel. *International Journal of Multilingualism, 3*(1), 7–30.

Bok, D. C., & Bok, D. C. (2009). *Beyond the ivory tower: Social responsibilities of the modern university*. Harvard University Press.

Central Bureau of Statistics. (2021). Social survey on languages. In *Statistical abstract of Israel 2021*. Israel Government.

Crystal, D. (1997). *English as a global language*. Cambridge University Press.

de Mejía, A. M. (2012). Immersion education: En route to multilingualism. In *The Routledge handbook of multilingualism* (pp. 216–230). Routledge.

Donitsa-Schmidt, S., Inbar, O., & Shohamy, E. (2004). The effects of teaching spoken Arabic on students' attitudes and motivation in Israel. *The Modern Language Journal, 88*(2), 217–228.

Donitsa-Schmidt, S., Amara, M., & Mar'i, A. A. R. (2022). Educating for democratic citizenship: Arabic in Israeli higher education as a case in point. In *Activist pedagogy and shared education in divided societies* (pp. 77–89). Brill.

García, O., & Lin, A. M. (2017). *Translanguaging in bilingual education* (pp. 117–130). Bilingual and multilingual education.
Hallel, M., & Spolsky, B. (1993). The teaching of additional languages in Israel. *Annual Review of Applied Linguistics, 13*, 37–49.
Halperin, L. (2015). *Babel in Zion: Jews, nationalism, and language diversity in Palestine, 1920–1948*. Yale University Press.
Kheimets, N. G., & Epstein, A. D. (2005). Languages of higher education in contemporary Israel. *Journal of Educational Administration and History, 37*(1), 55–70.
Mar'i, S. (1978). *Arab education in Israel*. Syracuse University Press.
Ministry of Education, Culture and Sport. (1995). "Policy for language education in Israel (in Hebrew)." Office of the Director General.
Ministry of Education, Culture and Sport. (1996). "Policy for language education in Israel (in Hebrew)." Office of the Director-General.
Mizel, O. (2021). 'I lost my identity in the halls of academia': Arab students on the use of Arabic in Israeli higher education. *Issues in Educational Research, 31*(3), 930–951.
Nahir, M. (1998). Micro language planning and the revival of Hebrew: A schematic framework. *Language in Society, 27*, 335–357.
Or, I. G. (2017). *Creating a style for a generation: The beliefs and ideologies of Hebrew language planners*. Ov (in Hebrew).
Or, I. G., & Shohamy, E. (2016). Asymmetries and inequalities in the teaching of Arabic and Hebrew in the Israeli educational system. *Journal of Language and Politics, 15*(1), 25–44.
Pierce, J. J., Peterson, H. L., & Hicks, K. C. (2020). Policy change: An advocacy coalition framework perspective. *Policy Studies Journal, 48*(1), 64–86.
Piller, I. (2016). *Linguistic diversity and social justice: An introduction to applied sociolinguistics*. Oxford University Press.
Sabatier, P. A. (1988). An advocacy coalition framework of policy change and the role of policy-oriented learning therein. *Policy Sciences, 21*, 129–168.
Safran, W. (2005). Language and nation-building in Israel: Hebrew and its rivals. *Nations and Nationalism, 11*(1), 43–63.
Shohamy, E. (2006). *Language policy: Hidden agendas and new approaches*. Routledge.
Shohamy, E. (2009). Language teachers as Partners in Crafting Educational Language Policies? *Íkala [online], 14*(22).
Shohamy, E. (2012). A critical perspective on the use of English as a medium of instruction at universities. In *English-medium instruction at universities: Global challenges* (pp. 196–210). Channel View Publications.
Shohamy, E., & Ghazaleh-Mahajneh, M. A. (2012). Linguistic landscape as a tool for interpreting language vitality: Arabic as a 'minority' language in Israel. In

D. Gorter, H. F. Marten, & L. V. Mensel (Eds.), *Minority languages in the linguistic landscape* (pp. 89–106). Palgrave Macmillan.

Spolsky, B., & Shohamy, E. (1999). Language in Israeli society and education. *International Journal of the Sociology of Language, 137*, 93–114.

Spolsky, B., & Shohamy, E. (2001). The penetration of English as language of science and technology into the Israeli linguistic repertoire: A preliminary enquiry. *Contributions to the Sociology of Language, 84*, 167–176.

Stavans, A. (2012). 5 challenges faced by a medium-sized language community in the 21st century: The case of Hebrew. *Survival and Development of Language Communities: Prospects and Challenges, 150*, 81.

Stavans, A., & Lindgren, E. (2021). Building the multilingual literacy bridge. In *Multilingual literacy* (pp. 260–286). Multilingual Matters.

Stavans, A., & Narkiss, D. (2004). Creating and implementing a language policy in Israel. In *C. Hoffman & J. Ytsma, Trilingualism in family, school and community* (pp. 139–165). Multilingual Matters.

Swirski, S. (1999). *Politics and education in Israel: Comparisons with the United States*. Falmer.

Tannenbaum, M., & Tahar, L. (2008). Willingness to communicate in the language of the other: Jewish and Arab students in Israel. *Learning and Instruction, 18*, 283–294.

Tannenbaum, M., Michalovich, A., & Shohamy, E. (2020). Toward a new multilingual educational policy in Israel: Attitudes and perceptions of teachers and students. *Modern Language Journal, 104*(3), 581–600. https://doi.org/10.1111/modl.12667

Tannenbaum, M., Shohamy, E., & Inbar-Lourie, O. (2022). *Advocacy strategies for a new multilingual educational policy in Israel* (pp. 1–13). Language Policy.

Yitzhaki, D. (2010). The discourse of Arabic language policies in Israel: Insights from focus groups. *Language Policy, 9*(4), 335–356.

Yitzhaki, D. (2013). The status of Arabic in the discourse of Israeli policymakers. *Israel Affairs, 19*(2), 290–305.

CHAPTER 9

Students' and Teachers' Perceptions of Diversity Education in Moroccan Higher Education Language Curricula: A Case Study

Soufiane Abouabdelkader ⓘ *and Mouhssine Ayouri*

1 Introduction

This chapter attempts to examine the state of diversity education principles and their implementation in higher education English language curricula from a Universal Design for Learning (UDL) perspective. In recent years, continuous discontent with the existing situation in Moroccan universities has been expressed by its stakeholders themselves. These dissatisfactions, as expressed by teachers, students, and politicians, suggest the existence of certain gaps that hamper the achievement of quality education assurance. The work done in the consecutive reforms in Moroccan higher education illustrates the worries and concerns of the government to improve the different aspects of higher education curricula. In their turn, researchers are aware of the changes brought forth by the changes in the

S. Abouabdelkader (✉)
Faculty of Letters, Chouaib Doukkali University, El Jadida, Morocco

M. Ayouri
Lycée Tariq Ibn Zyad, Azrou, Morocco

© The Author(s), under exclusive license to Springer Nature Switzerland AG 2023
H. Abouabdelkader, B. Tomalin (eds.), *Diversity Education in the MENA Region*, https://doi.org/10.1007/978-3-031-42693-3_9

world economies and policies and their impact on new language teaching curricula, pedagogies, and assessment principles and practices (Abouabdelkader, 2018; Larouz & Abouabdelkader, 2020). What makes people discontent about the ills of the system? And how can it be improved?

Researching diversity education in the Moroccan context is not a revolutionary adventure; it is not either a 'follow the trend' initiative. It is a continuation of the search for what might remedy the ills of learning and teaching and the disparities in educational achievement among the different social classes. Most of this research attributes these deficiencies to the mismatch between the principles of governance, sustainability, and their implementation in the educational curricula (El Hissi et al., 2018; Sellamy et al., 2023). The issues included in most outcries relate to general concepts such as professional guidance and educational assistance, the verification of which is hard to establish. Other concepts concerned include failure to consider students' needs and little regard for their concerns and prospects. To get closer to these issues, the investigation in this chapter is focused on teachers' and students' perceptions of the various aspects of these failures in terms of diversity education.

2 Diversity Education in the Language Curricula

The first thing needed at the outset is the identification of the concept itself and its connotation in this quest. As a compound notion, diversity education in language education is a comprehensive approach that combines teaching and learning for the achievement of the factors that create equitable and inclusive learning environments for all students. It includes various aspects including students' needs, motivation, and engagement, teachers' pedagogies and teaching strategies, and curricular orientations and practices. By combining diversity with education, a strong step is made to the promotion of cultural understanding and the preparation of students to engage with diverse communities.

Inspiration to carry out this search comes from Banks' Multicultural Education Framework (Banks, 2001) for its impartiality and usefulness in addressing how multicultural understanding impacts students' development in higher education. Among the factors involved in this endeavour, it is useful to stress the impact of an elaborate language curriculum on the development of students' learning outcomes in higher education. To serve these objectives, it is crucial to analyse these issues from frameworks and models of interaction such as Universal Design for Learning (UDL) that are consistent with the needs of learners. The argument under the choice of a useful theoretical design that incorporates several dimensions of diversity is evidence that English language instruction is multivariate and involves transdisciplinary knowledge.

The five dimensions of banks (Banks, 2001) multicultural education model include: content integration, knowledge construction, equity pedagogy, prejudice reduction and improving environment, and social structure. As reported in research (Cole & Zhou, 2014), these constructs are among the pillars of language learning, culture, and social structure. According to Cole and Zhou (2014):

> Content integration refers to the use of examples from various cultural groups to illustrate key concepts and theories. Knowledge construction means that instructors help students understand, investigate, and determine how the implicit cultural assumptions and biases influence the ways knowledge is constructed. Equity pedagogy means that instructors modify instruction to facilitate educational achievement for all students. Prejudice reduction focuses on how positive attitudes can be developed towards different groups. Empowering school culture and social structure refers to how educators, students, parents, and the community create a transformative ethos that enables students from diverse groups to experience equality. (p. 111)

The components raised by Cole and Zhou constitute some of the crucial dimensions of diversity education reported in this chapter.

To this end, a case study that investigates the impact of diversity education principles on learning English as a foreign language (EFL) by Moroccan university students. This case study is part of a project that makes the investigation of various aspects of diversity education issues in Moroccan higher education. By underscoring the importance of the stakeholders' perceptions of the English language curricula, this search seeks to examine teachers' and students' expectations from the materials, practices, and all the opportunities offered in the Moroccan higher education English language curricula from a diversity education perspective. It has been carried out with the objective of comparing students' perceptions of some diversity education issues with those of the faculty. By using a quantitative research design based on a survey questionnaire, the study aims to isolate how teachers and students view the English curricula, their contents, the pedagogies adopted, and the learning outcomes and their assessments. The factors investigated relate to diversity education principles and address their pertinence in the current English language courses. Comparison between the two samples investigated is achieved qualitatively, using different statistical measurements for each of the categories under study.

In view of the complexity of diverse education construct and the absence of a framework that caters for all community diversities, we try to adopt Bank's model (Cole & Zhou, 2014) and draw from other universal frameworks in search of a conceptualisation that fits the ingredient of the context under investigation.

3 Case Study Summary

This study poses the following research question and criteria as major targets:

RQ: How do students and teachers rate the language curricula and pedagogical practices in terms of their implementation of diversity, equity, and inclusion principles?

The five factors of the curriculum addressed are:

1. Curriculum Philosophy and Reform
2. Content Accessibility and Transdisciplinary Education
3. Inclusive and Equitable Pedagogy
4. Cultural Understanding and Community Involvement
5. Learning Outcomes and Assessment Purposes

Details of the design, structure, and methodology adopted in this case study for the purpose of this chapter are summarised below.

3.1 Methodology

The research design employed for this study uses a survey research design which utilised a Likert scale questionnaire. Descriptive statistics and T-test analysis were used to analyse the collected data and address the research questions related to the implementation of diversity, equity, and inclusion principles in Moroccan higher education language curricula and pedagogical practices.

A survey questionnaire was administered to a convenient sample of 191 students and 31 teachers from two faculties of Arts and Humanities in Morocco (Chouaib Doukkali University, El Jadida and Moulay Ismail University, Meknes). Participants provided ratings on the Likert scale to indicate their agreement or disagreement with statements pertaining to various dimensions of diversity, equity, and inclusion.

Descriptive statistics, such as means and frequencies, were employed to summarise and analyse the data, providing an overview of the participants' perceptions and ratings across the different aspects of interest. These analyses enabled the assessment of the current state of diversity, equity, and inclusion practices in Moroccan higher education. Additionally, a T-test analysis was conducted to examine whether there were any significant differences between the ratings of students and teachers regarding the implementation of diversity, equity, and inclusion principles. This second type of analysis provided insights into potential variations in perspectives between these two groups.

By utilising both descriptive statistics and T-test analysis, this research design ensured a comprehensive exploration of the research questions, allowing for a deeper understanding of the implementation of diversity, equity, and inclusion principles in the context of Moroccan higher education language curricula and pedagogical practices.

3.2 The Results

The research question (RQ) addressed in this case study is 'How do students and teachers rate the language curricula and pedagogical practices in terms of their implementation of diversity, equity, and inclusion principles?'

3.2.1 Diversity Education: Curriculum Philosophy and Reform

The ELT state of the art in Moroccan universities has been in constant change over the last four decades. A lot of improvements have been recorded, but a lot of gaps persist. This study is part of the continuing shifts and search for progress contributed by academics. It is assumed in this study that 'behind a good practice, there is always a good theory'. It is, therefore, crucial to make the philosophies at the forefront of any endeavour. As is the case in the analyses, starting with the foundations of a curriculum helps understand its underpinnings.

These results show that the existing English language curricula adopted in Moroccan higher education institutions caters of several dimensions of diversity. These features are mentioned in the National Charter of Education (NCET, 1999), reflecting the country's concern for the development of literacy and development of the country. The obtained results also provide evidence of the existing gaps that require improvement in these curricula.

Regarding the implantation of diversity education in these philosophical orientations of the curricula, the findings report a positive critical change of focus and interest. As shown in the analyses below, these results indicate that the diversity education principles set by the National Charter have been amply supported by students and teachers and that both students and teachers are more conscious of what needs to be implemented in concrete terms.

The results on philosophies and principles reported in the study (see Table 9.1) reflect harmony in the perceptions of both teachers and students in terms of adherence to the diversity issues investigated, suggesting that English language teaching in Moroccan HE institutions is at a satisfactory level consonant with the issues of equity and inclusion.

Table 9.1 showcases descriptive statistics on the implementation of diversity, equity, and inclusion principles in Moroccan higher education language curricula and pedagogical practices, as rated by teachers and students. As reported in the whole chapter, the tables displayed include several variables for each category: N (number of respondents), mean, median, minimum (Min), maximum (Max), and standard deviation (SD).

For the Teacher category, there were 31 respondents. The mean rating for teachers is 2.9774, indicating an average positive perception of the implementation of diversity, equity, and inclusion principles. The median rating is 3.0000, suggesting a relatively balanced distribution of ratings. The ratings range from a minimum of 2.00 (for Curr_i10) to a maximum of 4.20 (for Curr_i4). The standard deviations range from 0.58862 to 1.303, indicating some variability in ratings among the teachers. This finding, however, shows that there is a lot of variability among teachers in terms of their awareness of the contents of new paradigms, such as UDL, Learning Communities, and other collaborative learning theories, suggesting that most of them stick to the standards approach and philosophies brought by the National Charter of Education and Training. They also indicate that further professional development of the faculty is constantly required in higher education to debate the new upbringings of educational research.

Table 9.1 Descriptive statistics of curriculum philosophy and reform

Category		Curr_i1	Curr_i2	Curr_i3	Curr_i4	Curr_i5	Curr_i6	Curr_i7	Curr_i8	Curr_i9	Curr_i10	Curr_Mean
Teacher	N	31	31	31	31	31	31	31	31	31	31	31
	Mean	3.29	3.26	4.10	2.90	2.77	2.00	2.32	3.71	3.03	2.39	2.977
	Median	4.00	4.00	4.00	2.00	3.00	2.00	2.00	4.00	3.00	2.00	3.000
	Min	1	1	3	2	2	1	1	1	1	1	2.00
	Max	4	5	5	4	4	3	4	5	5	4	4.20
	SD	0.902	1.182	0.700	0.978	0.845	0.632	0.791	0.973	1.303	1.05	0.5886
Student	N	190	190	190	190	190	190	190	190	190	190	190
	Mean	3.39	3.97	4.12	3.45	3.63	3.07	3.62	3.08	3.25	3.18	3.4753
	Median	4.00	4.00	4.00	4.00	4.00	3.00	4.00	3.00	3.00	3.00	3.5000
	Min	1	1	1	1	1	1	1	1	1	1	1.50
	Max	5	5	5	5	5	5	5	5	5	5	5.00
	SD	1.037	0.860	0.830	1.143	0.999	0.992	0.984	0.939	1.053	1.06	0.58098

For the Student category, there were 190 respondents. The mean rating for students is 3.4753, indicating a slightly more positive perception compared to teachers. The median rating is 3.5000, suggesting a relatively balanced distribution of ratings. The ratings range from a minimum of 1.50 to a maximum of 5.00. The standard deviations range from 0.58098 to 1.143, indicating some variability in ratings among the students.

Analysing the mean ratings, both teachers and students generally rate the implementation of diversity, equity, and inclusion principles positively, with students having slightly higher mean ratings. This indicates that, on average, both groups perceive the implementation favourably. However, it is important to consider the variability within each group, as indicated by the standard deviations. The variability suggests that there are differences in opinions and perceptions among the respondents within each category.

Looking at the specific items rated, it is noteworthy that teachers rated the item "Our institution regularly reviews and revises the curriculum to reflect the diversity of cultures and perspectives represented in the classroom" (Curri_i6) relatively lower compared to other items. On the other hand, students rated this same item with a higher mean rating. This discrepancy suggests a potential difference in perception between teachers and students regarding the regular review and revision of the curriculum to reflect diversity. Further investigation would be required to understand the underlying reasons for this discrepancy.

Altogether, the data indicates a generally positive perception of the implementation of diversity, equity, and inclusion principles in Moroccan higher education language curricula and pedagogical practices. However, the data also reports that there are variations in ratings within each group and specific areas that may require attention. The post-Covid-19 pandemic has probably raised certain questions related to students' rights to the surface. The item-specific ratings highlight the importance of further exploring the differences between teachers and students, particularly in terms of curriculum review and revision. By the same token, they also reflect students' and teachers' awareness of and implication in these issues.

3.2.2 Content Accessibility and Transdisciplinary Education

Content accessibility and transdisciplinary education refer to the extent to which the English language curricular contents are accessible to all students in terms of genres and means, and whether they offer opportunities to students from different disciplines to learn from one another. Transdisciplinary collaborative work, on the other hand, is considered as a means which allows students to benefit from the knowledge and skills of their peers in other disciplines. This is basically applicable in engineering schools where several disciplines are set up as independent training for special courses. While content accessibility has been probed in HE curricula in connection with a clear set of norms (Abouabdelkader, S., 2023), transdisciplinary education in the English language teaching research in the Moroccan context needs to be promoted in the teaching of English for vocational purpose (ESP).

The results displayed in Table 9.2 (below) offer descriptive statistics on the ratings of teachers and students regarding the implementation of Content Accessibility and Transdisciplinary Education in Moroccan higher education language curricula and pedagogical practices. The mean ratings indicate a generally positive perception of the implementation by both teachers (mean = 3.2355) and students (mean = 3.4447). The median ratings for teachers and students are 3.3000 and 3.5000, respectively, suggesting relatively balanced distributions of ratings. The range of ratings varies from a minimum of 1.30 to a maximum of 5.00. The standard deviations show some variability in the ratings, with values ranging from 0.85188 to 1.380 for teachers and from 0.59739 to 1.112 for students.

These figures suggest that both teachers and students view the implementation of Content Accessibility and Transdisciplinary Education positively, with students having slightly higher mean ratings. As has been reported in this chapter, students display positive perceptions towards the means used by teachers in terms of content accessibility and facility. However, variations within each group indicate differences in opinions and perceptions. Notably, aspects such as Cont_i4 and Cont_i9 (see appendix) received relatively high ratings from both teachers and students, indicating strengths in these areas. Conversely, Cont_i1 and Cont_i5 (see Table 9.2) received lower ratings, highlighting the need for providing various courses pertaining to UDL principles as potential areas that require further attention and improvement in the implementation.

The descriptive statistics reported above demonstrate a generally positive perception of the implementation of Content Accessibility and Transdisciplinary Education in Moroccan higher education, emphasising the importance of continuous improvement efforts to enhance diversity, equity, and inclusion within curricula and pedagogical practices. This finding is also supported in a study which indicates that the recurring reforms made in Moroccan higher education have synergised the educational system and increased its quality features of diversity, equity, and inclusion

Table 9.2 Descriptive statistics of content accessibility and transdisciplinary education

		Cont_i1	Cont_i2	Cont_i3	Cont_i4	Cont_i5	Cont_i6	Cont_i7	Cont_i8	Cont_i9	Cont_i10	Cont_Mean
Teacher	N	31	31	31	31	31	31	31	31	31	31	31
	Mean	2.90	3.97	3.74	3.35	2.65	3.06	3.32	3.00	3.52	2.84	3.2355
	Median	2.00	4.00	4.00	4.00	2.00	3.00	4.00	3.00	4.00	3.00	3.3000
	Min	1	1	1	1	1	1	1	1	1	1	1.30
	Max	5	5	5	5	5	5	5	5	5	5	5.00
	SD	1.326	0.912	0.999	1.253	1.380	1.153	1.222	1.238	1.122	1.186	0.85188
Student	N	190	190	190	190	190	190	190	190	190	190	190
	Mean	3.14	3.74	3.87	3.67	3.36	3.23	3.49	3.37	3.38	3.20	3.4447
	Median	3.00	4.00	4.00	4.00	4.00	3.00	4.00	3.00	4.00	3.00	3.5000
	Min	1	1	1	1	1	1	1	1	1	1	1.00
	Max	5	5	5	5	5	5	5	5	5	5	4.90
	SD	0.995	0.923	0.878	1.068	1.112	0.906	0.985	1.020	1.010	1.104	0.59739

(Abouabdelkader, 2023; Fahim, et al. 2021). Low scores have also been obtained for some issues, suggesting there is a lot of work for the provision of accessible contents and transdisciplinary education. Policymakers and educators can utilise these insights to refine strategies and promote a more inclusive learning environment in Moroccan higher education institutions.

3.2.3 Inclusive and Equitable Pedagogy

The issues addressed under this rubric on Inclusive and equitable pedagogy address the extent to which the learning environment creates equitable opportunities that leverage students' learning outcomes, enhance their motivation, establish rapport between students and teachers, and enable them to face the challenges of the world of work on equitable grounds. It is assumed in the study that these categories are essential in English language learning in a context full of disparities.

The results concerning the 'inclusive and equitable pedagogy' categories investigated, as described in Table 9.3 (below), present descriptive statistics on the ratings provided by teachers and students regarding the implementation of Inclusive and Equitable Pedagogy in Moroccan higher education language curricula and pedagogical practices. Teachers expressed a moderate positive perception (mean = 3.4695) of the implementation, with a relatively balanced distribution of ratings as indicated by the median of 3.44. The ratings ranged from 2.33 as the minimum to 4.89 as the maximum. The standard deviations varied from 0.62572 to 1.207, indicating some variability in the teachers' ratings.

According to the results, students displayed a slightly more positive perception (mean = 3.4737) compared to teachers, suggesting the presence of disagreements on certain issues between the two categories of respondents. As can be seen in the table, the median rating of 3.5556 suggests a relatively balanced distribution of ratings among students. The range of ratings extended from 1.89 (for Curr_Mean) as the minimum to 4.78 (for several items) as the maximum. The standard deviations ranged from 0.58487 to 1.174, indicating variability in the students' ratings. Both teachers and students rated Inc_i3 and Inc_i4 (see appendix) relatively high, suggesting positive perceptions of these aspects of Inclusive and Equitable Pedagogy. However, both groups rated Inc_i1 (see appendix) lower, indicating 'English curricula: Prejudice and Discrimination Awareness' as a potential area that may require further attention and improvement in the implementation. One of the possible explanations,

Table 9.3 Descriptive statistics of inclusive and equitable pedagogy

Category		Inc_i1	Inc_i2	Inc_i3	Inc_i4	Inc_i5	Inc_i6	Inc_i7	Inc_i8	Inc_i9	Curr_Mean
Teacher	N	31	31	31	31	31	31	31	31	31	31
	Mean	3.19	3.87	4.19	3.68	3.42	3.32	3.45	3.10	3.00	3.4695
	Median	4.00	4.00	4.00	4.00	4.00	4.00	4.00	3.00	3.00	3.4444
	Min	1	2	3	2	1	1	1	1	1	2.33
	Max	5	5	5	5	5	5	5	5	5	4.89
	SD	1.167	0.885	0.543	0.979	1.148	1.194	1.207	1.165	1.155	0.62572
Student	N	190	190	190	190	190	190	190	190	190	190
	Mean	3.13	3.71	3.61	3.65	3.43	3.75	3.47	3.13	3.38	3.4737
	Median	3.00	4.00	4.00	4.00	4.00	4.00	4.00	3.00	4.00	3.5556
	Min	1	1	1	1	1	1	1	1	1	1,89
	Max	5	5	5	5	5	5	5	5	5	4,78
	SD	1.038	1.027	1.027	1.067	1.174	0.963	1.106	1.058	1.165	0.58487

though, of this difference, may be due to the fact that teachers are more knowledgeable of language teaching theories than students.

It is conclusive that the findings indicate a generally positive perception of the implementation of Inclusive and equitable pedagogy in Moroccan higher education. However, variations in ratings within each group and lower ratings for specific aspects highlighting 'English Curricula: Prejudice and Discrimination Awareness' as an area that could benefit from targeted interventions and enhancements.

What matters most is that the descriptive statistics reveal a favourable perception of the implementation of Inclusive and Equitable Pedagogy in Moroccan higher education that facilitate understanding for all learners. These insights underscore the importance of teachers' continual efforts to promote diversity, equity, and inclusion within curricula and pedagogical practices. Policymakers and educators can leverage these findings to refine learning strategies and foster an inclusive and equitable learning environment in Moroccan higher education institutions.

3.2.4 Cultural Understanding and Community Involvement

Cultural understanding and community involvement are two notable components of language learning. They refer to the extent to which students are able to recognise that every culture has its own way of looking at the world, avoid misunderstandings, and build meaningful relations without prejudices. Key factors that facilitate cultural understanding involve, for instance, students' engagement in activities that provide opportunities for them to interact with other groups or communities. In the foreign language context, especially in vocational institutions, such encounters can be achieved through learning communities that integrate students from different disciplines.

The purpose underneath analysis of the issues included in this category is to isolate the respondents' conceptions of the curriculum regarding the support provided for learners to assimilate what they are taught and make good use of it. Table 9.4 provides descriptive statistics on the ratings given by teachers and students regarding the implementation of Cultural Understanding and Community Involvement in Moroccan higher education language curricula and pedagogical practices. The table presents key findings related to the research question on the ratings of diversity, equity, and inclusion principles.

Table 9.4 shows that teachers expressed a relatively low perception of the implementation of the two components, cultural understanding and

Table 9.4 Descriptive statistics of cultural understanding and community involvement

Category		Cult_i1	Cult_i2	Cult_i3	Cult_i4	Cult_i5	Cult_i6	Cult_i7	Cult_i8	Cult_i9	Cult_i10	Cult_Mean
Teacher	N	31	31	31	31	31	31	31	31	31	31	31
	Mean	2.55	2.39	2.32	2.39	2.35	2.42	2.55	2.45	2.35	2.42	2.41
	Median	2.00	2.00	2.00	2.00	2.00	2.00	2.00	2.00	2.00	2.00	2.20
	Min	1	1	1	1	1	1	1	1	1	1	1.60
	Max	5	5	5	5	5	5	5	5	5	5	4.10
	SD	1.06	1.25	1.19	1.05	1.05	1.02	1.09	1.02	0.915	1.089	0.664
Student	N	190	190	190	190	190	190	190	190	190	190	190
	Mean	3.31	2.71	2.83	2.49	2.87	2.86	2.78	3.02	2.79	2.57	2.82
	Median	3.00	3.00	3.00	2.00	3.00	3.00	3.00	3.00	3.00	3.00	2.90
	Min	1	1	1	1	1	1	1	1	1	1	1.00
	Max	5	5	5	5	5	5	5	5	5	5	5.00
	SD	0.998	1.215	1.185	1.263	1.242	1.184	1.173	1.127	1.224	1.104	0.825

community engagement, in the curriculum, as indicated by a mean rating of 2.4194 and a median rating of 2.2000. The range of ratings varied from 1.60 (for Cult Mean) as the minimum to 4.10 (for Max) as the maximum. The standard deviations ranged from 0.66454 to 1.256, reflecting variability in the teachers' ratings. This divergence signifies that teachers' worries are less on the cultural understanding than it is on the teaching of thinking skills necessary to their studies; students, in turn, express their worries in terms of the instruments in use rather than the processes under way. As an aspect that aligns learning with diversity principles, cultural understanding is attended to by teachers in proportion to the means they have access to, leaving more freedom for students to reflect and react on their own.

Regarding students, the figures obtained in the analyses, among the 190 student respondents, display a mean rating of 2.8237, indicating a slightly more positive perception compared to teachers. The median rating of 2.9000 suggested a relatively balanced distribution of ratings. The range of ratings extended from 1.00 (for Min) as the minimum to 5.00 (for several items) as the maximum. The standard deviations ranged from 0.82515 to 1.263, indicating variability in the students' ratings.

Examining the specific items, both teachers and students rated the implementation of Cultural Understanding and Community Involvement relatively low. The mean ratings for teachers ranged from 2.32 to 2.55, while for students, they ranged from 2.49 to 3.31. These findings suggest a need for improvement in fostering cultural understanding and community involvement within the higher education language curricula and pedagogical practices in Morocco. This does not mean that they are excluded or not sufficiently comprehensive in the curriculum; it simply means that culture is round the clock in every language course and that it constitutes one of their major concerns.

The results highlight a potential disparity between the perceptions of teachers and students regarding the implementation of diversity, equity, and inclusion principles. While students generally rated the implementation more positively, both groups expressed relatively low ratings overall.

To wrap up, the descriptive statistics reveal that the implementation of Cultural Understanding and Community Involvement in some Moroccan higher education language curricula and pedagogical practices is perceived as relatively low. These results highlight the need for concentrated efforts to enhance the incorporation of diversity, equity, and inclusion principles that empower students with higher levels of the foreign language culture as well as opportunities for project task involvement. This teacher-bound pedagogical orientation consists of providing more effective conditions for learning, which is likely to enhance students' motivational drives and learning outcomes.

3.2.5   Learning Outcomes and Assessment Purposes
Finally, the issues of learning outcomes and assessment are considered in this chapter as two interrelated issues in language education. Learning outcomes refer to the categories of a curriculum that define the overall gains of a course. They are crucial components of a curriculum and constitute its main objectives and goals and go hand in hand with assessments.

It is assumed in this study that aligning learning outcomes with assessment contributes to students' engagement and motivation and ensures accountability for the language curriculum.

The results obtained in the study indicate that these issues are thornier than any other aspect of language instruction. Table 9.5 showcases descriptive statistics on the ratings provided by teachers and students regarding the implementation of Learning and Assessment Purposes in Moroccan higher education language curricula and pedagogical practices. The findings provide important insights into the perceptions of diversity, equity, and inclusion principles.

Among the 31 participating teachers, the ratings reflect a moderate perception of the implementation of efficacious learning outcomes and assessments in the current curricula. The mean rating of 2.8613 and the median rating of 2.8000 suggest a balanced distribution of ratings. The range of ratings extends from 2.00 to 3.80, indicating variability in the teachers' assessments. Standard deviations range from 0.59143 to 1.504, indicating diverse perspectives among teachers.

Likewise, the 190 student respondents indicate a slightly more positive perception compared to teachers. The mean rating of 3.1768 and the median rating of 3.2000 demonstrate a relatively consistent assessment. The range of ratings spans from 1.40 to 5.00, reflecting diverse evaluations among students. Standard deviations range from 0.56773 to 1.301, indicating variations in the students' viewpoints.

Upon examining specific items, both teachers and students rated the implementation of Learning and Assessment Purposes moderately. Teachers' mean ratings ranged from 2.19 to 3.48, while students' mean ratings ranged from 2.83 to 3.56. These results highlight the need for improvements in aligning learning and assessment purposes with diversity,

Table 9.5 Descriptive statistics of learning and assessment purposes

Category		Lear_i1	Lear_i2	Lear_i3	Lear_i4	Lear_i5	Lear_i6	Lear_i7	Lear_i8	Lear_i9	Lear_i10	Lear_Mean
Teacher	N	31	31	31	31	31	31	31	31	31	31	31
	Mean	2.74	2.90	3.48	3.19	2.94	2.39	2.19	2.94	2.68	3.16	2.861
	Median	3.00	3.00	4.00	3.00	3.00	2.00	2.00	3.00	2.00	3.00	2.800
	Min	1	1	1	1	1	1	1	1	1	1	2.00
	Max	4	4	5	5	5	5	5	5	5	5	3.80
	SD	0.893	1.106	0.890	1.108	1.063	1.054	1.327	1.504	1.376	1.369	0.5914
Student	N	190	190	190	190	190	190	190	190	190	190	190
	Mean	2.83	3.05	3.56	3.32	3.16	3.08	2.85	3.16	3.34	3.42	3.176
	Median	3.00	3.00	4.00	3.00	3.00	3.00	3.00	3.00	3.00	3.00	0.200
	Min	1	1	1	1	1	1	1	1	1	1	1.40
	Max	5	5	5	5	5	5	5	14	5	5	5.00
	SD	1.153	1.142	0.972	1.086	1.155	1.161	1.223	1.301	1.269	1.070	0.5677

equity, and inclusion principles in the higher education language curricula and pedagogical practices in Morocco. Notably, there appears to be a disparity between the perceptions of teachers and students regarding the implementation of these principles. While students generally expressed more positive ratings, both groups provided moderate assessments overall.

It is important to highlight that the descriptive statistics indicate a moderate perception of the implementation of Learning and Assessment Purposes in Moroccan higher education language curricula and pedagogical practices. These results underscore the importance of aligning learning and assessment strategies with diversity, equity, and inclusion principles. Similar results on assessment in higher education institutions have also been reported by other researchers and reported by the World bank World Bank (Abouabdelkader, S., 2023). Policymakers and educators should carefully consider these findings to enhance the integration of these principles in a systematically structured frame that optimises learning outcomes and promotes a higher education environment that is inclusive and equitable.

4 Conclusions

Based on the results obtained in the case study and those reported in the related literature, it is fair to conclude that several aspects of equity and inclusion issues related to language learning have been recently included in the university curricula investigated, as stipulated in the National Charter and the laws put forth by the ensuing reforms. By the same token, these findings indicate that some of them still require specification and consideration of individual learners' needs and concerns.

At the conceptual level, Moroccan HE students view language learning as a means of equipping all students with literacy skills – as recommended by the ministerial reports and guidelines – which involve communication skills and soft skills. Both in literary, linguistic, and applied linguistic studies, the focus of the curricula is oriented towards facilitating learning, providing equal opportunities to all students, and establishing bonds between learners and their environment. The positive aspects reported by both the faculty and the students include: (1) the provision of knowledge and skills that promote literacy skills that are adequate for each level of instruction and to all students, without any discrimination, and (2) the provision of learning materials that help students promote their knowledge of the anglophone world in association with the skills needed for effective communication and growth. (3) The inclusion of classics of literature and works that improve students' cultural understanding and familiarise them with international phenomena in the fields of science, technology, and education.

At the content and pedagogy levels, the conception of literacy skills is consistent with the philosophies and principles provided in the National Charter; they consist of the knowledge states that empower students with the skills that help them understand and produce information in English, and the issues addressed in the English-speaking civilisation and literature course are not confined to the Anglo-Saxon world; they also encompass literature and societal matters of the world at large.

Regarding the pedagogies related to the teaching of literacy skills, the state of the art of Moroccan higher education language curricula concerning diversity, equity, and inclusion is reported to be the responsibility of the faculty, based on their responsibility of providing what would be useful for each level of instruction and would stimulate the interest and motivation of the students. In fact, teachers also support these claims and say that their efforts are always oriented towards learner-centred approaches and collaborative language instruction to provide opportunities for all learners to overcome their worries and stimulate their energies.

Interestingly, however, the findings also reveal that teachers and students acknowledge that in the post-Covid-19 era, English language teaching pedagogies have witnessed a lot of positive change in this respect and that both are considering e-learning approaches as a better tool for developing independent learning that caters for all students. As shown in the results, all the participants have a positive attitude towards the use of information technologies to bridge the existing gap between students from poor and rich backgrounds. To serve diversity education principles, several positive accomplishments have been used to reduce the burden of getting computers of their own, but this remains an issue for students from poor backgrounds. Similarly, postgraduate students have been granted the privilege of using e-libraries. These power structures seek to help all students promote their learning and facilitate research and teaching management. In fact, these resources are beneficial to administrative staff, faculty, and students, and their use serves both the learning and professional development of teachers.

The major points agreed upon by all the teachers involved in the study are that the teaching of literacy skills should focus more on communication and intercultural skills that address students' needs. Most support is for pedagogical activities that provide enough freedom for learners to grow and flourish; more space for the exploration of different cultures, traditions, and perspectives; and more opportunities for the development of intercultural competence. These perceptions are reflective of the ethics and values of tolerance, understanding, and collaboration needed for effective English language learning.

In these terms, the notions of equity and inclusion are, therefore, made closely tied up with cultural understanding and community service, and carried out through the provision of an equitable pedagogy that fosters cultural understanding and inclusion of all learners. As revealed in the obtained findings, several measures have been reported which show that teachers and students recognise and support understanding of 'the other' and respect cultural differences. This is achieved through pedagogies that reject exclusion and marginalisation of certain students or certain phenomena, and that English Language course/studies include issues that debate culture and the principles of civic education.

Despite these positive features of language education, there is still need for further refurbishment and improvement of diversity principles (Chtatou, this volume), suggesting that further alignment is urged by the continuous development shifts in international economies and policies and that unfair assessment is one of the major causes of failure to learn languages for many students.

Finally, the English language learning landscape drawn in this chapter as reported in both the literature and the case study amply supports the importance of considering diversity education as an enlightening path towards the remediation of the ills of higher education language curricula and a useful tool for promoting students' engagement and growth.

Appendix

Questionnaire

Dear participant: The aim of this questionnaire is to assess the extent to which educators are incorporating the principles of diversity, equity, and inclusion in their teaching practices. The checklist used for this study has been modified and developed by our team of researchers. *If you consent to fill in this questionnaire,* we request your sincere and thoughtful responses to the statements included in each section. Your valuable participation in this study is highly appreciated.

Gender: Age: University/Institution: Educational Level:

Please rate your level of agreement with each statement on a scale of 1–5, *where 1 is strongly disagree and 5 is strongly agree.*

Statement	1	2	3	4	5

1. The language course meets the needs of students from diverse backgrounds and abilities.
2. The language course helps students to learn knowledge.
3. The language course helps students to develop their language skills.
4. The language class aims at preparing students to be independent.
5. The language class encourages teamwork, collaborative and experiential learning.
6. Our courses are designed to promote equity and inclusion by providing students with opportunities to explore and celebrate the diverse identities and backgrounds of all members of our community.
7. Our teachers facilitate a safe and welcoming learning environment that encourages respectful dialogue and fosters mutual understanding and appreciation of our differences.
8. Our institution provides an equitable, diverse, and inclusive educational experience for all students.
9. Our students voice their aspirations and needs and express their own critical abilities.
10. Our institution tests grade students' learning outcomes equitably.
11. The courses use a variety of instructional materials that reflect the diversity of cultures, concerns, and orientations of their students.
12. Teachers use resources and instruments such as books, videos, and websites that feature diverse characters and cultures.
13. Students are encouraged to read and use different resources that explain concepts and ideas adequately.
14. Activities are organised to encourage students to share their own experiences and perspectives in class discussions.
15. Websites are made available or suggested to all students to learn the subjects of the courses. Language contents for clarification.
16. The courses incorporate materials and resources that reflect the concerns of students from different disciplines.
17. Teachers provide students with opportunities to investigate and analyse knowledge from different disciplines.
18. Our students are encouraged to share and explore experiences of groups from diverse disciplines.
19. Teachers familiarise students with perspectives from different topics that reflect the complementarity of diverse disciplines in the courses.
20. Students are actively involved in common projects or learning communities from different disciplines.

(continued)

(continued)

Statement	1 2 3 4 5

21. The courses address issues of prejudice and discrimination when they arise in the classroom.
22. Teachers create a positive classroom environment and feedback for students from all backgrounds.
23. Students are to challenge their own biases and stereotypes about different people.
24. Teachers provide opportunities for students to interact with peers from diverse race, sex, and age in the classroom.
25. Events and activities are offered to promote positive relations inside and outside the classroom.
26. The language course provides opportunities for all students to use their knowledge and skills inside and outside the classroom.
27. The teaching methods provide equitable opportunities for all students regardless of their cultural or linguistic background.
28. Teachers provide appropriate support, such as books and exercises, for students with learning problems and disabilities.
29. Students are given clear and appropriate instructions that suit their needs.
30. Our teaching methods and materials ensure that all students can participate fully in classroom activities.
31. The language courses promote a sense of cultural understanding for all students.
32. Teachers provide opportunities for students and families to participate in planning and designing cultural events.
33. The courses actively encourage the spirit of language clubs and activities. Involving students, teachers, and staff.
34. Students and parents organise cultural events of common contests to the community.
35. The administration and staff celebrate and value the cultural diversity of our students through events and activities.
36. The teachers involve all students in partnerships with the community.
37. Students produce resources and materials through projects with external institutions.
38. The language tests incorporate students' projects in their evaluations.
39. Our students benefit from activities and programmes sponsored by the community.
40. The institution celebrates and values the cultural diversity of students and parents through events and activities.
41. The courses provide feedback only to students who perform well in the tests.
42. Teachers provide feedback and help to students on request only.
43. Low performers are asked to improve their performance through exercises.

(continued)

(continued)

Statement	1	2	3	4	5
44. Low performers are provided with remedial work and guidance for improvement.					
45. Students are coached by their peers to better their performance.					
46. Our school uses contents and language tests that match students' abilities and levels.					
47. The school provides accommodations and supports for students who may face cognitive or linguistic problems.					
48. Continuous assessments are constantly administered to measure student learning outcomes and progress.					
49. Teachers give feedback to all students and recognize the strengths and weaknesses of all students.					
50. Tests seek to evaluate students for administrative use.					

References

Abouabdelkader, S. (2018). Moroccan EFL university students' composing skills in the balance: Assessment procedures and outcomes. In A. M. Ahmed & H. Abouabdelkader (Eds.), *Assessing EFL writing in the 21st century Arab world: Revealing the unknown* (pp. 79–109). Palgrave Macmillan. https://doi.org/10.1007/978-3-319-64104-1_4

Abouabdelkader, S. (2023). Representation, engagement, and expression in Moroccan higher education curricula: Focus on reading comprehension. In H. Abouabdelkader & B. Tomalin (Eds.), *Diversity education in the MENA region: Bridging the gaps in language learning*. Palgrave Macmillan.

Banks, J. A. (2001). Citizenship education and diversity: Implications for teacher education. *Journal of Teacher Education, 52*(1), 5–16.

Cole, D., & Zhou, J. (2014). Do diversity experiences help college students become more civically minded? Applying Banks' multicultural education framework. *Innovative Higher Education, 39*, 109–121.

El Hissi, Y., Benjouid, Z., Haqiq, A., & Idrissi, L. L. (2018). Contribution of new technologies in the relationship between the governance and the social responsibility at the Moroccan university. *International Journal of Service Science, Management, Engineering, and Technology (IJSSMET), 9*(3), 1–13.

Larouz, M., & Abouabdelkader, S. (2020). Teachers' feedback on EFL students' dissertation writing in Morocco. In A. M. Ahmed, S. Troudi, & S. Riley (Eds.), *Feedback in L2 English writing in the Arab world: Inside the black box* (pp. 201–232). Palgrave Macmillan. https://doi.org/10.1007/978-3-030-25830-6_8

Sellamy, K., Fakhri, Y., & Moumen, A. (2023). What factors determine the academic orientation in Moroccan higher education? *Sustainability, 15*(8), 6866.

CHAPTER 10

How Culturally Diverse Is the Virtual Space? Towards Inclusive Pedagogy: A Case Study at the Arab Open University

Chahra Beloufa

1 Introduction

As universities and colleges around the world strive to create more diverse educational environments, cultural diversity in higher education has surged in prominence as a conversational issue in recent years. The presence of people from various cultural backgrounds as well as the appreciation and celebration of the distinctive viewpoints, experiences, and identities that each person offers to the community are all examples of cultural diversity. Cultural diversity in higher education includes a wide range of elements, such as race, ethnicity, nationality, religion, language, socioeconomic background, sexual orientation, and gender identity. The value of cultural diversity in higher education is found in its ability to improve all students' educational experiences. Students' awareness of the world can be expanded by exposure to different ideas, beliefs, and

C. Beloufa (✉)
The Arab Open University, Dammam, Saudi Arabia

experiences. To achieve cultural diversity in higher education, nevertheless, can be an intricate and challenging endeavor. Universities and colleges need to make an effort to build a supportive environment that embraces and supports students from all backgrounds. This entails ensuring that a diverse student body has access to the resources and services they need, as well as fostering an inclusive culture through curriculum design, policies, and practices. In this situation, it is crucial for higher education institutions to foster cultural diversity in a deliberate and proactive manner. This could entail actions like underrepresented group-specific recruitment and retention programs, multicultural faculty and staff training, and the creation of culturally sensitive curricula and pedagogies. Overall, cultural variety is crucial to an exceptional educational experience.

Culture, in the words of Durkheim (1915), "is the outward expression of religion," and it should go without saying that the two are interrelated, with one regularly influencing and developing the other. Similar in its approach, Smith (1982) points out that culture and religion are mutually constitutive and frequently inform one another, determining the impact of culture without taking into account its religious context will be fruitless and incorrect. Saudi Arabia's Kingdom (KSA) is regarded as a multicultural society. Due to the free movement of merchants and pilgrims throughout Saudi history, the Arabian Peninsula witnessed ethical and environmental diversity as well as multicultural exchange. Sunni, Shia, and other religious groups who were born in Saudi Arabia, as well as other religious groups from other religious backgrounds who came to work in KSA today, all contribute to the country's diversity.

Islam, being the nearly universal religion in the country, plays a significant role in influencing how education is delivered, interpreted, visualized, and valued in Saudi Arabia, despite the fact that the role of religion in education has sparked debate and controversy, and some elements argue that it limits the freedom of students and teachers to express their own beliefs and engage in critical thought. Saudi Arabia disclosed Saudi Vision 2030 (Vision 2030) in 2017, a strategic plan for education that would be completed by the year 2030. The Saudi economy will be diversified, and the country's tourism and education industries will grow. The development of civic values like respect, responsibility, creativity, belief in moderation, and tolerance, as well as the abilities necessary to assure future job success, is a key component of Vision 2030.

Since e-learning has become an increasingly common component of education in Saudi Arabia, the culture there has shown receptivity to its introduction. Given the size of the country's population and the need to accommodate each student's unique learning preferences, e-learning is seen as a flexible and effective way to impart education to pupils. E-learning is also thought to be an effective way to deliver education in isolated or rural areas where access to regular schools and universities is constrained. Additionally, e-learning gives students the opportunity to obtain education in a secure, comfortable, and familiar setting at a time that works for them. This study informs tutors and brings their attention to shifting their pedagogical practices, promoting cultural diversity during the different courses in Online Learning Environments. Therefore, when is it interesting to examine closely how students at the Arab Open University deal with cultural differences? In addition to that, I am also interested in studying the choices made by tutors when designing the course materials and whether these incorporate cultural inclusion topics and activities. I would stress by the end of the chapter on innovative digital tools that practitioners can use to implement diversity during their online lectures.

2 Cultural Diversity and Inclusion in Online Learning Environments

The growth of online education in the Middle East has been a dynamic process, influenced by several factors, including quick technological advancements, shifting socio-political environments, and a rising demand for high-quality education (Hamdan, 2014). This section provides an overview of those reasons and trends before delving deeper into the significant developments and drivers that have influenced the development of online learning in the area. Thanks to the widespread use of high-speed Internet, smartphone technology, and other digital technologies, the Middle East now has the infrastructure to support the expansion of online education (Weber, 2018). These technologies have made it possible for educational institutions to create and provide online courses and programs, as well as for students to have anytime, anywhere access to educational resources and take part in activities that call for collaborative learning. Moreover, the significant socio-political changes that have taken place in the Middle East over the past few years have had a significant impact on the region's educational system. Political unrest, economic hardship, and widespread population displacement are just a few of the circumstances that have boosted demand for flexible and accessible educational options (Hamdan, 2014). Learning online has become a potentially helpful way to deal with these problems and guarantee that a wide range of people can access high-quality education. The governments of the Middle Eastern nations have realized that online education has the potential to alter the educational system and enhance socioeconomic development. As a result, some countries in the region have started national e-learning initiatives and passed laws to encourage the use and integration of online learning within their individual educational systems (Khalil et al., 2020). Furthermore, massive Open Online Courses (MOOCs) and e-learning management systems are two online learning platforms that have become increasingly popular in the Middle East in recent years. Due to partnerships between regional, national, and worldwide providers of massive open online courses (MOOCs), Middle Eastern students now have access to a greater selection of educational options (Hamdan, 2014). Additionally, regionally specific e-learning platforms that address the region's unique cultural, linguistic, and contextual needs have emerged recently.

2.1 The Rise of Online Learning in Saudi Arabia

The Saudi Arabian government has invested significantly in the nation's digital education system as part of the Vision 2030 initiative, which is under the direction of Crown Prince Mohammed Bin Salman. The goal of this initiative is to strengthen the nation's economy and society by expanding the government's revenue streams, reducing reliance on foreign oil, and fostering knowledge-based industries like technology and education (Khan, 2016).

The Saudi government has made large expenditures in building the necessary infrastructure at the primary and secondary school levels, as well as at the postsecondary level, and has been aggressively promoting the use of online education (Al-Asmari & Rabb Khan, 2020). The COVID-19 outbreak contributed to a substantial acceleration of the movement toward online learning. To ensure that education would continue, educational institutions started implementing remote teaching and learning (Weber, 2018).

2.1.1 The National e-Learning Center (NECL)

Under the guidance of the Saudi Arabian Ministry of Education, the National E-Learning Center (NECL) was established in 2005 with the aim of promoting the growth of online education in the nation (Weber, 2018). The National E-Learning Center (NECL) was founded with the goals of assisting educational institutions in their adoption of e-learning initiatives, promoting the use of technology in educational settings, and creating rules and standards for e-learning (NECL, 2021). The following are some of the most important turning events in Saudi Arabia's history of online education:

- The first institution in the country to run fully online, the Saudi Electronic institution (SEU), was established in 2011. The first college in the nation to provide both undergraduate and graduate degrees in a range of subjects is SEU (SEU, n.d.).
- Since the launch of the "*Doroob*" National e-Learning Platform in 2012, users have had unrestricted access to a wide range of online educational resources, including interactive multimedia content, digital textbooks, and online courses (Doroob, 2021).
- The "*Tadarus*" platform was created in the year 2020. During the COVID-19 pandemic, Tadarus proved to be a virtual learning environment that will enable remote teaching and learning. It provides capabilities for content management, communication, and virtual classrooms.

Saudi Arabia has also actively sought partnerships with other institutions and organizations to develop its ecosystem for online learning. For instance, in order to provide Saudi students with access to thousands of online courses offered by the world's most esteemed educational institutions, the Saudi Arabian Ministry of Education has partnered with the American online education provider, Coursera (Moran, 2021). A variety of scholarship programs, like the King Abdullah Scholarship Program, have also been developed by the Saudi Arabian government to entice students to enroll in online and blended learning courses provided by prominent institutions across the world (Education Ministry, 2021).

2.1.2 The Arab Open University and Online Learning
In the Middle East, the Arab Open University (AOU) is a pioneering institution. It was established in 2002 with the intention of expanding access to and adaptability of higher education opportunities for a diverse student population across the Arab world (Anas, 2020). The American University in the Arab World (AOU) serves students from diverse cultural

and linguistic origins. It has its headquarters in Saudi Arabia and affiliates in numerous other Arab nations, including Kuwait, Lebanon, and Jordan (Al-Jarf, 2022).

The Academic Online University utilizes blended learning, which combines synchronous and asynchronous forms of online instruction (Anas, 2020). Students can take advantage of the flexibility of online education while retaining the ability to engage in real-time conversation with their instructors and peers (Al-Jarf, 2022). After obtaining recognition for its commitment to accessibility and inclusion, the Accessible Open University (AOU) in the Middle East has established itself as a leader in the field of promoting cultural diversity and inclusion within online learning environments. The educational organization consistently strives to improve the quality of the online learning opportunities it offers by implementing innovative pedagogical strategies and technological advances. This is done to enhance the overall educational experience of the institution's culturally diverse student body. Examples of such initiatives include the use of multimedia resources, interactive learning modules, and culturally diverse course materials that cater to the needs and interests of a population of students with a wide range of backgrounds and interests (Al-Essa, 2018). In addition, the AOU promotes cross-cultural contacts and collaborations among students by requiring them to collaborate on group projects, partake in online discussion forums, and engage in virtual classroom activities (Al-Jarf, 2022).

AOU instructors are provided with the necessary skills and knowledge to implement culturally responsive pedagogy. This indicates that they can identify the specific educational needs and scholastic preferences of their students from a variety of cultural backgrounds and adapt their teaching methods accordingly. Using this method, the institution is able to create an inclusive and supportive online learning environment for all students, regardless of their cultural or linguistic background. This environment promotes academic achievement and personal development for all students (Al-Essa, 2018). Thus, the Arab Open University functions as a model for educational institutions in the Middle East that seek to promote cultural diversity and inclusion in online learning environments. This is because Arab Open University was one of the first universities in the Gulf to offer exclusively online courses. Online education is capable of transcending cultural boundaries and fostering global understanding among students from diverse backgrounds. The blended learning approach, innovative use of technology, and commitment to culturally responsive pedagogy that are incorporated into the program demonstrate this potential.

3 Theoretical Perspectives on Cultural Diversity and Inclusion

Cultural diversity and inclusiveness are necessary for both traditional and virtual offline and online learning settings to be deemed effective (Banks & Banks, 2019). Many different theoretical stances emphasize the part that social and cultural contexts play in the formation of learning experiences, including Vygotsky's sociocultural theory (1978) and Bandura's social learning theory (1977). These theories contend that learners generate knowledge via their involvement in social interactions; hence, it is crucial for teachers to identify and value the many cultural backgrounds from which their students come in any classroom (Bandura, 1977; Vygotsky & Cole, 1978).

Learners from various cultural, linguistic, and ethnic origins are able to communicate with one another and learn from one another in the context of online learning environments, which afford these unique opportunities (Gudykunst, 2005). Research has demonstrated that students' critical thinking, creative thinking, and ability to solve problems may all improve when they are exposed to a culturally diverse online classroom environment (Denson & Zhang, 2010). In addition, being exposed to a wide variety of viewpoints and experiences may help foster empathy, global awareness, and cultural fluency (Banks, 2008). Enhanced Capabilities in Critical Thinking: Students are encouraged to assess and evaluate material from a variety of viewpoints when they are exposed to online learning settings that are culturally diverse. This helps students develop their ability to think critically (Denson & Zhang, 2010). Students who are given the opportunity to hear and consider arguments from a range of perspectives are better able to recognize and challenge their own preconceived notions and prejudices, as well as formulate arguments that are well-supported by evidence. Capacity for Enhanced Creativity as well as Problem-Solving: According to research conducted on the topic, varied groups are more likely to create new ideas and solutions than are groups with a similar composition. Students from a variety of cultural backgrounds are able to work together and offer their own unique viewpoints and methods to problem-solving in online learning settings, which can result in outputs that are more creative and successful (Denson & Zhang, 2010).

The Acquiring of Intercultural Competence: Students are able to build intercultural competence through participation in culturally diverse online learning settings. Intercultural competence refers to the capacity to successfully communicate, engage, and work with others from a variety of cultural backgrounds. Students have the opportunity to enhance their communication skills, become more adaptive and flexible in a variety of contexts, and gain a deeper knowledge of cultural differences and similarities when they interact with classmates who come from a variety of cultural backgrounds (Banks, 2008).

Developing a Sense of Community and Belonging: Learners can develop a sense of community and belonging when they participate in an online learning environment that is both inclusive and culturally relevant. When students have the experience of being valued and respected, they are more likely to be engaged and motivated to participate in learning activities, which ultimately leads to enhanced learning outcomes and a greater sense of pleasure (Ginns et al., 2013). Therefore, the presence of diverse cultures in online learning environments brings about a number of advantages. These advantages include the improvement of skills such as critical thinking, creativity, and problem-solving, as well as the growth of intercultural competence, global awareness, and a sense of belonging. Educators may provide students with online learning opportunities that are more effective, engaging, and inclusive for all students if they acknowledge and actively promote cultural diversity.

4 Culturally Responsive Pedagogy in Online Learning: Principles and Practices

The great range of cultural backgrounds, languages, and preferred learning styles that students bring to the classroom are acknowledged and celebrated by a teaching approach known as culturally responsive pedagogy. Regardless of the cultural traditions they come from, it aims to provide a learning environment that is welcoming to all students and gives them the tools they need to achieve academically and socially (Gay, 2018). Components of culturally responsive pedagogy include understanding the cultural backgrounds of students in online learning environments, accepting student differences, and using teaching strategies and materials that are culturally relevant (Gay, 2018).

One method to demonstrate respect for cultural diversity is by recognizing the enormous diversity of cultures among students and embracing the distinctive cultural perspectives and experiences that each student brings to the table. In addition, creating an environment for online education where students from various cultural backgrounds can feel welcomed, valued, and supported regardless of the subject being studied (Banks & Banks, 2019). For this reason, it is essential to put into practice course materials and teaching strategies that are meaningful and pertinent to students with a diversity of cultural backgrounds (Gay, 2018).

5 Online Learning Technologies and Cultural Diversity

Several technologies that can promote cultural inclusion and diversity in online learning environments are being used more frequently as a result of the rapid growth of online education. This section discusses how learning management systems (LMS), discussion boards, and multimedia technologies promote inclusivity and cultural diversity in online learning.

Learning management systems, such as Blackboard, Canvas, and Moodle, are platforms that are frequently used for the delivery of online courses and the management of educational content (Al-Azawei et al., 2016). These systems can be built in a way that makes it easy to facilitate culturally varied learning experiences by including elements that encourage inclusive instructional methods. The platform can be accessed by students in the language of their choice because the LMS can be altered to support a number of languages. A learning management system (LMS) can also be used to create differentiated learning paths, which provide students from various cultural backgrounds with access to curriculum materials and activities that are catered to their particular learning requirements.

Online discussion forums Students from vastly different cultural backgrounds can communicate and work together, thanks in large part to online discussion boards (2008) (Hew & Cheung). These platforms will give students the chance to interact with one another and exchange ideas, stories, and perspectives, which can promote intercultural dialogue. By encouraging an environment that is polite and open to dialogue, teachers can help create an inclusive learning environment for their pupils. Students will be able to express their cultural identities more freely and interact with a wider range of viewpoints as a result. Additionally, teachers can encourage student discussion of cultural issues using online discussion boards, developing both the students' cultural awareness and understanding. Tools for multimedia Using multimedia resources like movies, podcasts, and interactive simulations can further promote inclusivity and cultural diversity in online learning environments. These tools enable the delivery of course content in a range of formats, enabling instructors to cater to the different needs and preferences of students from various cultural backgrounds. If, for example, images, movies, and stories that represent a variety of cultures are presented, students may find it easier to connect with the material and gain a greater understanding of different cultural viewpoints (Castek & Beach, 2013). Multimedia resources can also be used to create cooperative learning activities like group projects and virtual simulations. These exercises can promote intercultural dialogue among students and help them become more culturally competent. The technology that enables online learning makes it possible to deploy tools that support cultural diversity and inclusion in learning environments. Utilizing the opportunities provided by learning management systems, online discussion forums, and multimedia tools, educators can create inclusive learning environments that accommodate the diverse needs and preferences of students who come from a variety of cultural backgrounds.

5.1 Multilingual Support and Translation Tools in Culturally Diverse Online Learning Environments

As online learning platforms continue to attract a diverse student body with students from a variety of linguistic backgrounds, it is becoming increasingly important to help non-native speakers surmount their language difficulties. Having support in multiple languages and translation tools can assist in bridging the communication divide between students in online learning environments with a diverse range of cultural backgrounds (Castaño-Muñoz et al., 2014).

The difficulty in comprehending course material and participating in online discussions is one of the obstacles encountered by non-native speakers when endeavoring to learn in online environments. Students who have trouble communicating because of language barriers may experience feelings of isolation, which can have negative effects on their motivation, engagement, and overall educational experience (Amiri & Ghonsooly, 2015). Consequently, it is of the utmost importance for instructors to implement strategies that cater to the diverse linguistic needs of their students.

One strategy for circumventing language barriers in online learning environments is the provision of instructional materials in multiple languages. This may involve translating textbooks, PowerPoint presentations, and any other available resources into the students' native tongues (Castaño-Muñoz et al., 2014). The incorporation of subtitles or transcripts within multimedia materials, such as video lectures and podcasts, can also aid non-native English speakers in understanding the content (Jónsdóttir et al., 2021). Integration of translation tools and materials that support multiple languages into the online learning environment is a further method. Integration of translation tools such as Google Translate into online discussion forums, chat rooms, and email systems may be required. This enables students to translate text and enhances their ability to communicate with both classmates and instructors (Dooly, 2017). In addition, providing non-native speakers with dictionaries, glossaries, and other reading materials can aid in the development of their language abilities.

In addition to cultivating a sense of community and enhancing language acquisition, it can be quite beneficial to encourage students from diverse linguistic backgrounds to support one another and collaborate. Organizing group activities that bring together native speakers and non-native speakers, for instance, is a fantastic way to foster cross-cultural understanding and language exchange (Dooly, 2017). Additionally, students can utilize online discussion forums devoted to language learning to practice their language skills, pose questions, and receive feedback from their peers. In the context of online education, the instructors play a crucial role in fostering an environment that is linguistically inclusive. Teachers can nurture students' language development and help them overcome language barriers by providing non-native speakers with individualized feedback and learning scaffolds (Amiri & Ghonsooly, 2015). Teachers must also be aware of the possibility of cultural bias in the materials they use to teach with and the methods they employ to evaluate students' performance, and they must work to make the educational environment more welcoming to students from a variety of linguistic backgrounds. To ensure the academic success of non-native speakers and encourage their participation, it is crucial to integrate multilingual support and translation technologies into culturally diverse online learning environments. Educators can create a linguistically inclusive online learning environment that fosters intercultural understanding and meets the specific needs of students from diverse linguistic backgrounds by implementing the following suggestions.

5.2 Case Studies and Best Practices in Culturally Diverse Online Learning Environments

5.2.1 Case Study 1: The Global Classroom Project

The Global Classroom Project links K-12 courses in many countries using a collaborative online learning platform in order to encourage global citizenship and cultural exchange (Lindsay & Davis, 2013). As part of this effort, students are urged to participate in cross-cultural discussions, online debates, and group projects with their classmates who have different cultural backgrounds. Educators employ a variety of digital tools, including video conferencing, online discussion forums, and shared online workspaces, to promote multicultural learning experiences.

Best Practices:

- It is important to promote collaboration and communication between peers from various cultural backgrounds.
- Using digital tools to encourage both asynchronous and real-time dialogues.
- Incorporate discussions of global issues and viewpoints into academic programs.

5.2.2 Case Study 2: University of British Columbia's Online Master of Educational Technology Program

The University of British Columbia (UBC) offers a Master of Educational Technology (MET) degree that is entirely online. Professionals working in the disciplines of education, healthcare, or business are the target audience for this program (Veletsianos, 2016). The program has a strong emphasis on cultural diversity and inclusion by utilizing a range of teaching strategies, learning materials, and assessment techniques that are specifically

designed to satisfy the diverse needs of students from various cultural backgrounds.
Best practices:

- Providing culturally relevant study materials and teaching content.
- Making flexible, accessible learning pathways available to accommodate different student preferences.
- Including a range of opinions and ideas in online discussions and activities.

5.2.3 Case Study 3: Singapore Management University's (SMU) Blended Learning Initiative

A blended learning method has been implemented into Singapore Management University's (SMU) undergraduate programs with the intention of promoting cultural inclusiveness and diversity among their student bodies (Gikandi & Morrow, 2016). In order to promote cultural awareness, intercultural communication, and collaborative learning among these students, who hailed from a range of cultural backgrounds, the initiative involved rethinking the course's content, pedagogy, and evaluations.
Best practices:

- One of the best practices is to incorporate case studies, examples, and knowledge that is culturally relevant into the curriculum.
- Encourage pupils to think about their own cultural identities and experiences as another effective practice.
- Giving pupils the chance to engage in cross-cultural dialogue and activities that prioritize cooperative learning.

Lessons Learned from Case Studies:

- The significance of creating a welcoming and tolerant online learning community that respects cultural differences and acknowledges their value.
- The requirement for educators to engage in ongoing professional development and training in order to successfully incorporate culturally responsive pedagogy and practices for online instruction.
- The role of technology in fostering cross-cultural communication and collaboration as well as providing access to a variety of educational resources and opportunities.

5.3 Cultural Diversity at the Arab Open University, Saudi Arabia

The present study is investigating the extent to which the online instructional design and pedagogy at the Arab Open University (AOU) take into account students' race, gender, country of origin, and language. The goal of this investigation was to determine whether or not these factors are taken into account during online lectures. The purpose of the study is to investigate how students' disparities in language and ethnicity expressed themselves in a virtual setting during online lectures and how tutors promoted those differences. The research design encompassed three data collection methods. The research purposefully uses a mixed-methods design to obtain a panoramic view of the phenomena investigated. Therefore, one has used quantitative and qualitative data collection forms to analyze holistically the research questions at stake. Greene et al. (cited by Johson and Onwuegbuzie, 2004) suggested five main rationales for conducting mixed-methods research:

1. Triangulation: the confirmation of results by different methods.
2. Complementarity: results from one method are used to enhance, elaborate, or clarify results from another method.
3. Initiation: where new insights are obtained which will stimulate new research questions.
4. Development: results from one method shape another method.
5. Expansion: expanding the breadth and the range of the research by using different methods for different lines of enquiry.

The participants are 60 students enrolled at the Arab Open University, Faculty of Language Studies, and five tutors who are assistant professors at the Department of English. The students and tutors are from different AOU branches in Saudi Arabia, belonging to Riyadh, Jeddah, Dammam, and Madinah. Anonymous sampling was used to ensure the objectivity and validity of the data collected.

Students and teachers at the Riyadh Branch of the Arab Open University were each given their own semi-structured questionnaire to fill out, and both were asked about their experiences with online-taught classes. The goal of these questionnaires was to get insights into the viewpoints held by both students and teachers regarding the manner in which cultural diversity was addressed in the context of the online learning environment. After collecting and analyzing the data from the questionnaires, common themes, patterns, and trends that were connected to the study question were identified and discussed.

An opened-ended teachers' questionnaire was designed to collect answers on teachers' practices and perceptions about cultural diversity in their courses. The questionnaire comprises seven questions designed with Microsoft Forms and sent to tutors electronically. The answers collected are five from tutors who are assistant professors at the department of English in the faculty of language studies at the Arab Open University. The tutors belong to different branches of AOU: Riyadh, Dammam, and Jeddah. The tutors teach different courses that comprise cultural topics and themes, such as AA100A, AA100B, and EL111. As for their experience, the tutors' experience at the AOU ranges from a minimum of six months to an average of three years. In addition to these tools, a purposive analysis of the AA100B course specifications was selected for analysis. The course specifications is evaluated to determine whether it contains components, questions, or activities that encourage cultural diversity and take into consideration differences in language and ethnicity. In order to identify the presence of culturally inclusive content in the present material, a content analysis approach was utilized as the methodology of choice.

5.4 *Cultural Diversity at the Arab Open University Online Lecturers: Attitudes and Considerations*

In the processing and interpretation of the information gleaned from the questionnaires, the study of the lecture materials, and the observations, both quantitative and qualitative approaches were used. The quantitative data from the questionnaires was summarized using descriptive tables, while the qualitative data from the questionnaires, as well as the examination of lecture material and observation, was analyzed using thematic analysis. Thematic analysis included data coding, the identification of emergent themes, and the interpretation of the findings in relation to the research question. This research design provided a thorough examination of how far cultural diversity and inclusion were addressed in the Arab Open University's online instructional design and pedagogy. The study uncovered how the AOU's online learning environment accommodated students' linguistic and ethnic differences by collecting rich and diverse data using a combination of semi-structured questionnaires, lecture material analysis, and observation. This information sheds light on how the

AOU's online learning environment accommodated students' linguistic and ethnic differences. The findings led to recommendations for instructors on how to enrich and construct a culturally diverse environment while students participate in online lectures.

The student survey responses provide fascinating insights into the cultural aspects of the online learning experience. These conclusions can be drawn from the data collected:

Diverse demographics The responders are a varied bunch, with 44% from Saudi Arabia and the remaining 56% from other countries, namely, Syria, India, Pakistan, Jordan, Yemen, Egypt, and Palestine. There is a chance for cross-cultural learning and interaction because of this diversity.

Cultural Sharing According to the survey, there is room for improvement when it comes to expressing and talking about cultural customs during online classes. In the survey 52% of respondents have not shared their cultural traditions with their tutor, compared to 48% who have. Only 57% of respondents reported that their tutors had encouraged them to discuss and compare different cultures in class.

Cultural Sensitivity More than half (54% of the respondents) reported feeling shocked when certain concepts or philosophies were first introduced in the class. This shows how the discussions and course material need to be more sensitive to cultural differences.

Interest in Global Cultures The majority of respondents, 91%, indicated a desire to learn more about global cultures, indicating a high level of interest and openness to cross-cultural learning.

Comparing Cultures According to the data, different tutors may encourage students to compare their own culture to that of others. While 39% of the respondents believed their teachers had encouraged them to draw such comparisons when talking about holy sites or recreational activities, 16% disagreed, and 45% weren't sure. According to the analysis of the questionnaire responses, there is room for improvement in terms of encouraging cultural sensitivity and sharing in the online learning environment, despite the fact that students have a keen interest in doing so. By encouraging students to share their cultural perspectives and fostering discussions that contrast and compare various cultural experiences, tutors can play a critical role in facilitating this.

6 Online Pedagogical Practices at the Arab Open University, Saudi Arabia

The tutors' responses were exported from Microsoft forms and put into tables. The data was then analyzed using Voyant Tools, which is an open-source, web-based application for performing text and data mining. Developed by Stéfan Sinclair at McGill University and Geoffrey Rockwell at the University of Alberta. This tool provides lightweight text analytics such as word frequency lists, frequency distribution plots, and KWIC (Key Word in Context) analysis. The objective is to fetch for frequency, look through the importance given to culture, and weigh the tutors' awareness of its importance by looking at the text ratio and density.

Tables 10.1 and 10.2 (below) are anonymous responses of five assistant teachers at the Arab Open University, Saudi Arabia. They both indicate their practices and considerations while designing and preparing for their courses.

Tutors admit that when introducing ideas on cultural encounters, they find students interested in exploring new themes and curious to learn about other cultures. One of the tutors highlights the importance of respecting other religions, this can be challenging particularly when students think it is useless to study or look at other religions. The fourth tutor points out this issue, for example, when addressing a taboo topic like

Table 10.1 Cultural considerations for course design

Questions 1	*Do you take into account your students' cultural experience when designing the course materials (slides)?*
Tutor 1 Response	Yes
Tutor 2 Response	Yes
Tutor 3 Response	Of course, I have to respect their beliefs and their background while I am presenting some ideas that clash with their beliefs, such as in the chapter on the Dalai Lama and tradition and dissent in English Christianity in part A.
Tutor 4 Response	Depends on the type of course material and the time we are given to cover it. If the course material that is being covered is culturally sensitive, then addressing the cultural aspects and taking into consideration the student's cultural backgrounds is essential.
Tutor 5 Response	Yes

Table 10.2 Students' cultural awareness

Question 2	Do you find students responsive when introducing ideas on cultural encounters, world's cultures, religions? How would you describe their attitudes and reactions?
Tutor 1	Yes. I find them interested in such topics. Such ideas open their eyes to so many experiences of cultural encounters that they daily witness around them locally and globally. They show more understanding and awareness of these encounters.
Tutor 2	Yes, they are always eager to learn about other societies
Tutor 3	Yes, sometimes it is religious and as a tutor I always remind them of the importance of respecting other people's beliefs.
Tutor 4	Overall, it is not challenging as long as I explain to them that they should look at it from the perspective of understanding a different culture. However, if the material examines taboo topics, like homosexuality, students show unwillingness to look at it objectively from the lens of the other's culture.
Tutor 5	Most of them don't respond and I do believe it is because they don't train to give their opinions.

homosexuality, students refute and may find it shocking. Some students do not respond, as the fifth tutor asserted. They lack cultural understanding and are not trained enough to explore other cultures. Table 10.3 provides further information on how students respond to cultural and philosophical notions.

In addition to using Voyant tools and to gain a deeper understanding of the obtained data, an inductive coding (see Fig. 10.1) was used, where the codes were selected from the raw data itself. This method would allow the research to come up with new themes and explore possible theories.

Figure 10.1 shows the coding scheme developed to categorize and analyze the data, focusing on themes and concepts related to cultural diversity, teaching methods, and student engagement. The tutors' questionnaire responses were also coded based on emerging themes and concepts related to cultural diversity, teaching methods, and student engagement. A tutor's response emphasizing respect for students' cultural backgrounds was coded as CD, while responses detailing the use of culturally diverse materials or inclusion of cross-cultural discussions were coded as TM (Teaching Methods). Instances where tutors mentioned student reactions or engagement with cultural diversity topics were coded as SR (Student Reactions), capturing students' active engagement with the subject matter. Additionally, examples of inclusivity resources used by tutors were coded as IR (Inclusivity Resources). Through systematic coding of course

Table 10.3 Students and philosophical concepts

Question 3	How do students respond to cultural ideas and philosophical theories on leisure, the notion of sacredness, etc.?
Tutor 1	The discussion of philosophical concepts such as leisure and sacredness resulted in positive responses on the part of students. They began to understand the philosophical background of such topics and analyze the intended goal behind the activities which are related to these concepts.
Tutor 2	Interested
Tutor 3	The majority find the course is an interesting one, especially part B.
Tutor 4	Philosophical topics tend to be the most challenging for students to understand. However, I think that the root cause is that the examples in the textbook are culturally centered. Students respond better when the examples given are from their own culture.
Tutor 5	Some of them are active and share their travel experience and cultural diversity encountered or have read about. Others are either shy to respond or have no idea about these topics.

Fig. 10.1 The process of inductive coding

content and questionnaire responses, the study facilitated a comprehensive examination of the presence and emphasis of cultural diversity in online lectures. We counted the occurrences of each theme in the tutors' responses and calculated the percentage of each theme/code for every question.

7   Cultural Awareness and Cultural Sensitivity: The Need of Urgent Implementation at the AOU

Different courses at the Arab Open University incorporate themes discussing Western culture, Western philosophies, and ancient histories. These cultural themes are aimed not only at preparing the students to be graduates in the field of humanities, yet to make them explore the world, compare, and understand these differences. This research has examined students' cultural awareness and how teaching cultural themes Online is undertaken by tutors. According to the overall results, the present study points out important issues that urgently need to be remedied by tutors and syllabus designers at AOU. The sample population of the study is characterized by its rich diversity of backgrounds, and this influences a lecture delivery considering the different cultures of students during the lecture. The majority of students highlighted that they are shocked when some topics are introduced. That is why this study is valuable as it alerts tutors to navigate the crucial experiences and themes introduced when preparing for the course, taking cultural sensitivity into account. Another aspect that could be noted during the design of this study and its undertaking is how some students question the different cultural themes covered in the different courses. As a tutor at the Arab Open University, in different occasion, whether in AA100B *Past and Present Course*, or EL118 which is a reading course, students sometimes when being introduced to ancient civilizations and their practices, or beliefs, they stress the inutility of these topics which has prompted the researcher to conduct the present study. Cultural sensitivity has to be addressed and reflected in the design of the material used Online during VC classes. In the tutors' responses, one has observed that all tutors mostly use illustrations and videos. Online lectures are challenging when it comes to introducing cultures or discussing a sensitive topic of religion or a taboo topic for students. With the emergence of new digital tools, cultural diversity can be explored with vital techniques and platforms, particularly collaborative projects that can bridge the cultural differences encountered within a course.

8 Towards the Incorporation of Cultural Diversity Via Digital Tools

Based on our discussion in this chapter, I would like to suggest vital practices to consider when designing courses and teaching Online. At the Arab Open University, tutors need to conduct workshops for students on *Cultural Sensitivity* where students from different cultures will collaborate with one another creating projects and searching cultural scenarios. This projects can be created Online also and shared through different platforms. As one's study covers the online aspect of lectures, practical suggestions are made to offer tutors the opportunity to further develop features of cultural diversity in their classes:

1. *Virtual Field Trips*: Virtual field trips can allow students to explore cultural sites and landmarks around the world without leaving the classroom. Many museums, historical sites, and cultural organizations offer virtual tours and exhibits that can be accessed online.
2. *Video Conferencing*: Video conferencing tools can be used to connect students with people from different cultures and backgrounds. Teachers can arrange virtual conversations with guest speakers, students from other countries, or experts in a particular field to promote cross-cultural communication and understanding.
3. *Online Collaborative Tools*: Online collaborative tools, such as Google Docs, can be used to facilitate group work and collaborative projects that incorporate diverse perspectives. These tools can allow students from different cultural backgrounds to work together and share their knowledge and experiences.
4. *Cultural and Diversity Apps*: There are many mobile apps available that promote cultural diversity and inclusion. These apps can provide information about different cultures, languages, and customs, as well as provide opportunities for students to connect with peers from different cultural backgrounds.
5. *Digital Storytelling*: Digital storytelling tools can be used to allow students to share their own cultural stories and experiences. These tools can allow students to create videos, podcasts, or other multimedia presentations that showcase their cultural heritage and perspectives.
6. *Cultural and Diversity Apps*: There are many mobile apps available that promote cultural diversity and inclusion. These apps can pro-

vide information about different cultures, languages, and customs, as well as provide opportunities for students to connect with peers from different cultural backgrounds.

Online collaborative tools that can be used to facilitate group work and collaborative projects. Here are some examples:

1. *Google Docs*: Google Docs is a free online tool that allows students to collaborate on documents, spreadsheets, and presentations in real-time. This tool is easy to use and can be accessed from any device with an internet connection.
2. *Padlet*: Padlet is an online bulletin board that allows students to collaborate and share ideas using text, images, and videos. This tool is versatile and can be used for a variety of projects, including brainstorming, group discussions, and project planning.
3. *Trello*: Trello is a project management tool that allows students to organize and collaborate on projects. This tool uses a visual board format to help students track progress and communicate with one another.
4. *Slack*: Slack is a messaging platform that allows students to communicate and collaborate in real-time. This tool is particularly useful for group projects that require frequent communication and coordination.
5. *Figma*: Figma is a design tool that allows students to create and collaborate on digital designs, such as websites, apps, and graphics. This tool is particularly useful for design projects that require collaboration and feedback from multiple team members.
6. *Miro*: Miro is a virtual whiteboard that allows students to collaborate and share ideas using text, images, and other media. This tool is useful for brainstorming, project planning, and group discussions.
7. *Canva*: Canva is a design tool that allows students to create and collaborate on visual designs, such as posters, infographics, and social media graphics. This tool is easy to use and can be accessed from any device with an internet connection.
8. *Basecamp*: Basecamp is a project management tool that allows students to organize and collaborate on projects. This tool includes features such as to-do lists, group chats, and file sharing and can be accessed from any device with an internet connection.

In addition to tools, educators shall be supported with training to advance their understanding of e-learning strategies, online pedagogy, and the use of a variety of educational technology tools. Educators should also be provided with ongoing training and opportunities for professional development. As for the course content that is inclusive and culturally sensitive, curriculum developers and teachers at the AOU should make sure that e-learning materials are inclusive, sensitive to cultural differences, and pertinent to the many different learning needs of students. The syllabus shall not exclude cultural differences or Western cultural civilizations as per the Saudi 2030 vision to become the touristic destination with international visitors from all over the world. It has to be balanced in terms of incorporating both Western and Arabic cultural themes so that students would be engaged in a comprehensive and rich experience where would value theirs, appreciate the others' cultures. Therefore, the university shall accommodate this plan by preparing students to be culturally aware. It is essential for teachers to prepare and check their approach before presenting information in a culturally sensitive and appropriate manner. The following main points are to be considered:

1. Recognize the cultural context: Teachers should research the cultural setting of the subject they are teaching.
2. Examining stereotypes: Instructors should refrain from presenting or generalizing about a culture. It is crucial to convey information in a courteous, respectful, and culturally aware manner.
3. Recognize your own prejudices and how they could affect how you present the information. Teachers should be conscious of their own biases. Approaching the subject with an open mind and a desire to learn is crucial.
4. Use inclusive language: When talking about cultural issues, teachers should use inclusive vocabulary. This entails using language that is gender-neutral, abstaining from using derogatory phrases, and being conscious of how language affects various cultures.

9 Conclusion

The goal of this study was to look into the impact of cultural diversity on e-learning experiences and the role tutors play in the process of creating a culturally inclusive environment for students in Saudi Arabia. An extensive review of the relevant literature, an examination of the primary data collected via questionnaires, and an assessment of numerous online learning platforms all contributed to the effective completion of the research objectives. The results of this study show how vital it is in the context of e-learning to recognize and appreciate the cultural diversity among participants. The presence of students from a diverse range of cultural origins in the classes studied provided several opportunities for cross-cultural learning and interaction. Despite this, there is still room for growth in the e-learning environment in terms of promoting cultural exchange, sensitivity, and comparison. The student questionnaire results show that, while there is a strong desire to learn about other cultures, not all students feel encouraged to offer their cultural perspectives or participate in conversations comparing different cultural experiences. This is demonstrated by the fact that, while there is a considerable interest in learning about different cultures, there is also a large interest. Tutors' contributions substantially contribute to the creation of a culturally inclusive environment. They can improve the e-learning experience by encouraging students to share their cultural traditions, facilitating debates that compare and contrast different cultural experiences, and being aware of the possibility of students experiencing cultural shock as a result of the course content or discussions. E-learning platforms can also help to achieve this goal by creating culturally inclusive instructional design and delivering materials that promote intercultural understanding and communication. Finally, the recognition and incorporation of cultural diversity into the educational process are critical to the success of e-learning programs in Saudi Arabia and elsewhere. This is true regardless of where the initiatives are carried out. E-learning has the potential to be a strong tool for enhancing global understanding, tolerance, and appreciation for the diversity and depth of human experiences. This can be accomplished by implementing culturally inclusive procedures and encouraging intercultural exchange.

REFERENCES

Al-Asmari, A. M., & Rabb Khan, M. S. (2020). E-learning in Saudi Arabia: Past, present and future. *Near and Middle Eastern Journal of Research in Education, 2014*(1), 2.

Al-Azawei, A., Parslow, P., & Lundqvist, K. (2016). Barriers and opportunities of e-learning implementation in Iraq: A case of public universities. *The International Review of Research in Open and Distributed Learning, 17*(5).

Al-Essa, N. S. (2018). The impact of using Edmodo as a blended learning medium on promoting Saudi EFL female secondary school students' English grammar. *Arab World English Journal, 221*, 1–112. https://doi.org/10.24093/awej/th.221

Al-Jarf, R. (2022). Developing students' global awareness in EFL reading and speaking. *Online Submission, 4*(1), 31–38.

Amiri, M., & Ghonsooly, B. (2015). The relationship between English learning anxiety and the students' achievement on examinations. *Journal of Language Teaching and Research, 6*(4), 855–865.

Anas, A. (2020). Perceptions of Saudi students to blended learning environments at the University of Bisha, Saudi Arabia. *Arab World English Journal, 6*, 261–277. https://doi.org/10.24093/awej/call6.17

Arab Open University. (n.d.). Arab Open University - KSA. https://www.arabou.edu.sa/Pages/default.aspx

Bandura, A. (1977). *Social learning theory*. Prentice Hall.

Banks, J. A. (2008). Diversity, group identity, and citizenship education in a global age. *Educational Researcher, 37*(3), 129–139.

Banks, J. A., & Banks, C. A. M. (Eds.). (2019). *Multicultural education: Issues and perspectives*. John Wiley & Sons.

Castaño-Muñoz, J., Duart, J. M., & Sancho-Vinuesa, T. (2014). The internet in face-to-face higher education: Can interactive learning improve academic achievement? *British Journal of Educational Technology, 45*(1), 149–159.

Castek, J., & Beach, R. (2013). Using apps to support disciplinary literacy and science learning. *Journal of Adolescent & Adult Literacy, 56*(7), 554–564.

Denson, N., & Zhang, S. (2010). The impact of student experiences with diversity on developing graduate attributes. *Studies in Higher Education, 35*(5), 529–543.

Dooly, M. (2017). Telecollaboration. In *The handbook of technology and second language teaching and learning* (pp. 169–183).

Doroob. (2021). Retrieved April 29, 2023, from http://doroob.sa/

Education Ministry. (2021). *The Kingdom of Saudi Arabia*. Ministry of Education. Retrieved April 29, 2023, from https://moe.gov.sa/(X(1)S(nydys4cjuij0o2ruvrjit3yb))/en/pages/default.aspx

Gay, G. (2018). *Culturally responsive teaching: Theory, research, and practice*. Teachers College Press.

Gikandi, J. W., & Morrow, D. (2016). Designing and implementing peer formative feedback within online learning environments. *Technology, Pedagogy and Education, 25*(2), 153–170.

Ginns, P., Martin, A. J., & Marsh, H. W. (2013). Designing instructional text in a conversational style: A meta-analysis. *Educational Psychology Review, 25*, 445–472.

Gudykunst, W. B. (Ed.). (2005). *Theorizing about intercultural communication*. Sage.

Hamdan, A. K. (2014). The reciprocal and correlative relationship between learning culture and online education: A case from Saudi Arabia. *The International Review of Research in Open and Distributed Learning, 15*(1).

Jónsdóttir, A. A., Kang, Z., Sun, T., Mandal, S., & Kim, J. E. (2021). The effects of language barriers and time constraints on online learning performance: An eye-tracking study. *Human Factors,* 00187208211010949.

Khalil, R., Mansour, A. E., Fadda, W. A., Almisnid, K., Aldamegh, M., Al-Nafeesah, A., et al. (2020). The sudden transition to synchronized online learning during the COVID-19 pandemic in Saudi Arabia: A qualitative study exploring medical students' perspectives. *BMC Medical Education, 20,* 1–10.

Khan, M. U. H. (2016). Saudi Arabia's vision 2030. *Defence Journal, 19*(11), 36.

Lindsay, J., & Davis, V. A. (2013). *Flattening classrooms, engaging minds: Move to global collaboration one step at a time.* Allyn & Bacon.

Moran, J. (2021, December 16). Saudi Arabia's National Elearning Center partners with Coursera to launch nationwide skill training program. *Coursera Blog.* Retrieved April 29, 2023, from https://blog.coursera.org/saudi-arabias-national-elearning-center-partners-with-coursera-to-launch-nationwide-skill-training-program/

Saudi Electronic University (SEU). (n.d.). Retrieved April 29, 2023, from https://seu.edu.sa/en/home/

Smith, P. (1982). In Search of a multicultural society: Culture and education in multicultural societies.

Veletsianos, G. (Ed.). (2016). *Emergence and innovation in digital learning: Foundations and applications.* Athabasca University Press.

Vygotsky, L. S., & Cole, M. (1978). *Mind in society: Development of higher psychological processes.* Harvard University Press.

Weber, A. S. (2018). Saudi Arabia. *E-Learning in the Middle East and North Africa (MENA) Region,* 355–381. https://doi.org/10.1007/978-3-319-68999-9_16

NELC الإلكتروني للتعلم الوطني المركز | NELC: National E-Learning Center. المركز الوطني للتعلم الإلكتروني National E-Learning Center. (2021). Retrieved April 29, 2023, from https://nelc.gov.sa/en/nelc

PART IV

Diversity Education and Intercultural Communication Issues in Language Learning in the MENA Region

CHAPTER 11

The Mediatization of Education: Classroom Mediation as an Agent of Change in Middle Eastern Higher Education Systems

Hussein AlAhmad and *Elias Kukali*

1 Introduction

The majority of Arab first- and second-year university students in the Middle East have attended public schools and experienced large classes with traditional learning modes; most of them come from single-sex public schools that are segregated based on learner or teacher gender (Al-Zarah, 2008; Atia, 2018). In first-year university classrooms where students from private and public schools merge, this poses serious challenges for students and teachers alike, given their diverse cultural backgrounds, varying levels of personal and linguistic skills, and attitudes. Unlike public schools, private schools nurture a culture that emphasizes personal and linguistic skills equally to pedagogical achievements. Additionally, most reputable Arab universities adopt English as the

H. AlAhmad (✉) • E. Kukali
Arab American University, Ramallah, Palestine
e-mail: hussein.alahmad@aaup.edu

auxiliary medium of instruction. Hence, the prolonged reduction of teamwork and linguistic skills amongst heterogeneous groups of several backgrounds leads to emotional and rational limitations that are expected to hinder their ability to interact and reproduce knowledge (AlAhmad, 2021c; Wilkens, 2011). In such a heterogeneous Teaching and Learning (T&L) environment, there materialize numerous *T&L barriers* of subcultural, linguistic, emotional, and rational nature that hinder students' effective learning. The chapter explores the indispensable relationship between the two different, albeit interrelated, and intersected fields of teaching-learning and media-communication. The aim is to identify teaching aids and best practices that might play a role in fostering an environment whereby "we understand education initially as a communicative system that is dedicated to the acquisition of new and future relevant knowledge in lifelong processes of appropriation" (Marci-Boehncke & Rath, 2020: p. 5). In treating the aforesaid T&L barriers, the concept of *a 'schooling model'*, or a *'school educational model'* encompasses the educational theoretical approaches a school adopts and the approved teaching methods being used within its classrooms, which determine how the school operates, also its curriculum's cognitive and behavioural focus, as well as its pedagogy in general (Fitriani & Istaryatiningtias, 2020; Ghani, 2013).

In an era of unprecedented mediatic turn, a promising solution in fostering a motivative, innovative, and productive T&L environment is *'classroom mediation'*, a critical concept that emphasizes teachers' attempts to incorporate the two fields of communication and education in integrating heterogeneous and multi-cultural classrooms into a melting pot of interactive T&L milieu (AlAhmad, 2021b). In classroom mediation, teachers are seen as facilitators of T&L, providing their students with motivative, innovative, and productive media-aided T&L techniques and best practices (*classroom mediation dynamics*) that can powerfully engage them in authentic opportunities to learn from each other, think creatively, stimulate novel learning skills, and enhance their ability to control themselves both rationally and emotionally in a healthy and democratic environment (Lundby, 2014; Rawolle, 2010; Rawolle & Lingard, 2014; Walsh & Apperley, 2014). Classroom mediation draws on *'Mediatisation'* as a metatheory that explores the interrelationship between the *media logic* and the *pedagogical logic* in order to understand its societal impact. The *Media logic* refers to the intended quest of the media dominance of information processing, presentation, and storytelling techniques in varied societal interaction processes to take advantage of its own mediums, formats, and representations to become more competitive in the ongoing struggle to capture people's attention to designated issues and goals. The *Pedagogical Logic*, however, is most commonly understood as the systematic approach to understanding teaching and knowledge acquisition in light of the theory and best practices of T&L and how this might influence, or be influenced by, the cognitive and behavioural development of teachers and learners alike. Mediatization "incorporates a plurality of interrelating concepts and processes and suggests a complex interplay of media forces on and in education" (Rawolle & Lingard, 2014, p. 597). Classroom mediation is one key concept among these, which builds on classroom mediation dynamics as facilitators for class management and student engagement in a successful T&L (Forsler, 2020). In classroom mediation, a teacher's role goes beyond content expertise and traditional methods of lecturing to be student-centred, focused on excellence and critical skills, constantly exploring gaps among students in the T&L process, and adjusting their teaching methods accordingly.

2   Chapter Aims

The chapter emphasizes the importance of classroom mediation in T&L in Higher Education (HE) as a theoretical object of inquiry and conceptual elaboration. Emphasizing first- and second-year classrooms, the chapter inspects the application of these concepts as agents of change in the T&L process and their relation to the theory of education in terms of fostering effective education. The chapter also examines the premise that media facilitates "a priori" conditions for effective communication to promote cognition and knowledge acquisition, socio-cultural dimension, and instructional dimension in T&L (Breiter, 2014; Friesen & Hug, 2011; Hjarvard, 2014; Thompson, 2018). Ultimately the chapter aims at finding how all that might play a role in achieving T&L's desired *cognitive, pedagogical,* and *behavioural* goals or dimensions (henceforth T&L dimensions) and its societal impact and regional development.

In the T&L process, the *cognitive dimension* encompasses the developing individual's mental skills through knowledge acquisition, comprehension, application, analysis, synthesis, and evaluation (Anderson et al., 2001). The *pedagogical dimension*, however, aims at implementing a well-organized set of methods, strategies, and approaches to promote student learning and enrich the overall system of education (Kapur, 2020). The *behavioural dimension* deals with learning activities as modifiers for individual behaviour through an appropriate system of rewards and encouragement to achieve social interactions among students of varied backgrounds in a classroom (Leroy & Ramanantsoa, 1997; Milem et al., 2005). The organized and integrated interaction between these dimensions is nominated to foster *synergistic mechanisms* in the T&L process, primarily those intended to promote student' *engagement, motivation, productivity,* and *innovation*. These mechanisms are integrated in the T&L to mitigate socio-cultural and school-inherited disparities in students' learning styles (*T&L-inherited barriers*) that are likely to hinder levels of students excel in the T&L. Classroom mediation can boost the three main dimensions in the T&L process, primarily by raising teachers' awareness of the discrepancies among their students, endorsing alternative individualized learning styles, and fostering students' engagement in the T&L activities. As articulated by the Glossary of Education Reform, student engagement refers to "the degree of attention, curiosity, interest, optimism, and passion that students show when they are learning or being taught, which extends to the level of motivation they have to learn and progress in their education (Education Reform, 2016)."

3 Queries and Hypotheses

The chapter examines whether and to what extent the incorporation of classroom mediation dynamics in T&L might play a role in mitigating T&L-inherited barriers. There is a prediction that there will be significant differences in Palestinian undergraduate students (henceforth undergraduates) *cognitive, pedagogical, and behavioural* learning achievements, attributed to school milieu/location, school type, and schooling model. This prediction will be tested as follows:

H_1: There is a significant main effect of school milieu/location on the cognitive, pedagogical, and behavioural learning achievements among undergraduates while controlling the effects of the covariate variable of classroom mediation level at an alpha level of 0.05.

H_2: There is a significant main effect of the undergraduate schooling model on their cognitive, pedagogical, and behavioural learning achievement while controlling the effects of the covariate variable of classroom mediation level at an alpha level of 0.05.

H_3: There is a significant main effect of school type on the cognitive, pedagogical, and behavioural learning achievement among university students while controlling the effects of the variable of classroom mediation level at an alpha level of 0.05.

H_4: There is a significant difference in the degrees of cognitive, behavioural, and pedagogical achievements in undergraduates learning, in terms of undergraduates' levels of engagement, innovation, productivity, and motivation when classroom mediation is applied in T&L.

4   Literature and Theory

The word *educate* comes from Latin, indicating an active process of 'upbringing or training (Bennett, 2019).' The word *teach*, however, comes from German to convey the passive activity of showing, declaring, or persuading (ibid.). The difference between the terms has resulted in various instructional strategies, ranging from active to passive, from which teachers can choose to deliver designated content successfully. The core life skills are said to be better gained when appropriately incorporated into the education process. UNICEF, UNESCO, and WHO identified these skills as effective communication, self-awareness, critical and creative thinking, decision-making, problem-solving, interpersonal relationship, empathy, stress coping, and emotions (Singh, 2003). Classroom mediation is theorized to aptly foster these skills in T&L, maximizing its efficiency and also minimizing adverse effects on T&L quality and outputs (Felder & Henriques, 1995; Shabiralyani et al., 2015).

UNICEF (2016) identified a four-dimensional learning approach tailored to the Middle East and North Africa T&L needs: *'Learning to Know'* (Cognitive Dimension), *'Learning to Do'* (Instrumental Dimension), *'Learning to Be'* (Individual Dimension), and *'Learning to Live Together'* (Social Dimension). This approach expanded to encompass a set of twelve – built on evidence – life-long core skills that underline the importance of classroom mediation. Most of these skills can be acquired and sustained via designated forms of T&L that recognize multiple learning pathways. Reflecting on the effectiveness and inter/relatedness of these skills and concepts to classroom mediation and T&L in Palestinian undergraduate programs is relevant because, in T&L, gaps in acquiring these skills often occur between the learning styles of students and the teaching style/strategies of instructors (Rahal & Palfreyman, 2009). These gaps further reinforce within heterogeneous classrooms due to shortcomings related to various lingual, cross-cultural, and communication deficiencies among students (Wahyudi, 2018). Classroom mediation, which is postulated to appropriately handle such gaps in T&L through the efficient application of media aids designed to improve learning and maximize efficiency (Felder & Henriques, 1995; Shabiralyani et al., 2015), also helps teachers minimize gaps between students with varied backgrounds, e.g., *active* learners, who learn better in situations requiring them to interact, and *reflective* learners, who learn better when teachers engage them in discussions (Felder, 1988).

Classroom mediation means more than communicating; it acts as an agent of change. "Change agency has become an integral and essential part of advancing learning, instruction, and performance (Savoy & Carr-Chellman, 2014, p. 618)." As change agents, the role of mediation in educational innovation is promising, with many teachers still dealing with content expertise as an essential ingredient they need for effective teaching (Backlund, 2008). For others, however, it is about relying merely on making traditional methods more accessible to facilitate T&L rather than exploring new techniques and technologies to support students' learning (Backlund, 2008). In addition, there is a demand for interactive T&L processes to motivate students' critical thinking and promote their in-class participation to engender *positive change* at the level of *attitudes* for teachers as facilitators of the educational system and students as its direct product (AlAhmad, 2021b; Ndongko & Agu, 1985).

For Savoy and Carr-Chellman (2014), "Communication has evolved [...] to a more collaborative communication network that allows participants to be involved in the change decisions and development (p. 624)." Mediatization emerged as a concept with considerable promise for education research (Rawolle & Lingard, 2014). It broadly refers to how media are increasingly involved in change processes and ongoing societal interaction, including understanding media employment in education. Mediatization of education refers to the combination of sub-processes that are fundamentally concerned with how technological advances in the media might influence the way policy-making in other sectors operates, e.g., education, politics, religion, and more (AlAhmad, 2021a). As a process, mediatization is likely to happen by shaping/framing education forms, content, processes, and policy to fit other varied forms, techniques, and attributes of digital media, alternatively, by setting an educational media agenda, recruiting emerging communication technologies (Rawolle & Lingard, 2014). To frame, for Entman (1993), is "to select some aspects of a perceived reality and make them more salient in a communicating text, in such a way as to promote a particular problem definition, causal interpretation, moral evaluation, and/or treatment recommendation for the item described (Entman, 1993, p. 52)." For Raychuk as well: "A frame is an abstraction that works to organize or structure message meaning, it also refers to the way media as gatekeeper organizes and presents the ideas, events, and topics they cover (Raychuk, 2011)."

In this chapter, the analytical discussion draws on mediatization as its analytical lens in exploring the T&L process within a *"mediatized classroom,"* a classroom where diverse educational tasks and concrete and abstract instructional concepts are increasingly enacted, embedded, and performed through visual dynamics, semiotic expressions, and info-rich representations, facilitated by media auxiliaries and communication strategies in more effective and innovative models (Breiter, 2014). Classroom mediation draws on *Mediatization* as a metatheory that explores the interrelationship between the media logic and the pedagogical logic in order to understand its societal impact. The *Media logic* refers to the intended quest of the media dominance of information processing, presentation, and storytelling techniques in varied societal interaction processes to take advantage of its own mediums, formats, and representations to become more competitive in the ongoing struggle to capture people's attention to designated issues and goals. The *Pedagogical logic*, however, is most commonly understood as the systematic approach to understanding teaching and knowledge acquisition in light of the theory and best practices of T&L and how this might influence, or be influenced by, the cognitive and behavioural development of teachers and learners alike.

In vibrant systems like education, the mediatization of education gains additional importance when considering teaching as a sophisticated interactive process, where "teachers are constantly imparting new knowledge or transmitting information (Prozesky, 2000, p. 2)." This importance stems from the "growing dependence of education and education policy on the media and its new technologies, and the reduced autonomy of education from changes in the media and its logic (Lingard & Rawolle, 2014; Rawolle & Lingard, 2010)." The concept of the mediatized classroom also refers to "representations and images" (Rawolle & Lingard, 2014, p. 597), where teachers and students can effectively partake in an evocative learning process (Waldeck et al., 2001). In a mediatized classroom, students are likely to learn better through a multidimensional interactive and preferred approach "by seeing and hearing; reflecting and acting; reasoning logically and intuitively; memorising and visualising" (Felder, 1988, p. 674; see also: Breiter, 2014). In such a context, for the media to set its agenda in support of the T&L process is paramount (Muste, 2016) and is likely to result in a variety of valuable outcomes, primarily improving interaction among students, between students and teachers, also among teachers, to decide on what is best for students to learn, and *how*. Relating to the recent advancements achieved in educational affairs, the mediatized classroom has gained more momentum and so extended to assimilate pivotal issues like the application of theories, principles, and paradigms of *mediated communication* in advancing the process of education (UKEssays, 2018). To this end, literature on mediatization links our understanding of the interrelationship between the media, its effects on the educational process and policy setting, to theories of teaching practice on one side, and research in media and communications studies (Benson & Nevue, 2005; Couldry, 2012) and media role in education on the other side (Blackmore & Thorpe, 2003). Batterham (2000) traced the patterns of interactions between media and other key societal players in an attempt to inspect how, also the degree to which such interaction might be dominated by '*agents*' in one field (like media experts and communicators) or another field (teachers, policymakers or politicians). Rawolle and Lingard (2014) expanded on Batterham's efforts to suggest a range of effects that mediatization normally engenders in society, to which they refer as '*mediatisation effects.*' These effects relate to patterns of *change* within the field of media and communication, also the field of education policy, as well as other effects related to the patterns of – or resulted from – interaction between the two fields (p. 604). For them, "the selection of particular technologies in classrooms, lecture theatres, and other sites of learning is a stake that normalizes future generations of technology users, and one that has cascading effects on the education of teachers and their students, including different dispositions required to be a part of an education system (p. 596)." Similarly, Friesen and Hug (2011) emphasize the significant shifts in education resulting from the emergence of new media techniques and communication technologies, accompanied by the purposeful and innovative application of technological platforms in universities and other educational institutions.

The mediatization of education – and other social processes – employs "media logics," including media norms and practices, primarily representations and pitching stories that fit within the media framing of issues and setting its *agenda*. In this direction, Stack (2016) argues that mediatization "is part and parcel of how universities brand themselves in hopes of improving their rankings (p. 4)." Bishop et al. (2004) explored the role of communication and technology in the T&L process, integrating the works of renowned scholars like Hannafin (1984), Quintana et al. (2006), Stickler and Hampel (2010), Hannafin (2012). In the *Handbook of Research on Educational Communications and Technology*, Savelyeva (2015) offers a set of T&L approaches wherein teachers can *mediate* the T&L in the classroom. Their primary focus is to enable teachers to identify relevant communication resources and technology and foster an interactive T&L climate to boost students' understanding and participation in an innovative context, i.e., to mediatize practices, situations, and processes.

5 Method

To ensure a representative sample, a multistage probability sampling technique was applied; in the first stage, the population included twelve Palestinian universities in the West Bank (WB) (see Table 11.1), dividing universities into clusters based on their geographical location and ownership type (public, private, or NGO).

Table 11.1 Distribution of universities across ownership type, campuses, and geographical locations

Universities	Ownership types	Campuses	Geographical location
Arab American University	Private	Jenin	North WB
		Ramallah	Central WB
Palestine Ahliya University		Bethlehem	South WB
Al-Zaytoonah University of Science and Technology		Salfit	North-Mid WB
Dar al-Kalima University for Arts and Culture		Bethlehem	South WB
An-Najah National University	Public	Nablus	North-Mid WB
Hebron University		Hebron	South WB
Palestine Polytechnic University		Hebron	South WB
Quds University		Jerusalem	Central
Al-Quds Open University		Nationwide	Nationwide
Palestine Technical University–Kadoorie		Tulkarem	West-Mid WB
Birzeit University	NGO	Birzeit	Central WB
Bethlehem University		Bethlehem	South WB

Table 11.2 shows a subset of six campuses that belong to three universities, two of which have campuses nationwide, that were selected among the twelve Palestinian universities.

A systematic random sample of students from each university was drawn. Afterward, a random number was chosen – using the Excel RANDBETWEEN option – from each list of university students, and then the sample was selected according to a pre-specified regular interval, dividing population size "N" by sample size "n." Six hundred students from all clusters were approached through an online survey conducted using Google Forms over a period of three weeks between March 25 and April 15, 2023. An online survey was used for data collection because it is cost-effective and time-efficient, and a list of students with their e-mails was available. The proportion of students who responded to the survey was 427, with a reasonable response rate of 72.0%. Infographics presented in Fig. 11.1 summarize the characteristics of the sample.

For technical and contextual limitations, the sample excluded Al-Quds Open University and Al-Istiqlal University (a military and security sciences-oriented university) for their exclusive approaches in T&L. A particular focus of the inspection is on the available ingredients of classroom mediation and how teachers employ them in *mediating* the interaction (T&L activities) between teachers with varied instructional styles and their students with varied socio-cultural backgrounds and inherited learning styles. This is crucial in addressing gaps resulting from such mismatches and also in determining the extent to which available 'classroom mediation techniques and best practices' (hereinafter classroom mediation dynamics) are fit for mitigating/bridging resulting gaps in T&L, primarily those hindering teachers' efforts in creating and fostering a motivational, productive, and innovative climate that is necessary for optimizing T&L dimensions.

Table 11.2 Cluster selection of universities for research study

Universities	Ownership types	Campuses	Geographical location
Arab American University	Private	Jenin	North West Bank (WB)
Palestine Technical University–Kadoorie	Public	Ramallah Tulkarem	Central WB West-Mid WB
Bethlehem University	NGO	Bethlehem	South WB

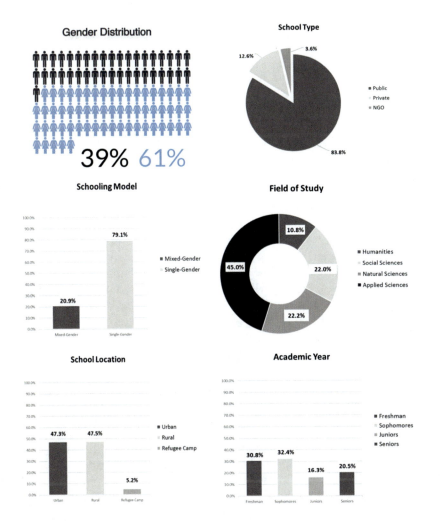

Fig. 11.1 Key characteristics of the sample

The survey included multiple indexes/measurements reflecting the search queries and theoretical postulations. Students were asked to rate their agreement on a five-point Likert scale for these measurements. First, the questionnaire was face-validated by three experts in the field. Then it was tested on a convenient sample of 20 students to ensure that the items were clear, relevant, and appropriate for the study population. Then, reliability tests of all scale items were assessed using Cronbach's alpha and revealed a good internal consistency, as presented in Table 11.3:

After collecting the data, discriminate and convergent validities were assessed for the Teaching and Learning (T&L) dimensions and mechanisms using a series of correlation analyses. Results indicate that the T&L Dimensions were highly correlated with each other ($r > 0.80$, $p < 0.001$), supporting their convergent validity. Additionally, the T&L Dimensions exhibited low to moderate correlations with the learning mechanisms ($r = 0.30$ to 0.60, $p < 0.001$), proving their discriminate validity. Each scale represents the mean values of all items pertaining to that scale.

In testing hypotheses, the MANCOVA statistical technique was employed, with the cognitive, pedagogical, and behavioural T&L dimensions as dependent variables and the school location, type, and schooling model as independent variables. In addition, the level of mediatization was included as a covariate variable to control for its potential effects on the dependent variables. Finally, Wilks' lambda test was used to assess the significance of the overall effect of the independent variable(s) on the dependent variable(s) while controlling for the effect of one or more covariates.

6 Findings and Discussion

The main findings emphasize classroom mediation as an agent of constructive change and process development in T&L in undergraduate classrooms at the sampled universities. With the case of socio-cultural disparities and inherited barriers among students, the premise that classroom mediation facilitates students' engagement in a more motivative, innovative, and productive T&L process proved to be valid. This is conditioned to adequate employment of classroom mediation dynamics in fostering

Table 11.3 Summary of indexes reliability estimates

Scale		Number of items	Cronbach's alpha
T&L dimensions	Behavioural	3	0.880
	Cognitive	3	0.875
	Pedagogical	3	0.898
T&L mechanisms	Engagement	2	0.778
	Innovation	2	0.892
	Productivity	4	0.892

cognitive, behavioural, and pedagogical dimensions. The following discussion aims at verifying the hypotheses postulated earlier in the chapter.

6.1 School Milieu and Its Pertinence to the Variances in Learning Achievements

This section inspects the effects of the school milieu/location (urban, rural, or refugee camp) on the three T&L dimensions while controlling the classroom mediation level. It measures these dimensions on a 5-point scale and controls for the students' classroom mediation level while meeting the normality, linearity, and multicollinearity assumptions. The Box's M test for equality of covariance matrices was not significant (Box's $M = 6.86$, $F(12, 17774) = 0.14.38$, $p = 0.30$), indicating that the assumption of homogeneity of covariance matrices across groups was also met. Likewise, Wilks' criterion showed no significant differences in the learning dimensions based on school location (Wilks' $\Lambda = 0.99$, $F(6, 944) = 6.49$, $p = 0.55$, partial $\eta 2 = 0.00$) once the level of classroom mediation was taken into account. However, the covariate variable had a significant effect on T&L's level of mediatization (Wilks' $\Lambda = 0.96$, $F(3, 472) = 0.83$, $p = 0.00$, partial $\eta 2 = 0.04$) on the three key T&L dimensions. This indicates that the level of classroom mediation positively impacts undergraduates' learning experiences, regardless of their previous school location.

These findings also suggest that, when classroom mediation is appropriately employed, a school's location is not a significant factor in predicting learning outcomes and that educators should focus on implementing a variety of effective mediation dynamics in classroom activities and teaching practices rather than worrying about the presumed educational contexts. This is necessary to boost undergraduates' learning outcomes and improve all students' learning outcomes, regardless of their school location. Although there were no significant differences in learning outcomes pertaining to school location (see Fig. 11.2), the adjusted mean values indicate that undergraduates who studied in refugee camps performed better on the pedagogical and cognitive learning dimensions, while those who studied in urban areas scored higher on the cognitive dimension but lower on the behavioural dimension. Notwithstanding, these differences did not reach statistical significance.

This finding implies that the level of mediatization of the T&L process should be considered when implementing behavioural and pedagogical dimension improvements in various school locations. Furthermore,

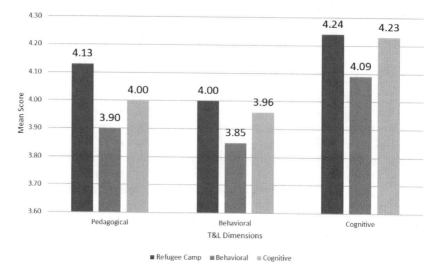

Fig. 11.2 Mean scores on T&L dimension by school location

educators and policymakers should prioritize integrating appropriate technological tools and teaching strategies to enhance levels of classroom mediation, regardless of the school milieu.

6.2 *The Impact of Segregated vs. Mixed-Gender Schooling Model on T&L Achievement*

The inspection in this section focuses on how different schooling models (single vs. mixed-gender) might affect the three learning dimensions while factoring in the T&L's mediatization level. In addition, the analytical model met the necessary assumptions for accuracy. Results show no significant difference between the schooling models (Wilks' $\Lambda = 0.99$, $F(3, 473) = 2.23$, $p = 0.08$, partial $\eta 2 = 0.01$), while the level of media aids usage by students in classrooms had a significant impact on their learning (Wilks' $\Lambda = 0.96$, $F(3, 472) = 0.83$, $p = 0.00$, partial $\eta 2 = 0.04$) across all three dimensions. This indicates classroom mediation as a crucial factor for students' learning achievements, regardless of gender orientation in their school.

Notwithstanding, a significant variance between the two schooling models was identified through the 'between-subjects effects' test in favour of the behavioural dimension ($F(1, 476) = 4.14$, $p = 0.043$, partial $\eta2 = 0.01$), implying that the schooling model may have an impact on the behavioural dimension, but not on the cognitive or pedagogical dimensions. Therefore, a univariate F-test using an alpha level of 0.05 was conducted to investigate the impact of each effect on the behavioural dimension. While controlling for the covariate effect of the mediatization level of the T&L process, the results favoured mixed-gender education (mean value = 3.89) more than single-gender education (mean value = 3.77), as indicated in the pairwise comparison (see Table 11.4).

6.3 The Impact of School Type and Mediatization Level on T&L Dimensions

The three learning dimensions were inspected in relation to public and private schools while controlling for media aids usage and ensuring the data met statistical assumptions. It was observed that NGOs and private schools were combined because only a small number of students ($n = 14$) attended the NGOs. This decision was supported by the commonalities in

Table 11.4 Pairwise comparison of schooling model across T&L dimensions

Dependent variable			Mean difference (I-J)	Std. error	Sig.[b]
Cognitive	Single-gender education	Mixed-gender education	−0.139	0.090	0.125
	Mixed-gender education	Single-gender education	0.139	0.090	0.125
Behavioural	Single-gender education	Mixed-gender education	−0.205[a]	0.101	0.043
	Mixed-gender education	Single-gender education	0.205[a]	0.101	0.043
Pedagogical	Single-gender education	Mixed-gender education	−0.055	0.105	0.599
	Mixed-gender education	Single-gender education	0.055	0.105	0.599

Based on estimated marginal means
[a]The mean difference is significant at the 0.05 level
[b]Adjustment for multiple comparisons: Bonferroni

their mission, values, and regulatory environments. However, there may be differences in their governance, funding sources, and accountability mechanisms that need to be taken into account.

Findings indicate no significant difference in covariance matrices between the two groups ($F(12, 17774) = 0.14.38$, $p = 0.30$), demonstrating their similarity. In addition, the Box's M test for equality of covariance matrices was insignificant (Box's $M = 6.06$, $F(6, 105389) = 6.07$, $p = 0.43$), indicating the assumption of homogeneity of covariance matrices across groups was also met. Therefore, Wilks' criterion is applied to determine if there was a significant difference in learning mechanisms based on school type (Wilks' $\Lambda = 0.98$, $F(3, 473) = 2.45$, $p = 0.06$, partial $\eta2 = 0.02$). However, when the level of classroom mediation was taken into account, results were significant (Wilks' $\Lambda = 0.96$, $F(3, 472) = 0.62$, $p = 0.00$, partial $\eta2 = 0.04$). This assumes that the level of the mediatization of education process has an impact on learning outcomes, even when controlling for school type.

The Wilks' lambda test showed no significant differences between public and private schools for the three learning dimensions. However, the test of 'between-subjects effects' indicates a significant difference between the two types of schools for the cognitive dimension ($F(1, 473) = 6.03$, $p = 0.014$, partial $\eta2 = 0.01$). This suggests that school type may affect the cognitive dimension but not the behavioural or pedagogical dimension. To further investigate, a univariate F-test was conducted with an alpha level of 0.05 while controlling for the mediatization level of the T&L process. Again, the results favoured private schools over public schools in the cognitive dimension. These findings were reflected in the estimates and pairwise comparison tables, with a mean value of 4.37 for private school graduates and 4.13 for public school graduates.

Data analysis revealed that students who attended private schools had an advantage in the cognitive dimension (learning outcomes), but there were no significant differences between students from both types of schools regarding behavioural or pedagogical learning outcomes. This suggests that educators and policymakers should take a more holistic approach to education that considers a school's values, resources, community involvement, and cognitive learning outcomes. Improving cognitive learning outcomes in public schools should remain a focus, but it should not be at the expense of other vital aspects of education. Furthermore, data analysis proved that the degree of classroom mediation significantly affects all aspects of learning outcomes. Therefore, it is crucial to consider the level of classroom mediation when creating educational programs and interventions. Educators can use technology and media in their teaching methods to improve learning outcomes. This also assumes that students become familiar with media aids to complement their learning beyond the classroom.

6.4 Classroom Mediation's Impact on Promoting T&L Dimensions and Mechanisms

This section analyses classroom mediation in relation to the realization and promotion of learning dimensions and mechanisms (T&L gaols) among Palestinian students. To determine if any significant differences materialize in the degrees of T&L dimensions (cognitive, behavioural, and pedagogical) and mechanisms (engagement, innovation, productivity, and motivation), a t-test was conducted, and Table 11.5 summarizes its results.

Results show that specific mediation techniques, such as Virtual Lab Solutions, Online Interactive Polls, Interactive Maps, and eLearning Moodle, were more effective in enhancing various learning aspects (dimensions/goals and mechanisms) than other techniques; improved ($p.< 05$), except for Virtual Lab Solutions and the engagement component. These tools can enhance the learning experience by providing interactive and engaging materials to help students better understand and retain information. Additionally, these tools may offer a more flexible and convenient way of learning that allows students to access educational materials from anywhere and at any time. Nonetheless, the study found that PowerPoint and Prezi, and LCD projectors had a significant ($p.< 05$) impact on productivity and motivation mechanisms only, while Smart Boards had a significant impact ($p.< 05$) on productivity. Such results stem from the fact that, while PowerPoint and Projector lack the interactive dynamics of mediation, many teachers in the sampled universities might not be willing to or capable of running Smart Boards tactfully and meaningfully.

The mean values in Table 11.5 identified Virtual Lab Solutions, Online Interactive Polls, and Interactive Maps as the most motivating tools. The two tools are also powerful for undergraduates in improving their productivity, engagement, and innovation. In addition, the study found that virtual lab solutions, online interactive polls, and interactive maps effectively enhance the pedagogical goals of their T&L. As for the behavioural and cognitive dimensions, both interactive polls and maps were also effective. This finding concurs with the theoretical discussion over the feasibility of

Table 11.5 Summary of T-Test results for the mean value of students answering "yes" to the media technique used

Dependent/independent variables		PowerPoint, Prezi	LCD projector	Smart board	Virtual lab solutions	Interactive maps	Online interactive polls	eLearning Moodle
T&L dimensions	Cognitive	4.17	4.17	4.15	4.26*	4.33*	4.32**	4.24**
	Behavioural	3.91	3.91	3.93	4.10*	4.15**	4.17***	3.97*
	Pedagogical	4.00	4.00	4.04	4.24***	4.21*	4.22***	4.04*
T&L mechanisms	Engagement	3.99	3.99	3.98	4.10	4.11*	4.17**	4.05**
	Innovation	4.04	4.04	4.05	4.23*	4.24*	4.24***	4.07**
	Productivity	3.91*	3.91*	3.97*	4.08*	4.16***	4.14***	3.95*
	Motivation	4.23*	4.23*	4.20	4.37*	4.35*	4.38**	4.27**

* $p < 0.05$, ** $p < 0.01$, *** $p < 0.001$

Note: Numbers in this table represent the mean value of students answering "yes" about the use of media technique in classrooms classroom mediation dynamics as postulated by Ndongko and Agu (1985), Felder (1988), Felder and Henriques (1995), Shabiralyani et al. (2015), AlAhmad (2021c). It also supports Savoy and Carr-Chellman's (2014) theorization of classroom mediation as an agent for change in education systems and an essential ingredient in effective teaching (Backlund, 2008).

7 Conclusions

The chapter emphasizes classroom mediation as an agent in mitigating students' inherited barriers and fostering students' engagement in a more motivative, innovative, and productive T&L process to promote the cognitive, behavioural, and pedagogical dimensions in the T&L process. The chapter validates the premise that best practices in classroom mediation provide an avenue for educators and students alike to optimize these *dimensions* within undergraduate classrooms in the sampled Palestinian universities. In inspecting the effects of school location in the Palestinian community, the chapter utilized Box's M test for equality of covariance matrices, which was not significant, indicating that the assumption of homogeneity of covariance matrices across groups was also met. Wilks' criterion showed no significant differences in the learning dimensions based on school location, indicating the efficiency of classroom mediation when being considered. However, there was a significant effect of the covariate variable of T&L's level of mediatization on the three T&L dimensions, indicating that the level of classroom mediation positively impacts students' learning experiences, regardless of their previous school location. There is a call for educators and policymakers to consider the level of mediatization when implementing improvements in the T&L process at both behavioural and pedagogical dimensions, regardless of the school location.

Data recorded no significant difference between the schooling models at the school gender orientation level. In contrast, classroom mediation significantly impacted students' learning across all three T&L dimensions, indicating classroom mediation as a crucial factor in students' learning achievements, regardless of their school gender orientation. However, the significant variance between the two schooling models was identified through the 'between-subjects effects' test in favour of the behavioural dimension, implying that the schooling model may impact the behavioural dimension, but not the cognitive or pedagogical dimensions. No significant difference in covariance matrices between the two groups was identified, demonstrating their similarity. The Box's M test for equality of covariance matrices was insignificant, indicating the assumption of homogeneity of covariance matrices across groups was also met.

At the level of T&L mechanisms, Wilks' criterion is used to determine if a significant difference in learning mechanisms relates to school type (private and NGOs vs. public); results were significant, assuming the level of the mediatization of the education process has an impact on learning outcomes. At the same time, the Wilks Lambda test shows no significant differences between public and private/NGO schools for the three learning dimensions; however, the test of 'between-subjects effects' indicated a significant difference between the two categories of schools for the *cognitive* dimension, suggesting school type may affect the cognitive dimension in favour of private/NGOs but not the behavioural or pedagogical dimension. F-test was conducted with an alpha level of 0.05 while controlling for the mediatization level of the T&L process; results favoured private schools over the public in the *cognitive* dimension, with no significant differences between students from both categories of schools regarding *behavioural* or *pedagogical* learning outcomes, suggesting the adoption of a more holistic approach to education that considers a school's values, resources, community involvement, and cognitive learning outcomes. As for the classroom mediation dynamics, t-test results indicated that Virtual Lab Solutions, Online Interactive Polls, Interactive Maps, and eLearning Moodle were more effective in enhancing both T&L dimensions and mechanisms than other dynamics. This finding concurs with the theoretical discussion over the feasibility of mediation dynamics as agent for change in education systems.

The above conclusions can be synthesized in a set of theoretical arguments as a 'mediatized classroom' model informed by the essential assumptions in the theory of mediatization of education. These arguments crystalize the *cognitive, pedagogical, and behavioural* dimensions in the T&L process, as well as their subordinate mechanisms of *motivation, innovation, and productivity*.

(a) Exposing students to information via varied resources, perspectives, and representations is expected to boost their cognitive capabilities, mental skills, and ability to detect, interpret, and synthesizing new knowledge.
(b) Engaging students in well-structured language tasks and sociocultural practices via media-aided knowledge acquisition and

application techniques is likely to help modify individual behaviour to achieve productive social interactions among students from varied socio-cultural backgrounds and inherited disparities between teaching and learning.

(c) As a staging process, classroom mediation incorporates a well-organized set of methods, strategies, and approaches that enable students to choose and pursue individual interests. It also exposes them to essential skills in decision-making, self-monitoring, checking attention, and taking responsibility for learning.

(d) The mediatization of T&L processes makes it more motivational (minimizes stress and increases students' participation and persistence of goal-directed behaviour), more productive (enables teachers to monitor students' understanding), more innovative (solving real problems in a genuine, simple, and economical way promotes students' autonomy and ownership of the learning process), and more productive (optimize the level of effort put into accomplishing academic excel).

Finally, the impact of school location, profit orientation, and gender orientation on learning outcomes may not be as significant as traditionally thought of, to the extent that other factors, such as 'level of mediatization,' may be of stronger prediction. Further research is needed to explore the relative importance of different predictors of learning outcomes in different contexts.

References

AlAhmad, H. (2021a). A mediatised conflict: The Mediatisation of Palestinian Split in pan-Arab transnational satellite TV journalism. *The Turkish Journal of Middle East Studies, 8*(2), 151–181. https://doi.org/10.26513/tocd.873752

AlAhmad, H. (2021b). The role of educational communication in promoting a student-centered learning style in multicultural classrooms: A reflective essay on learning and teaching in higher Education. *International Journal of Research in Education and Science, 7*(3), 838–851. https://doi.org/10.46328/ijres.2374

AlAhmad, H. (2021c). The role of educational communication in supporting teaching and learning within multi-cultural heterogeneous classroom. *Journal on Social and Education Sciences (IJonSES), 7*(3), 838–851. https://doi.org/10.46328/ijres.2374

Al-Zarah, L. N. (2008). *An investigative study of the female initial teacher preparation programme in Saudi Arabia in an Islamic context: Perceptions of the key participants*. University of Durham.

Anderson, L. W., et al. (2001). *A taxonomy for learning, teaching, and assessing: A revision of Bloom's taxonomy of educational objectives. A T.* Pearson, Allyn & Bacon.

Atia, M. (2018). *Why girls achieve academically more than boys in the Arab world? The effect of gender segregation and bullying in schools on gender achievement*. University of Twente. Available at: https://essay.utwente.nl/79413/1/Mina%20Atef%20Moussa%20Atia_MA_EST.pdf

Backlund, P.M. (2008). Pedagogy, communication in. In *The International Encyclopedia of Communication*. https://doi.org/10.1002/9781405186407.wbiecp017

Batterham, R. (2000). *The chance to change: Final report*. Australian Government Printing Service (AGPS). https://bluetongue1.files.wordpress.com/2007/12/2000-chance-to-change-robin-batterham-final-report-pmseic.pdf

Blackmore, J., & Thorpe, S. (2003). 'Media/ting change: The print media's role in mediating education policy in a period of radical reform in Victoria, Australia', *Journal of Education Policy, 18*(6), pp. 577–595. https://doi.org/10.1080/0268093032000145854.

Bennett, C. (2019). *Methods for presenting subject matter*. Available at: https://www.thoughtco.com/methods-for-presenting-subject-matter-8411. Accessed: 12 Feb 2023

Benson, R., & Neveu, E. (2005). Introduction: Field theory as a work in progress. In R. Benson and E. Neveu (Eds.), *Bourdieu and the journalistic field* (pp. 1–29). Polity Press.

Bishop, M. J., et al. (Eds.). (2004). *Handbook of research on educational communications and technology*. Lawrence Erlbaum Associates Publishers.

Breiter, A. (2014). Schools as mediatized worlds from a cross-cultural perspective BT – Mediatized worlds: Culture and Society in a Media Age. In A. Hepp & F. Krotz (Eds.), *Mediatized worlds* (pp. 288–303). Palgrave Macmillan UK. https://doi.org/10.1057/9781137300355_17

Couldry, N. (2012) *Media society world: Social theory and digital media practice*. Polity Press.

Education, R. (2016). *Student engagement*. Available at: https://www.edglossary.org/student-engagement/. Accessed: 26 Apr 2023

Entman, R. (1993). Framing: Toward clarification of a fractured paradigm. *Journal of Communication, 43*(4), 51–58.

Felder, R. M. (1988). Learning and teaching styles in engineering education. *Engineering Education, 78*(7), 674–681.

Felder, R. M., & Henriques, E. R. (1995). Learning and teaching styles in foreign and second language education. *Foreign Language Annals, 28*(1), 21–31. https://doi.org/10.1111/j.1944-9720.1995.tb00767.x

Fitriani, S., & Istaryatiningtias, I. (2020). Promoting child-friendly school model through school committee as parents' participation. *International Journal of Evaluation and Research in Education (IJERE), 9*(4), 1025–1034. https://doi.org/10.11591/ijere.v9i4.20615

Forsler, I. (2020). 'The mediatization of education: A transparency dilemma?', *IV Seminário Internacional de Pesquisas em Miditarização e Processos Sociais, Online (8 occations), November 4, 2020 – January 20, 2021.* Media and Communication Studies, School of Culture and Education, Södertörn University: Instituto Humanitas Unisinos. Available at: https://midiaticom.org/anais/index.php/seminario-midiatizacao-resumos/article/view/1165

Friesen, N., & Hug, T. (2011). In J. Fromme, S. Iske, & W. Marotzki (Eds.), *After the mediatic turn: McLuhan's training of the senses and media pedagogy today BT – Medialität und Realität: Zur konstitutiven Kraft der Medien* (pp. 83–101). VS Verlag für Sozialwissenschaften. https://doi.org/10.1007/978-3-531-92896-8_6

Ghani, M. F. A. (2013). Development of effective school model for Malaysian school. *International Journal of Academic Research, 5*(5), 131–142. https://doi.org/10.7813/2075-4124.2013/5-5/b.20

Hannafin, M. J. (1984). Guidelines for using locus of instructional control in the design of computer-assisted instruction. *Journal of Instructional Development, 7*(3), 6–10.

Hannafin, M. (2012). Student-centered learning. In N. Seel (Ed.), *Encyclopedia of the sciences of learning* (pp. 3211–3214). Springer. https://doi.org/10.1007/978-1-4419-1428-6_173

Hjarvard, S. (2014). Mediatization and cultural and social change: An institutional perspective. In K. Lundby (Ed.), *Mediatization of communication: Handbooks of communication science* (pp. 199–226). De Gruyter Mouton. https://doi.org/10.1515/9783110272215.199

Kapur, R. (2020). *Goals and objectives of pedagogy.* Accessed online, March 3, 2023, at: https://www.researchgate.net/publication/345156302_Goals_and_Objectives_of_Pedagogy (Accessed: 5 March 2023).

Leroy, F., & Ramanantsoa, B. (1997). The cognitive and behavioural dimensions of organizational learning in a merger: An empirical study. *Journal of Management Studies, 34*(6), 871–894. https://doi.org/10.1111/1467-6486.00076

Lundby, K. (2014). *Mediatization of communication.* Available at: http://www.degruyter.com/viewbooktoc/product/180158

Marci-Boehncke, G., & Rath, M. (2020). Education with digital culture. *Medienjournal*, *44*(1), 5–17. Available at: https://elibrary.utb.de/doi/abs/10.24989/medienjournal.v44i1.1924

Milem, J.F., Chang, M.J., & Antonio, A.L. (2005). *Making diversity work on campus: A research-based perspective*, Association of American Colleges and Universities. Available at: https://old.coe.arizona.edu/ameri/climate/model/behavioral. Accessed: 20 Mar 2023

Muste, D. (2016). 'The role of communication skills in teaching process', in *Education, reflection, development*. Fourth. UK: Future academy: www.FutureAcademy.org.UK. https://doi.org/10.15405/epsbs.2016.12.52

Ndongko, T. M., & Agu, A. A. (1985). The impact of communication on the learning process: A study of secondary schools in Calabar municipality, Cross River state of Nigeria. *International Review of Education – Internationale Zeitschrift ffir Erziehungswissenschaft – Revue Internationale de Pddagogie*, *XXXI*, 205–221.

Prozesky, D. R. (2000). Communication and effective teaching. *Community Eye Health*, *13*(35), 44–45.

Quintana, C., et al. (2006). Learnercentered design: Reflections on the past and directions for the future. In R. K. Sawyer (Ed.), *The Cambridge handbook of the learning sciences* (pp. 119–134). Cambridge University Press.

Rahal, T., & Palfreyman, D. (2009). Assessing learning styles of students at Zayed University. *Learning and Teaching in Higher Education: Gulf Perspectives*, *6*(2) http://www.zu.ae.ae/lthe/lthe06_02_01_rahal.htm

Rawolle, S. (2010). Understanding the mediatisation of educational policy as practice. *Critical Studies in Education*, *51*, 21–39. https://doi.org/10.1080/17508480903450208

Rawolle, S., & Lingard, B. (2014). *Mediatization and education: A sociological account*. https://doi.org/10.1515/9783110272215.595

Raychuk, A. (2011). 'Framing, Agenda-Setting and Priming in Media', group МЛа. Accessed online, 12 Feb 2017, at: Academia: htt. Available at: https://www.academia.edu/9827598/Framing_Agenda-Setting_and_Priming_in_Media

Savelyeva, T. (2015). M. Spector, D. Merrill, J. Elen, Bishop (Eds). Handbook of Research on educational communications and technology. *Technology, Knowledge and Learning*, *20*, 123–128.

Savoy, M. R., & Carr-Chellman, A. A. (2014). Change agency in learning, instruction, and performance. In D. Jonassen et al. (Eds.), *Handbook of research on educational communications and technology* (4th ed.). Springer.

Schulz, W. (2004). Reconstructing Mediatization as an analytical concept. *European Journal of Communication*, *19*(1), 87–101. https://doi.org/10.1177/0267323104040696

Shabiralyani, G., et al. (2015). Impact of visual aids in enhancing the learning process case research: District Dera Ghazi Khan. *Journal of Education and Practice, 6*(19), 226–233. https://files.eric.ed.gov/fulltext/EJ1079541.pdf

Singh, M. (2003). *Understanding life skills*, p. 8. UNESCO document 2004/ED/EFA/MRT/PI/69.

Stack, M. (2016). *Global university rankings and the Mediatization of higher Education*. Palgrave Macmillan. https://doi.org/10.1057/9781137475954

Stickler, U., & Hampel, R. (2010). CyberDeutsch: Language production and user preferences in a Moodle virtual learning environment. *CALICO Journal, 28*(1), 49–73.

Thompson, J. B. (2018). Mediated interaction in the digital age. *Theory, Culture & Society, 37*(1), 3–28. https://doi.org/10.1177/0263276418808592

UKEssays. (2018). 'No Title', *Theories of Communication in Education* [Preprint]. Available at: https://www.ukessays.com/essays/education/theories-communication-education-3147.php?vref=1

UNICEF. (2016). *Life skills and citizenship education transforming education through life skills and citizenship education*. Al-Issa. Available at: https://www.unicef.org/mena/life-skills-and-citizenship-education.

Wahyudi, R. (2018). *Situating English language teaching in Indonesia within a critical, global dialogue of theories: A case study of teaching argumentative writing and cross-cultural understanding courses*. Victoria University of Wellington. http://repository.uin-malang.ac.id/5786/

Waldeck, J., Kearney, P., & Plax, T. (2001). Teacher e-mail message strategies and students' willingness to communicate online. https://doi.org/10.1080/00909880128099

Walsh, C., & Apperley, T. (2014). Digital culture and education. *Digital Culture & Education, 5*, 132–133.

Wilkens, K. (2011). *Higher education reform in the Arab world*. The Brookings Project on U.S. Relations with the Islamic World.

CHAPTER 12

When Inequalities Are Reversed: Algeria's Gender Inequity in Education

Wafaa Taleb

1 Historical Background

Algerian women only truly had access to education in the very last years of colonization. The Jules Ferry laws on secular, free, and compulsory schooling applied to the French departments of Algeria from February 1883. The year 1882 marked the beginning of the separation of the School and the State in France. In 1962, on the eve of independence, only 30% of Algerian children were in school, while 98% of the children of European origin were in school (Mansouri-Acherrar, 1996, 180). Among Algerians in school, girls made up less than a third.

This segregationist application of the fundamental principles of Third Republic schools was to be founded for all Algerians but had a contradictory discourse, torn between the desire to exclude Algerians from the benefit of education by "restricting them to fields" and the need to civilize them and therefore assimilate them. To their detriment, native Algerian girls suffered additional segregation. Customs that are considered

W. Taleb (✉)
University of Oran 2, Mohamed Ben Ahmed, Oran, Algeria

retrograde were used as an authoritative argument against the education of girls. That is, it was commonly stated not to shock the natives or to "declass" their daughters. The establishments that were be opened had to correspond to the will of the parents (Mansouri-Acherrar, 1996).

In fact, at least until the interwar period, the rare schools open to Algerian girls were mainly workshops intended for the learning of domestic work. It was not until the war of national liberation and the Plan of Constantine in 1959 that the requirement of the universal education of Algerians was enacted. The Constantine Plan was an ambitious project that aimed to increase wages, housing, and public infrastructure across colonial French Algeria. It was an overarching program meant to target all levels of Algeria's society.

Although the numbers continuously increased, the enrollment of girls during colonization was particularly low (see Table 12.1).

2 Post-Independence Algeria: Principles Governing Algerian Education System

The principles governing the Algerian educational system are defined by the Algerian constitution. It is stipulated in the Algerian constitution, in particular its article 53, that education is an inalienable right. Education is also compulsory and should be free for all school-age children up to the age of 16.

Education is one of the major prerogatives assigned to the State, which allocates a substantial budget to it. Families are exempt from any tuition fees, notwithstanding the cost of school books, which are sold at a price covering only production costs. In addition, students receive an annual tuition bonus.

Table 12.1 Evolution of the number of Muslim boys and girls enrolled in public primary schools (6–13 years)

Year	Schoolable	Schooled	Rate	Boys	Girls	Girls%
1911	1,067,537	40,858	3.8	37,331	3527	8.63
1936	1,264,655	88,492	7.9	75,837	12,655	14.30
1948	1,939,563	175,569	9.8	133,420	42,149	24.00
1954	1,833,623	306,737	16.7	225,289	81,448	26.55

Source: Table compiled from several sources (Desvages, 1972; Kateb, 2005; Kadri, 2007; Djebbar, 2008)

The school system is characterized by centralization in terms of programs, methods and timetables. However, the management of establishments and personnel is decentralized.

Law No. 08-04 of 23 January 2008 on the orientation law on national education consecrates, through articles 10, 11, 12, 13, and 14, the guarantee of the right to education:

Article 10: The State guarantees the right to education to each and every Algerian without discrimination based on sex, social origin, or geographical origin.

Article 11: The right to education is concretized by the generalization of basic education and by the guarantee of equal opportunities in terms of conditions of schooling and continuation of studies after basic education.

Article 12: Education is compulsory for all girls and boys aged 6–16 years. However, the duration of compulsory education may be extended by two years, as needed, to accommodate disabled students.

The State ensures, in collaboration with the parents, the application of these provisions. The breaches of parents or legal guardians expose them to a fine ranging from 5000 to 50,000 Algerian dinars.

Article 13: Education is free at all levels in establishments belonging to the public sector of national education.

In addition, the State provides support for the education of underprivileged students by allowing them to benefit from multiple forms of aid, particularly in terms of scholarships, textbooks and school supplies, food, accommodation, transportation, and health care at school.

3   Description of the Education System in Algeria

The Algerian education system is divided into several levels: preparatory, primary, middle (or college) secondary, and superior (higher education). Access to higher education is conditioned by obtaining a baccalaureate degree or an equivalent foreign diploma.

In 1962, Algeria had only three higher education establishments (in Algiers, Oran, and Constantine) with fewer than 2000 students, of which only 1% were women, and there were fewer than 250 teachers. It was only after independence (1963) that the Algerian government began to rebuild its country and its education system. After the creation of the Ministry of Higher Education and Scientific Research in the 1970s, universities were gradually established. The university network represented 107 universities in 2015 and more than 1,500,000 students, 60% of whom were women, and it had a total of 54,000 teachers (MEN).

3.1   Equal Educational Opportunities in Algeria

Due to the expansion of the school network and a proactive policy of hiring Algerian female teachers, the education policy enacted in Algeria since independence has had the effect of enabling students' equitable access to education regardless of their sex and their class of origin. Progressively higher participation has been the result of the democratization of education, first in elementary school, then in secondary education, and eventually in higher education.

Since the first years of independence, the state has made efforts to generalize schooling from the age of six. The education of a girl was rare; it is a right that many Algerian women did not have. We can cite here a few causes that have pushed some parents not to send their daughters to school or not to encourage them to attend school:

- The remoteness of schools from home.
- The still widespread idea that boys had more right to study and that girls should stay at home to help their mothers.
- The desire to marry off a daughter as soon as possible.
- The fact of not having the means to get all their children into school and therefore "sacrificing" the girls.
- The fear, quite simply, that there would be talk about a father letting his daughter go to school.

Currently, these reasons, and others, still exist, but they have become rarer. Society has evolved, and mentalities have also evolved; the State is investing in educational structures, and so many factors have turned the tide. Beyond all these aspects, there is the awareness of Algerian girls who, for several decades, have decided almost silently to lead a revolution, to change their fate, their status, and their lives. Their only weapon is their studies; not only do they seem to have understood it but, moreover, they are convinced that it is their only salvation.

The introduction of universal access to education, which was made mandatory and free for children between the ages of 6 and 16, has unquestionably been the government program that has contributed the most to the betterment of the position of women since Algeria's independence in 1962. Given the 1960s' demographic environment, achieving this goal was extremely difficult. The Algerian population was young (47% were under the age of 15 in 1966) as a result of its exceptionally rapid expansion, and enrollment rates increased quickly until a drop in fertility gradually slowed the rate.

As shown in Table 12.2, The participation of girls in the primary cycle is still lagging behind that of boys; the sex ratio at this level of education was 91 girls for 100 boys in 2014 (CNES, 2016), and even if their participation progressed continuously, it is slow and does not reach parity. This is because of the low rate of schooling for girls, particularly in rural areas and the poorest regions, generally located in the mountainous areas, the high plains, and the desert steppes, where the school infrastructure remains underdeveloped, and where the economic conditions and the sociocultural environment create some attitudes that are not very favourable to girls' education. Thus, in Tamanrasset, in the extreme south of Algeria, the enrollment rate for girls is 76% versus 82.5% for boys and 87.6% versus 91.3% in Relizane (in the north) (ONS, 2008).

Table 12.3, however, shows that in secondary education, from the mid-1990s, there was a reversal of the trend in the participation of girls, where their presence became greater than that of boys, with 136 girls for 100 boys in 2014 (CNES, 2016).

Table 12.4 indicates that the higher success rates of girls at the end of the secondary cycle are the primary reason for the increased percentage of girls in high schools and universities. The higher graduation rates for females in Algeria have long remained hidden. Information that might have provided insight into their evolution could not be retrieved using the data made available by the Ministry of Education. There is also an absence of data on success rates for the baccalaureate or the fundamental teaching licence since 2007 (a diploma that certifies nine years of primary and middle-school education).

Table 12.2 Evolution of the participation rate of girls in the primary cycle from 1962/1963 to 2010/2011

1919–1963	*1972–1973*	*1982–1983*	*1992–1993*	*2002–2003*	*2010–2011*
36.37%	38.74%	42.42%	45.35%	46.96%	47.37%

Source: ONS

Table 12.3 Number of female/male students in all cycles 2017/2022

Year	2017	2018	2019	2020	2021	2022
Number of students in all cycles	8,732,608	8,924,230	921,160	9,562,916	1,002,265	10,433,348
Female	4,298,087	4,386,650	450,031	4,698,045	4,947,963	5,166,605
Male	4,434,521	4,537,580	471,139	4,864,871	5,074,702	5,266,743

Source: United Nations Human Rights Council

Table 12.4 Evolution of the participation rate of girls from 1970/1971 to 2010/2011

Year	Primary cycle females (%)	Middle cycle females (%)	Secondary cycle females (%)
1970–1971	37.86	27.93	27.53
1975–1976	39.82	35.03	28.29
1980–1981	41.92	39.01	36.75
1985–1986	43.55	41.28	42.43
1990–1991	44.83	41.63	46.63
1995–1996	46.12	44.40	50.44
2000–2001	46.82	48.06	56.15
2005–2006	47.04	48.99	58.38
2010–2011	47.37	48.95	57.56

Source: ONS

The information provided yearly by the Algerian press on the results of the baccalaureate or the Brevet d'études Fondamentales (BEF) (a diploma that certifies nine years of primary and middle-school education), which are reported by the Ministry of National Education but never formally published, are to be used to track the recent developments of these two indicators. In 2005, 38% of girls and 35% of boys successfully completed the BEF. They were 58% for girls and 42% for boys in 2015 (Fig. 12.1a).

Despite fairly similar success rates for the general baccalaureate (43.7% for girls and 39% for boys) and the technical baccaleaureate (70% versus 67.6%, respectively), 61% of baccalaureate holders were girls in 2007, the last year in which the Ministry of Education and the ONS published results by gender. This was primarily because more girls than boys were enrolling in high school. However, since 2007, the situation has drastically worsened for boys in terms of baccalaureate success rates.

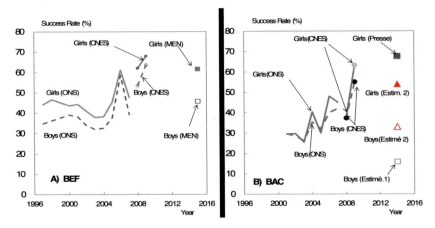

Fig. 12.1 (a) Success rate (%) for the Brevet d'études Fondamentales (BEF) and (b) success rate for the Baccalauréat Général (BAC) by Sex. Algeria, 1997–2015. (Source: 1997–2007 ONS, different publications; 2008–2009, CNES, unpublished document; 2014 Algerian press; 2015, MEN, in Ouadah-Bedidi (2018, 90))

Since then, the only data sources have been the information that the Algerian press has reported based on remarks made by the Ministry of Education when the baccalaureate results are announced. These data demonstrate that while academic achievement for boys significantly declined between 2007 and 2014, it gradually increased for girls over those same years. By 2013, 64% more girls than boys had completed their baccalaureate. Most significantly, in 2014, the press reported a 45.01% total national success rate and a very high rate for girls (67.61%). There have been numerous fruitless attempts to locate data on the number of applicants, the number of candidates, and the number of admissions to recognized institutions by sex.

However, it is possible to recalculate the number of girls who have passed the baccalaureate and determine the number of boys based on gender data that was provided by the press on the number of candidates enrolled in May 2014 (APS, 30-05-2014) and on the published success percentage for girls. Regarding the success rate for boys, it can be inferred that only 14% of the candidates who took the baccalauréat passed. Thus, one could infer that 85% of baccalaureate holders were female by 2014.

However, the most recent National Report on Human Development unequivocally demonstrates that success appears to have decreased over the past few years for both sexes (CNES, 2016).

In 2021, out of 375,594 students, 191,121 passed the baccalaureate, a rate of 51.15%. Once again, the trends were reaffirmed since we noted a success rate of nearly 64% among girls with 122,944 winners. The boys come quite far behind at just over 36% with 69,177 admitted (MEN).

4 Boys Dropping Out of School: An Emerging Issue?

In its 2018 report, the Algerian League for the Defence of Human Rights said that 400,000 children drop out of educational institutions in the country every year (Middle East Monitor, 2018). Dropouts occur for several reasons; despite the huge sums of money the state has allocated to this sector.

In a statement to mark the National Day of Knowledge on 16 April on which Algerians commemorate the death of the Head of the Algerian Muslim Ulema Association, Sheikh Abdelhamid Ben Badis, the Algerian Ministry of Education stated that "official statistics indicate that 400,000 children drop out of school annually, and only 250,000 go on to professional training (training in crafts)."

The report added that "school dropouts are especially high in the countryside because of the remoteness of schools and high poverty rates … We have also noted that in many regions, the classrooms are not equipped with electricity, water or heating, or lack toilets and school medical health care."

There are 8.5 million students in the three stages of education in Algeria (primary, intermediate, and secondary), according to the latest statistics for the current academic year. The school dropout rate is 4.7%. The human rights organization pointed out that there are other reasons for school dropouts, such as "the problem of over crowdedness in classrooms, as the maximum number of students within one classroom reaches about 48 students."

According to the organization, school dropout is the most serious problem in the country's educational system. The report also noted that the education sector is facing a crisis despite the substantial funds the state has allocated to this sector, with a budget of seven billion dollars annually.

The report added that the evidence is in the latest report that was issued by the United Nations Educational, Scientific and Cultural Organization (UNESCO) in 2017, which ranked Algeria in the 119th position out of 140 Arab and foreign countries in terms of the quality of education.

In the 1990s, when the issue of low school enrollment and the short duration of schooling for girls was at the centre of the debate, particularly in underdeveloped and developing countries, in industrialized countries, and in the same period, a new concern emerged, that of boys dropping out of school. Indeed, the repetition and school dropout rates indicated a male predominance, raising questions among the researchers.

> A new phenomenon has emerged in certain countries where gender disparities in education are turning in favour of girls, and therefore against boys, both in terms of participation and performance. This is particularly evident in countries that have achieved universal access and have high participation rates for both girls and boys, at least at the primary stage of schooling. (Jha & Kelleher, 2006, 3–4)

This problem of the failure of boys, even if it has been the subject of numerous publications and research works (Browne & Mistos, 1998; Wilson, 2004; Jha & Kelleher, 2006; Sax, 2009; Auduc, 2009), does not have high visibility, and the abandonment of studies is most often approached in the omission of one of its main characteristics, which mainly concerns boys. As Bereni and Chauvin et al. stated, "School sociology has long ignored the gender variable, focusing too much on the question of the production of social inequalities thought of in terms of class" (2008, 95).

In Algeria, the situation of boys is particularly worrying, and the figures concerning school dropouts reveal the disparities between the sexes in the school system (see Graph 12.1 below).

These dropout rates among the school population, which constitute a major problem of the educational system in Algeria, are accompanied by repetition rates in primary and middle school, which show significant disparities between the sexes, sometimes reaching middle to ten percentage points away between girls and boys (UNICEF, 2014; see Graph 12.2 and Chart 12.1 below). Algeria is one of the countries where the gender gap in grade repetition is the largest (UNESCO, 2010).

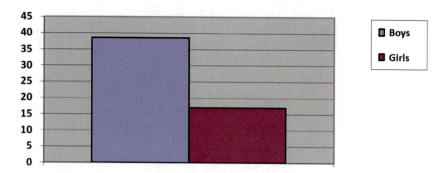

Graph 12.1 Dropout rate before the last year of middle school by gender in 2011. (Source: UNICEF (2014))

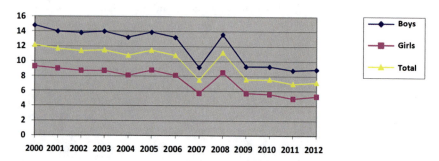

Graph 12.2 Primary repetition rate from 2000 to 2012. (Source: Calculation based on MEN data (UNICEF, 2014))

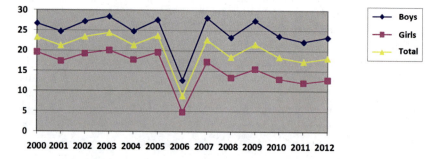

Chart 12.1 Average repetition rate from 2000 to 2012. (Source: Calculation based on MEN data (UNICEF, 2014))

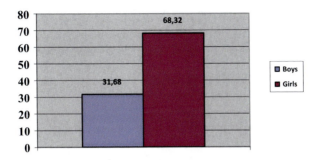

Chart 12.2 Baccalaureate pass rate in 2015. (Source: Algeria Press Service (APS))

The gap thus widens as one advances in the years of study. This trend is also confirmed by the baccalaureate results, for example, in 2015, the success rate for girls was 68.32% versus 31.68% for boys (see Chart 12.2).

Thus, hundreds of thousands of students, especially boys, many of whom are still at the age of compulsory schooling, leave school before obtaining a diploma. However, these exits without qualifications have harmful consequences on their future life, on their ability to integrate in a sustainable way in an increasingly complex society, and with a labour market whose requirements are growing. Indeed, it is useful to recall the vulnerability of undereducated and unqualified populations, as well as the risk of social marginalization, unemployment, and precariousness that they face.

5 Gender and University Attendance

The Programme for International Student Assessment (PISA) by the Organisation for Economic Co-operation and Development's (OCDE) measures 15-year-olds' ability to use their reading, mathematics, and science knowledge and skills to meet real-life challenges. Beyond mere attendance, the results of the PISA survey show that girls not only have better academic performance and more positive attitude towards school and learning but also nurture higher expectations of themselves (OCDE, 2015).

The observation of disparities between girls and boys in education is marked in higher education, where the sex ratio continues to fall from 331 boys for 100 girls in 1976 to 69 boys for 100 girls in 2004 (Kateb, 2011). Moreover, the average ratio of female to male students in higher-level education in Algeria from 2004 to 2021 was estimated to be 1.32%, with a minimum of 1.07% in 2004 and a maximum of 1.41% in 2020. The latest value from 2021 is 1.4%. For comparison, the world average in 2021 based on 41 countries is 1.17% (UNESCO, 2022).

Girls thus constitute the majority of the university student population. This increase in the number of women seems to indicate a greater investment in longer study cycles leading to diplomas, which is explained by higher grades and pass rates than for boys (Kateb, 2011).

In other countries, the same phenomenon is observed at different times. According to a vast number of studies, women now outperform men in most Western societies in terms of educational achievement (Buchmann & DiPrete, 2006; Buchmann et al., 2008; Organization for Economic Co-operation and Development (OECD), 2012). In many Western countries, women now outperform men in terms of educational achievement, according to a number of studies (Buchmann et al., 2008; OECD, 2012; Snyder & Dillow, 2011). In addition, trends in practically all Western countries even lead to greater advantages for women in education, notwithstanding inequalities in size and speed.

In the United States, for instance, Snyder and Dillow (2011) showed that since 1982, women have outperformed men in terms of educational attainment. According to statistics on the gender gap in education across all of Europe, they are roughly comparable to those for the United States (Helbig, 2012).

It is therefore clear that in the space of a few years, girls' schooling caught up with that of boys' in several countries; according to Establet, "few things in the social world have changed so clearly and so quickly" (1988, in Terrail, 1992, 646).

In Algeria, girls outnumber boys in terms of success rates, and more girls than boys are enrolling in universities. Of the 1,090,592 students in Algerian institutions who were on pace to graduate during the 2011–2012 academic year, 60% were female (ONS, 2013). No more than 10% of girls were enrolled in universities during the 1981–1982 academic year; this number increased to 50% in the early 1990s (Mansouri-Acherrar, 1996) and over 60% by the 2010–2011 academic year (ONS, 2012).

Even in fields of study that once seemed to be reserved only for boys, girls are now present. In a few years, they have made up half of the students enrolled in universities, up from 36% in 1993–1994 after graduation. There were 148 girls per 100 boys in the natural and earth sciences,

140 in literature, and 133 in the medical sciences in 2010–2011, for example, making some fields of study more gender-focused than others.

The advantage of women is equally obvious in regard to university degrees. From the 2016–2017 academic year, girls represented 65.31% of graduates across all fields of study (ONS, 2018; see Tables 12.5 and 12.6). Girls make up an overwhelming majority in various fields, accounting for 65% of graduates in the humanities, social sciences, and medicine, 80% in the natural and earth sciences, and 83% in languages. Girls are performing significantly better than boys even in the "hard sciences," a field that was historically dominated by men (68% in 2009–2010 and 70% in 2010–2011; see Table 12.5). Only the "technology," "veterinary," and "applied sciences" fields still lean towards men.

6 Understanding Gender Disparities in Education: Contributions from Studies

The analyses of psychosocial orientation, which offer three primary explanatory registers, are the most relevant theoretical frameworks for explaining the differences between boys and girls in the educational system.

The first highlights the feminization of the teaching field and the consequent lack of masculine role models that young males can look up to. According to research conducted in Tunisia, the proportion of women employed in the teaching profession is one of the factors most strongly associated with girls' academic performance (Lockheed & Mete, 2007). In contrast, boys are said to "search in vain, in primary school, for figures of male identification in a universe that is overwhelmingly female" (Bisaillon, 1992, 7, in Bouchard & Saint-Amant, 1993, 21).

Strong feminization of the teaching profession is observed in practically all countries. This phenomenon is probably explained by the desire of women to move towards a profession that allows them to adapt their professional life and their family life, the responsibility of this being socially attributed to them. In Algeria, even if the same phenomenon is observed, it is marked by great regional disparities; for example, if the percentage of female teachers in primary education in 2010–2011 is 54%, from one wilaya to another, this rate is very variable; for example, in Adrar (in southern Algeria), it is 27%, and in Algiers (the capital city), it is 85% (ONS, 2014).

Table 12.5 Proportion of girls enrolled in university and of students holding university degrees, by discipline, from 2004–2005 to 2010–2011

	2004–2005	2005–2006	2006–2007	2007–2008	2008–2009	2009–2010	2010–2011
Enrolled in university	56.9	56.1	57.6	58.5	58.5	58.7	58.8
On track to graduate[a]	57.4	56.7	58.3	59	59	59.3	59.5
Graduated by discipline	61.1	60.4	60.4	61.1	63.4	65	64.7
Hard sciences	64	60.6	60.6	61.7	64.2	67.7	70.5
Applied sciences	48.9	45.9	45.9	28.4	32.2	38.7	30.8
Technology	37.2	35.9	35.9	36.6	34.8	36.2	35.9
Medical sciences	58	59.8	59.8	61.6	62.4	66.4	65.3
Veterinary sciences	52.3	42.9	42.9	45	45.3	48.6	44.1
Natural/earth sciences	73.1	76.5	76.5	73	73.8	76.9	80
Social/human sciences	60.8	61.9	61.9	61.4	63.8	65.9	65
Language and literature	83.7	79.2	79.2	82.3	82	83.8	82.6

Sources: ONS, based on statistics from MESR. Years 2004–2005 and 2005–2006 (ONS, annual report no. 26); years 2007–2008 to 2010–2011 (ONS, annual report no. 29)
[a]Graduation: the first university degree after three years of studies

Table 12.6 The evolution of graduates: 2014/2015 to 2016/2017

Field	Total graduates			Percentage of females		
	2014/2015	2015/2016	2016/2017	2014/2015	2015/2016	2016/2017
Hard sciences	15,709	16,459	16,431	11,363	12,033	12,457
Applied sciences	122	0	–	34	0	–
Technology	62,539	58,971	61,893	27,025	25,446	27,274
Medical sciences	7044	5348	7458	4895	3846	5744
Veterinary sciences	1344	1844	1380	814	963	677
Nature/earth sciences	30,796	30,307	34,183	24,820	24,672	27,387
Social sciences/humanities	138,137	131,671	132,648	88,816	83,651	83,397
Letters and languages	56,285	48,083	49,107	45,961	39,653	41,204
Total	311,976	292,683	303,100	203,728	190,264	197,940
%	100	100	100	65.30	65.01	65.31

Source: Ministère de l'enseignement supérieur et de la recherche scientifique (ONS, 2018)

Indeed, according to the Ministry of Education, in the academic year 2017/2018, among a total of 101,388 teachers in high schools, 66,054 were women (see Table 12.7). Moreover, there were 16,729 women teaching foreign languages (French, English, German, Spanish, and Italian) in 2017/2018.

Table 12.7 Teaching staff in secondary education by sex and discipline: 2015/2016 to 2017/2018

Subjects taught	Teaching staff in secondary education			Of which: Women in secondary education		
	2015/16	2016/17	2017/18	2015/16	2016/17	2017/18
Arabic letters	11,600	11,659	11,713	8782	9010	9199
Philosophy	4979	5040	5094	3540	3662	3785
Social sciences (history and geography)	8354	8471	8544	5193	5415	5638
Islamic sciences	5052	5124	5169	2401	2418	2447
French language	9600	9685	9702	7298	7431	7521
English language	9384	9527	9561	7686	7842	7968
German language	634	652	681	447	456	473
Spanish language	733	769	807	588	606	651
Italian language	147	172	190	90	106	116
Mathématics	11,636	11,676	11,640	6787	7081	7301
Physic sciences	11,123	11,116	11,054	6127	6388	6734
Technology	193	145	148	50	51	54
Natural and life sciences	10,149	10,040	10,048	7605	7703	8043
Physical education & sport	5448	5529	5565	446	437	447
Drawing (art education)	286	258	261	124	116	115
Music (music education)	217	214	243	126	134	151
Tamazight	430	509	522	288	354	365
Management and economy	2868	2979	3025	1699	1801	1901
Computer science	855	1231	1638	476	741	1024
Civil engineering	1424	1441	1448	480	513	555
Electrical engineering	1999	1945	1852	664	674	700
Mechanical engineering	1841	1775	1672	305	315	334
Process engineering	794	804	811	466	501	532
Total	99,746	100,761	101,388	61,668	63,755	66,054
Of which: Foreign	05	03	01	00	00	00

Source: ONS (2018)

The second explanatory register relates to gendered socialization and stereotypes that shape feminine and masculine habits. Girls' academic success would be attributed to the typically feminine values—discipline, order, and docility—that are instilled in them from a young age and that predispose them to be better students than boys. They would benefit more from what the school has to offer since they would be better able to adapt to institutional norms and standards. According to researchers, teachers help build sexual stereotypes in the classroom and are responsible for the low academic performance of males due to their expectations and preconceptions about their performance (Jha & Kelleher, 2006; Duru Bellat, 1994).

The third explanatory register focuses on how young students see masculinity and femininity as well as how attitude towards school change during adolescence since for some people, having a successful academic career and being a man are somehow at odds with one another. Unlike "the social definition of femininity… [which] more easily matches the expectations of the institution" (Felouzis, 1990, in Terrail, 1992, 665).

> Boy groups also exercise control over socially appropriate male behaviour. In this case, doing well at school can be denounced as "feminine". The alternative, schematically, is then either to reject school by displaying virile behaviour (challenging authority in particular), or to succeed in "masculine" subjects, i.e., science or sport. Boys are therefore exposed to a real dilemma: to appear virile or to be a good student. (Duru-Bellat, 2010, 201)

This is particularly true in working-class areas, where academic success risks call into question the virility of boys. The Anglo-Saxons speak of "laddish anti-learning culture," and counter-school culture (anti-school culture) like Paul Willis (2011) who carried out work on young men from the working class, in which he questions the mechanisms of resistance to the school order, as elaborated and perceived by these young people, as well as the process of self-elimination in which they voluntarily enrol.

Thus, it appears that the influence of the processes of socialization and construction of gender on the development of the relationship to school and knowledge is considerable. It is by internalizing cultural models and social expectations that girls and boys adopt behaviour appropriate to their gender and social class.

To this must be added the change in mentalities and social practices in favour of equality. Indeed, the influence of feminist movements and the decline of discrimination against girls in society have led to a change in the attitude of parents concerning the education of their daughters (Kateb, 2005, 2011), and it can be assumed that the growing presence of female role models in labour market work impacts the motivation and academic and professional ambitions of young girls.

Moreover, it should be noted that women's investment in studies has become possible because they have prolonged their celibacy. In fact, the average age at marriage continues to decline, as well as the average age of the first pregnancy in Algeria, which were 30 and 31.8 in 2015, respectively (ONS, 2015).

> Fecundity management and women choosing to marry and to have their first child at a later age are demographic factors that have allowed greater participation of women in higher education and a reduction in drop-out-rates. (Vincent-Lancrin, 2008, 279)

6.1 Age, Wealth, Geographical Disparities, and Gender Reversal

Studying the differences between (generations) towns and rural areas, which are greatly influenced by lifestyle and other socioeconomic factors, and the differences between territories, which are heavily influenced by regional characteristics, would be interesting.

According to the National Office of Statistics (2008), the population living in urban areas, both among women and men, is characterized by a much higher level of education than that of those living in rural areas. The share of uneducated people drops to 16.2% in urban areas, whereas it reaches 29.7% in rural areas. Similarly, the urban population stands out with a relatively high number of people reaching secondary and university levels.

The level of education of the population increases with age, and only 16.8% of people reach the secondary level and 7% of university graduates at the national level. Moreover, 21.9% of young people aged between 20 and 24 years have a secondary level, and 17.8% have a university level.

There are no major differences between regions. However, there are significant differences in the level of education of the population according to the household standard of living.

The poorest 20% of households are characterized by a very low level of education, reflecting a proportion of people with no level of education of 38.3% compared to 11.6% among more affluent people (see Table 12.8).

Table 12.8 Level of education of the population aged 10 and over, ALGERIA, 2006

Variables		None	Primary	Middle	Secondary	Higher education	Number of persons
Region	Centre	21.0	23.8	30.4	17.2	7.6	49,956
	Est	23.6	22.7	29.3	17.2	7.2	44,353
	Ouest	24.8	25.5	27.7	15.6	6.4	32,946
	Sud	22.9	24.3	29.8	17.1	5.9	14,280
Stratum	Urbain	17.4	22.1	30.6	20.3	9.5	79,460
	Rural	29.8	26.3	27.8	12.3	3.8	62,075
Gender	Masculin	16.2	25.7	34.1	17.1	6.8	71,277
	Féminin	29.7	22.1	24.6	16.5	7.2	70,258
Age	10–14 ans	1.8	58.0	39.5	0.7	0.0	18,632
	15–19 ans	4.1	13.5	47.3	31.9	3.2	19,544
	20–24 ans	7.2	16.5	36.6	21.9	17.8	20,031
	25–29 ans	10.4	16.3	35.8	23.9	13.7	16,300
	30–34 ans	14.2	16.4	33.5	27.2	8.7	13,162
	35–39 ans	21.5	25.7	24.7	20.7	7.4	11,053
	40–44 ans	30.5	27.9	21.1	15.2	5.2	9586
	45–49 ans	41.0	26.4	15.5	12.0	5.1	7643
	50–54 ans	49.1	28.9	10.4	6.9	4.7	7350
	55–59 ans	59.8	24.0	7.3	4.5	4.5	5193
	60 ans & +	85.1	10.7	2.4	1.1	0.8	13,038
Index quintile richness	Poorest	38.3	28.7	23.8	7.3	1.9	27,365
	Second	26.6	27.1	30.5	12.4	3.4	28,105
	Average	21.1	24.7	32.4	16.4	5.4	28,449
	Fourth	17.6	22.4	31.7	20.7	7.6	28,762
	Richest	11.6	17.0	28.3	26.6	16.5	28,855

Source: ONS (2008)

The secondary and university levels increase with the standard of living of the households to reach more than 42% of the population belonging to the 20% wealthiest households in contrast to only 9.2% of poorer households.

Concerning the schooling of 6–15-year-olds, survey data show a gross enrollment rate of 92.4% of the entire population in this age group. Differences are observed according to sex in favour of boys, whose rate reaches 93.1% versus 91.6% for girls (ONS, 2008).

Graph 12.3 (below) shows the enrollment rates by age and sex. The progression of schooling takes place in the same way for 6–10-year-olds, regardless of the gender of the child. The school enrollment rate reaches

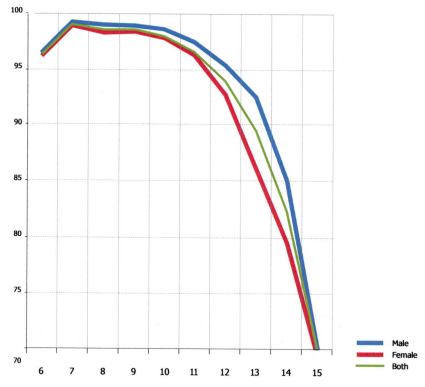

Graph 12.3 School enrollment rate by age of 6–15 years and by gender, ALGERIA, 2006. (Source: ONS (2008))

its maximum value when children reach ten years of age for boys and girls. Beyond the age of ten, this rate drops gradually, and more rapidly in girls. At the ages of 11, 12, 13, and 14, the gap between the schooling of boys and that of girls is increasingly pronounced, in favour of boys. At the age of 15, there is an identical school enrollment rate of 75% for both genders.

This again proves that several factors influence the level of schooling, the place of residence, the level of education of the mother and, in particular, the wealth index. According to place of residence, the gap between urban and rural areas is approximately five points. In urban areas, there is no gender difference, unlike in rural areas, where the rate is less than 90% for girls.

The level of education of the mother also seems to have a significant influence on both the overall schooling rate and that of girls. Significant differences are observed according to the level of education of the mothers. The most discriminating factor in terms of children's schooling remains the household's level of wealth, in the sense that the schooling rate increases significantly with the rise in the household's level of economic wealth. The poorest households stand out clearly with a very low level of schooling for boys and even more so for girls (81.5%), a difference of more than 11 points compared to the national average.

This leads us to conclude that if access to schooling seems to be done equally between boys and girls for three quarters of the wealthiest households, the same is not true for the poorest households. Indeed, the gap between the enrollment rate of girls and that of boys widens as the level of household wealth decreases, reaching six points of difference in favour of boys in the poorest households (see Table 12.9).

Among young people aged 15–19, the male population is characterized by the predominance of the level of average education, and girls seem to be much better educated; the share of those reaching the secondary level represents 37.2%, whereas it is only 26.7% for boys (ONS).

Among the 20–24-year-olds, there is a higher proportion of women with secondary education compared to men (22% versus 13.1% for men). However, there remains a nonnegligible proportion of women without education (11.3% versus only 3% for men). The same trend is observed with those aged 25–29, with a larger share of uneducated women (ONS).

The level of education increases significantly across generations, especially among women. This demonstrates the efforts made in the field of education through the various generations since independence.

Table 12.9 School enrollment rate of 6–15-year-olds

Part relative des enfants âgés de 6–15 ans scolarisés, MICS3 ALGÉRIE, 2006

Variables		Masculin		Feminin		Total	
		Scolarisation rate	Number of children	Scolarisation rate	Number of children	Scolarisation rate	Number of children
Region	Centre	93.3	5753	93.3	5513	93.3	11,265
	Est	93.1	5735	90.9	5614	92.0	11,349
	Ouest	91.8	4040	89.5	3877	90.7	7917
	Sud	95.3	2226	93.1	2148	94.2	4374
Strate	Urbain	94.8	9490	95.8	9074	95.3	18,565
	Rural	91.2	8264	87.0	8077	89.1	16,341
Age	6	96.2	1443	95.8	1473	96.0	2916
	7	98.3	1573	98.1	1418	98.2	2991
	8	98.2	1606	97.6	1547	97.9	3153
	9	98.1	1556	97.7	1598	97.9	3154
	10	97.8	1824	97.3	1728	97.5	3552
	11	96.9	1873	95.9	1850	96.4	3723
	12	95.3	1966	93.1	1934	94.2	3900
	13	92.9	1978	87.8	1929	90.4	3908
	14	86.9	1948	82.5	1876	84.7	3824
	15	75.0	1986	74.8	1798	74.9	3784
Mother's level of education	None	90.8	8838	87.5	8620	89.2	17,457
	Primary	93.6	3760	94.1	3676	93.8	7435
	Middle	96.1	2718	97.0	2569	96.6	5287
	Secondary	98.0	1953	97.6	1873	97.8	3827
	Higher	98.4	444	97.4	372	97.9	815
	NSP	55.5	42	75.4	41	65.3	83

Quintile of the index of richness						
Poorest	88.7	4115	81.5	4008	85.1	8123
Second	92.0	3743	91.1	3572	91.5	7315
Middle	94.0	3497	94.9	3470	94.4	6968
Forth	95.4	3233	96.1	3133	95.7	6366
Richest	96.9	3167	97.5	2967	97.2	6134

Source: ONS (2008)

7 THE STUDY OF LANGUAGES: A FEMALE SPECIALTY

It is generally assumed that women are able to learn languages at a faster rate than men. Much empirical evidence suggests that the female brain is more suited to language learning, even from birth (Dionne et al., 2003).

In Algeria, only 45% of high school graduates enrol in literature, philosophy, foreign languages, and management courses, compared to 55% who obtain a baccalaureate in scientific and technical courses. However, more than 60% of new students choose social sciences, humanities, and foreign languages. Moreover, 21.66% of baccalaureate holders from the fields of technical, experimental, and mathematical sciences voluntarily ask to switch to social sciences, humanities, and foreign languages studies (MESR, 2022).

Females have better motivation. Given how difficult it is to establish motivation, this is arguably the most contentious argument supporting gender differences in language learning. According to some studies, this is because boys and girls both regard languages as being feminine topics, with males choosing more traditionally masculine disciplines such as math and physics. The prevalence of female language teachers, who serve as role models for females, frequently supports this notion. Studies continue to affirm that females' and males' brains have key differences, especially when it comes to learning new languages. Are women advantaged in the linguistic field? Why would they learn a foreign language more easily? According to a 2011 study by the Ministry of Higher Education and Research, there were 74.1% of women in languages, against 25.9% of men, but also 70.8% of women student in letters and language sciences.

Thus, there is a majority of women in the literary streams, while a majority of men choose a scientific stream. So how can these stark statistics be explained? Why would women feel more comfortable learning languages?

To determine the role of the sex variable in foreign language learning success, it is important to review and connect data gathered from several tests and studies, all of them dealing with boys' and girls' achievement, attitudes and motivation as regards foreign languages. In the light of the data analysed, the hypothesis put forward for consideration is that girls' achievement in foreign language learning is enhanced by the interaction of different factors. Each factor is activated in a different way for boys and for girls, with the result that girls are equipped with a combined network of variables whose mutual influence is ultimately responsible for their success in learning foreign languages and the growing number of female language students that exceeds that of males.

7.1 Neurological and Cognitive Factors: Verbal Intelligence and Aptitude

Since the term's definition is also up for debate, it is difficult to pinpoint the role of aptitude in language learning. In general, and as Stern observes "the concept of aptitude for languages is derived from everyday experience that some language learners appear to have a 'gift' for languages which others lack" (1990, 367). It is clear that aptitude alone (as with other elements) cannot define achievement in terms of the relationship between aptitude and success in language learning. However, Krashen recognises a bad language learner "might be the result of both attitudinal factors […] as well as low aptitude" (1988, 38). Thus, the question to be asked is "is there any correlation between sex and aptitude that might favour achievement?"

Neurophysiological research has demonstrated that there are gender disparities in how the brain functions, with women outperforming men in verbal tasks and men outperforming women in nonverbal tasks in tasks involving visual and spatial skills: "According to behavioural tests and clinical data, women appear to be less lateralized for language functions, yet as a group they are superior to men in language skills" (Springer & Deutsch, 1989, 224). Female superiority in colour-naming tests in both native and foreign languages, as noted by Yang (2001), may be due to gender differences in the development of cognitive abilities, as well as differences in learning styles. In this regard, Jiménez Catalán (2003) notes that research on vocabulary learning strategies suggests that males prefer visual and tactile learning while females prefer auditory learning. Powell (1979) notes that girls are superior to boys in all facets of the linguistic process in the case of boys' and girls' verbal abilities, indicating a better potential for language learning.

The amount of data available is quite tiny, so the advantage of girls in verbal processing may not be as great as thought, despite the fact that research on the subject indicates that sex differences start very early. Dale (1976) came to the conclusion that there aren't many, if any, differences between boys and girls in the preschool and early school years after reviewing the evidence on sex differences in language development. The author asserts, however, that "around the age of ten or eleven years, girls establish a definite pattern of superior verbal performance, which continues through the high-school and college years" (1976, 311). Dale highlights the occurrence of a "consistent, though modest difference" in the assessment of verbal abilities, including spelling, punctuation, verbal originality, comprehension of challenging written texts, and logical verbal relationships. Girls' perceived higher verbal abilities in adolescence are likely due to extralinguistic variables like society or personality.

The facts lead to the conclusion that, while males and females have the same linguistic potential as humans (aptitude in a broad sense), females' linguistic talents appear to be more susceptible to being pushed in order to achieve higher levels of linguistic competence.

7.2   Attitude, Motivation, and Personality

Although attitudes do not directly affect learning, they do lead to motivation, which does affect learning according to Spolsky (1990, 49). A learner's positive attitude fosters the growth of strong motivation, which is correlated with competence. As a result, attitude is related to achievement through motivation. A person's tendency to react favourably or unfavourably to an object is referred to as their attitude. In this regard, the studies by Pritchard (1987), Powell and Littlewood (1983), and Powell and Batters (1985) all suggest that girls are more receptive to the language than boys are, as well as to the speakers and the culture. It is generally agreed upon that females' positive attitudes and strong levels of motivation are key factors in their success.

According to Van Els et al. (1984, 116), motivation is defined as "those factors that energize behaviour and give it direction." Although there are many kinds of motivation, Gardner and Lambert's (1972) distinction between integrative and instrumental motivation is still widely regarded. While the latter assumes a good attitude towards the speakers and the culture, the former is tied to practical issues (find a job, pass an exam), which motivate the learner's activity. Achievement has been demonstrated to be correlated with integrative motivation.

Girls often have more favourable attitudes towards learning a language, according to the contributions examined (Burstall, 1975). Boys' motivations are typically of an instrumental nature; for instance, they choose a foreign language because they need "a subject to fill in the timetable" (Powell & Littlewood, 1983, 36) or because of the grades they received in previous years (Palacios Martínez, 1994). In contrast, girls tend to demonstrate integrative reasons for studying foreign languages (namely their interest in the speakers and the cultures of those languages). However, one sort of instrumental motivation is consistently linked to girls in the majority of surveys: the conviction that language proficiency would be useful to them in a future career or field of study.

Self-confidence is almost universally cited in the research as being crucial to foreign language learning and overall achievement. The authors Dulay, Burt, and Krashen expressly state that "the self-confident, secure person is a more successful language learner" (1982, 75) with regard to the connection between self-confidence and language learning. Additionally, Krashen adds that motivation and self-assurance are related because, in theory, "the self-confident or secure person will be more able to encourage intake and will also have a lower filter" (1988, 23). In brief, it is projected that self-confidence would be correlated with foreign language learning success, along with related factors like fear and inhibition.

Studying linguistic self-confidence has revealed gender differences: generally speaking, girls demonstrate greater confidence in their linguistic competency for language learning and also have a tendency to appraise themselves more favourably. Boys seemed less confident in their capacity to learn a second language, according to Powell and Batters (1985).

Van der Meulen (1987) cites a number of studies that show girls aged seven to ten score higher on perceptions of their own talents, particularly their reading and spelling ability. Last but not least, it's intriguing to consider Powell's (1979) association between ability and assurance in his argument that boys' underachievement may be caused by girls' better ability and consequent confidence.

7.3 Social Factors: The Environment

Girls' success in foreign language learning may also be attributed to societal expectations. According to Powell and Littlewood (1983), who looked into the potential link between attitude and social class, the latter "played no significant role in the distinction of attitude scores" (1983, 36), so, for instance, all girls demonstrated the same attitude towards French regardless of their social class (i.e., a more positive attitude than boys, which ultimately contributed to their linguistic achievement).

According to Francis (2000, 88), "increased ambition, coupled with a feeling that opportunities in the workplace are skewed against them, is what has provided girls with new motivation for achievement at school."

Girls still have to meet different expectations for their future vocations and social responsibilities, which may explain why they perform better in language learning than boys. This explanation comes from a sociological perspective. It is undeniable that there is a distinction between the activities of men and women, with women continuing to maintain a dominant role at home.

It is also true that boys and girls are trained to assume different occupational expectations and different relations to power throughout early childhood, despite the advancements achieved towards equal employment possibilities and pay. With girls "tend[ing] to opt for artistic or 'caring' professions, and boys opting for occupations that were scientific, technical, or business oriented," Francis acknowledges that the gender divide is still present in future career choices (2000, 90). In addition, as Crawford (1995, 88) pointed out, "social patterns are mirrored and even exaggerated by mass media."

According to the sex-role differentiation hypothesis, "men specialize in instrumental or task behaviours and women specialize in expressive or social activities" (1982, 145), for which, on the other hand, they appear neurologically better prepared. This is relevant too to boys' and girls' expected social roles and behaviour in Algerian society. Holmes contends that women are given the responsibility of serving as role models for proper behaviour in the community (1992, 172). Both theories can be combined in the argument that women fulfil the role of models through a variety of verbal interaction-heavy tasks performed in private settings, such as childrearing.

To put it another way, both society and the home promote girls' interest in language because it is necessary for their future responsibilities as mothers and emotional pillars of the family. Girls' communication abilities are therefore improved as a result of their expected social behaviour. In fact, it has been suggested that girls' preference for languages is significantly influenced by society's role divide, which itself may have a neurological or evolutionary basis. This division, in turn, shapes professional sex stereotypes. Van Alphen proposes the following relationship between work division and speech pattern:

> Women apparently learn a speech style which is more appropriate for the domestic sphere: it is supportive, harmonizing, open-hearted, "cooperative". Men apparently learn a speech style more appropriate for the domain of public discussion: it is dominant, fast, loud and "competitive". Those

differences in speech styles reinforce the (unacceptable) division of labour between women and men: men are more visible in, and ideologically defined by, the public sphere, whereas women are relegated (either actually or ideologically) to the domestic sphere. (1987, 71)

Parental jobs appear to have an impact on the importance parents place on language development and the importance they instil in their boys or girls. Parents' evaluation also replicates societal expectations for occupations, as Pritchard notes, which results in girls receiving "more overt encouragement to learn languages than boys" (1987, 70). The unique roles that society assigns to men and women will be reflected in these vocational expectations, as was already indicated.

8 Conclusion

The analysis of the various statistical data on national education shows, on the one hand, an evolution in the rates of schooling and in the lengthening of the duration of schooling, but it also reveals high rates in grade repetition and school dropout, as well as significant gender gaps. Regarding access to education, these disparities are to the disadvantage of girls, particularly in rural areas, where enrollment rates are lowest, but in regard to school life expectancy and graduation, the figures for these measures show that boys drop out of school more than girls and are less likely to graduate. Repetition is also more frequent among the male school population. Moreover, the analysis also shows a strong feminization of the teaching profession marked by large regional disparities between the northern and southern regions of Algeria.

Article 53 of the constitution and Article 12 of the National Education Orientation Law n°08-04 of 23 January 2008 both provide compulsory education for children aged 6–16 and gender parity. These texts are not honoured, as seen by the gender discrepancies in the educational system of today and the high school dropout rate.

Regarding the lack of schooling, the most apparent reasons for these shortcomings are related to the inadequacy of school infrastructure, as suggested by the low schooling rates in the most isolated and least urbanized regions as well as the mother's level of education and the level of household wealth. It is challenging to find satisfactory answers to the questions of school abandonment and the historical reversal of gender inequities, but these topics also present intriguing study opportunities.

The analysis further shows the strong attraction of female students for language studies in Algerian universities. There are some obvious distinctions between males and females, according to research on how the sex variable relates to foreign language learning in higher education in Algeria. The broad findings of the analysis are that girls consistently outperform boys in terms of overall achievement in languages. Compared to boys, girls are much more likely to choose to study foreign languages.

Moreover, boys are better at spatial activities than girls, while girls often outperform boys in verbal tasks (hearing, speaking, reading, and writing). Girls regularly show greater enthusiasm in learning foreign languages than boys do, as well as a clear preference for the language's culture. Boys' incentives for learning the language are typically utilitarian, whereas ladies' objectives are typically integrative. Furthermore, girls are noticeably more assured in their ability to learn the language. Boys, on the other hand, seem to be more critical of their linguistic skills.

Finally, the sexism of occupations in society still promotes language study as a feat for females. Girls consequently tend to view languages as having greater vocational relevance. In other words, individuals tend to have a stronger belief that learning a language will benefit them in their future professions. These findings seem to imply that a variety of learner and environmental variables affect both boys' and girls' contrastive achievement in foreign language learning and thus explain the growing number of female language students in Algerian universities, which exceeds that of males.

References

Auduc, J. L. (2009). *Sauvons les garçons!* Descartes & Cie.
Bereni, L., Chauvin, S., Jaunait, A., & Revillard, A. (2008). *Introduction au gender studdies; manuel des études sur le Genre.* DeBoek.
Bouchard, P., & Saint-Amant, J. C. (1993). La réussite scolaire des filles et l'abandon des garçons: un enjeu à portée politique pour les femmes. *Recherches féministes,* 6(2), 21–37.
Browne, K., & Mitsos, E. (1998). Gender differences in education: The achievement of boys. *Sociology Review,* September, 27–31.
Buchmann, C., & DiPrete, T. A. (2006). The Growing Female Advantage in College Completion: The Role of Family Background and Academic Achievement. *American Sociological Review,* 71(4), 515–541. https://doi.org/10.1177/000312240607100401

Buchmann, C., Di Prete, T. A., & Mcdaniel, A. (2008). Gender inequalities in education. *Annual Review of Sociology, 34*, 319–337. https://doi.org/10.1146/annurev.soc.34.040507.134719

Burstall, C. (1975). Factors affecting foreign language learning: A consideration of some relevant research findings. *Language Teaching and Linguistics Abstracts, 8*, 105–125.

CNES. (2016). *Rapport National sur le Développement Humain 2013–2015*. CNES.

Crawford, M. (1995). *Talking difference: On gender and language*. Sage Publications, Inc.

Dale, P. (1976). *Language development: Structure and function*. Holt, Rinehart and Winston.

Desvages, H. (1972). La scolarisation des musulmans en Algérie (1882-1962) dans l'enseignement public français, étude statistique. *Cahiers de la Méditerranée, 4*(1), 55–72.

Dionne, G., Dale, P. S., Boivin, M., & Plomin, R. (2003). Genetic evidence for bidirectional effects of early lexical and grammatical development. *Child Development, 74*, 394–412.

Djebbar, A. (2008). Le système éducatif algérien: miroir d'une société en crise et en mutation. In T. Chenntouf (Ed.), *L'Algérie face à la mondialisation* (pp. 164–207). CODESRIA.

Dulay, H., Burt, M., & Krashen, S. D. (1982). *Language two*. Newbury House, Rowley.

Duru Bellat, M. (1994). Filles et garçons à l'école, approches sociologiques et psychosociales. *Revue Française de Pédagogie, 109*, 11–141.

Duru-Bellat, M. (2010). Ce que la mixité fait aux élèves. *Revue de l'OFCE, 114*, 197–212. https://doi.org/10.3917/reof.114.0197

Francis, B. (2000). *Boys, girls and achievement: Addressing the classroom issues*. Routledge.

Galbraith, R. C., Olsen, S. F., Duerden, D. S., & Harris, W. L. (1982). The differentiation hypothesis: Distinguishing between perceiving and memorizing. *The American Journal of Psychology, 95*(4), 655–667. https://doi.org/10.2307/1422191

Gardner, R. C., & Lambert, W. E. (1972). *Attitudes and motivation in second language learning*. Newbury House Publishers.

Helbig, M. (2012). Boys do not benefit from male teachers in their reading and mathematics skills: Empirical evidence from 21 European Union and OECD countries. *British Journal of Sociology of Education, 33*(5), 661–677. https://doi.org/10.1080/01425692.2012.674782

Holmes, J. (1992). *An introduction to sociolinguistics*. Longman. https://www.ohchr.org/en/hr-bodies/upr/dz-index

Jha, J., & Kelleher, F. (2006). *Boys' underachievement in education, an exploration in selected commonwealth countries*. Commonwealth of Learning.

Jiménez Catalán, R. M. (2003). Sex differences in L2 vocabulary learning strategies. *International Journal of Applied Linguistics, 13*(1), 54–77.
Kadri, A. (2007). Histoire du système d'enseignement colonial en Algérie. In F. Abecassis, G. Boyer, B. Falaize, G. Meynier, & M. Zancarini-Fournel (Eds.), *La France et l'Algérie: leçons d'histoire* (pp. 19–39). ENS Éditions.
Kateb, K. (2005). *École, population et société en Algérie*. L'Harmattan.
Kateb, K. (2011). Scolarisation féminine massive, système matrimonial et rapports de genre au Maghreb. *Genre, sexualité & société, 6*. http://gss.revues.org/1987
Krashen, S. (1988). *Second language acquisition and second language learning*. Prentice Hall.
Lockheed, M. E., & Mete, E. (2007). Tunisia: Strong central policies for gender equity. In M. A. Lewis, & M. E. Lockheed (Eds.), *Exclusion, Gender and Education, Case studies from the developing world. A companion volume to Inexcusable Absence*. Center for Global Development.
Mansouri-Acherrar, L. (1996). La scolarisation des filles en Algérie. *Recherches internationales, 43–44*(Hiver-printemps), 179–190.
Middle East Monitor (MEMO). (2018). *Algeria: 400,000 children drop out of school annually*. https://www.middleeastmonitor.com/20180417-algeria-400000-children-drop-out-of-school-annually/
Ministère de l'Education Nationale (MEN). Downloaded from https://www.education.gov.dz/fr/systeme-educatif-algerien/
Ministère de l'Enseignement Superieur et de la Recherche (MESR). (2022). https://www.mesrs.dz/index.php/fr/accueil/
OCDE. (2015). *L'égalité des sexes dans l'éducation: Aptitudes, comportement et confiance*. PISA, Editions OCDE.
OECD. (2012). *Closing the Gender Gap: Act Now*. OECD Publishing.
OECD. (2015). *Education at a Glance 2015: OECD Indicators*. OECD Publishing. https://doi.org/10.1787/eag-2015-en.
Office National des Statistiques (ONS). (2008). *Suivi de la situation des enfants et des femmes, Enquête nationale à indicateurs multiples, Rapport Principal* (édition 2008). ONS. Retrieved from https://mics-surveys-prod.s3.amazonaws.com/MICS3/Middle%20East%20and%20North%20Africa/Algeria/2006/Final/Algeria%202006%20MICS_French.pdf
Office National des Statistiques (ONS). (2012, 2013, 2015). L'Algérie en quelques chiffres. ONS. Retrieved from: https://www.ons.dz/IMG/pdf/AQC_R_2015_ED_2016.pdf
ONS. (2014). *Annuaire statistique de l'Algérie, résultats 2010–2012* (Vol. 30, édition 2014). ONS. Retrieved from the site of L'office Nationale des statistiques http://www.ons.dz/IMG/pdf/AnRes10-12No30.pdf
ONS. (2018). *Annuaire statistique de l'Algérie, résultats 2018–2019* (Vol. 871, édition 2018). ONS. Retrieved from the site of Office Nationale des statis-

tiques. Downloaded from https://www.ons.dz/IMG/pdf/education_nat2018-2019.pdf

Ouadah-Bedidi, Z. (2018). Gender inequity in education in Algeria: When inequalities are reversed. *Journal of Education & Social Policy, 5*(2), 84–105.

Palacios Martínez, I. M. (1994). *La Enseñanza del Inglés en España*. Universidad de Santiago de Compostela.

Powell, R. C. (1979). Sex differences in language learning: A review of the evidence. *Audio-Visual Language Journal, 17*(1), 19–24.

Powell, R. C., & Batters, J. D. (1985). Pupils perceptions of foreign language learning at 12+: Some gender differences. *Educational Studies, 11*(1), 12–23.

Powell, R. C., & Littlewood, P. (1983). Why choose French? Boys' and girls' attitudes at the option stage. *The British Journal of Language Teaching, 21*(1), 36–39.

Pritchard, R. (1987). Boys' and girls' attitudes towards French and German. *Educational Research, 29*(1), 12–23.

Sax, L. (2009). *Boys adrift: The five factors driving the growing epidemic of unmotivated boys and underachieving young men*. Basic Books.

Snyder, T. D., & Dillow, S. A. (2011). *Digest of education statistics 2010 (NCES 2011–2015)*. National Centre for Education Statistics, Institute of Education Sciences, U.S. Department of Education.

Spolsky, B. (1990). *Conditions for second language learning*. Oxford University Press.

Springer, S., & Deutsch, G. (1989). *Left brain, right brain*. Freeman.

Stern, H. H. (1990). *Fundamental concepts in language teaching*. Oxford University Press.

Terrail, J. P. (1992). Destins scolaires de sexe: une perspective historique et quelques arguments. *Population, 3*, 645–676.

UNESCO. (2010). *Recueil de données mondiales sur l'éducation 2010, statistiques comparées sur l'éducation dans le monde*. UNESCO.

UNESCO. (2022). *UNESCO's efforts to achieve gender equality in and through education, 2021 highlights*. UNESCO.

UNICEF. (2014). *Algérie, rapport national sur les enfants non scolarisés*. UNICEF. https://reliefweb.int/report/algeria/alg-rie-rapport-national-sur-les-enfants-non-scolaris-s

United Nations Human Rights Council. *Universal periodic review – Algeria*. https://www.ohchr.org/en/hr-bodies/upr/dz-index

Van Alphen, I. (1987). Learning from your peers: The acquisition of gender-specific speech styles. In D. Brouwer & D. de Haan (Eds.), *Women's language, socialization and self-image* (pp. 58–75). Foris Publications.

Van Der Meulen, M. (1987). Self-concept, self-esteem and language: Sex differences in childhood and adolescence. In D. Brouwer & D. de Haan (Eds.), *Women's language, socialization and self-image* (pp. 29–42). Foris Publications.

Van Els, T., Bongaerts, T., Extra, G., Van Os, C., & Jansen-Van Dieten, A. (1984). *Applied linguistics and the learning and teaching of foreign languages*. Edward Arnold.

Vincent-Lancrin, S. (2008). The reversal of gender inequalities in higher education: An on-going trend. In *OCDE, higher education to 2030, Volume 1: Demography* (pp. 265–298). OECD.

Willis, P. E. (2011). *L'école des ouvriers. Comment les enfants d'ouvriers obtiennent des boulots d'ouvriers* (L'ordre des choses, 456p). Agone, coll.

Wilson, D. (2004). Human rights: Promoting gender equality in and through education. *Prospects, 34,* 11–27. https://doi.org/10.1023/B:PROS.0000026677.67065.84.

Yang, Y. L. (2001). Sex and language proficiency level in color-naming performance: An ESL/EFL, perspective. *International Journal of Applied Linguistics, 11*(2), 238–256.

PART V

Sustainability: Student Potential and Communication Ability in the Balance

CHAPTER 13

Diversity and Inclusivity in Tertiary Language Education—The Case of Turkey—Turkiye

Ozlem Yuges

1 Introduction

Stretching across the Middle East and into Southern Europe the Ottoman Empire was one of the great empires of the western world until its demise after the First World War in 1918 but was then revitalised and revolutionised in 1923 as the Republic of Turkey under the rule of Mustafa Kemal, known worldwide as Kemal Ataturk. Throughout its period as a republic, education has always played an important part in building the elites of Turkish society.

Now, in the age of globalisation and the dominance of English as a lingua franca as the global language of business, the teaching of English at university level has become even more important both as a degree in its own right and as the language used in the teaching of degrees in other subjects.

Turkey, or as it is now known, Turkiye, has a working population of about 33.3 million out of a total population of 83,539 in 2023, making it

O. Yuges (✉)
Language Trainer and Intercultural Consultant, London, UK

© The Author(s), under exclusive license to Springer Nature Switzerland AG 2023
H. Abouabdelkader, B. Tomalin (eds.), *Diversity Education in the MENA Region*, https://doi.org/10.1007/978-3-031-42693-3_13

293

the third largest labour force in Europe. Its gross domestic product is estimated as the 16th largest in the world by the International Monetary Fund and it is regarded as one of the world's newly emerging economies.

In the last few decades, the whole world has turned its attention towards globalisation. This has led education systems to re-examine their perceptions and tailor their teaching in order to incorporate sensitivity and diversity in education with the aim of enabling people from other cultural backgrounds to assimilate. Nevertheless, not everyone has welcomed globalisation with open arms. Some parts of society have sought to preserve and protect their identities, culture and customs and resist outside influence. One reason is the danger of linguicide, the death of local languages, as the leading British Linguist David Crystal put it in his book, Language Death, published in 2000. Crystal predicted that by the twenty-second century 5500 of the 6000 languages spoken around the world will have died out. English as an international language will be one of the survivors.

An important dimension of globalisation has been the need to reform education with a greater focus on understanding members of other communities we interact with and optimising our communication skills. This is particularly the case with the teaching and learning of English as a foreign language, as a language of international communication and business. Research by David Crystal and others has revealed that the number of non-native users of English worldwide far exceeds the number of native speakers a response to the fact that English has become the international language of communication. In his book Language Death published in 2000 Crystal predicted that of the 6000 languages spoken in the world today 5500 would become dead languages by the twenty-second century. One of the survivors will be English as an international language, so, how has Turkey developed its teaching of English and other languages at both school and university and college level?

2   Changes in Language Training in Turkey

In 2011 the Turkish Government announced major changes to the language training curriculum in Turkish primary and secondary schools with effects on language training in colleges and universities. The revisions focused on the theoretical framework and each grade and suggested changes in the curriculum, target language skills, evaluation of tasks and activities as well as testing and evaluation. Turkey works on a 12 grade, Sinif in Turkish, primary and secondary education system. English language teaching used to be introduced in the fourth grade but under the new system would be brought forward to the second and third grades in primary schools.

According to the new approach, the language training curriculum would be based both on teaching basic language skills but also on values education, focusing on real communication situations and using the language in real life.

The curriculum itself followed the Common European Framework of Reference for Languages, Language Learning, Teaching, Assessment (CEFR) published by the Council of Europe in 2001 and amended and updated in 2021. The aim of the change in syllabus was to encourage students to see English as a means of communication rather than just a system to be studied, changing the focus in the classroom from students learning the language to using it as well.

In implementing this, the Turkish language teaching system as well as learning the rules also focused on the adoption of teaching materials which contained authentic situations and also on teaching methods which emphasised the development of speaking and listening skills through "hands on" activities using acting out, simulations and other "live" activities in the classroom responding to students' interests and aspirations. Following the initial focus on developing speaking and listening skills, reading and writing skills were introduced in higher grades as the students' knowledge and foreign language use requirements expanded. The new English language teaching syllabus listed the types of activity and language skills development appropriate for use in class under the new curriculum.

3   Language Training and Language Use in Higher Education

In 2003 major curriculum changes were already being introduced in some Turkish universities. In Innovation as a Curriculum Renewal Process in a Turkish University, Yasemin Kirkgöz, describes changes in Çukurova University's Centre for Foreign Languages (CFL), (Kirkgöz, 2003). English as an international language has become an important part of university curricula with both English language training and qualifications and university courses in some non-language learning subjects being taught in English.

In doing so, students learned speaking, listening, reading, and writing skills, their instructors being trained in in-service teaching skills by the university in cooperation with the British Council.

A key part of the reforms in CFL was curricular development. The old curriculum focused on the language structure. The revised curriculum, developed by CFL taught language structure through the development of language skills, based on needs analysis exploring the key skills students needed to develop to complete their studies successfully and their perceived success in mastering those skills. A survey of students' needs supported by interviews with instructors revealed that they needed more challenging instructional materials and productive learning, content-based materials, more autonomy, and better acculturation training. Students needed more opportunity to practise their English and experienced difficulties with mastering vocabulary. Interacting with classmates showed limitations of their fluency and reading comprehension and as a result led to a lack of motivation.

CFL designed a new task-based and content-based learning curriculum and introduced multi-skills portfolios to assess student performance but also to encourage their autonomy and their use of language. The portfolio included both an instructional task that students had to complete and also a reflection section where students could reflect their own work and apply it to their own futures. Kirkgöz saw the introduction of the portfolio as a major innovation encouraging independent, self-directed learners, promoting their language skills, and making the teaching programme more responsive to students' needs. Introduced over the course of two years the new curriculum project revitalised the teaching of foreign languages at tertiary level, especially English as an international language (Kirkgöz, 2003).

4 A Multilingual Labour Force

As globalisation has grown and increasingly dominated the international economy, Turkiye has become an attractive investment opportunity for multinational companies. As a result, the learning and use of foreign languages has become increasingly important. What is the foreign language teaching methodology and content? How is the Turkish government aiming to improve it?

Turkish is the official language of Turkiye but Kurdish is also an important language. However, the expansion of industry and the growth of foreign investment has led to an increasing number of foreigners living and working in Turkiye and increased the number of languages in use, especially English. The other main foreign languages taught are French, German, and Spanish.

According to Aydin (2013 cited in Erbas, 2019: 24), "Turkiye's population is comprised of diverse ethnic groups which has increased rapidly over the years, and integration regarding the backgrounds of these ethnic groups into the curriculum has become an increasingly important issue for the Turkish educational system. The recent growth of ethnic groups in Turkiye, with regards to the population, has demonstrated the need for increased awareness pertaining to future teachers' abilities to teach issues regarding diversity in diverse classroom settings and teaching multiculturalism via teacher education programmes". Since this research in Aydin's article in 2013, it can be clearly stated that teacher education has not yet progressed enough to help students present themselves at a reasonable language level.

As a language trainer and intercultural consultant working at a leading language school in London UK, I hear from undergraduate and postgraduate students from Turkiye now studying or working in the UK about their problems with speaking English. Here are some examples.

- I can't hear people. I need to work on my listening.
- I don't have enough vocabulary to express myself; I try to translate but can't find the right expressions to get the message across because my teachers or friends look at me and ask me to repeat what I say. I find it difficult to construct sentences and most of the time I forget auxiliary verbs in my sentences.
- Even if I know the vocabulary, I still don't know how to construct sentences.
- Even though I know the grammar, I still don't know how to use it according to time and context.
- I feel embarrassed because all the other students from other countries are better than me; they improve fast, but I don't know how to catch up with them.
- I feel helpless as I don't know how to improve myself; I feel abandoned by the teachers because they didn't teach us how to be independent learners.

- When I speak with my peers, I sometimes don't realise that I am very direct and offend my friends because in Turkiye it is normal when we are honest for example.

All the issues raised by students at the graduate level should have been addressed at an earlier stage in their education. Private and state universities provide a preparatory classroom for students to reach a certain level for their university written and oral communication. Therefore, language teaching methodology should involve embedding grammar into different contexts so that students practise different skills. Most of the time, students believe that they understand how grammar works. However, they simply become familiar with the rules and lack the ability to put it into practice when communicating. In other words, they don't grasp the culture of the language with its "form" and adding "meaning" according to different contexts. It is crucial to help them to build a vocabulary bank to be effective communicators by using words to describe various types of expressions to be polite, diplomatic, kind, and sensitive to help them become users of the language they are learning in diverse contexts and to become, in effect, citizens of the world. It is imperative to help learners become aware of their surroundings and to adapt accordingly.

4.1 International Students in Turkey

Every academic year, thousands of students choose to go to internationally recognised universities in Turkiye to expand their network internationally, to enhance their future career prospects and to foster lifelong connections with people from all around the world. This encourages individuals to become more competent in the English and the Turkish language.

In Turkiye, there are several English medium and private universities which offer degrees to international students at undergraduate, master's, and PhD levels.

There are universities in Turkiye "whose mode of instruction is solely English or English and Turkish" (Global Scholarships, 2023). This is designed to enable international students to conveniently transition into life in Turkiye. This also enables the individuals to immerse themselves into Turkish culture whilst studying. In some universities, all departments are taught in English while others only have some departments which teach specific courses in English. For instance, in the following universities, English is required for vocational courses and for proficiency English: Boğaziçi University; Middle East Technical University (METU); İzmir High Technology Institute; İstanbul Technical University (İTÜ); İstanbul University; Marmara University; Eskişehir Anadolu University; Yıldız Technical University; Hacettepe University; Ankara University; Izmir Ege University; and Gaziantep University. Also, there are some English-taught study programmes which include Bilkent University; Koç University; Sabanci University; TED University (TEDU); Istanbul Shir University.

4.2 Language Training in Higher Education

Apart from Turkish and English universities also run courses to learn other languages such as Arabic, German, French, and Spanish. Turkish tertiary education systems for languages follow the Common European Framework of Reference (CEFR) and they offer the qualification BA, BSs, MA, MSc, PhD, and other training programmes. It is compulsory for everybody to take certain internationally recognised exams for university entrance such as IELTS and TOEFL for English. According to their levels, students either study a one or two-year foundation programme or they immediately start at graduate level if their score is high enough (CEFR B2). The question is, how effective is the language training in achieving a degree of fluency and how is diversity and inclusion improved by bridging the language gap? The whole education system appears to follow international standards and yet this is not necessarily reflected in the quality of teaching and learning languages. For instance, Turkish students, who travel to the UK to develop their English language, often find real difficulties in successful communication.

One of the primary reasons individuals study higher education is to develop a deeper understanding in their targeted subject area(s) and to foster transferable skills. This gives people the opportunity to communicate with like-minded people, to exchange ideas; to improve critical thinking and problem-solving skills; to present themselves in higher education via discussions, presentations, group work, field trips; and to conduct thorough research. This would help university students become confident and competent with using their own initiative as individuals and to be able to work effectively in group settings with people from diverse backgrounds, from different ethnicities in this increasingly globalised society.

The question then becomes, as succinctly posed by Professor Geoff Layer, do these "universities have the power to transform lives?" (Layer, 2017: 3).

How do universities bridge the gaps in English language learning in diverse learning environments to break language barriers to learning and socialising? In addition, are these international students autonomous enough to develop the key skills described above at tertiary education level?

Also, in classrooms there are national students who are competent in English and bilingual students whose mother tongues may be of Kurdish or Balkan descent. There are also international students with little to no knowledge of the Turkish language, and their English needs to be tailored for higher education level in productive and receptive skills.

For instance, diversity is not synonymous with equity, nor is it interchangeable with inclusion in curriculum design. Each of these areas has its own specificities, criteria, and bearings. In view of these subtle distinctions, the issues related to diversity education that have been explored in this book include the principles of inclusion, equity and all the related approaches adopted in language learning which either hamper or leverage human rights, sustainability, and promotion of the human capital.

5 Culture Clash?

According to the Turkish Statistical Institute, about 1.3 million foreigners live in Turkiye, with residence or work permits, many of them refugees from conflicts in other parts of the Middle East and Asia, in particular Iraq and Afghanistan. According to the Statistical Institute most of the immigrants are living in Istanbul, Ankara, and Antalya. Like all societies, there can be difficulties for the Turkish people in adapting to foreigners and for foreigners adapting to Turkish life and ideas. Some parts of society have sought to preserve and protect their identities, culture, and customs. Education systems have required reshaping to deal with diversity and the transition towards a more diverse and inclusive society has become a bumpy road. Thus, it has been a painful period of time for the newcomers working hard to blend in with the locals. This has certainly created a lot of emotion amongst students and academic staff and administrators alike.

As described in previous paragraphs, many teachers, managers, and teacher trainers have approached the situation actively to reform the education system by introducing inclusivity in diverse educational environments. This was designed to improve the quality of teaching and learning, and thus, to transform society by reshaping people's outlook through classroom settings. In all parts of the world, fellow educators have made it their mission to adjust their outlook in order to address the challenges to communication which have emerged from diversity. They have met unfamiliar characters, who grew up with different customs and distinct cultural habits, for example, people who react to and tell jokes differently. In some places, the locals have expected the newcomers to adapt to their environment while others believed that both sides needed to compromise and meet each other half-way to ensure harmony.

As Simon Anholt writes in his book about national identity, image, and reputation as part of its aspiration to be part of the European Union Turkey is conscious of its need to encourage immigration from other countries and accept people from different regions, cultures, and religions (Anholt, 2010). However, not all educators willingly welcome individuals from different backgrounds and some have resisted accepting the reality of differences. As globalisation and the need to recognise and accept diversity is still relatively new, it seems that it is not easy for educators around the world to see themselves as global citizens. They hold onto their traditional principles of teaching and methodology. This can delay the adoption of new curricula and methodologies in classrooms.

6 Diversity and Inclusivity in Teaching and Teacher Training

Due to its geographical position, Turkiye has been a destination for immigrants for thousands of years, and thanks to globalisation, it has become a popular destination in recent years and especially popular for international students seeking to study at university level.

This has naturally influenced and shaped diverse education and teacher development which is the result of these social changes in Turkish society. Globally and nationally the whole world is going through ongoing developments in science, education, business, and tourism as well as advances in technology. This naturally forced every sector to restructure and adapt to the new globalised era. Together with this, according to Turkkahraman, "teacher training process, the core of education, has gained crucial importance within the sphere of the ever-increasing international competition together with globalization, since well-trained students and quality education could be provided by teachers, who occupy a very important role among the main strategic human resources" (Turkkahraman, 2014: 26).

According to Sheets, (2005 cited in Sheets, 2009: 1) "Diversity Pedagogy Theory (DPT), is a set of principles that point out the natural and inseparable connection between culture and cognition. In other words, to be effective as a teacher, you must understand and acknowledge the critical role culture plays in the teaching-learning process". This indicates how it is essential for teachers to acknowledge the differences in culture and use this to observe and adapt their teaching style to "facilitate learning".

The integration of diversity education, at undergraduate, postgraduate and doctorate levels, certainly helps educators recognise pluralism which every student embodies. This needs to be reflected in educational resources used to teach every unique individual. These distinct identities, reflected in "social class, race, gender", can be used as a resource instead of a means to discriminate (Nieto, 2023; Jackson, 2015: 145). Thus, educators need to keep up to date with current trends and this ensures that their methodology reflects developments in current social changes.

Nieto (2000: 180) highlights that the need for "teacher education programmes to place diversity front and centre" (Nieto, 2000: 180). He goes on, "To have knowledge of another culture does not mean to be able to repeat one or two words in a student's language, nor is it to celebrate an activity or sing a song related to their culture. To acknowledge and respect is to be able to understand and apply this knowledge to everyday classroom activities. It is to be able to make changes or modifications in one's curriculum or pedagogy when the needs of the students have not been served. It is to be patient, tolerant, curious, creative, eager to learn, and most important, non-authoritarian with students. In order for a teacher to promote excellence in education, there has to be a real and honest connection between the needs and cultural values of teachers and students. This is culturally responsive education".

Nieto and Roman highlight the fundamental role language educators play in diverse classroom environments. To be effective in teaching, Nieto (2000, 180) states that all educational institutions must "radically transform their policies and practice" and focus on teacher educational programmes which "need to take a stand on social justice and diversity, make social justice ubiquitous in teacher education, and promote teaching as a life-long journey of transformation" (ibid.). Hence, in order to be compatible with the current teaching requirements, language educators need to have to have the following competences:

- **"Linguistic competence**: the ability to apply knowledge of the rules of a standard version of the language to produce and interpret spoken and written language.
- **Sociolinguistic competence**: the ability to give to the language produced by an interlocutor –whether native or not – meanings which are taken for granted by the interlocutor or which are negotiated and made explicit by the interlocutor.
- **Discourse competence**: the ability to use, discover and negotiate strategies for the production and interpretation of monologue or dialogue texts which follow the conversations of culture of an interlocutor or are negotiated as intercultural texts for particular purposes" (Byram 197:48 model, cited in Lewandowska-Tomaszczyk & Pulazewska, 2014:325).

Based on my recent research into Turkish tertiary and foundation language courses, I have discovered that curriculums, methodologies, and formal exams as well as teaching materials have been structured to meet global standards. However, this has not been done effectively enough to ensure inclusivity. For instance, despite having diverse classes in Turkish universities, teaching methodologies and materials are still not sufficiently accessible to individuals from different cultural backgrounds with different mindsets. Teaching resources and methodologies do not fully meet the needs of the students who are still in transition. This gap in learning creates anxiety which stifles language acquisition. Memory is essential to learning a new language and stress can wipe out short-term memory. Therefore, a step towards inclusivity in education would require the use of needs analysis and verbal feedback at the end of each lesson for five to ten minutes to improve the quality of teaching and learning. Office hours for graduate students is life changing because it gives them the chance to get answers to any questions. Teaching principles and methods need to cover different teaching styles, involve feedback, and relate these to the assessments that practitioners set for their targeted students and teacher trainees.

This situation has led Turkish society to keep the Turkish state as a nation to maintain its position as a strong state. Even though Turkiye has welcomed individuals from different backgrounds, the policy and sense of patriotism helped the country remain nationalistic and maintain Turkish values. Nevertheless, at the same time, this constant insecurity and tension has led a large chunk of society to adopt an attitude of intolerance in order to uphold traditional Turkish ideals and identity.

In the last few decades, with the emergence of globalisation and mobilisation around the globe, the concept of diversity education has come to the forefront, and constant reform of educational principles and practices has helped to recognise people in multicultural societies in educational settings. Language educators, researchers, the United Nations (UN) and the European Commission have been dedicated to working to improve the quality of teaching and learning for many nations to reach global standards and even go further beyond national standards. Nevertheless, this has been a difficult process and most countries have not gone far enough to reform educational practices to meet these new inclusive international standards in educational settings and this includes Turkiye. For instance, there is a struggle to accept multilingualism, as many in Turkish society may see acceptance as a threat to their national identity and this attitude can also be reflected in educational settings and may make it more difficult to accept minorities. According to Kaya and Harmanyeri, in their report, Tolerance and Cultural Diversity Discourses in Turkiye (European Commission, 2010), "the term 'minority' is a very polemical concept in Turkiye and has a negative connotation in the popular imagery as it is often recalled as the main source of the fall of the Ottoman Empire" (Kaya et al., 2010: 8). Consequently, this makes it difficult to accept diversity and to sufficiently give full rights to individuals to speak their indigenous or minority languages which has created tension for several generations. However, the current government has given the right to all people to speak their mother tongue and feel free to represent themselves.

A few years back, this attitude led a major portion of society to be less open to the idea of learning the language of other nations or to accept changes in the educational system. Political ideologies and policies in educational reforms constantly left Turkish society behind with their progress of developing, learning, and understanding other cultures and languages effectively until recent years.

As such, according to Kaya and Harmanyeri (2010: 8), of the European Institute Istanbul Bilgi University, "tolerance is nothing but a myth in Turkiye" (Kaya and Harmanyeri, ibid.). Subsequently, considering the 2010 report, it can be said that it may not be easy for many educators to empathise with national minorities and international students. They would need to be trained to learn how to see each individual as a world citizen. This results in having low performance in students' language learning as it takes years for them to integrate and think in English.

According to Ozmat and Senemoglu, "Studies on English language proficiency levels in Turkey are underwhelming. The English language proficiency levels of Turkish students are below expectations based on average TOEFL scores in the country, which are rather low. In 2011, the average TOEFL score among Turkish students was 77, which resulted in a ranking of 93 out of 161 countries using the 193 H-index score (TEPAV and British Council, 2013). An examination of the 2014 English Proficiency Index results showed that Turkey ranked 47th out of 63 countries and last among European countries (Education First English Proficiency Index, 2015). Additionally, the English language portions of the Undergraduate Placement Exam results are rather low. For example, the average score in 2017 was 22.73. The average of the correct responses is one-fourth of the number of questions (Student Selection and Placement Center, 2017). Regarding these international and national exam results of Turkey and previous research results summarized above, it can be concluded that there are problems in teaching and learning English as a foreign language in our country" (Ozmat and Senemoglu (2021: 2).

For example, when I teach Turkish students, they usually ask "how do we say this in English?". They try to translate the message directly and fail to consider the fact that certain phrases or specific ways of speaking may not be culturally polite, appropriate, or even acceptable in an English setting, which creates great conflict when communicating. As such, their inability to adopt an inclusive mindset towards other cultures stifles their progress in language learning. Turkish tertiary education at proficiency level needs to focus more intensively on language and culture.

A 2010 report by UNESCO further sheds light on Turkiye's current lack of progress in incorporating inclusivity sufficiently in their higher educational system. They too attribute this slow progress to pre-existing attitudes towards diversity in many language classrooms.

UNESCO points out "the various complexities, tensions, and inadequacies in the conceptualization of inclusive education in Turkish public primary schools that study participants have observed and experienced. In light of the findings, possible reasons behind the gap between theory and practice and the discrepancies between Western and Turkish interpretations of inclusive education in Turkiye are discussed. In the current inclusive education system in Turkiye, the challenge of modifying deeply held attitudes at both personal and institutional levels, providing clearly constructed inclusive education policies and approaches, offering appropriate training to key stakeholders, and making adequate resources available appear to be the primary issues for moving forward with full inclusion initiatives" (Ciyer, 2010: 2).

The current Turkish government has made great efforts to overcome diversity issues in Turkish education, in particular in relation to encouraging gender equality in schools. Promoting Gender Equality for girls and boys throughout the education system is a project funded by the European Union and the Government of Turkiye with the aim of making the education system gender sensitive in its education policy, curricula, teaching materials and teacher training. According to a report on the project published by the British Council, Gender Sensitive School Standards were introduced in the school system, a Leadership and Training for Female Teachers programme was started and participants attested to the positive influence the programme had on them in their attitudes to gender sensitivity in education management (British Council, 2023). To make this an active principle in language education, however, what is needed is student engagement, classroom activities to get students talking about their own lives and their own interests using the language they are learning. Students also need exposure to examples of authentic language, the language usage of the communities whose language they are studying.

These requirements are also the result of globalisation which has led to problems of inclusivity in education in most societies in the twenty-first century. Thus, their findings still hold true today as Turkish students who have studied in higher education since 2010 still speak the English language at the CEFR A2 level. From my research, there is clear evidence that there have been countless attempts to aid Turkish educators and the leadership. The Turkish government and a number of European governments have funded the educational sector to further enhance inclusivity. However, the slow development of individuals' levels of language skills indicates that there has not been substantial change. This can create conflict and tension between teachers and students in learning environments. Turkish students feel isolated and embarrassed amongst their peers from other educational backgrounds, and they try to put pressure on teachers to work to find a mutual understanding between the students. In order to enhance development in language learning, there needs to be further reform in Turkish education so that students become familiar with learning to understand the concept of plurilingualism, and to develop a diverse mindset. By developing an inclusive mindset in the students, these individuals will be able to develop their English language and adopt vocabulary to sufficiently fit into Western culture.

When language educators are trained, institutions (trainers) need to offer programmes to each participant to fully equip them with the skills to communicate and create an environment where every individual adopts a sensitivity to and understanding of one another. Gaining the necessary knowledge and skills for culturally diverse classrooms is imperative as, "the current understanding of intercultural communicative competence has been shaped by decades of research by anthropologists, scholars, psychologists and educators, in an effort to improve the quality of communication in the classroom. Or training room" (Yuges, 2020: 45). In a diverse educational setting, educational principles and practices must be reviewed regularly to address the needs of international language educators, who need to be able to adjust themselves according to classroom dynamics. This can be done by observing students' behaviour, emotional states, learning abilities, strengths, and weaknesses in learning the language in all skills.

7 Difficulties Experienced by Turkish Students

The issues facing language education in Turkey are manifested when Turkish students study abroad. From my own experience in teaching and training Turkish graduate students in the UK, I have found that many of them have difficulty in recognising basic vocabulary, common phrases, collocations, and other fixed expressions. There is a common misconception where they believe that by understanding grammar alone will enable them to speak the language. However, they miss out on the culture of the target language which reflects the native speakers' mindsets and approach to the language. This prevents them from using certain expressions where a native speaker would not hesitate to fit a particular context.

The crucial point is that all learners need to learn how to adjust themselves to a globalised world which undergoes constant social change. Neither teachers nor students can ignore the reality of constant social change and ignore people who come from various backgrounds. Intercultural sensitivity and behaviour are vital to international understanding, even when using a common language like English, and should take pride of place.

8 Barriers to Communication

English as a language of global communication plays a fundamental role in both international and Turkish universities. According to (Nazir & Ozcicek, 2022: 214), "the determinant government efforts of Internationalization of Turkish education system started in 1990s with the project, namely the Grand Student Project" (Ozoglu, 2015: 3). Ozoglu goes on to state that the government put several measures in place to attract international students and over time the number of applicants grew. International student enrolments to Turkish universities are currently mainly from "African countries, Arabs, Balkans, or Turkic countries. But this trend saw a huge shift after 2010 for as the Turkish government introduced different scholarships and other programs for international students and paid special attention to the higher education studies" (Ozoglu, ibid.). Considering how Turkiye is already a diverse country filled with multiple ethnicities, with the new arrivals, barriers to communication in language classrooms amongst students and between students and teachers reached its peak.

9 Conclusions and Next Steps

Developing communication techniques and skills at the leadership level is one of the keyways of reaching international standards. As universities receive international students, then initiatives at this level must be genuine and leaders must have their own unique voice to create a useful educational setting to guide lecturers or teachers. As Thomas Roulet, Associate Professor at the University of Cambridge in the UK, points out, learning compelling communication skills at the level of leadership is to be able to "convey important ideas, build consensus and ultimately foster positive social change" (Roulet, 2023).

There needs to be a unique way of approaching a particular group of educators in each educational setting by considering the teams' different ethnic backgrounds. In that way, every part of the team in the institution would learn the skills to increase the quality of teaching and learning by contributing their own experiences and ideas in combination with the institution's principles.

The Turkish Ministry of Education has set the curriculum to ensure inclusivity and this needs to be reviewed according to demographics and the needs of students according to their course programme. This will create an inclusive teacher education and language learning environment. The curriculum should meet international standards; however, it needs to also be relevant to the student studying a specific course as the language pedagogy and resources used must be distinct for each subject.

To address this, I believe students at foundation level need to be able to gain a certain level of competency. This would be reflected in their ability to independently prepare presentations, speak fluently and accurately participate in academic and intellectual discussions. When they are on graduate programmes, the university could provide extra booster classes and tutorials to go through their writing to be able to write at academic English level. Sometimes, spending a couple of minutes with one student on a one-to-one basis could save a lot of time and could bring success to that student through constant feedback.

The following proposals will help ensure the implementation of Ministry of Education policies:

1. **Curricular reform:** Ensure that the curriculum encourages the opportunity to use the language being taught to encourage student interaction focusing on their personal experiences and interests. The curriculum should create an allow time for this.
2. **Student engagement:** Ensure that classroom methodology allows time (maybe as little as 10–15 minutes a session) to allow students to use the language they are learning to express their own ideas and experience.
3. **Teacher training:** Ensure that teacher training courses and in-service training introduce teaching methods and technology to train teachers in how to involve their students by enabling them to use the language they are learning to exchange their experiences and their interests with others in the group. Teachers can be taught to organise intercultural exchanges and exchanges about personal interests and experiences in class using small group activities.

In short, educational policy designers need to ensure that diversity and inclusivity are practised in the language learning classroom the curriculum, the teaching materials and classroom activities create opportunities for student engagement in the language learning process by doing language learning activities appealing to personal background and interests.

To sum up, according to Sanger and Gleeson, "diversity presents an opportunity to foster deeper learning for our students and ourselves"

(Sanger & Gleason, 2020: 31). Responding positively to diversity and inclusion and improving English and other languages competence will help build a pathway towards diminishing mistaken assumptions and prejudice. As they go on to say, the teacher's job, now more than ever, is to use diversity and inclusivity to enrich the learning process, embrace differences, and help students benefit from one another.

REFERENCES

Anholt, A. (2010). *Places*. Palgrave Macmillan.
Beerkens, M. & Udam, M. (2017). *Stakeholders in higher education quality assurance: richness in diversity?* Downloaded from: https://www.researchgate.net/publication/312476986_Stakeholders_in_Higher_Education_Quality_Assurance_Richness_in_Diversity
British Council. (2023). *Promoting gender equality in education, Turkey*, available at: https://www.britishcouncil.org/society/womens-and-girls-empowerment/our-work/promoting-gender-equality-education-turkey
Ciyer, A. (CLASH 2010). Developing Inclusive Education Policies and Practices in Turkey: A Study of the Roles of UNESCO and Local Educators, UNESCO, https://core.ac.uk/download/pdf/79559394.pdf
Crystal, D. (2000). *Language death*. Cambridge University Press.
Erbas, Y. H. (2019). A qualitative case study of multicultural education in Turkey: Definitions of multiculturalism and multicultural education. *International Journal of Progressive Education*, 15(1). https://doi.org/10.29329/ijpe.2019.184.2. © 2019 INASED Available at: https://files.eric.ed.gov/fulltext/EJ1219364.pdf
European Commission. (2020). https://ec.europa.eu/migrant-integration/library-document/tolerance-and-cultural-diversity-discourses-Turkiye_en
Global Scholarships. (2023). *5 Best English-Taught Universities in Turkey*. Available at: https://globalscholarships.com/best-english-taught-universities-turkey/
Ingilizce Dersi Ogretim Programi. (2018). Ankara, T.C. Milli Egitim Bakanligi.
Jackson, S. A. (Ed.). (2009). *Routledge International Handbook of Race, Class, and Gender*. Routledge. https://www.google.co.uk/books/edition/Routledge_International_Handbook_of_Race/bxEWBAAAQBAJ?hl=en&gbpv=1&dq=racial/ethnic,+social+class,+gender&printsec=frontcover
Jackson, S. A. (2015). *Routledge International Handbook of Race, Class, and Gender*. Routledge.
Kaya, A. & Harmanyeri, E. (2010). *Tolerance and cultural diversity discourses in Istanbul Bilgi University European Institute*. Published by the European University Institute Robert Schuman Centre for Advanced Studies ACCEPT PLURALINGUISM 7th Framework Programme Project. Available at: https://ec.europa.eu/migrant-integration/library-document/tolerance-and-cultural-diversity-discourses-turkey_en

Kirkgöz, Y. (2003). Innovation as a curriculum renewal process in a Turkish University. In A. Rice (Ed.), *Revitalising an established program for adult learners*. TESOL language Development Series.

Layer, G. (2017). *Inclusive teaching and learning in higher education as a route to excellence*. Downloaded from https://assets.publishing.service.gov.uk/government/uploads/system/uploads/attachment_data/file/587221/Inclusive_Teaching_and_Learning_in_Higher_Education_as_a_route_to-excellence.pdf

Lewandowska-Tomaszczyk & Pulazewska (2014) (eds. / Hrsg.) Intercultural Europe – Arenas of Difference, Communication and Mediation. Stuttgart, Germany.

Nazir, T., & Ozcicek, A. (2022). Language barrier, language related issues and stress among international students in Turkish universities. *International Journal of Advanced Multidisciplinary Research and Studies*, 2(2), 213–218. ISSN: 2583-049X – corresponding author: Dr Thseen Nazir downloaded from: https://www.researchgate.net/publication/359391721_Language_Barrier_language-related_issues_and_Stress_among_International_Students_in_Turkish_universities

Nieto, S. (2000). *Placing equity front and center: Some thoughts on transforming teacher education for a new century*. Journal of Teacher Education, 51, 180. https://doi.org/10.1177/0022487100051003004. by the American Association of Colleges for Teacher Education Available at: https://www.researchgate.net/publication/249704655_Placing_Equity_Front_and_Center/link/55f0207d08ae199d47c0579c/download

Nieto S. (2023). *Diversity education: Lessons for a just world*. Rozenberg Quarterly: Rozenberg Edition ISBN 978 90 3610 128 8 – Unisa edition ISBN 978 1 86888 567 1 https://rozenbergquarterly.com/diversity-education-lessons-for-a-just-world-sonia-nieto/?print=pdf

Ozmat, C., & Senemoglu, N. (2021). Difficulties in learning English by EFL students in Turkey. *Ankara University Journal of Faculty of Educational Sciences: Year 2021*, 54(1), 141–173. https://doi.org/10.30964/auebfd.742803. E-ISSN: 2458-8342, P-ISSN: 1301-3718 Available at: https://dergipark.org.tr/tr/download/article-file/1573988

Roulet, T. (2023). https://advanceonline.cam.ac.uk/courses/compelling-communication-skills?utm_medium=cpc&utm_source=google&utm_campaign=ccs_geo1_jan2023&gclid=Cj0KCQiAt66eBhCnARIsAKf3ZNGA6naWDX4yRmJJhvTsl7bog0veu3A-5e4Phb0hqyZswcS1Awpqgg4aAjAIEALw_wcB

Sanger, C. S., & Gleason, N. W. (2020). *Inclusive pedagogy and universal design approaches for diverse learning environments*. Palgrave Macmillan.

Sheets, R. H. (2009). *What is diversity pedagogy?* Available at: https://files.eric.ed.gov/fulltext/EJ847137.pdf

Turkkahraman, M. (2014). *International Journal on New Trends in Education and Their Implications* April 2014 volume: 5 issue: 2 article: 3 ISSN 1309-6249. Akdeniz University, Education faculty, Antalya, Turkiye http://www.ijonte.org/FileUpload/ks63207/File/03.turkkahraman-.pdf

Veugelers, W., & de Groot, I. (2019). *Theory and Practice of Citizenship Education.* koninklijke brill nv, leiden, 2019. https://doi.org/10.1163/9789004411944_002. Downloaded from Brill.com07/14/2021 05:13:29AM. Available at: file:///C:/Users/oyuge/Downloads/1.%20Education%20for%20Democratic%20Intercultural%20Citizenship]%20Chapter%202%20%20Theory%20and%20Practice%20of%20Citizenship%20Education.pdf

Yuges, O. (2020). Enhance the development of intercultural communicative competence in business and study environments. *TLC Journal Training, Language and Culture,* 4(1), 44–54. https://rudn.tlcjournal.org/issues/4(1)-04.html

WEBSITE

https://expatguideTurkiye.com/english-medium-universities-in-Turkiye/

CHAPTER 14

Understanding and Maximizing Diversity Education in the MENA Region

Mohamed Chtatou

1 Education in the MENA Region

The MENA region is one of the most conflict-affected areas in the world. It has faced and continues to face interrelated challenges posed by protracted conflict situations and socioeconomic, political, natural resource management, and climate change issues.[1] The MENA region has one of the largest populations of youth and children in the world as well as the highest youth unemployment rate, as it were.[2] Conflicts in the region have exacerbated inequalities and have had an impact on youth and children.

---

[1] Whitaker, Brian (2009). *What's Really Wrong with The Middle East*. Saqi Books.
[2] Dadush, Uri (2018, December). Youth Unemployment in the Middle East & North Africa, and the Moroccan case. *OCP Policy Center, PP-18*/12, 1–28. Retrieved from https://www.policycenter.ma/sites/default/files/OCPPC-PP-18-12.pdf

---

M. Chtatou (✉)
International University of Rabat, Rabat, Morocco

© The Author(s), under exclusive license to Springer Nature Switzerland AG 2023
H. Abouabdelkader, B. Tomalin (eds.), *Diversity Education in the MENA Region*, https://doi.org/10.1007/978-3-031-42693-3_14

This region is also the homeland of excessive wealth[3] (petro-monarchies of the Gulf) and excessive poverty[4] in the rest of the Arab world.

For many Arab countries, one of the most sensitive post-independence priorities is to meet the need for education and training. Indeed, even if population growth has slowed down in recent decades, young people under 25 years of age represent a very large share of the population of the Arab world: up to 66% of the population in Yemen; 42% in Tunisia; 51% in Egypt, etc. The democratization of education is therefore a challenge and a major one, indeed.[5]

On what concerns the place of diversity in education in the Arab world, Rouchdi Labib argues:[6]

> *We are still able, at this time, to discern, even in a rough way, some of the changes that are likely to occur in the future and to plan our educational programs accordingly. However, we anticipate that the process will accelerate to the point where we will have to constantly modify our plans. At that point, some form of mechanism will have to be put in place to permanently adapt educational programs to the rapid pace of human life and experience. In such a context, stability in education will not mean the immutability of educational objectives, content, or curriculum, but rather the development of a policy that allows it to evolve continuously and at the desired pace.*

In many ways, the democratization of education did not mean democracy of its philosophy and content because most of the political systems of the MENA region were not democratic and the educational systems lacked diversity and were country-centric with a nationalistic tinge.[7] The

[3] Kamrava, M., Nonneman, G., Nosova, A. & Valeri, M. (2016, November). Ruling Families and Business Elites in the Gulf Monarchies: Ever Closer? *Chatham House*. Retrieved from https://www.chathamhouse.org/sites/default/files/publications/research/2016-11-03-ruling-families-business-gulf-kamrava-nonneman-nosova-valeri.pdf

[4] Khouri, Rami G. (2019). Poverty and Inequalities Continue to Plague Much of the Arab Region. *IEMed Mediterranean Yearbook 2019*. Retrieved from https://www.iemed.org/publication/poverty-and-inequalities-continue-to-plague-much-of-the-arab-region/

[5] Bougharriou, N., Benayed, W. & Gabsi, F.B (2019). Education and democracy in the Arab world. *Econ Change Restruct 52*, 139–155. https://doi.org/10.1007/s10644-017-9221-6

[6] Labib, Rouchdi (1980). L'Éducation dans le monde arabe: vers l'unité dans la diversité. *Perspectives: revue trimestrielle d'éducation*, X (4), 525–532. Retrieved from https://unesdoc.unesco.org/ark:/48223/pf0000042859_fre

[7] Chzhen, Yekaterina (2013). Education and democratisation: tolerance of diversity, political engagement, and understanding of democracy. Paper commissioned for the *EFA Global Monitoring Report 2013(4), Teaching and learning: Achieving quality for all*. UNESCO. Retrieved from https://unesdoc.unesco.org/ark:/48223/pf0000225926

minorities like the Amazigh in North Africa[8] and the Kurds in the Middle East and a myriad of other ethnic groups remained outside of the system because cultural diversity was seen as a threat to national unity. So, education was an illustration of dictatorship, not to say a means of its glorification, and the end result was the formation of docile citizens and the demonization of the critical mind and critical appraisal of governance and society.[9] Undemocratic regimes used, also, orthodox religion to make obedience and obsequiousness the salient aspects of education in its primary, secondary, and tertiary forms.

The adult literacy rate has improved to an average of 80% in the region.[10] However, this figure does not reflect significant contrasts, both between and within countries. In Iraq, illiteracy affects more than a third of the population at certain times! In Bahrain and Jordan, few children leave school early, but only two out of three make the transition from primary to secondary school in Tunisia and Algeria. Thus, while literate, their level of education remains low, and access to skilled employment is compromised. Gender inequalities are also very high and vary from country to country. The Palestinian Autonomous Territories, Bahrain, Jordan, Lebanon, and the United Arab Emirates have achieved parity in school enrolment rates, but the female illiteracy rate is 77% in Iraq, 76% in Yemen, 65% in Morocco, and 71% in Mauritania.[11]

In Morocco, the territorial coverage of pre-schooling remains very disparate. It is more marked in urban areas (69.9%) than in rural areas (20%). Not surprisingly, urban children are 3.5 times more likely to be enrolled than rural children. Similarly, families with large siblings are more likely than others to be out of school. In the same vein, it should be noted that

---

[8] Chtatou, Mohamed (2020, August 21). Amazigh Identity in Morocco and Algeria. *FUNCI*. Retrieved from https://funci.org/amazigh-identity-in-morocco-and-algeria/?lang=en

[9] Campante, F. R. & Chor, D. (2012). Why Was the Arab World Poised for Revolution? Schooling, Economic Opportunities, and the Arab Spring. *Journal of Economic Perspectives*, 26(2), 167–88. Retrieved from https://pubs.aeaweb.org/doi/pdfplus/10.1257/jep.26.2.167

[10] (Arab Development Portal. November 2020). Education. Retrieved from https://www.arabdevelopmentportal.com/indicator/education

[11] ElSafty, Madiha (2005). Gender Inequalities in The Arab World: Religion, Law, or Culture? *Jura Gentium*. Retrieved from https://www.juragentium.org/topics/islam/mw/en/elsafty.htm

the chances of access to pre-schooling increase with the educational level of the head of the household.[12]

Governments generally seek to establish national education and teaching systems in order to create a basis for economic and social development. If the budget reserved for education can be important (5% of the country's income on average) and makes it possible to reach massive enrolment objectives, the efforts nevertheless seem insufficient in the light of international evaluations and rankings.

Speaking of education in the Arab World, Arab.org writes quite rightly:[13]

> EDUCATION *in the Arab countries is where the paternalism of the traditional family structure, the authoritarianism of the state and the dogmatism of religion all meet, discouraging critical thought and analysis, stifling creativity and instilling submissiveness.*

While the 2004 Arab Human Development Report -AHDR - observed:[14]

> *Communication in education is didactic, supported by set books containing indisputable texts in which knowledge is objectified so as to hold incontestable facts, and by an examination process that only tests memorisation and factual recall.*

On what concerns curricula, teaching and evaluation methods, the AHDR noted, also:[15]

> *Do not permit free dialogue and active, exploratory learning and consequently do not open the doors to freedom of thought and criticism. On the contrary, they*

---

[12] Chtatou, Mohamed (2015). A Moroccan success story tainted with some shortcomings. Background paper prepared for the *Education for All, Global Monitoring Report 2015, Education for All 2000–2015*, 1–15. UNESCO. Retrieved from https://unesdoc.unesco.org/ark:/48223/pf0000232463

[13] (Arab.org, 2018, February 25). The stifling of ideas. Retrieved from https://arab.org/educational-reform-arab-world/

[14] (Reliefweb, 2005, April 1). *The Arab Human Development Report 2004 (AHDR 2004).* Retrieved https://reliefweb.int/report/world/arab-human-development-report-2004?gcli d=CjwKCAjw6IiiBhAOEiwALNqncYWOGODnT9KEZ7-IFjIkdUtIrwoabUL8jVdW9lgt2 2jinrmZcxbrDBoCfacQAvD_BwE

[15] Ibid.

weaken the capacity to hold opposing viewpoints and to think outside the box. Their societal role focuses on the reproduction of control in Arab societies.

2 Education for Sustainable Development

Education is the key to achieving many other sustainable development goals. When people have access to quality and diversity education, they can break the cycle of poverty. Education, therefore, helps to reduce inequality and achieve gender equity.[16]

Sustainability Education is often referred to as Education for Sustainable Development (ESD),[17] which has been defined as:

> *Education for Sustainable Development allows every human being to acquire the knowledge, skills, attitudes and values necessary to shape a sustainable future.*
>
> *Education for Sustainable Development means including key sustainable development issues into teaching and learning; for example, climate change, disaster risk reduction, biodiversity, poverty reduction, and sustainable consumption.*
>
> *It also requires participatory teaching and learning methods that motivate and empower learners to change their behaviour and take action for sustainable development. Education for Sustainable Development consequently promotes competencies like critical thinking, imagining future scenarios and making decisions in a collaborative way.*
>
> *Education for Sustainable Development requires far-reaching changes in the way education is often practised today.*

Looking at these indirect definitions of formal, non-formal, and informal education, it seems clear that education must be an ongoing process that combines all these levels. What are the problems of education?

---

[16] Liu, D., Jemni, M., Huang, R.; Wang, Y., Tlili, A. & Sharhan, S. (2021). *An Overview of Education Development in the Arab Region: Insights and Recommendations towards Sustainable Development Goals (SDGs)*. Smart Learning Institute of Beijing Normal University. Retrieved from http://www.alecso.org/publications/SLIBNU-ALECSO_BOOK.pdf

[17] (United Nations Educational, Scientific and Cultural Organization (UNESCO), 2014). *UNESCO roadmap for implementing the global action programme on education for sustainable development*. UNESCO. Retrieved from https://unesdoc.unesco.org/ark:/48223/pf0000230514

Problems facing teachers include managing the needs of students, lack of parental support, and even criticism from an audience that may be largely unaware of their daily lives. Educational inequalities, regardless of their origins, shape the future of individuals. However, to the same degree, inequalities in social, ethnic, and gender origins can continue to influence the destinies of individuals.[18]

Considering the needs and potentialities of a heterogeneous school public, the issue is posed with the necessary distance to avoid the traps of angelizing the educational environment. The plurality of the approaches developed makes it possible to point out the major stakes involved in the construction of education and training for diversity in the context of tensions and debates in society.

It is necessary, nevertheless, to question the evidence that is attached to the valorization of diversity in education. Through certain significant experiences, one must identify the advances and obstacles that mark the implementation of intercultural projects in different political and ideological contexts. The relationship between migrant populations to schools must be questioned from both the students' and the teachers' perspectives.

It is, also, vital to present avenues of intervention, based on skills to be developed or actions to be promoted at the classroom or school level. The question of the tools required to consider the needs and potential of a heterogeneous school population is raised.

The rise of the Education for All movement and the need to accommodate certain students identified as having a disability is linked to the emergence of universal pedagogical practices.[19] Given the diversity of learner profiles, how can university pedagogy be rethought to promote learning and success for all students from an equitable perspective?[20]

---

[18] Leicht, Alexander et al. (2018). From Agenda 21 to Target 4.7: The development of education for sustainable development. *Issues and trends in Education for Sustainable Development*, 25–38. Retrieved from https://unesdoc.unesco.org/ark:/48223/pf0000261801

[19] Cologon, Kathy & Carly Lassig (2019). Universal approaches to curriculum, pedagogy and assessment. In Graham, Linda (Ed.). *Inclusive Education for the twenty-first Century* (1st ed., chapter 8). Routledge.

[20] Schreiber, Jörg-Robert & Siege, Hannes (2016). *Curriculum framework: Education for sustainable development*. Engagement global. Retrieved from https://www.globaleslernen.de/sites/default/files/files/link-elements/curriculum_framework_education_for_sustainable_development_barrierefrei.pdf

3 Diversity in the Arab World

But where is the cultural diversity in the Arab world? This diversity is multiple; it is first ethnic, with Arabs, Kurds, Syriacs, Amazigh/Berbers, and since the end of the nineteenth century, Armenians. Then, it is tribal, with tribes crossing borders. There is of course a religious diversity with a majority of Muslims, but also Christian minorities, there are still small Jewish minorities, the majority of them having populated the newly conquered territories of Palestine. Arabness is a crucible, the result of a rich mix of African, Hellenic, Roman, or Ottoman contributions. Moreover, historically, and as Samir Kassir says, "*the cultural community is organized around a plurality of urban centers of cultural production.*"[21] Furthermore, there is linguistic diversity in the registers of the Arabic language itself between literary Arabic and the multitude of spoken dialectal languages which, moreover, conceal a little-known oral literature heritage, but there is, also, Amazigh/Berber languages, Kurdish or Armenian. And finally, there is a diversity between towns and the countryside which carries the seeds of conflicts between the groups.[22]

The Arab world has known periods of coexistence, notably under the Ottoman Empire, which presented a model of coexistence between communities, the Ottoman *millet*[23] gave privileges to religious minorities. But, after the fall of the empire, there was an "ethnicization" of communities, the Maronites in Lebanon as well as today's Shiites, Kurds in Iraq, and Amazigh/Berbers in the Greater Maghreb. the problem arose when ethnic or religious or linguistic groups posed their national identity as a

---

[21] Kassir, Samir (2004, p. 46). *Considérations sur le malheur arabe*. Sindbad.

[22] Yahiaoui, D., & Al Ariss, A. (2017). Diversity in the Arab World: Challenges and Opportunities. In Özbilgin, M. F., & Chanlat, J-F. (Eds.). *Management and Diversity, Vol.3: International Perspectives on Equality, Diversity and Inclusion* (pp. 249–260). Emerald Publishing Limited. Retrieved from https://doi.org/10.1108/S2051-233320160000003010

[23] The Ottoman term "*millet*" refers to a legally protected religious community. It also refers to minorities (see people of the Book and *dhimmi*). It comes from the Arabic word "*milla*" or "*mellah*" (feminine singular) and "*millet*" (plural), which means faith-based community (also sometimes called "*taifa*," طائفة). In modern Turkish, "*milliyet*" means nation. The "*millet*", implemented by the Ottoman power to control the populations living there, took into account their organized religions, whose hierarchs it appointed or confirmed. Language could play a role, but it was primarily religion that defined the "*millet*".

Cf. Ágoston, Gábor & Masters, Bruce (1982). Millet. In *Encyclopaedia of the Ottoman Empire* (pp. 383–4). Holmes & Meier.

central identity under the French influence, but especially under the influence of German and Italian unification. Cultural diversity only becomes a problem when it is posed in terms of identity ideology. Peaceful coexistence in a culturally diverse environment is conditioned by the dismantling of allegiances due to oppression, whether external through foreign domination or internal through the domination of one group over the others.

The experience of certain Arab States, according to Ghassan Salamé,[24] often badly entrenched, weakened in need of democratic legitimacy. This experience has failed miserably to change States into nations and to help them acquire particular myths necessary for their social cohesion. The regime in place manipulates the State to legitimize and present itself as the bearer of a founding myth whether it be Arabism, Islamism or other. If we refer to a few admittedly complex evaluation criteria which make it possible to determine or measure respect for cultural diversity within of a country, the analysis for the Arab world risks leading us to conclude that this diversity is in danger or, at least, is threatened.

It is, also, measured by respect for linguistic diversity and the culture of minorities[25] and community groups. The conversion to the Muslim religion of the majority of the peoples of these countries from the seventh century allowed the Arabic language, a language with sacred connotation because of the Koran, to supplant any other language in the region and belittle them as was the case with Kurdish and Amazigh/Berber but even Syriac and Aramaic specific to the Christian minorities of the Middle East. The practice of a multitude of languages dialects, most often the only language of most disadvantaged layers, deepens the gap and creates discrimination between the people and the elites who master the literary language. As for the minorities, whether ethnic (Amazigh/Berbers, Kurds, Armenians, or migrant workers) religious (Copts, Jews), or political (Palestinian refugees or others) they are stifled, marginalized, and their cultural rights denied. In Syria more than three hundred thousand Kurds fail to obtain official nationality documents, while in Iraq the new Iraqi constitution will allow the Kurds to benefit from recognition complete with Kurdish as the country's second language. And it is the same for the

---

[24] Salamé, Ghassan (1996, pp. 98–105). *Appels d'empire: ingérences et résistances à l'âge de la mondialisation.* Fayard.

[25] Thornberry, Patrick & Gibbons, Dianne (1966). Education and Minority Rights: A Short Survey of International Standards. In *International Journal on Minority and Group Rights,* 4(2), 115–52. Retrieved from http://www.jstor.org/stable/24674532

Amazigh/Berbers in Morocco, where the recognition of their cultural specificity is fully enacted now with the State decision to make the teaching of Tamazight (Amazigh/Berber language) compulsory in 2008. In addition, the presence of a large Asian population in the Gulf countries, in particular, gives rise to discrimination and violations of freedoms (withdrawal of passports, abuse of women, ban on religious practices for non-Muslims, and omission of payment of salaries). Racism and feudalism govern the master-slave relationship between Asian migrant workers and their local employers with greatest impunity.

Within Sunni Islam, there is discrimination against Shiite minorities in the Gulf countries, even when they are in the majority as in Iraq and Bahrain, where ethnic or religious diversity overlaps with social differences and social conflicts are most often disguised by the confessional. With the exception of Lebanon where the presence of a large Christian minority has allowed the construction of a multi-faith State in which cultural diversity, especially that of minorities, is respected. But as is, also, the case in Jordan and Egypt where they only benefit from a jurisdiction that is under the authority of the religious authorities for personal status.

Cultural diversity also requires respect for rights and equal opportunities between men and women. However, we encounter a great disparity in the status enjoyed by women between countries like Tunisia or Lebanon, and Saudi Arabia. Arab women struggle to make it onto the public scene, as in Kuwait where they ended up gaining the right to vote and eligibility by 2005, but women who participate in political life in Arab countries are still very low, the proportion of women in parliament is 6%. Some would say that this rate is not so bad, compared to that of the United States or England where it does not reach 10%. But even more seriously, of the 65 million illiterate people in all Arab countries, 75% are women.[26] A very serious analysis of the various reasons for the deficit of democracy in the Arab world asserts that the essential factor in this deficit is related to the status of women. The absence or hindrances to female expression, also linked to social censorship, amputates cultural diversity from a source of creativity and originality, with women remaining confined to craft trades.

In this regard Lina Abirafeh argues in *Global Dialogue*[27]:

---

[26] Abirafeh, Lina (2019, June 21). Gender and Inequality in the Arab Region. *Global Dialogue*. Retrieved from https://globaldialogue.isa-sociology.org/
[27] Ibid.

While gender inequality is an unfortunate global reality, the Arab region faces not only the greatest gap, but also significant challenges in redressing this inequality. The region has long suffered economic and political insecurities, compounded by socio-cultural obstacles and a system of entrenched patriarchy. This toxic combination stalls – and in many cases, reverses – progress toward gender equality.

4 Inclusive Education

UNESCO defines inclusive education as a transformation process that ensures full participation and access to quality learning opportunities for all children, young people, and adults, respecting and valuing diversity, and eliminating all forms of discrimination.[28] Inclusive education is an approach that promotes learning environments adapted to all, including those disabled. This requires respect for diversity, an adaptation of teaching, parental involvement, and changing school policies and strategies.

Inclusive education emerged in the 1990s.[29] Since then, educators have sought to educate students with difficulties or so-called disabilities in the most normal context possible. Rejecting normalization, inclusive education is a process of increasing the participation of all learners and reducing their exclusion from educational institutions, the curricula they offer, and the cultures and communities that ground them.[30]

Taking an inclusive approach to education means valuing diversity and removing barriers to learning, to support success for all. Inclusive education, therefore, goes beyond the issue of access to education, although this is an essential condition for participation. Nor does it deal exclusively with the issue of people with disabilities, but considers the differences of all

---

[28] Definition adopted from the Cali Commitment, Outcome Document of the 2019 UNESCO International Forum on Inclusion and Equity in Education.
Cf. (UNESCO, 2019). International Forum on Inclusion and Equity in Education, Cali, Colombia, 2019. UNESCO. Retrieved from https://unesdoc.unesco.org/ark:/48223/pf0000370910

[29] Beauregard, F., & Trépanier, N. (2010). Le concept d'intégration scolaire… mais où donc se situe l'inclusion? In Trépanier, Nathalie & Paré, Mélanie (Eds.). *Des modèles de service pour favoriser l'intégration scolaire* (pp. 31–56). Presses de l'Université du Québec.

[30] Ainscow, Mel & Miles, Susie (2008). Vers une éducation pour l'inclusion pour tous: prochaine étape? *Perspectives: revue trimestrielle d'éducation comparée*, XXXVIII 1 / 145, (38), 15–34. Retrieved from https://unesdoc.unesco.org/ark:/48223/pf0000178967_fre

learners (ethnic, linguistic, cultural and religious background, gender, disability or disorder, special ability, etc.).[31]

Inclusive education is based on the principle of equity, which means giving everyone the resources they need to succeed in meeting the demands placed on them. Students with diverse learning profiles are now accessing university education all over the MENA region, a thing that was not possible in the recent past. All students may encounter difficulties affecting their learning at some point in their academic career, whether or not they are considered to have a disability. The inclusive approach to education promotes the expression of difference and encourages the university community to question its pedagogical practices in order to promote the success of all. Flexible and universal teaching practices help reduce barriers to learning.

For Jason Carroll these practices are:[32]

1. *Know your students' strengths and barriers;*
2. *Use digital materials when possible;*
3. *Share content in a variety of ways;*
4. *Offer choices for how students demonstrate their knowledge;*
5. *Take advantage of software supports;*
6. *Low and No Tech options do exist; and*
7. *Learn from others.*

The rise of inclusive education is based on multiple influences.[33] In particular, the recognition of the right to education which has made inclusion the subject of international agreements (UNESCO, 2009):[34]

> *Inclusive education is a process that involves the transformation of schools and other centres of learning to cater for all children – including boys and girls,*

---

[31] Vienneau, R. (2002). Pédagogie de l'inclusion: fondements, définitions, défis et perspectives. *Éducation et francophonie, 30*, 257–286. Retrieved from https://www.erudit.org/fr/revues/ef/2002-v30-n2-ef06208/1079534ar/

[32] Carroll, Jason. (2022, December 6). 7 Universal Design for Learning Examples and Strategies for the Classroom. *Texthelp*. Retrieved from https://www.texthelp.com/resources/blog/7-ways-to-introduce-udl-into-your-classroom/

[33] Slee, Roger (2013, July). Meeting Some Challenges of Inclusive Education in an Age of Exclusion. *Asian Journal of Inclusive Education, 1*(2), 3–17. Retrieved from https://ajiebd.net/wp-content/uploads/2016/08/roger_slee.pdf

[34] (UNESCO, 2009). *Policy guidelines on inclusion in education*, ED.2009/WS/31. UNESCO. https://unesdoc.unesco.org/ark:/48223/pf0000177849

students from ethnic and linguistic minorities, rural populations, those affected by HIV and AIDS, and those with disabilities and difficulties in learning and to provide learning opportunities for all youth and adults as well. Its aim is to eliminate exclusion that is a consequence of negative attitudes and a lack of response to diversity in race, economic status, social class, ethnicity, language, religion, gender, sexual orientation and ability. Education takes place in many contexts, both formal and non-formal, and within families and the wider community. Consequently, inclusive education is not a marginal issue but is central to the achievement of high-quality education for all learners and the development of more inclusive societies. Inclusive education is essential to achieve social equity and is a constituent element of lifelong learning.

Similarly, research in the field of disability studies has redefined disability as a situation produced by the interaction between an individual and his or her environment, thus recognizing the impact of teaching practices and other institutional factors in the emergence of educational difficulties and even exclusion. Research in this field aims at developing so-called universal teaching practices.[35] Accommodations for students with disabilities can be grafted onto these practices, but the lack of obligation for a student to disclose a condition that could place him or her in a disability situation invites us to think of the practice from the perspective of inclusive education from the start.

In this regard, UNESCO believes:[36]

that every learner matters equally. Yet millions of people worldwide continue to be excluded from education for reasons which might include sex, gender orientation, ethnic or social origin, language, religion, nationality, economic condition or ability. Inclusive education works to identify all barriers to education and remove them and covers everything from curricula to pedagogy and teaching. UNESCO's work in this area is firstly guided by the UNESCO Convention against Discrimination in Education (1960) as well as Sustainable Development Goal 4 and the Education 2030 Framework for Action which emphasize inclusion and equity as the foundation for quality education.

---

[35] Opertti, Renato. (2017). *15 clues to support the Education 2030 Agenda. Current and critical issues in the curriculum 14.* UNESCO-IBE. Retrieved from https://unesdoc.unesco.org/ark:/48223/pf0000259069

[36] (UNESCO, 2023). Inclusion in Education. Retrieved from https://www.unesco.org/en/inclusion-education

Inclusive education can improve learner's academic success, strengthen his/her social-emotional development, foster acceptance of others, and thus contribute to more inclusive societies. Based on the above definition, it is clear that inclusive education serves the goals of education for all, ensures equality of opportunity among learners, and promotes equality and equity in learning.

What are the three main principles of inclusive schools? There are, indeed, 3 levers to act for an ever more inclusive school:

- **Improve** the identification of students with special educational needs;
- **Strengthen** the support of students with special educational needs; and
- **Develop** a culture of inclusive education among staff.

For example, in 2011,[37] Morocco incorporated the principle of non-discrimination based on disability and equal access to modern, inclusive, and quality education[38] into its new Constitution.[39] However, in Morocco, only 30% of people with disabilities have access to education.

Inclusive education is about looking at the ways in which MENA schools, classrooms, programs, curricula, and courses are designed so that all children can participate and learn. Inclusion is, also, about finding different ways of teaching so that all learners are actively involved in the classroom. It also means finding ways to develop friendships, relationships, and mutual respect among all learners, and between learners and teachers in the school.

---

[37] Constitution of the Kingdom of Morocco, 2011, Art. 34.

Article 34: The public powers enact and implement the policies designed [destinies] for persons and for categories of specific needs. To this effect, it sees notably: to respond to and provide for the vulnerability of certain categories of women and of mothers, of children, and of elderly persons; to rehabilitate and integrate into social and civil life the physically sensory-motor and mentally handicapped and to facilitate their enjoyment of the rights and freedoms recognized to all.

[38] Ibid., Article 31.

[39] Since the 1980s, Morocco has engaged in a legal process for people with disabilities (PWDs), which includes the right to employment, education, training, and accessibility. Morocco ratified the UN Convention on the Rights of Persons with Disabilities in April 2019.

5 Inclusive Education for Whom?

An analysis of statistical data on school-age children who do not attend school shows that a large number of boys and girls[40] never attended school or left school early without completing their compulsory schooling. Globally, according to UNESCO statistics for 2017[41] it was found that one in five children is not in school and that there are approximately 263 million children and adolescents outside the education and training system. This number is distributed by educational level: 63 million boys and girls of elementary school age, 61 million of middle school age, and 139 million of high school age.

All children who do not attend school are considered, for whatever reason, to be victims of barriers to schooling. For the different education systems, the following categories of children are concerned:

- Street children;
- Children from poor families;
- Girls (especially in rural areas);
- Children of nomads;
- Orphaned children;
- Disabled children;
- Children with learning disabilities;
- Children with HIV;
- Children from refugee families;
- Children affected by disasters; and
- Children from ethnic minorities.

Children with disabilities are among the most marginalized and excluded children, whose right to a quality education is often disregarded.

---

[40] (UNICEF & CSEFRS, 2015). Tous à l'école, Moyen-Orient et Afrique du nord, Initiative mondiale en faveur des enfants non scolarisés. Résumé du rapport national sur les enfants non scolarisés. UNICEF. Retrieved from https://www.unicef.org/mena/media/6576/file/Morocco%20Country%20Report%20on%20OOSC_FR.pdf%20.pdf

[41] (UNESCO, Institut de statistique de l'UNESCO (UIN), 2017). Données pour les objectifs de développement durable. UNESCO. Retrieved from https://unstats.un.org/sdgs/files/report/2017/TheSustainableDevelopmentGoalsReport2017_French.pdf

Objectives

- To define the categories of children and adolescents who face obstacles that deprive them of their right to education;
- To identify the barriers that block the schooling of all groups of children and adolescents and their characteristics; and
- To identify the role of education actors in removing barriers to schooling.

Basic Questions

- Which categories of children and adolescents are most likely to encounter barriers that deprive them of their right to access education?
- What are these barriers to education and what is their nature? and
- What can principals do to remove barriers that are relevant to their roles and functions?

Ensuring the right to education is the fundamental pillar of children's rights as well as a complex process requiring the convergence of a range of measures of social policies and more particularly of educational policies. These policies defined by the general orientations of the national strategies remain dependent on the visibility that national actors have of the situation of children in the MENA region, particularly on the availability of intelligible information bases that can lead to more effective political action in the fight against the social exclusion of children.

Aware of the importance of information as a tool for defining the orientations of social and educational policy measures, and with the support of the UNESCO Institute for Statistics, UNICEF has launched the Global Initiative on Out-of-School Children.[42] This initiative aims to make information available on characteristics of out-of-school children, factors associated with school exclusion, and the description of policy measures aimed at guaranteeing the right to education particularly in the basic cycles.[43]

---

[42] (UNESCO, Institut de statistique de l'UNESCO (UIN), 2017). Données pour les objectifs de développement durable. UNESCO. Retrieved from https://unstats.un.org/sdgs/files/report/2017/TheSustainableDevelopmentGoalsReport2017_French.pdf

[43] (UNESCO Institute for Statistics (UIS) & United Nations Children's Fund (UNICEF), 2011). Global Initiative on Out-of-School Children: UNICEF and the UNESCO Institute for Statistics. UNESCO. Retrieved from https://unesdoc.unesco.org/ark:/48223/pf0000217147

6   Barriers to Education

As numerous as they may be, the reasons that hinder the schooling of children of the MENA region are due to either a problem of access to the school or the inability of the school to keep the children.

Barriers to schooling in the Arab world are classified into two distinct categories:

6.1   Barriers Related to the Environment

- This category of barriers contains all physical, geographical, and human factors (relational factors that do not encourage schooling), mainly:
- The distance of the school from the student's place of residence;
- Lack of sanitary facilities;
- Lack of accessibility facilities in the school for children with motor disabilities;
- The unhealthy climate that prevails in general in the school in terms of relationships and communication; and
- The inability of the family to pay the school fees.

6.2   Institutional Barriers

These include negative representations and attitudes that impede the encouragement of schooling, mainly:

- Parents' lack of confidence in school and schooling;
- Parents consider that children's work to help the family materially is much better than the time wasted in school
- The prevalence of discriminatory practices among children within the school
- The prevalence of hasty judgments by some principals; and
- Recognition of the inability to fit in and keep up with the pace because of the existence of a particular disability.

By ratifying the International Convention on the Rights of the Child in 1993, Morocco recognized the right to education for all children, including those with disabilities (articles 23, 28, and 29). In line with these commitments, the new Constitution of the Kingdom of Morocco of July 1, 2011, affirms the rights and freedoms of people with disabilities, which implies, in terms of education, the establishment of an inclusive education system.

7 Intercultural Education

The term intercultural appeared for the first time in 1975 in official texts in France. In the 1980s it gave rise to varied and sometimes contradictory intercultural approaches, activities, and pedagogies. In the years 1975–1977, it fueled discussions at the Council of Europe around certain basic principles, such as intercultural dialogue, the rejection of ethnocentrism, adherence to the principle of cultural relativism, and its transposition to school activities in the interest of the integration of children of immigrants.

Subsequently, the Council of Europe developed various projects relating to intercultural education, such as: Democracy, human rights, minorities: educational and cultural aspects (1997),[44] Education for democratic citizenship (2000),[45] The new intercultural challenge of education: religious diversity, dialogue in Europe (2002).[46] The Council of Europe, thus, plays a driving role in the implementation of intercultural approaches in European countries.

The systematization of intercultural education is advocated, mainly for the development of concepts and practices within the framework of education for human rights and against intolerance and racism in the Arab region. While multiculturalism, is the natural state of society, which can only be diverse, interculturalism, is characterized by reciprocal relations

---

[44] (Council of Europe, OSCE/ODIHR, UNESCO, OHCHR, 2009). *Human Rights Education in the School Systems of Europe, Central Asia and North America: A Compendium of Good Practice*. OSCE Office for Democratic Institutions and Human Rights (ODIHR). OHCHR. Retrieved from https://www.ohchr.org/sites/default/files/Documents/Publications/CompendiumHRE.pdf

[45] (Council of Europe, 2010). *Council of Europe Charter on Education for Democratic Citizenship and Human Rights Education Recommendation CM/Rec (2010)7 adopted by the Committee of Ministers of the Council of Europe on 11 May 2010 and explanatory memorandum*. Council of Europe Publishing. Retrieved from https://rm.coe.int/16803034e3

[46] Faas, Daniel, et al. (2014). Intercultural Education in Europe: Policies, Practices and Trends. *British Educational Research Journal, 40*(2), 300–18. Retrieved from http://www.jstor.org/stable/24464053

and the ability of entities to build common projects, assume shared responsibilities, and forge common identities.

8 Intercultural Education for Diversity

Cultural differences cannot be defined on the basis of objective data, classifications, categories, or characteristics that one would oppose. They can be apprehended in their relationship, their interaction, their interference, and their intersubjectivity. It is indeed the relationships that contribute to attributing cultural characteristics and not the other way around. It is, therefore, the relationship to the Other that takes precedence since it gives meaning to everyone and not the characteristics of each culture.[47]

Intercultural approaches are at the heart of educational policies and more generally of contemporary societies. Indeed, the presence of many students from migrant or minority cultures poses pedagogical, social, and political challenges for both the school institution and the teachers.

If other cultures are different from ours, it is their variation that interests the anthropologist. Knowledge of cultural differences (with methodological tools avoiding an unequal treatment of differences) allows him to model a culture, the first stage of a work whose objective is to understand cultural variations and therefore the processes or dynamics that make it possible to decipher complex situations or contexts.

When cultural diversity—and therefore its complexity—is apprehended by a division of the heterogeneous into smaller and supposedly homogeneous units, we deviate from the scientific approach of the anthropologist to fall into sectarianism, ethnicity, nationalism, and fundamentalism. This systematization, which produces an artificial homogeneity, will then obscure the fact that it is above all heterogeneity that characterizes the nature of any society, and even more so when it comes under democracy. Heterogeneity is the norm of any society.[48]

Cultural diversity can give rise to comparison with the objective of measuring differential gaps beyond their singularities. Already in 1952,

---

[47] Talbot, Laurent (2011). Prendre en compte la diversité des élèves. *Les Dossiers des Sciences de l'ducation*, 26, 7–12. Retrieved from http://journals.openedition.org/dse/1058

[48] Abdallah-Pretceille, Martine (1999). *L'éducation interculturelle* (pp. 57–58). Presses universitaires de France.

The question of the treatment, by the school, of cultural heterogeneity is a major issue. It is necessary to learn to think cultural diversity in the universality/singularity tension. The author takes stock of the theoretical contributions and acquired experience.

C. Levi-Strauss mentioned the error of comparing human societies based on the characteristics of Western civilization, such as mechanization.[49]

Education is one of the areas in which cultural influences are most marked. We do not teach and learn in the same way in France as in Italy, in the United Kingdom, in Germany, or in the Arab World as in the United States. But the alliance of digital technologies, marketing, and an immense need for education will perhaps soon change this state of affairs: the MOOCs are arriving in force from the United States.[50] And all of Europe is trembling, while the nationals of the countries of the South are rubbing their hands to finally be able to access courses distributed free of charge by renowned or obscure, but American universities.

The time has come to react. The economic stakes are probably immense in the medium term, but the cultural stakes are much more so, and as of today. It is obviously not a question of rejecting everything that comes from the United States, but rather of thinking about ways to value the best of what we have and that we wish to share with the other peoples of the world. Clearly, we will have to join forces, learn to work together, come to terms with our respective cultures. Companies that have establishments in different countries know well the gap between the multicultural ideal and its daily reality when everything, from meeting time to greetings between colleagues, is potentially subject to misunderstanding and conflict.

In times of crisis, there is a tendency to withdraw, a stiffening in postures and speeches. Yet it is at times like these that we have to seek ideas elsewhere, observe new practices, not to copy them but to examine the interest of integrating them into our own capital. This creative dynamic deserves to be better known wherever it is at work, and especially in the

---

[49] Lévi-Strauss, Claude (1987). *Race et histoire* (pp 47–49). Denoël.

[50] A MOOC (an acronym formed from the initials of massive open online course) is an open type of distance learning capable of accommodating a large number of participants. The term MOOC has become part of everyday language; it is now recognized by the main dictionaries. There are two main types of massive open online courses: xMOOCs, which aim to validate the skills acquired by issuing a certificate of achievement, and cMOOCs, which have open learning objectives and in which participants largely create the content. These cMOOCs are based on connectivity theory and open pedagogy, which rely on networks of content and individuals.

Cf. Kaplan, Andreas M. & Haenlein, Michael (2016). Higher education and the digital revolution: About MOOCs, SPOCs, social media, and the Cookie Monster. *Business Horizons, 59*(4), 441–50.

Cf. Walsh, Taylor (2011). *Unlocking the Gates: How and Why Leading Universities Are Opening Up Access to Their Courses*. Princeton University Press.

educational field, so as not to suggest that only those who shout very loudly have good ideas.

9 Special Education

Studies suggest that people with disabilities represent 15% of the world's population. In the Arab World, this figure varies between 2% and 5%, depending on the definition of disability. Since this definition is still limited in the region, this percentage remains below the reality, whereas with a broader definition that includes the visible and the invisible such as psychosocial disability and any other kind of disability, it would reach 15% in the region.

> *The disability is not in the person, but in the barriers that are put in front of him. There are physical barriers, environmental barriers, communication barriers and technology barriers, but above all there are barriers in the attitudes of those who are afraid of the difference. There are also institutional barriers where discrimination takes place in many areas, whether in school, at work or even in public and political life* . (Notes Fadi el Halabi[51])

People with disabilities in the Arab World are victims, to varying degrees, of marginalization and ostracism, even though they have struggled to gain equal rights as citizens to make the most of their personal potential. There is a need to focus on accessibility (the ability to move freely in a chosen environment), equal opportunity in education, work, and housing, and stopping the various forms of violence and aggression to which they are particularly vulnerable.

If the disabled in the Arab World are given equal access to school, they can lead rewarding lives and contribute to the social, cultural, and economic vitality of their community. Education is the gateway to full participation in society. It is particularly of vital importance to people with disabilities, who often suffer exclusion because of their increased exposure to the risk of poverty compared to their non-disabled peers. They have to overcome more barriers because of their disabilities and the many constraints imposed by society.

---

[51] Sader, Sarah (2023, January 5). Un premier manuel en langue arabe sur le handicap au Liban. *L'Orient-Le Jour*. Retrieved from https://www.lorientlejour.com/article/1323531/un-premier-manuel-en-langue-arabe-sur-le-handicap-au-liban.html

Enshrined in the Universal Declaration of Human Rights (1948), education is a fundamental right. Several declarations and conventions have highlighted the importance of education for people with disabilities: The Salamanca Declaration for Special Needs Education of 1994,[52] as well as Article 24 of the Convention on the Rights of Persons with Disabilities (UNCRPD) adopted in 2006.

For language training to be accessible to a disabled person,[53] it is necessary to consider the following cases:

- For mental and/or cognitive disabilities, language training also needs to be adapted. These handicaps can indeed manifest themselves by difficulties of memorization, attention, and/or comprehension. They can also involve specific dysfunctions like dyslexia. Some may, as a result, alter the learning process;[54]
- In the case of visual impairment, audio media of all kinds—including music, audiobooks, podcasts, etc.—will be preferred. Their use promotes oral comprehension and improves pronunciation for a person with significant visual impairment; and
- For hearing-related disabilities, the teacher will have to adapt the volume of their voice. He or she will also adapt his or her pace to the listening skills of the student. This time, the use of a camera during videoconference lessons can greatly facilitate understanding. In addition, written and visual media will be preferred. This may involve the use of video recordings subtitled in the language studied.

In principle, all people have the same right to education. They are disproportionately deprived of it, which compromises their ability to fully

---

[52] (Centre for Studies on Inclusive Education, 2020). The UNESCO Salamanca Statement. CSIE. Retrieved from http://www.csie.org.uk/inclusion/unesco-salamanca.shtml#:~:text=In%20June%201994%20representatives%20of,inclusion%20to%20be%20the%20norm

(UNESCO, 1994). World Conference on Special Needs Education: Access and Quality, Salamanca, Spain. UNESCO. Retrieved from https://unesdoc.unesco.org/ark:/48223/pf0000098427

[53] Guérin, Emmanuelle (2013). La validité de la notion de « handicap linguistique » en question. Le français aujourd'hui, 183(4), 91–104. Retrieved from https://www.cairn.info/revue-le-francais-aujourd-hui-2013-4-page-91.htm

[54] Sundberg, Mark L. & Partington, James W. (2010). *Teaching Language to Children with Autism or Other Developmental Disabilities Perfect Paperback*. AVB Press.

enjoy their rights as citizens and to play a meaningful role in society, primarily through paid employment.

There is a need to ensure that Arab educational professionals working directly with people with disabilities ought to have a better knowledge of the issue of disability and what it implies in terms of a pedagogical approach. The capacity-building activities carried out must enable these educators to take into consideration the educational needs of people with disabilities and help them to understand the issues at stake and to accompany them in changing their pedagogical practices to promote school inclusion.

Inclusive education for persons with disabilities is a process that addresses the diverse needs of all learners by increasing participation in learning and reducing exclusion from and through education. It is a pedagogical approach that seeks to change the system. Thus, in order to make schools inclusive, practices and management tools must take into consideration this approach as well as the educational needs of the handicapped.

On the topic of promoting the education of young people with disabilities in the Arab World, Maha Khochen-Bagshaw writes that the following forms of education are common for the education of children with disabilities: special schools, inclusive schools, special classrooms, and special resource rooms. She argues also that the enrolment of children with disabilities in vocational education and in other forms of informal education is still under-researched across the Arab region.[55]

A book entitled: *"The Issue of Disability in the Arab World: A Roadmap to the Future"* (translated from Arabic) authored by Fadi Halabi was published in 2023 in Lebanon.[56] It deals with themes that have never been addressed before in the Arab world such as citizenship and disability, art, inclusion, the sexual life of people with intellectual disabilities. It also includes a study of religious texts.

---

[55] Khochen-Bagshaw, Maha (2022). *Promoting the inclusion of children and young people with disabilities in education in the Arab region: an analysis of existing developments, challenges and opportunities.* UNESCO Office Beirut. Regional Office for Education in the Arab States. UNESCO. Retrieved from https://unesdoc.unesco.org/ark:/48223/pf0000383309

[56] Halabi, Fadi (2023). *Mas'alat al-ʿaqa fi al-ʿâlem al-ʿarabî* (La question du handicap dans le monde arabe: une carte de route vers l'avenir). Dâr Sâ'ir ash-Sharq.

Referring to the convention on persons with disabilities launched by the United Nations in 2006, the book includes all types of disabilities and both policy and legal terminology. Fadi Halabi elaborates:[57]

> We're limited to the traditional disability framework which is physical, sensory, auditory, and mental, whereas disability needs to include people with autism, cancer survivors, it can include chronic fatigue, and it can include a lot of spectrums and psychological issues like depression and anxiety.

10 Educational Material to Trivialize the Difference in the Arab Society

When they are young, children do not see the difference, or at least do not stop to think about it. We must take advantage of this look to trivialize the difference. How can we do this? First, by giving them the opportunity to see it! The representation of people with disabilities remains too low in our society and, if we look at toys, it is almost non-existent! Making toys available to children in the Arab world representing people different from them is already allowing them to understand, naturally, that there is a great diversity of people and that everyone has a place!

Dolls with the physical characteristics of children with Down syndrome can be made available to children. They make it possible to sensitize the children with the difference by including the concept of handicap in a natural way in the situations of plays. Simple two-piece puzzles to promote inclusive education, empathy, and social skills. The puzzles must feature girls and boys doing different activities. Based on the principle of equality, these puzzles will help to transmit values of respect and tolerance, promoting gender diversity from an early age.

Arab children must be, also, introduced to a magnificent magnetic construction set made of very resistant wood, to create all kinds of modern families and to approach co-education in general. The Arab child will be able to mix and create many little characters and invent stories. These products ought to be designed to last. Easy to grip and assemble: the attraction or repulsion of the pieces is very sensitive and therefore induces the placement of the pieces. Teaching and valuing cooperation improve

---

[57] Sader, Sarah (2023, January 5). Un premier manuel en langue arabe sur le handicap au Liban, op. cit.

communication and transmit important values such as respect and openness.

Develop Empathy Children are often simply not aware of what other people are going through or feeling. Developing empathy means teaching the Arab children to put themselves in the other person's shoes and to see things from their point of view. When encouraged to change their perspective, children are immediately more likely to be accepting and caring. To develop this essential skill, we can propose to our children small play sessions that deprive them of a sense of putting themselves in the place of a person with a disability, for example, and thus understand the difficulties that this person may encounter... but also of all that we can share with him or her. An excellent way to develop empathy and solidarity![58] There are many different pathologies that an empathy educational approach can affect[59] positively in language learning.[60] Here are a few examples:

- **Autism spectrum disorders**: Autism is a developmental disorder that affects communication and social interaction. Children with autism can benefit from specialized educational programs, behavioral therapies, and social skills training.
- **Attention deficit hyperactivity disorder (ADHD)**: ADHD is a neurological disorder that affects attention, impulsivity, and hyperactivity. Children with ADHD can benefit from medication, behavioral therapy, and academic accommodations.
- **Learning disabilities**: Learning disabilities are conditions that affect the ability to read, write, perform mathematical calculations, or learn languages. Students with learning disabilities can benefit from specialized teaching, accommodations, and assistive technologies.
- **Emotional and behavioral disorders**: Emotional and behavioral disorders are conditions that affect a child's social, emotional, and behavioral functioning. Children with emotional and behavioral disorders can benefit from counseling, behavioral therapy, and social skills training.

---

[58] Dörnyei, Z. & Hadfield, J., (2013). *Motivating Learning*. Pearson

[59] Jaray-Benn, Csilla (2019, February). Empathy as a Source of Motivation in Language Learning and Language Teaching. *Hltmag, 21*(1). Retrieved from https://www.hltmag.co.uk/feb19/empathy-as-a-source-of-motivation

[60] Rodriguez, Elizabeth (2022). *Language Learning and Empathy*. [Master's thesis, Bethel University], Spark Repository. Retrieved from https://spark.bethel.edu/etd/783

- **Physical disabilities**: Physical disabilities can include conditions that affect mobility, such as cerebral palsy or muscular dystrophy, as well as conditions that affect vision or hearing. Students with physical disabilities can benefit from accommodations, assistive technologies, and physical therapy.[61]
- **Speech and language disorders**: Speech and language disorders can affect a child's ability to communicate effectively. Children with speech and language disorders can benefit from speech therapy, assistive technologies, and accommodations.

Develop Inclusion We must help children with toys understand that the only thing we all have in common is our differences! And that this diversity is an opportunity. Because this way of looking at the other and the world is in itself a source of empathy, benevolence, and openness. Our Differences Are our Similarities Show the Arab children, with toys and games, to what extent the notion of "difference" ultimately means nothing! We are all different from our neighbor, our friend, or even our loved ones in certain aspects. What criterion(s) should be considered to say whether a person is *"different from us"* or not? *"I love football, he does not at all," "I am a fan of Harry Potter, she didn't read it."* By listing with the children everything that can distinguish us from others, we very quickly realize the incongruity of this notion! What Binds us But above all, in a second step, we advise you to list with them everything that brings them together: *"we are human beings, we are children, we live in such a city, etc."* And then, by the way, don't we all feel, sometimes, a little different? From members of our family when we have the impression that they do not understand us? From our class friends because we don't have the same tastes as them?... Encourage Acceptance Fostering acceptance is about accepting difference as part of life and taking action to make society more inclusive. In particular, by allowing all children, whether they have a disability or not, to play and grow together! To do this, it is up to us to make the environments in which our children evolve—our crèches, our schools, our parks—more ergonomic, accessible to all, adapted to specific needs… in a word, inclusive! Toys to Trivialize Differences Let's start by stopping perpetuating stereotypes and preconceived ideas through the choice of toys we offer our children, and turn to games, which will allow them all to

[61] Bachara, G. H. (1976). Empathy in Learning Disabled Children. *Perceptual and Motor Skills, 43*(2), 541–542. Retrieved from https://doi.org/10.2466/pms.1976.43.2.541

have fun together! Very small children do not see the difference, do not stop there in any case. The representation of people with disabilities remains too low in our society and, if we look at toys, it is almost nonexistent! Providing children with toys representing people different from them is already allowing them to understand, naturally, that there is a great diversity of people and that everyone has their place! Let's Play as Equals Use simple puzzles to promote inclusive parenting, empathy and learning social skills. The puzzles feature girls and boys performing different activities. Based on the principle of equality, these puzzles help to transmit values of respect and tolerance, promoting diversity from an early age. In fine, Arab educators are expected to provide more games to educate about diversity, and to develop openness values and cooperation. Learning cooperation improves communication and transmits important values such as respect, empathy, and openness.

11   Country Cases in the MENA Region

For the purpose of illustrating the way diversity issues are addressed in the MENA region, focus in this section is on three countries, Lebanon, Egypt, and Morocco.

11.1   *Living Together (*Vivre Ensemble*) in Lebanon*

Cultural and religious diversity in Lebanon has always defined the social fabric and constituted a defining element of the national identity. Religious affiliation also plays an important role in the formation of the personality, ideas, and behavior of the Lebanese citizen, influencing even his relations with others and his public sphere. The Lebanese constitution advocates the respect of this spiritual dimension as well as religious diversity, by guaranteeing the freedom of belief on the one hand, and the respect by the State of all rites and traditions on the other.[62] Thus, the Constitution stipulates that no legitimacy would be granted to any authority contradicting by its nature or activity the Pact of Common Life.[63]

---

[62] The Lebanese Const. art. 9. Retrieved from http://www.presidency.gov.lb/English/LebaneseSystem/Documents/Lebanese%20Constitution.pdf

[63] The Lebanese Const. introduction, j. Ibid.

This national reality is in accordance with international charters; in fact, the UNESCO's Universal Declaration on Cultural Diversity[64] considers cultural diversity to be a source of exchange, renewal, and innovation whose existence is indispensable for human beings, just as biological diversity is indispensable for living beings. Thus, the declaration emphasizes policies aimed at promoting social coherence and peace by guaranteeing the participation and interaction of all citizens, regardless of their background, in the framework of an active civil society embracing this diversity.[65] Indeed, according to the report of the UNESCO International Commission on Education for the twenty-first century,[66] education should be a lifelong process whose main objectives include the promotion of the principles of coexistence and the maintenance of relations with individuals or groups of different backgrounds.

In addition, in article 26, which calls for the right to education for all, the Universal Declaration of Human Rights[67] insists on a global education that must aim at the development of the human personality, the strengthening of human rights and fundamental freedoms, and shall promote understanding, tolerance, and friendship among all nations, racial or religious groups.

Education for living together (*vivre ensemble*) in Lebanon is thus the response to the constitutional rules establishing the national entity in accordance with international instruments and the spiritual values advocating the development of humanity and the civilization of mankind. It provides the young generations with the ability to live in the light of globalization, rapprochement, and interaction between peoples. Moreover, this education is in itself a strategic objective of primary importance in view of the seriousness of the aftermath of wars and internal conflicts on

---

[64] (UNESCO, November 02, 2001). UNESCO Universal Declaration on Cultural Diversity. UNESCO. Retrieved from https://en.unesco.org/about-us/legal-affairs/unesco-universal-declaration-cultural-diversity

[65] Ibid, art.1 and 2.

[66] (UNESCO, 1996). *Education: The Treasure Within"*, report of the International Commission on Education for the Twenty-first Century. UNESCO publications.

Delors, Jacques, et al. (1998). *Learning: the treasure within; report to UNESCO of the International Commission on Education for the Twenty-first Century (pocketbook edition)*. International Commission on Education for the Twenty-first Century. UNESCO. Retrieved from https://unesdoc.unesco.org/ark:/48223/pf0000110780

[67] (United Nations, December 10, 1948). Universal Declaration of Human Rights. UN. Retrieved from https://www.un.org/en/about-us/universal-declaration-of-human-rights

the Lebanese society, social cohesion as well as on individuals and their confidence in their country and in others.

This explains the importance of education for living together, which goes beyond the simplicity of a certain religious culture or the approach of citizenship by its individual or legal dimension separated from the Lebanese reality. It is an education that is based on strengthening the capacity of young people to perceive the religious diversity in the Lebanese context as part of the common national heritage and to be aware of its factors that reinforce belonging to a unifying national entity. Education for living together is based on the promotion of the values of inclusive citizenship that embraces cultural and religious diversity by highlighting its spiritual roots and global human dimensions so that it becomes a tool of dissuasion against fanatical and intolerant mentalities.[68]

This approach to Education for Living Together in the light of inclusive citizenship goes hand in hand with the educational reform plan adopted by the Council of Ministers in 1994 and with the educational programs provided for by decree no. 10227 of June 8, 1997. The emphasis is on the formation of a citizen who:

- Draws his spiritual heritage from the Abrahamic religions and is attached to human values and ethics.
- Is aware of his national history far from any obtuse segregation in order to
- to achieve a united and open society.
- Works for the promotion of the public interest and submits to the rules of the Covenant of Common Life
- Works for the consolidation of the spirit of peace among
- individuals.

To achieve the desired objectives of education, it is essential to have an agreement, even unanimity, between all parties involved (starting from the students themselves, their parents, to educators, trainers, directors, and decision-makers of educational policies and programs in both the private and public sectors) towards a common approach to this fundamental issue. Thus, this National Charter for Education for Living Together (Charte

---

[68] Faruki, Kemal A. (1974). The National Covenant of Lebanon: Its Genesis. *Pakistan Horizon*, 27(3), 19–31. Retrieved from http://www.jstor.org/stable/41403854

Nationale pour l'Education au Vivre Ensemble)⁶⁹ within the framework of Inclusive Citizenship was elaborated to embody the determination of the above-mentioned partners in the face of this challenge and this common responsibility. The charter presents the conceptual framework, policies, and mechanisms that can lead to the desired objectives in harmony and efficiency.

Despite such documents as the above-mentioned Charter, Nemer Frayha argues that the Lebanese government must work harder in the field of education to safeguard national cohesion.[70]

11.2 Special Education in Egypt

Social and political systems in Egypt are changing rapidly. In 2011, a series of events underscored the need for fundamental changes in the status of young people in this country. Members of the Disability Rights Movement, along with other actors in Egyptian society, all expressed their desire for change. They successfully campaigned for the establishment of the National Council for Disability Affairs. However, the Covid-19 pandemic has weakened the country's economic situation, delaying potential progress in the field of disability.

"*In Egypt, most people with mental disabilities stay at home,*" says Eglal Chenouda, director of the SETI (Support, Education, Training for Inclusion) disability center affiliated with the Caritas Foundation, explaining that there is a severe lack of facilities for the disabled in the country.[71]

Although there are no official statistics, Caritas estimates that there are 14 million disabled people in Egypt, three quarters of whom are mentally disabled, and that only 2–3% of them receive the necessary care. The country has a population of nearly 93 million people.[72]

---

[69] Lebanese Republic, Ministry of Education and Higher Education, (1993, March 15). CHARTE NATIONALE POUR L'EDUCATION AU VIVRE ENSEMBLE AU LIBAN: Dans le cadre de la citoyenneté inclusive de la diversité. Retrieved from https://adyanfoundation.org/wp-content/uploads/2019/08/Charte-Nationale-pour-lEducation-au-Vivre-Ensemble-FR.pdf

[70] Frayha, Nemer (2003). Education et cohésion sociale au Liban. *Perspectives: revue trimestrielle d'éducation comparée*, XXXIII (1), 77–88. Retrieved from https://unesdoc.unesco.org/ark:/48223/pf0000130146_fre

[71] Le Point/AFP (2017, August 1). En Egypte, le parcours du combattant pour les handicapés mentaux. *Le Point/AFP7*. Retrieved from https://www.lepoint.fr/monde/en-egypte-le-parcours-du-combattant-pour-les-handicapes-mentaux-01-08-2017-2147292_24.php#11

[72] (CARITAS Egypt). http://www.caritasegypt.com/

However, the care of mentally disabled people from early childhood is crucial for their well-being. This is what SETI offers, among other structures that are still too rare: psychomotor monitoring of children, training in care for families, professional training, and discussion groups. Families are also confronted with the stigma surrounding mental disability.

President Sissi had announced 2018 as the year for the disabled. Moreover, in 2017,[73] a new law on the disabled was enacted with the aim of ensuring the right of about 11 million disabled people to a dignified life and providing them with more social and legal protection.

In addition, the Ministry of Education has defined some criteria for the integration of disabled students in public and private schools. Thus, students with visual impairments (blind and visually impaired or with Irlen syndrome), hearing impairments, and mentally handicapped students whose intelligence level is not lower than 65 or higher than 84 according to the Stanford-Binet scale will be eligible for integration. Similarly, all degrees of motor disability and cerebral palsy are accepted in integration schools, excluding severe cases of paralysis. Autism and hyperactivity cases must have approval from health insurance, and public or university hospitals.

On the other hand, students with multiple disabilities will not be admitted to integration schools, with the exception of cases of motor impairment, since this type of disability does not affect the educational process. In addition, according to this regulation, the total number of disabled children should not exceed 10% of the total number of students in the class with a maximum of four students per class all with the same type of disability. And according to the Education Law, the age of enrolment in the first grade of primary school must be between six and nine years.

Until now, only 2.8% of children with disabilities were enrolled in school, a reality that will change, according to MP Heba Hagras,[74] chairwoman of the Social Solidarity Committee in Parliament and member of the National Council for the Affairs of the Disabled, especially since the

---

[73] Arab Republic of Egypt (2020). *Law on the Rights of Persons with Disabilities, Law No. 10 of 2018* (Fist edition). National Council of Women. Retrieved from http://ncw.gov.eg/Images/PdfRelease/Law%20No%2010%20of%202018%20For%20Rights%20o-122020403910677.pdf

[74] Abdel-Hamid, Chaimaa (2018, October 9). Les handicapés ont aussi leur place à l'école. *Al-Ahram Hebdo.* Retrieved from https://hebdo.ahram.org.eg/NewsContent/1/130/29464/Egypte/Egypte/Les-handicap%C3%A9s-ont-aussi-leur-place-%C3%A0-l%E2%80%99%C3%A9cole.aspx

new measures meet the constitutional requirement of Article 81, which states that the State must guarantee all rights to people with disabilities, whether economic, social, cultural, educational and even in terms of entertainment and public services.

In addition to government initiatives, Caritas Egypt is active in various areas related to the education of the underprivileged. In the field of education, it has an 18-month training program. In addition to learning to read and write, beneficiaries learn about health and hygiene, as well as civic rights. Over the years, peer education and economic awareness components have been added, as well as the creation of village libraries. The program primarily reaches women. It has approximately 10,000 new learners each year.

In the social field, it has set up a program for street children. Through its centers in Cairo and Alexandria, Caritas works to reintegrate them into their families and provide them with school education or vocational training. The refugee service aims to improve the social level of refugees according to the standards set by the United Nations Refugee Agency (UNHCR).

Caritas Egypt also has a program in Hagganah, a slum in Cairo, that integrates girls into a school of high standards, including good conduct and education, run by the Sisters of Charity of St. Vincent de Paul. This program has had a positive impact on the entire Hagganah community. The first group of girls will enter college in 2021.

In the area of health, the SETI Center is addressing the problem of mental disabilities in children and adolescents. It also provides leadership training, preparation of rehabilitation programs, and vocational training for some adults.

11.3 Morocco, an Example of Diversity Education in the MENA Region

Multiculturalism is the second nature of Morocco, a country where Muslims (Arabs, Amazighs, and Black Africans), Jews and Christians have lived in total harmony for over 2500 years. Indeed, while the Amazigh people lived in the country for over 8000 years of known history, Jews arrived in the aftermath of the destruction of their First Temple in 586 BC. After that, migrations followed, and the strongest of them was what happened after signs appeared of exile, deportation, and expulsion of Jews and Muslims from Andalusia in 1492 and from Portugal in 1497 following the *Reconquista*.[75] The Arabs conquered Spain at the end of the seventh century, after sweeping across North Africa and the Middle East in the name of Islam.

The Moroccan Black Guard descended from black captives brought to Morocco from West Africa, who were settled with their families in special colonies, at Mashra' ar-Raml, to have children and to work as indentured servants.[76] They were known as "'Abîd al-Bukhârî" and were formed by Sultan Moulay Ismaïl (1645–1727). Endowed with incredible power during the reign of the latter, they were to play a preponderant role after his reign, installing and deposing sultans, or even reigning in their place.

Since the inception of the first Muslim dynasty in Morocco, the Idrisids (788–974), the reigning sultan took the title of *Amîr al-Mu'minîne* (The Commander of the Faithful) and not that of *Amir al-Muslimîne* (The Commander of the Muslims) because Morocco was inhabited by Muslims, Jews and Christians and the monarch was entirely responsible for their safety and well-being.[77]

The Moroccan diversity is expressed in full in the Constitution of 2011 that recognizes explicitly in the Preamble the different cultures of the country:[78]

A sovereign Muslim State, attached to its national unity and to its territorial integrity, the Kingdom of Morocco intends to preserve, in its plentitude and its diversity, its one and indivisible national identity. Its unity is forged by the convergence of its ArabIslamist, Berber [amazighe] and Saharan-Hassanic [saharo-hassanie] components, nourished and enriched by its African, Andalusian, Hebraic and Mediterranean influences [affluents]. The preeminence accorded to the Muslim religion in the national reference is consistent with the attachment of the Moroccan people to the values of openness, of modera-

---

[75] Chtatou, Mohamed (2019). The Expulsion of Sephardic Jews from Spain in 1492 and their Relocation and Success in Morocco. *Researchgate*. Retrieved from https://www.researchgate.net/publication/335652520_The_Expulsion_of_Sephardic_Jews_from_Spain_in_1492_and_their_Relocation_and_Success_in_Morocco

[76] El Hamel, Chouki (2013, pp. 162–163). *Black Morocco: A History of Slavery, Race, and Islam*. Cambridge University Press.

[77] Chtatou, Mohamed (2009). La diversité culturelle et linguistique au Maroc. *Asinag*, 2, 149–161. https://www.ircam.ma/sites/default/files/doc/asinag-2/mohamed-chtatou-la-diversite-culturelle-et-linguistique-au-maroc-pour-un-multiculturalisme-dynamique.pdf

[78] Moroccan Const., preamble (2011). Retrieved from https://www.constituteproject.org/constitution/Morocco_2011.pdf

tion, of tolerance and of dialog for mutual understanding between all the cultures and the civilizations of the world.

In the same vein Tamazight is recognized as an official language alongside Arabic.[79]

Also reference to Judaism and to the Jewish Moroccan Heritage and the Holocaust is available in Moroccan school curricula and Hebrew is taught as a language and literature in some Moroccan universities. Not to mention of course that king Mohammed VI has for over two decades undertaken a program for the renovation of all religious sites of Moroccan Judaism.[80]

Hassan II Foundation for Moroccans Living Abroad Education (Fondation Hassan II Pour les Marocains Résidant à l'Etranger) was created in 1990 by the late King Hassan II and chaired by HRH Princess Lalla Meryem, the Hassan II Foundation for Moroccans Living Abroad is governed by law N ° 19–89 promulgated by dahir N° 1-90-79 of 20 Hijja 1410 (July 13, 1990). It is a non-profit institution, endowed with legal personality and financial autonomy. Its purpose is to work to maintain the fundamental links that Moroccans residing abroad have with their homeland and to help them overcome the difficulties they encounter as a result of their emigration.

To this end, the Foundation deploys a range of programs in the cultural, legal, economic, and social fields, which mobilize more than 700 people, including more than 600 abroad.

The Education and Cultural Diversity Division is in charge of teaching the Arabic Language and Moroccan Culture (L'Enseignement de La Langue Arabe et de La Culture Marocaine –ELACM) to the children of Moroccans living abroad. Indeed, the attachment of Moroccans residing abroad to learning the Arabic language and Moroccan culture remains strong despite their remoteness.

To further strengthen this attachment to the values of the country of origin, the "Cultural Stay" has been set up as a natural extension of the ELACM, in the sense that it offers participating children the opportunity to experience the richness of their culture of origin.

---

[79] Ibid., art. 5 pp. 6–7.
[80] Chtatou, Mohamed (2023). The Moroccan-Israeli Geostrategic Relationship: From a Harmonious Past to a Promising Future. *Orbis*, 67(2), 228–246. Retrieved from https://www.sciencedirect.com/science/article/abs/pii/S0030438723000066

The Education and Cultural Diversity division also accompanies the Moroccan community on the spiritual path by sending a delegation of religious scholars and preachers for religious coaching in the host countries, particularly during the sacred month of Ramadan.

11.4 Cultural Diversity in Teaching Languages in Morocco

Cultural diversity in Morocco is particularly marked by language factors.

11.4.1 Linguistic Diversity

The linguistic situation of Morocco experiences a variety of Romance and Semitic languages which form a complex linguistic situation. Accordingly, the French language is one of the languages spoken and used by a large number of Moroccans; such a language is said to be widespread in Morocco and does not really have the status of a foreign language.

In fact, there are certain classes in Morocco that use French language only. However, French only affects a small number of Moroccans who are wealthier, more educated and who have had dealings with France. Arabic is the official language of Morocco, it is the language of education and culture and there are a large number of people who only speak the Arabic language in their daily dealings.

In Morocco, the linguistic situation is very complex but also reflects the social diversity and cultural richness that characterize this country. In the linguistic market in Morocco, one notices more than one mother tongue (Amazigh and Arabic), as well as several dialectal languages used. Each language has a particular status. The weight of these languages in the linguistic market is determined by their status, their social uses, and on the other hand by the attitude of the speakers towards them.[81]

The linguistic landscape by which Morocco distinguishes itself is varied. This landscape shows a division of the languages in two distinct groups: the local languages and foreign ones which are imported either by history or by modernity. Moha Ennaji writes, in this regard, that this linguistic diversity is:[82]

---

[81] Bijeljac-Babic, R. (1985). *L'utilisation des langues maternelles et nationales en tant qu'instrument d'enseignement, d'alphabétisation et de culture: expériences dans des pays en développement d'Afrique et d'Asie.* UNESCO.

[82] Ennaji, Moha (2010). Hybridité, langue et migration. Le paradigme Maghreb-Europe. In: Toro, Alfonso de (Ed.), et al. *Repenser le Maghreb et l'Europe. Hybridations-Métissages-Diasporisations* (pp.91–104). L'Harmattan.

marked by four important ingredients: Berber, Arabic, French, and Islam. Berber and dialectal Arabic reflect the popular culture, while classical Arabic, French and Islam represent the culture of knowledge.

The languages in Morocco can be divided into two groups. The first one includes the "local" or "maternal" languages, namely, Arabic and Amazigh. The second group consists of foreign languages such as French, and Spanish which were introduced by the colonizers and English by the culture of globalization.

11.4.2 Tamazight

In Morocco, Tamazight is the mother tongue of 28% of the population according to the census of 2004; it is spoken more in rural than in urban areas.

The Moroccan government decided to introduce Amazigh into elementary school in September 2003,[83] opting for its compulsory teaching, its progressive generalization, and the standardization of the language to be taught. Thus, the teaching of Amazigh is officially part of the curriculum.[84]

Long-held hopes that formalization would lead to the teaching of Tamazight in all elementary school remain unfulfilled. 550,000 students were enrolled in Tamazight in 2010, however, this figure had fallen to about 350,000 by 2022. There has been no increase since then.[85]

According to Ahmed Boukous, rector of the Institut Royal de la Culture Amazighe (IRCAM)[86] the pedagogical approach adopted is:[87]

---

[83] Akinou, Mohamed (2021, October 1). Tamazight, an Official Language of Morocco, Is Getting More Attention. *Al-Fanar Media*. Retrieved from https://www.al-fanarmedia.org/2021/10/tamazight-an-official-language-of-morocco-is-getting-more-attention/

[84] Boukous, A (2005). L'amazighe dans l'éducation: Enjeux d'une réforme. In Rispail, M. (Ed.). *Les langues maternelles: Contacts, variations et enseignement* (pp. 249–259). L'Harmattan.

[85] Chtatou, Mohamed (2022, April 8). Promouvoir, protéger et revitaliser la langue amazighe. *Le Monde Amazigh*. Retrieved from https://amadalamazigh.press.ma/fr/promouvoir-proteger-et-revitaliser-la-langue-amazighe/

[86] (Institut Royal de la Culture Amazighe -IRCAM-, 2023). Retrieved from https://www.google.com/search?q=Institut+Royal+de+la+Culture+Amazighe+%E2%80%93IRCAM&oq=Institut+Royal+de+la+Culture+Amazighe+%E2%80%93IRCAM&aqs=chrome..69i57j0i22i30j69i6513.6243j0j7&sourceid=chrome&ie=UTF-8

[87] Boukous, Ahmed (2007). L'enseignement de l'amazighe (berbère) au Maroc: aspects sociolinguistiques. *Revue de l'Université de Moncton*, 81–89 & 84–85. Retrieved from https://www.erudit.org/fr/revues/rum/2007-rum2172/017709ar.pdf

> *The approach adopted is inspired by the pedagogy of skills. The designers of the manuals start from the assumption that the teaching of Amazigh must aim at mastering the learner's communication skills, mainly oral skills and secondarily written skills, both in terms of expression and comprehension. Progressively, once the oral, reading and writing strategies have been acquired, the learner is introduced to cultural competence through activities that can be supported by tales, rhymes, sayings and poetry.*

And he goes on to say:[88]

> *On the technical level, the pedagogical progression is based on a specification grid relating to the functions assigned to language learning through the identification of language acts appropriate to the level of the learner and the notions that need to be conveyed through adequate linguistic and rhetorical means.*

The University of Agadir was the first to offer degrees in Tamazight in 2006. Many universities followed suit: Oujda, Nador, Rabat, Casablanca, Aïn Chock and Fez. Tamazight teacher training centers exist in Tangier, Casablanca, Marrakech, Agadir and Nador. Since 2011, there is a diploma to become a teacher of Tamazight through a course on Tamazight and its didactics. But in 2022, the policy began to require Tamazight teachers to also pass exams in Arabic and French as well as in science and mathematics. Yet those who teach Arabic and French are not required to learn Tamazight, creating an implicit but obvious hierarchy. This policy has also resulted in the qualification of some teachers after only 45 days of training in Tamazight, raising concerns about the quality of teaching. According to most commentators, the lack of political will is to blame.[89]

These ups and downs in the implementation of Tamazight in education are reflected at the national level. When Morocco made Tamazight official alongside Arabic as a national language, it also promised a law that would define the implementation of Tamazight and its integration into education and public life. This law took another eight years to see the light of day. Even now, although each government ministry is required to issue a concept note detailing how it will implement the development of

---

[88] Ibid., p. 85.
[89] Barqach, El Mustapha (2020). La gestion de la variation linguistique au Maroc: le cas de l'amazighe et de son enseignement. In For lot, Gilles & Louise Ouvrard (Eds.). *Variation linguistique et enseignement des langues: Le cas des langues moins enseignées.* Presses de l'Inalco. Retrieved from http://books.openedition.org/pressesinalco/40104

Tamazight in its area, so far none has issued such a note, and the promised National Council of Moroccan Languages and Culture has not been established yet.

According to Silvia Quattrini, North Africa Manager and language rights focal point of the Minority Rights Group organization:[90]

> *Despite the existing obstacles, the implementation of the Amazigh language policy in Morocco remains an interesting example in the African landscape. If adequate human and financial resources were allocated, the revitalization of the Amazigh language could become a point of reference not only for its neighboring countries, as is often already recognized, but for the entire African continent. The government of Morocco should pave the way for a significant implementation of Tamazight in its educational system and in all areas of public life.*

The linguistic and pedagogical training of Amazigh teachers is both urgent and necessary. The objective is the initial training of all future teachers of Amazigh. The training considers two aspects: an adapted linguistic competence and the pedagogy of teaching Amazigh to elementary school students.

Continuing education will serve to support initial training and at the same time to update the pedagogical knowledge of teachers in the didactics of Amazigh.

This training is complemented by academic information seminars and assistance provided by inspectors, educational advisors, and trainers. In order to teach the Amazigh language, existing teachers will have to be qualified according to procedures defined at the pedagogical or academic level.

The development of programs and textbooks can only be done adequately in a progressive and coherent way from the point of view of conception, realization, and validation. Thus, the didactics of Tamazight language is based on a pedagogy that integrates the student in his sociocultural environment, a pedagogy that ensures his psycho-linguistic and cognitive balance, and also a pedagogy that aims to teach the child knowledge, know-how and interpersonal skills.

---

[90] Quattrini, Silvia (2023, February 21). Revitalizing Tamazight: The role of language education policies in Morocco. *Minority Rights Group*. Retrieved from https://minorityrights.org/2023/02/21/revitalizing-tamazight-the-role-of-language-education-policies-in-morocco/

12 Diversity Education, How to Go About it in Class?

Plural classrooms are the "the new normal" in the Arab world and teachers need to be better supported and prepared to deal with the different situations that arise in the classroom. While there is a growing body of literature on what teachers should learn, it is important to examine their day-to-day work in pluralistic classrooms, their feelings and emotions, the situational triggers that make it difficult for them to work in these classrooms, and the barriers that teachers and students must overcome to maintain positive relationships. To do this, it is necessary to move from the theoretical to the practical sphere, where doubts, uncertainties, and disagreements are addressed. The "lived worlds (field reality)" must be thoroughly examined before a course of action can be proposed.[91]

12.1 Diverse Classrooms

The concept of "diversity tact" could be used to describe the reality that teachers face in diverse classrooms in the Arab region, where they must respond appropriately and with practical wisdom to each situation that presents itself to them. Express "diversity tact" can help teachers revisit salient situations that have occurred in the classroom, to consider alternative readings of the facts, and to reflect on other ways of acting.

It must be said that both educational decision-makers and educators must view diversity in students and curricula as a strength both at school and at university levels and work towards its realization in the following ways:

- **Integration in education**: processes of integration of students with a migrant background in educational systems.
- **Integration through education**: the links between education/training systems and skills development as important determinants of migrants' ability to integrate their host communities.

---

[91] Arnesen, Anne-Lise, Bîrzea, Cézar, Bernard Dumont, Essomba, Miguel Àngel, Furch, Elisabeth, Vallianatos, Angelos, & Ferrer, Ferran (2008). *Teachers education: Policies and practices for teaching socio-cultural diversity Survey's report on initial education of teachers on socio-cultural diversity*. Council of Europe Publishing. Retrieved from https://www.coe.int/t/dg4/education/diversity/source/volume_1_en.pdf

- **Education for social cohesion**: the role of education systems in promoting social cohesion.

And answer the following questions:

- Are there any programs or initiatives to encourage teachers to work in disadvantaged educational institutions (schools, universities, etc.?); and
- What approaches/practices are taken to allocate resources to disadvantaged educational institutions so that minority and handicapped students have the means to compensate for this disadvantage?

An important point to consider is that diversity in the classroom must be presented to teachers as a learning opportunity for them as well. Working in disadvantaged schools should not be seen as a sacrifice, but rather as an opportunity to reap the benefits of diversity.

12.2 Incentive

Financial incentives are commonly used to attract teachers to disadvantaged schools. For example, in Spain there is a (regional) points credit system that allows teachers who work in certain plural schools in certain regions to earn more points than they would otherwise have earned.

In certain regions to obtain more points that they can use to gain a promotion in an administrative area or to be transferred to another school. The system also provides for an increase in pay after six years, depending on the number of points. Turkey has a similar system.

In the United States, the Department of Education provides federal loan debt forgiveness for young teachers working in so-called Title 1 schools,[92] which are located in the most disadvantaged areas, where 65% of students are eligible for free or reduced-price meals. This means that the government will forgive a student loan debt if the young teacher chooses to work in one of these schools. This measure is intended to encourage young teachers to work in multi-grade classrooms.

---

[92] U.S. Department of Education (2008). *Parents/Prepare My Child for School. Improving Basic Programs.* Operated by Local Educational Agencies (Title I, Part A). Retrieved from https://www2.ed.gov/programs/titleiparta/index.html

Attracting teachers to more rural areas is also difficult. Norway's Arctic University has conducted a pilot project called "Small Steps Ahead," focusing specifically on rural areas of the country, which have difficulty finding qualified teachers. The program can help young graduates find affordable housing and relocate to remote areas of the country. Once they have their master's degree, future teachers are encouraged to move to rural areas. Since the teaching profession is not as well paid as other professions in Norway, it is still difficult to encourage students to choose it.[93]

12.3   Experiential Learning

Professional development activities that focus on diversity should be based on experiential learning. Teachers need to be exposed to different situations, scenarios and values in order to develop awareness and empathy for their students. In-service teacher education and professional development should be based on an active learning approach.

Promising professional development approaches and activities include exposing teachers to a foreign language course to increase empathy for the language of instruction and empathy for students with immigrant backgrounds and the linguistic and cultural challenges they face. The simulation can also prepare teachers to deal with different situations.

Another promising approach is for teachers to go into the students' environment. For example, in New York City, teachers went into the neighborhoods where their students came from, allowing them to not only better understand their students' home environment and cultural background, but also to reverse the roles.

Giving teachers regular feedback on their teaching practices and facilitating collaboration among teachers within and between schools are important steps in helping them deal with various classroom issues and to develop a network of mutual aid.

---

[93] Bendix-Olsen, Kurt & Bonderup, Mette (2022). *Constructions of disability, involvement and participation in social case-management work with children*. 1. Abstract from 2nd International Childlife Conference, Oslo, Norway. Retrieved from https://www.ucviden.dk/ws/portalfiles/portal/162731265/Program_Childlife.pdf
https://en.uit.no/om/strategi2030

12.4   Evaluation Process

Education specialists should also be interested in the indicators and assessment mechanisms in place to measure diversity in the classroom by examining the following questions:

- How is diversity defined across countries?
- What indicators are used to collect data on teaching in plural classrooms?
- What evaluation mechanisms exist to measure the effectiveness of teaching in pluralistic classrooms?

There is a need to develop teachers' knowledge and skills. In addition, teachers expressed concern about the pressure on them to manage diversity in their classrooms and their ability to provide inclusive instruction.

Nevertheless, it is necessary to ask how to measure diversity, whether it is something that can be controlled or just a state, and whether it can be considered a natural characteristic or a set of characteristics.

In perspective, diversity must be incorporated into the curriculum and evaluated constantly, and it is not enough for schools to just celebrate different cultural holidays as an approach but it must become a salient part of the curriculum.

Summative evaluation, which, like formative evaluation, uses assessment in the context of learning. It continues to play an important role in classrooms and schools, but also in high-stakes central examinations. Assessments can tend to favor different groups of students based on a variety of factors such as socioeconomic status, gender, ethnicity, and language (e.g., using complex language that is difficult for non-native speakers to understand, or by using multiple-choice tests). It is therefore important to develop the skills and knowledge of teachers so that they can integrate cultural and general differences among their students in assessments. Since there is always a risk of bias in an assessment, it is essential to use a variety of assessments so that students have multiple ways to demonstrate their abilities.

A standardized assessment can be used to monitor whether a system is meeting the needs of students. Monitoring at the national level, which is well established, involves assessments and surveys of parents and teachers as well as longitudinal research. System-wide monitoring can help address equity issues and target resources and public action on schools and students.

Different types of evaluations and follow-up measures can be used in countries. Formative assessment, for example, places students at the center and allows them to monitor their own learning and act on it to improve. It is incorporated into the routine and daily practices of teachers, who use it to see what students have learned and can do, and how they can best help them learn.

For summative assessments, it is important to develop the skills and knowledge of teachers to incorporate cultural and general differences among their students into their assessments. Since there is a risk of bias in an assessment, it is essential to use a variety of assessments so that students have multiple ways to demonstrate their abilities.

13 Conclusion

In spite of the fact that the Arab States have been extremely timid in considering cultural diversity in their global policy, these countries have nevertheless voted unanimously for the text of the Convention on the Protection and Promotion of the Diversity of Cultural Expressions of UNESCO,[94] but their adhesion to this text is biased. Why biased? Firstly, because this convention is not sufficiently binding to oblige the States to respect its clauses, not more than they respect the other conventions, especially those on human rights. Then, because the concept of diversity is often used as a way of claiming respect for Arab cultural expressions in international markets and, above all, as a system for asserting the Arab voice on the international political scene. Their approach does not necessarily encompass diversity within the country, it can just as easily serve, in some cases, as an alibi to denounce and fight against the invasion of foreign cultural products, thus justifying the practice of censorship.

Oppression and lack of democracy in most Arab countries are the most harmful threats to political pluralism and, moreover, to cultural diversity and, therefore, diversity education in all levels (primary, secondary, and tertiary). It is therefore hoped that the adoption of the UNESCO Convention will make civil society in each of the Arab countries aware of

---

[94](UNESCO, 2005, October 20). *Convention on the Protection and Promotion of the Diversity of Cultural Expressions*. UNESCO. Retrieved from https://en.unesco.org/creativity/sites/creativity/files/passeport-convention2005-web2.pdf

the role that it must play in the defence and the respect of its diversity as well as in the claim of its right to access to that of others. In addition, and despite the predominance of a democratic system in Western countries, the approach to this diversity is probably almost as biased there. Let's also hope that this same Convention will make Western countries aware that the respect of cultural diversity does not pass only by the defence of their cultural expressions and contents facing the mercantile hegemony of the multinationals but, that it also induces the re-composition of a multicultural identity integrating the contributions of the social and community groups which compose their countries today.

The era of globalization entails numerous challenges to accept plurality, differences, and the management of cultural diversity, especially with the return of the cultural ingredient to the field of political action in a context in which culture occupies a central place in the world after the Cold War.

Globalization has attempted to generalize many cultural values, practices and expressions, while many Arab and Western countries seek refuge in cultural uniqueness and identity. Therefore, cultural factors have had their impact on the design of national, regional and international policies.

In this way, diversity and pluralism have become the most important characteristics of contemporary societies. This has required the enactment of laws and the adoption of policies that consider cultural diversity and protect the rights of religious and ethnic minorities in order to avoid "cultural" tensions and sectarianism and preserve social cohesion. However, this process faces complications and setbacks. Some studies indicate that one in three conflicts that occur in the world today is due to "cultural" or "religious" causes.

In the midst of current challenges and with the triumph of the logic of the market, the unification of cultural norms, and the influence of new information technologies, new phenomena have appeared in which the defence of identity and national processes are mixed, the protests of the new social movements, the claim for cultural rights and the challenges of managing the phenomena resulting from immigration.

In this context, numerous factors have combined to generate differences whose consequences have not been slow to appear, such as the challenges posed by ethnic nationalism to the State, which often creates a climate of mistrust between the majority and minorities, in the face of the need for the contribution of all components of society in the development of its future and a common culture and identity seeking recognition, rights, justice, equality, and full citizenship.

This means that cultural diversity seconded by diversity education are an essential component of the structures of all societies and its management is a challenge, since States and nations coincide in the richness of their cultural fabric, but differ in the modalities of their management, which requires taking advantage of successful experiences.

REFERENCES

Abdallah-Pretceille, M. (1999). *L'éducation interculturelle* (pp. 57–58). Presses universitaires de France.

Abdel-Hamid, C. (2018, October 9). *Les handicapés ont aussi leur place à l'école.* Al-Ahram Hebdo. Retrieved from https://hebdo.ahram.org.eg/NewsContent/1/130/29464/Egypte/Egypte/Les handicap%C3%A9s-ont-aussi-leur-place-%C3%A0-l%E2%80%99%C3%A9cole.aspx

Abirafeh, L. (2019, June 21). *Gender and inequality in the Arab region.* Global Dialogue. Retrieved from https://globaldialogue.isa-sociology.org/

Ágoston, G., & Masters, B. (1982). Millet. In *Encyclopaedia of the ottoman empire* (pp. 383–384). Holmes & Meier.

Ainscow, M., & Miles, S. (2008). Vers une éducation pour l'inclusion pour tous: prochaine étape? *Perspectives: Revue trimestrielle d'éducation comparée, XXXVIII 1/145*, (38), 15–34. Retrieved from https://unesdoc.unesco.org/ark:/48223/pf0000178967_fre

Akinou, M. (2021). *Tamazight, an official language of Morocco, is getting more attention.* Al-Fanar Media. Retrieved from https://www.al-fanarmedia.org/2021/10/tamazight-an-official-language-of-morocco-is-getting-more-attention/

Arab Development Portal. (2020 November). *Education.* Retrieved from https://www.arabdevelopmentportal.com/indicator/education

Arab.org. (2018, February 25). *The stifling of ideas.* Retrieved from https://arab.org/educational-reform-arab-world/

Arnesen, A.-L., Bîrzea, C., Dumont, B., Essomba, M. À., Furch, E., Vallianatos, A., & Ferrer, F. (2008). *Teachers education: Policies and practices for teaching socio-cultural diversity. Survey's report on initial education of teachers on socio-cultural diversity.* Council of Europe Publishing. Retrieved from https://www.coe.int/t/dg4/education/diversity/source/volume_1_en.pdf

Bachara, G. H. (1976). Empathy in learning disabled children. *Perceptual and Motor Skills, 43*(2), 541–542. https://doi.org/10.2466/pms.1976.43.2.541

Barqach, E. M. (2020). La gestion de la variation linguistique au Maroc : le cas de l'amazighe et de son enseignement. In G. Forlot & L. Ouvrard (Eds.), *Variation linguistique et enseignement des langues : Le cas des langues moins enseignées.*

Presses de l'Inalco. Retrieved from http://books.openedition.org/pressesinalco/40104

Beauregard, F., & Trépanier, N. (2010). Le concept d'intégration scolaire... mais où donc se situe l'inclusion ? In N. Trépanier & M. Paré (Eds.), *Des modèles de service pour favoriser l'intégration scolaire* (pp. 31–56). Presses de l'Université du Québec.

Bendix-Olsen, K., & Bonderup, M. (2022). *Constructions of disability, involvement and participation in social case-management work with children*. 1. Abstract from 2nd International Childlife Conference. Retrieved from https://www.ucviden.dk/ws/portalfiles/portal/162731265/Program_Childlife.pdf, https://en.uit.no/om/strategi2030

Bijeljac-Babic, R. (1985). *L'utilisation des langues maternelles et nationales en tant qu'instrument d'enseignement, d'alphabétisation et de culture : expériences dans des pays en développement d'Afrique et d'Asie.* UNESCO.

Boukous, A. (2005). L'amazighe dans l'éducation : Enjeux d'une réforme. In M. Rispail (Ed.), *Les langues maternelles : Contacts, variations et enseignement* (pp. 249–259). L'Harmattan.

Boukous, A. (2007). L'enseignement de l'amazighe (berbère) au Maroc : aspects sociolinguistiques. *Revue de l'Université de Moncton*, 81–89. Retrieved from https://www.erudit.org/fr/revues/rum/2007-rum2172/017709ar.pdf

CARITAS Egypt. (n.d.). http://www.caritasegypt.com/

Carroll, J. (2022, December 6). *7 Universal design for learning examples and strategies for the classroom.* Texthelp. Retrieved from https://www.texthelp.com/resources/blog/7-ways-to-introduce-udl-into-your-classroom/

Centre for Studies on Inclusive Education. (2020). *The UNESCO Salamanca Statement.* Retrieved from http://www.csie.org.uk/inclusion/unesco-salamanca.shtml#:~:text=In%20June%201994%20representatives%20of,inclusion%20to%20be%20the%20norm

Chtatou, M. (2009). La diversité culturelle et linguistique au Maroc. *Asinag, 2*, 149–161. https://www.ircam.ma/sites/default/files/doc/asinag-2/mohamed-chtatou-la-diversite-culturelle-et-linguistique-au-maroc-pour-un-multiculturalisme-dynamique.pdf

Chtatou, M. (2015). A Moroccan success story tainted with some shortcomings. Background paper prepared for the *Education for All, Global Monitoring Report 2015, Education for All 2000–2015*, 1–15. UNESCO. Retrieved from https://unesdoc.unesco.org/ark:/48223/pf0000232463

Chtatou, M. (2019). *The expulsion of Sephardic Jews from Spain in 1492 and their relocation and success in Morocco.* Researchgate. Retrieved from https://www.researchgate.net/publication/335652520_The_Expulsion_of_Sephardic_Jews_from_Spain_in_1492_and_their_Relocation_and_Success_in_Morocco

Chtatou, M. (2022, April 8). *Promouvoir, protéger et revitaliser la langue amazighe.* Le Monde Amazigh. Retrieved from https://amadalamazigh.press.ma/fr/promouvoir-proteger-et-revitaliser-la-langue-amazighe/

Chtatou, M. (2023). The Moroccan-Israeli geostrategic relationship: From a harmonious past to a promising future. *Orbis, 67*(2), 228–246. Retrieved from https://www.sciencedirect.com/science/article/abs/pii/S0030438723000066

Cologon, K., & Lassig, C. (2019). Universal approaches to curriculum, pedagogy and assessment. In L. Graham (Ed.), *Inclusive education for the 21st century (chapter 8)* (1st ed.). Routledge.

Council of Europe. (2010). *Council of Europe Charter on Education for Democratic Citizenship and Human Rights Education Recommendation CM/Rec (2010)7 adopted by the Committee of Ministers of the Council of Europe on 11 May 2010 and explanatory memorandum.* Council of Europe Publishing. Retrieved from https://rm.coe.int/16803034e3

Council of Europe, OSCE/ODIHR, UNESCO, OHCHR. (2009). *Human rights education in the school systems of Europe, Central Asia and North America: A compendium of good practice.* OSCE Office for Democratic Institutions and Human Rights (ODIHR). OHCHR. Retrieved from https://www.ohchr.org/sites/default/files/Documents/Publications/CompendiumHRE.pdf

Dadush, U. (2018). Youth unemployment in the Middle East & North Africa, and the Moroccan case. *OCP Policy Center, 18/12*, 1–28. Retrieved from https://www.policycenter.ma/sites/default/files/OCPPC-PP-18-12.pdf

Delors, J., et al. (1998). *Learning: the treasure within; report to UNESCO of the International Commission on Education for the Twenty-first Century (pocketbook edition).* International Commission on Education for the Twenty-first Century. UNESCO. Retrieved from https://unesdoc.unesco.org/ark:/48223/pf0000110780

Dörnyei, Z., & Hadfield, J. (2013). *Motivating learning.* Pearson.

Egypt, Arab Republic of. (2020). *Law on the Rights of Persons with Disabilities, Law No. 10 of 2018* (1st ed.). National Council of Women. Retrieved from http://ncw.gov.eg/Images/PdfRelease/Law%20No%2010%20of%202018%20For%20Rights%20o-122020403910677.pdf

El Hamel, C. (2013). *Black Morocco: A history of slavery, race, and Islam* (pp. 162–163). Cambridge University Press.

ElSafty, M. (2005). Gender inequalities in the Arab world: Religion, law, or culture? *Jura Gentium.* Retrieved from https://www.juragentium.org/topics/islam/mw/en/elsafty.htm

Ennaji, M. (2010). Hybridité, langue et migration. Le paradigme Maghreb-Europe. In A. de Toro et al. (Eds.), *Repenser le Maghreb et l'Europe. Hybridations-Métissages-Diasporisations* (pp. 91–104). L'Harmattan.

Faas, D., et al. (2014). Intercultural education in Europe: Policies, practices and trends. *British Educational Research Journal, 40*(2), 300–318. Retrieved from http://www.jstor.org/stable/24464053

Faruki, K. A. (1974). The National Covenant of Lebanon: Its genesis. *Pakistan Horizon, 27*(3), 19–31. Retrieved from http://www.jstor.org/stable/41403854

Frayha, N. (2003). Education et cohésion sociale au Liban. *Perspectives : revue trimestrielle d'éducation comparée, XXXIII, 1*, 77–88. Retrieved from https://unesdoc.unesco.org/ark:/48223/pf0000130146_fre

Goals (SDGs). (n.d.). Smart Learning Institute of Beijing Normal University. Retrieved from http://www.alecso.org/publications/SLIBNU-ALECSO_BOOK.pdf

Guérin, E. (2013). La validité de la notion de « handicap linguistique » en question. *Le français aujourd'hui, 183*(4), 91–104. Retrieved from https://www.cairn.info/revue-le-francais-aujourd-hui-2013-4-page-91.htm

Halabi, F. (2023). *Mas'alat al-ʿiaqa fi al-ʿâlem al-ʿarabî (La question du handicap dans le monde arabe : une carte de route vers l'avenir)*. Dâr Sâ'ir ash-Sharq.

Institut Royal de la Culture Amazighe –IRCAM. (2023). Retrieved from https://www.google.com/search?q=Institut+Royal+de+la+Culture+Amazighe+%E2%80%93IRCAM&oq=Institut+Royal+de+la+Culture+Amazighe+%E2%80%9 3IRCAM&aqs=chrome..69i57j0i22i30j69i65l3.6243j0j7&sourceid=chrome &ie=UTF-8

Jaray-Benn, C. (2019). Empathy as a source of motivation in language learning and language teaching. *Hltmag, 21*(1) Retrieved from https://www.hltmag.co.uk/feb19/empathy-as-a-source-of-motivation

Kamrava, M., Nonneman, G., Nosova, A., & Valeri, M. (2016). *Ruling families and business elites in the Gulf monarchies: Ever closer?* Chatham House. Retrieved from https://www.chathamhouse.org/sites/default/files/publications/research/2016-11-03-ruling-families-business-gulf-kamrava-nonneman-nosova-valeri.pdf

Kaplan, A. M., & Haenlein, M. (2016). Higher education and the digital revolution: About MOOCs, SPOCs, social media, and the Cookie Monster. *Business Horizons, 59*(4), 441–450.

Kassir, S. (2004). *Considérations sur le malheur arabe* (p. 46). Sindbad.

Khochen-Bagshaw, M. (2022). *Promoting the inclusion of children and young people with disabilities in education in the Arab region: An analysis of existing developments, challenges and opportunities.* UNESCO Office Beirut, Regional Office for Education in the Arab States. Retrieved from https://unesdoc.unesco.org/ark:/48223/pf0000383509

Khouri, R. G. (2019). *Poverty and inequalities continue to plague much of the Arab region*. IEMed Mediterranean Yearbook 2019. Retrieved from https://www.iemed.org/publication/poverty-and-inequalities-continue-to-plague-much-of-the-arab-region/

Lebanese Const., art. 9. (n.d.). Retrieved from http://www.presidency.gov.lb/English/LebaneseSystem/Documents/Lebanese%20Constitution.pdf

Lebanese Republic, Ministry of Education and Higher Education. (1993, March 15). *Charte nationale pour l'education au vivre ensemble au liban : Dans le cadre de la citoyenneté inclusive de la diversité*. Retrieved from https://adyan-foundation.org/wp-content/uploads/2019/08/Charte-Nationale-pour-lEducation-au-Vivre-Ensemble-FR.pdf

Leicht, A. et al. (2018). From Agenda 21 to Target 4.7: The development of education for sustainable development. *Issues and trends in Education for Sustainable Development*, 25–38. Retrieved from https://unesdoc.unesco.org/ark:/48223/pf0000261801

Lévi-Strauss, C. (1987). *Race et histoire* (pp. 47–49). Denoël.

Liu, D., Jemni, M., Huang, R.; Wang, Y., Tlili, A. & Sharhan, S. (2021). An Overview of Education Development in the Arab Region: Insights and Recommendations towards Sustainable Development Goals (SDGs).

Moroccan Const., preamble. (2011). Retrieved from https://www.constituteproject.org/constitution/Morocco_2011.pdf

Opertti, R. (2017). 15 clues to support the Education 2030 Agenda. Current and critical issues in the curriculum 14. UNESCO-IBE. Retrieved from https://unesdoc.unesco.org/ark:/48223/pf0000259069

Point Le/AFP. (2017). *En Egypte, le parcours du combattant pour les handicapés mentaux*. Le Point/AFP. Retrieved from https://www.lepoint.fr/monde/en-egypte-le-parcours-du-combattant-pour-les-handicapes-mentaux-01-08-2017-2147292_24.php#11

Quattrini, S. (2023). *Revitalizing Tamazight: The role of language education policies in Morocco*. Minority Rights Group. Retrieved from https://minorityrights.org/2023/02/21/revitalizing-tamazight-the-role-of-language-education-policies-in-morocco/

Reliefweb. (2005). *The Arab Human Development Report 2004 (AHDR2004)*. Retrieved from https://reliefweb.int/report/world/arab-human-development-report-2004?gclid=CjwKCAjw6IiiBhAOEiwALNqncYWOGODnT9KEZ7-IFjIkdUtIrwoabUL8jVdW9lgt22jinrmZcxbrDBoCfacQAvD_BwE

Rodriguez, E. (2022). *Language Learning and Empathy*. [Master's thesis, Bethel University], Spark Repository. Retrieved from https://spark.bethel.edu/etd/783

Sader, S. (2023, January 5). *Un premier manuel en langue arabe sur le handicap au Liban*. L'Orient-Le Jour. Retrieved from https://www.lorientlejour.com/

article/1323531/un-premier-manuel-en-langue-arabe-sur-le-handicap-au-liban.html

Salamé, G. (1996). *Appels d'empire : ingérences et résistances à l'âge de la mondialisation* (pp. 98–105). Fayard.

Schreiber, J.-R., & Siege, H. (2016). *Curriculum framework: Education for sustainable development*. Engagement Global. Retrieved from https://www.globaleslernen.de/sites/default/files/files/link-elements/curriculum_framework_education_for_sustainable_development_barrierefrei.pdf

Slee, R. (2013). Meeting some challenges of inclusive education in an age of exclusion. *Asian Journal of Inclusive Education, 1*(2), 3–17. Retrieved from https://ajiebd.net/wp-content/uploads/2016/08/roger_slee.pdf

Sundberg, M. L., & Partington, J. W. (2010). *Teaching language to children with autism or other developmental disabilities perfect paperback*. AVB Press.

Talbot, L. (2011). Prendre en compte la diversité des élèves. *Les Dossiers des Sciences de l'Education, 26*, 7–12. Retrieved from http://journals.openedition.org/dse/1058

Thornberry, P., & Gibbons, D. (1966). Education and minority rights: A short survey of international standards. *International Journal on Minority and Group Rights, 4*(2), 115–152. Retrieved from http://www.jstor.org/stable/24674532

U.S. Department of Education. (2008). *Parents/prepare my child for school*. Improving Basic Programs. Operated by Local Educational Agencies (Title I, Part A). Retrieved from https://www2.ed.gov/programs/titleiparta/index.html

UNESCO. (1994). *World Conference on Special Needs Education: Access and Quality, Salamanca, Spain*. Retrieved from https://unesdoc.unesco.org/ark:/48223/pf0000098427

UNESCO. (1996). *Education: The treasure within, report of the International Commission on Education for the Twenty-first Century*. UNESCO.

UNESCO. (2001 November 2). UNESCO Declaration on Cultural Diversity. UNESCO. Retrieved from https://en.unesco.org/about-us/legal-affairs/unesco-universal-declaration-cultural-diversity

UNESCO. (2005). *Convention on the protection and promotion of the diversity of cultural expressions*. UNESCO. Retrieved from https://en.unesco.org/creativity/sites/creativity/files/passeport-convention2005-web2.pdf

UNESCO. (2009). *Policy guidelines on inclusion in education, ED.2009/WS/31*. UNESCO. https://unesdoc.unesco.org/ark:/48223/pf0000177849

UNESCO. (2019). *International Forum on Inclusion and Equity in Education, Cali, Colombia, 2019*. UNESCO. Retrieved from https://unesdoc.unesco.org/ark:/48223/pf0000370910

UNESCO. (2023). *Inclusion in education*. UNESCO. Retrieved from https://www.unesco.org/en/inclusion-education

UNESCO, Institut de statistique de l'UNESCO (UIN, 2017). *Données pour les objectifs de développement durable.* UNESCO. Retrieved from: https://unstats. un.org/sdgs/files/report/2017/TheSustainableDevelopmentGoals Report2017_French.pdf

UNESCO -Institute for Statistics (UIS) & United Nations Children's Fund. (2011). *Global initiative on out-of-school children: UNICEF and the UNESCO Institute for Statistics.* UNESCO. Retrieved from https://unesdoc.unesco. org/ark:/48223/pf0000217147

UNICEF & CSEFRS. (2015). *Tous à l'école, Moyen-Orient et Afrique du nord, Initiative mondiale en faveur des enfants non scolarisés. Résumé du rapport national sur les enfants non scolarisés.* UNICEF. Retrieved from: https://www. unicef.org/mena/media/6576/file/Morocco%20Country%20Report%20 on%20OOSC_FR.pdf%20.pdf

United Nations, December 10, (1948). *Universal Declaration of Human Rights.* UN. Retrieved from https://www.un.org/en/about-us/universal-declaration-of-human-rights

United Nations Educational, Scientific and Cultural Organization (UNESCO. (2014). *UNESCO roadmap for implementing the global action programme on education for sustainable development.* UNESCO. Retrieved from https://unesdoc.unesco.org/ark:/48223/pf0000230514

Vienneau, R. (2002). Pédagogie de l'inclusion : fondements, définitions, défis et perspectives. *Éducation et francophonie, 30(2),* 257–286. Retrieved from https://www.erudit.org/fr/revues/ef/2002-v30-n2-ef06208/1079534ar/

Whitaker, B. (2009). *What's really wrong with the Middle East.* Saqi Books.

Yahiaoui, D., & Al Ariss, A. (2017). Diversity in the Arab world: Challenges and opportunities. In M. F. Özbilgin & J.-F. Chanlat (Eds.), *Management and diversity, Vol. 3: International perspectives on equality, diversity and inclusion* (pp. 249–260). Emerald Publishing Limited. https://doi.org/10.1108/S2051-233320160000003010

CHAPTER 15

Conclusion: The Way Forward

Hassan Abouabdelkader and Barry Tomalin

After completing the works selected for the purpose of this book, we thought it would be useful for any reader to get a glimpse of their content, not only to stir their attention to browsing the contents, but also to check the extent to which it has achieved its objectives.

The works included in this volume have honoured their promise to investigate the impact of diversity education in the MENA region. They illustrate the importance of raising the stakes of language education to issues that used to be mostly used by politicians and decision makers and hardly approachable by the rest of the people, especially in developing countries.

These works have offered us a new vision of language learning and teaching pedagogy that addresses the integrity and wellbeing of learners, the aspirations of educational policy makers and the work of practitioners of the English and other languages teaching profession. All the chapters of the book are witness to pragmatic achievements offering committed

---

H. Abouabdelkader (✉)
Ecole Nationales Supérieure d'Arts et Métiers, Moulay Ismail University, Meknes, Morocco

B. Tomalin
Glasgow Caledonian University London, London, UK

© The Author(s), under exclusive license to Springer Nature Switzerland AG 2023
H. Abouabdelkader, B. Tomalin (eds.), *Diversity Education in the MENA Region*, https://doi.org/10.1007/978-3-031-42693-3_15

visions of the future of language learning and education in general. With no exception, they all have unbiasedly described the realities of diversity, equity, and inclusion as experienced in their respective countries.

It is argued in this book that, in addition to the implementation of diversity education policy in the MENA countries, the most effective impact comes from the teachers' pedagogical practices and the teaching materials in use in and outside the classroom. Similarly, the writers of the work presented in this volume stress the importance of understanding the social and cultural background of learners and providing them with appropriate opportunities in the classroom or lecture hall. They also indicate that the development of this area is oscillating between hope and fear on the grounds of lacking evidence-based policies that give the learners their due.

In the Introduction of the book, Hassan Abouabdelkader illustrates the difficulty of defining the concepts alone without referencing. He identifies the issues of primary importance to the promotion of language education in the region, arguing that the concepts of diversity, equity and inclusion have come to education through the window of language learning to repair the disequilibrium inherited from older teaching pedagogical practices. This chapter debates the importance of implementing diversity principles by providing opportunities for learners to display their potential and get in tune with the demands of the twenty-first century. According to many of the authors these accommodations are highly important requirements in syllabus and teaching materials design, pedagogical practices, and assessment.

Explanations and tangible illustrations of these concepts are provided by Barry Tomalin in the second chapter of the book, explaining diversity, equity, and inclusion and their function in teaching. He contends that students from the MENA region and indeed from around the world may feel unable to express themselves freely due to constraints imposed by difficulties in adapting to the new learning environment and the need for educational authorities, materials producers, and teachers to recognise and take into account the cultural and diversity differences of students in the classroom, which is demonstrated by several contributors.

Chapter 3 seeks to demonstrate through a case study how students' perceptions of reading comprehension (RC) modules reflect the importance of aligning language teaching curricula with the needs of learners. Rich pedagogical issues are raised in Chap. 3 concerning how to make reading comprehension a viable part of a language teaching course. By investigating student representation, engagement, and the expression of the reading comprehension modules, this chapter provides the findings of a case study related to pertinent questions which address the extent to which the modules are accessible, doable, and usable by all students. Most of the dimensions raised by the author have deep implications for learning. These analyses indicate that RC material and pedagogy design needs to take into consideration their value and relevance for the learners and their pertinence to their culture and their understanding. The chapter demonstrates the influence of higher education curricula orientations, teaching materials and pedagogies on students' learning outcomes. In this chapter by Soufiane Abouabdelkader the guidelines and principles of the Universal Design for Learning (UDL) paradigm provide some appropriate pedagogical practices which address motivational drive and engagement, and finally, include accommodations which appeal to all learners.

In a similar vein, the chapters and case studies which follow stress that re-evaluating language policies is indispensable for creating an inclusive educational environment in the MENA countries and that adopting language policies that consider the linguistic diversity of students and recognise the importance of both local and global languages positively impacts learners' development and growth.

Within the tradition of illustrative evidence on the practices that succinctly apply to diversity education, Deborah Swallow in Chap. 4 argues that the provision of solutions to students is not automatic and that teachers have an important role to play in ensuring diversity and inclusion of students from different backgrounds studying in the MENA region. This chapter portrays the repercussions of Incorporating diversity principles in the region as a means of empowering students who migrate to international universities around the world.

In a global historical review of the teaching of English in the MENA region within a globalised world, Sagrario et al. stress the value of integrating relevant cultural content in the curricula. They urge the policy makers to address the resource gap as a determinant factor in the promotion of language learning by investing in infrastructure and professional development to ensure equitable opportunities that leave "no one behind".

As illustrated in several case studies, Fawziya Al Zadjali and Sharita Viola Furtado in Chap. 7 describe the state of diversity in Oman, suggesting that inclusive language policies are aware of the importance of enhancing students' opportunities for academic success and preparing them for a globally interconnected world. By rethinking language as a medium of instruction, these studies argue that institutions' acknowledgement and development of intercultural understanding and a sense of inclusion and equity contribute to the promotion of quality education, equality, and inclusion.

In short, the issues covered in this book offer insights into the state of diversity and inclusion in higher education as illustrated in the teaching approaches and the curricular orientations in several countries of the region. Theoretically, the existing research in the area corroborates the findings of the present book. As reported by (Bray and Hajar, 2023), the values and behaviours in this region vary significantly both interculturally and philosophically, and the learning of languages places additional demands on teachers, learners, and material writers in terms of diversity management, equity and inclusion.

New realities, often unnoticed in the field of language education, have been depicted and succinctly analysed in this volume. As Anat Stavans in Chap. 8 attests, Israel has been a multilingual, multicultural, and multi-ethnic country since its foundation with Hebrew, Arabic and English as its dominant languages, as well as other languages being taught. Israel is a plurilingual country in which diversity is very important given the different communities that live there. Anat Stavans divides the organisation of the management of linguistic diversity into three tiers: the first tier, macro level language policies and language education policies; the second tier, mezzo level schools and institutes including tertiary education and the third tier, micro level teachers and instructors in the lecture hall and the classroom. She goes on to reflect on how different communities in the country manage diversity in language education and also focuses on how the Arabic speaking community manages the language and its teaching at the local level (community and family), the glocal level (both global and local for the large Arabic speaking minority in Israel) and the global level (internationally with special regard to the Arabic speaking world). A key feature in managing diversity and inclusion in the T&L (Teaching and Learning) process is the use of mediation in the language class and in Chap. 11 Hussein AlAhmad and Elias Kukali apply the principle to teaching in Palestine tertiary education in the state of Israel, where English is frequently not just the language taught but also the language of delivery of a number of courses. Having explained the mediation principle and how it operates they emphasise the importance of classroom mediation in reducing student's personal barriers and fostering their commitment and engagement with the teaching environment and the language they are studying. They argue that the level of classroom mediation has a positive impact on students' learning experience—and results. They also stress how students educated in an environment of different gender orientation and other social differences can increase motivation and engagement with tertiary education through the process of classroom mediation.

In Chap. 12, Wafaa Taleb also discusses gender inequality, focusing on the changes in Algerian education since 1962. His survey shows that the number of female teachers has increased immensely in schools and in tertiary education and that women students are more likely to graduate than male students. In fact, 60% of Algerian university students are female. He also notes that, according to statistics, girls are much more likely to opt for foreign language study than boys and see it as a real asset to their future professions. In tracing the gender revolution in Algerian education Taleb shows how gender inequality can almost be eliminated in any MENA region country.

Chapters 9 and 13 focus on the relations between language students and teachers and focus on how diversity, equity and inclusion can improve teaching and ensure commitment and engagement by the students. In Chap. 9, Soufiane Abouabdelkader and Mouhssine Ayouri return to Morocco to explore how teachers and students respond to diversity in higher education.

They make the point that although the National Charter makes clear how education policy has changed to respond to diversity, equity and inclusion needs in tertiary education there is still a requirement for language teaching faculties in educational institutions to support teachers and students in recognising diversity and implementing it in the language learning process to achieve better student engagement with the result of greater success in their studies. They also explore the influence of the adoption of hybrid-education strategies, combining both classroom and online learning activities, particularly during the Pandemic phase, and discuss the influence of diversity management on online teaching and learning. They point out how the introduction of information technology and online learning strategies can help bridge the gap between students from richer and poorer backgrounds although some difficulties, such as access to new and updated computers or access to e-libraries, remain. However, they conclude that from the point of view of both staff and students the use of online resources can enhance student learning skills and the professional development of teachers.

In Chap. 13, the point about improving better relations between teachers and students through the understanding and implementation of diversity practices is pushed home by Ozlem Yuges in her case study of students in Turkiye and Turkish students studying abroad. Turkiye is a country which has accepted very large numbers of immigrants from neighbouring states and a has large number of Turkish students who go to study abroad. She emphasises the importance of diversity in sustaining commitment and engagement in the learning process and shows that the issues arise not at the level of educational policy but at the level of educational practice. Teachers tend to teach the system of grammar, vocabulary and pronunciation but often fail or do not have classroom time to adapt what they have taught to the students' personal backgrounds and interests. She cites the criticisms of students abroad complaining about being unable to understand their teachers because they talk too fast or the content is too complicated and they can easily get discouraged and disengaged from the learning process. Ozlem Yuges goes on to suggest teaching techniques where students can work in small groups to exchange information about their own lives and interests and activities using the language they have learned, which they can then share with the whole class. For her the key is better teacher training and classroom management encouraging a feeling of inclusion and equity on the part of the students in their efforts to learn the language and succeed in their studies. Above all, she argues, teaching teachers active listening skills so that they learn to really listen to their students and allow them to display not just their linguistic knowledge but also their emotions and how they feel about the topic they are presenting or discussing.

Finally, Chaps. 10 and 14 address the big picture.

In Chap. 10 Chahra Beloufa discusses inclusive pedagogy and asks about the diversity of the virtual space and Mohamed Chtatou finishes off by looking at how to maximise diversity education in the MENA region as it moves forward. For Chahra Beloufa the adoption of e-learning in tertiary education is an essential tool in promoting intercultural knowledge and exchange of ideas and experiences between students and between teachers and learners. Basing her case study on Saudi-Arabia where Prince Mohammed bin Salman has declared the development of e-learning in education as core to the advance of his national digital education project for 2030, she stresses the value of e-learning as a way of improving the exchange of cultural experiences between students as a vital way to increase student engagement and to enhance global understanding, tolerance, and appreciation of others.

In Chap. 14, Mohamed Chtatou provides a comprehensive stance on diversity education in the MENA region. He endorses the recommendations provided in all the chapters and stresses the importance of recognising cultural diversity and commends the UNESCO Convention on the Protection and Promotion of the Diversity of Cultural Expressions which took place in Paris in 2005. However, in identifying the challenges many MENA societies face in recognising internal cultural diversity, he argues that recognising and accepting cultural diversity within national borders as well as externally is a vital component of national security and that the development of diversity, equity and inclusion is an essential key to achieving this, educationally and politically.

To conclude this final overview, we would like to thank our contributors immensely for sharing their knowledge, their experience, and their research with us and apologise for any gaps in the coverage, which we hope to fill in future editions. We would like to offer our special thanks to Mohammad Tamimy of Shiraz University in Iran for writing the Forward to the book. We must never forget that we are one species on one planet with a variety of ways of expressing ourselves according to our background and experience. We need to pay attention to this as a way of assuring our continuance in a globalising society. Encouraging diversity, equity, and inclusion in the language learning classroom in education is a key (some would say *the* key) to doing so successfully.

Reference

Bray, M., & Hajar, A. (2023). *Shadow education in the Middle East: Private supplementary tutoring and its policy implications* (p. 122). Taylor & Francis.

Index[1]

A
Active learners, 236
Algeria, 5, 101, 104, 257–286, 315
Amazigh/Berber languages, 105, 319, 321, 347, 349
Anti-racism, 14
Arab Open University (AOU), 203–226
Arabic, 18, 19, 104, 105, 107, 109, 111, 115, 117, 122, 128, 131, 133, 134, 142, 150–154, 156, 157, 159, 160, 162, 164–175, 225, 299, 319, 319n23, 320, 334, 345–348, 366
Arab World, 105, 135n2, 165, 207, 314, 316, 319–321, 328, 331, 332, 334, 335, 350
Assessment, 3, 5, 6, 8, 17–20, 22, 31, 32, 37, 39, 42, 43, 53, 54, 78, 80, 81, 85, 86, 92–94, 111, 115, 123, 124, 167, 169, 180, 182, 183, 194, 196, 198, 214, 226, 282, 303, 353, 354, 364
Assessment purposes, 182, 194–196
Attitude, 37, 38, 90, 108, 115, 124–126, 137, 142, 181, 197, 217–218, 231, 236, 261, 267, 273, 274, 280, 282–283, 303–306, 317, 324, 328, 332, 346
Autochthonous Arabic-speaking population, 151

B
Baccalauréat, 113, 261–264, 267, 280
Barriers to schooling, 326–328
Behavioural dimension, 233, 243, 245, 249, 250
Beliefs and customs, 16, 70
Blended learning, 207, 208, 215
Burnout, 66, 67

---

[1] Note: Page numbers followed by 'n' refer to notes.

C

Classroom mediation, 231–251, 366, 367
Classroom mediation dynamics, 232–234, 240, 242, 249, 250
Cognitive dimension, 233, 235, 243, 246, 247, 250
Community involvement, 182, 191–194, 246, 250
Comparing cultures, 218
Compulsory education, 160, 259, 285
Content accessibility, 182, 186–189
Context and purpose of the English language use, 170
Cooperative learning, vii, viii, 17, 21, 50, 212, 215
Cooperative Project-Based Learning (CPBL), 110
Cultural background, 14, 22, 63, 80, 93, 123, 203, 208–212, 214, 215, 220, 223, 224, 231, 294, 303, 352, 364
Cultural behaviour, 64
Cultural boundaries, 208
Cultural differences, 131–133, 198, 205, 210, 215, 218, 222, 225, 330
Culturally based beliefs, 14
Culturally responsive pedagogy, vi, vii, 208–211, 215
Cultural understanding, 7, 48, 81, 92, 93, 180, 182, 191–194, 197, 198, 220
Culture shock, 66–73

D

Decolonising the curriculum, 17–22
Diglossia, 165, 166
Disabilities in the Arab World, 332, 334
Discrimination, 1, 14, 15, 29, 92, 196, 259, 273, 320–322, 332
Disparities, 2, 9, 38, 84, 91, 92, 106, 109, 112, 115, 180, 189, 193, 196, 216, 242, 251, 265, 267, 269–277, 281, 285, 321
Distance, 65, 89, 318, 328, 331n50
Diversity, v, 1, 14, 48, 63–73, 79, 100, 121–143, 149, 180, 203, 293–310, 314, 364
Diversity and inclusion, vi, viii, 8, 13–24, 63, 64, 73, 84, 205–210, 212, 214, 217, 223, 299, 310, 365, 366
Diversity education, vi–viii, 1–9, 29, 37, 77–94, 179–198, 300, 302, 304, 313–356, 363–365, 368, 369
Diversity education reforms, 81–83
Diversity, equity, and inclusion (DEI), 2, 10, 14, 31–32, 77, 86, 182–184, 186, 187, 191, 193, 194, 196–198, 364, 369
Diversity in the Arab World, 319–322
Dropout, 87, 264–266, 285

E

Educational media agenda, 236
Education quality assurance, 81
Education system, v, vi, 7, 103, 108, 112, 114, 153, 155, 156, 160, 165, 169, 206, 231–251, 258–264, 294, 299, 300, 305, 306, 308, 326, 329, 351
Efficacy, 37, 77, 80
E-learning in Moroccan higher education, 89
eLearning Moodle, 247, 250
Emotional barriers, 232
English language teacher trainees, 169–175
ENGLISH or €NG£I$H?, 157–160
Enrolment, 258, 261, 265, 276–279, 285, 308, 315, 316, 334, 342

Equitable pedagogy, viii, 182, 189–191, 198
Ethnocentrism, 68, 329
Ethnolinguistic vitality, 169, 171
Ethnorelativism, 68
Experiential learning, 352

F
Feminization, 269, 285
Foreign language learning, 63, 280, 283, 286
Framing education, 236

G
Gender, 2, 8, 14, 15, 23, 24, 80, 83, 91, 107, 116, 121, 123, 126, 143, 154, 199, 216, 231, 244, 249, 251, 257–286, 302, 306, 315, 317, 318, 322–324, 335, 353, 367
Gender identity, 203
Geopolitical, 159, 164, 173, 175
Goal-directed behaviour, 251

H
Hebrew, 150–154, 156, 157, 159, 161–165, 167–175, 345, 366
Heritage, 27, 102, 103, 110, 115–117, 150, 152–156, 223, 319, 340
Heterogeneous Teaching and Learning (T&L) environment, 232

I
Identity, vii, 1, 20, 82, 100, 104–106, 111, 115, 117, 126, 128, 142, 150, 152, 154, 165, 166, 169, 172, 175, 203, 212, 215, 273, 294, 300–304, 319, 320, 330, 338, 344, 355
Implementation of a multilingual LEP, 169–175
Inclusion, v, 2, 4, 5, 7, 9, 14–17, 31, 32, 80, 85, 86, 88, 89, 91, 125, 132, 136, 138–139, 141–142, 150, 175, 184, 197, 198, 205, 208, 211, 220, 300, 306, 323–325, 334, 337, 366–368
Inclusive education, 84, 104, 108, 305, 322–327, 329, 334, 335
Individual and societal prospects, 149, 175
Individual Dimension, 235
Instrumental Dimension, 235
Interactive Maps, 247, 250
Isolation, 65, 213

J
Jewish immigration, 151
Jewish Moroccan Heritage, 345

L
Language assessment, 85, 92, 93, 111
Language education policy (LEP), 17, 107, 149, 155–157, 164–175, 366
Language education policy (LEP) agency, 169–175
Language in schools, 111, 112, 163–167
Language policy (LP), 5, 7, 18, 81, 100, 107–111, 115, 116, 118, 152, 153, 155, 157–159, 163, 166, 167, 175, 349, 365, 366
Languages at Universities and Colleges, 160–163
Languages of higher education (HE), 8, 77–94, 157–160, 179–198

Languages of Israel, 150–157, 162, 173
Language teachers between "ideal and real," 168–175
Learners' abilities and outcomes, 149, 175
Learning communities, 18, 84, 184, 191, 215
Learning management systems (LMS), 211, 212
Learning outcomes, 2, 4, 6, 8, 37, 38, 53, 78, 80–83, 85, 86, 92–94, 114, 180–182, 189, 194–196, 210, 243, 246, 247, 250, 251, 365
Lebanon, 101, 102, 208, 315, 319, 321, 334, 338–341
Linguistic autobiographies, 173–175
Linguistic diversity, 7, 117, 149, 152, 155, 175, 319, 320, 346–347, 365, 366
Linguistic diversity in education, 149–175
Loneliness, 64, 65, 67

M
Marginalization, 117, 162, 198, 267, 332
Means of engagement, 41, 47–49
Means of expression, 41, 49–52, 54, 92
Media logic, 232, 237, 238
Mediated classroom, 237, 238, 250
Mediated communication, 238
Mediatisation, 232
Mediatisation effects, 238
Medium of instruction, 7, 14, 106, 115, 122, 133, 150, 153, 155, 162, 232, 365–366
Meta-theory, 232, 237
Mezzo level, 149, 157–167, 173, 366

Migrant workers, asylum seekers, and refugees, 151
Minority, 15, 18, 107, 116, 150, 152, 160, 162, 166, 171, 172, 175, 304, 315, 319–321, 319n23, 324, 326, 329, 330, 351, 355, 366
Mixed-gender schooling model, 244–245
Monolingualism, 100
Morocco, 5, 30, 40, 78, 81–84, 100, 101, 104, 111–115, 183, 193, 196, 315, 321, 325, 325n39, 328, 338, 343–349, 367
Mother tongue, 150, 155, 156, 300, 304, 346, 347
Motivation, 4, 28, 37, 80, 83, 110, 136, 142–143, 180, 189, 194, 197, 213, 234, 235, 247, 250, 274, 280, 282–283, 296, 367
Multilingualism, 100, 155, 158, 159, 169, 175, 304
Multilingual self-perception, 169–175
Multilingual support, 212–214

N
National E-Learning Center (NECL), 206–207
Nationalism, 66, 108, 330, 355
National language, 64, 151, 348
National language policy (LP), 149, 152–155, 175

O
Online discussion forums, 208, 211–214
Online education in the Middle East, 205
Online Interactive Polls, 247, 250
Online learning in Saudi Arabia, 206–209

P

Pairwise comparison, 245
Pedagogical dimension, 233, 243, 245, 246, 249, 250
Pedagogical logic, 232, 233, 237
Pedagogy, 1–5, 7, 9, 14, 15, 20–24, 31, 33, 36, 38, 39, 42, 43, 51, 53–55, 78, 80, 81, 84–86, 90, 123, 180, 181, 197, 198, 203–226, 232, 302, 309, 318, 324, 329, 331n50, 348, 349, 363, 365, 368
Prejudice and Discrimination, 189, 191
Primary cycle, 261

R

Reading comprehension (RC), 90, 167, 296, 364, 365
Reflective learners, 236
Representation, 19, 233, 237, 238, 250, 328, 335, 338, 365

S

Salamé, Ghassan, 320
School enrolment, 265, 276–279, 315
Schooling model, 232, 234, 242, 244, 245, 249
School-inherited disparities, 234
Secondary cycle, 261
Second language (L2), 15, 16, 63, 64, 69, 70, 122, 150, 156, 164, 167, 175, 283, 320
Segregated schooling model, 244–245
Social Dimension, 235
Socio-cultural disparities, 242
Special education in Egypt, 341–343
Standardization and proliferation of Hebrew, 151
Start-up Nation, 157–160
Stereotypes, 17, 225, 273, 284, 337
Strategic Vision, 112, 114
Student engagement understanding, 369
Subjective English language assessment (CANDO), 170
Sunni Islam, 321

T

Teacher training, vii, 5, 15, 17, 18, 22, 23, 109, 114, 163, 165, 168, 301–307, 309, 348, 368
Teaching and Learning (T&L) inherited barriers, 234
Teaching and Learning (T&L) mechanisms, 250
Teaching materials, 7, 15, 17–19, 21, 23, 49, 86, 114, 131, 167, 295, 303, 306, 309, 364, 365
Tertiary education, 13, 64, 299, 300, 305, 366–368
3 plus policy, 155
Tools for Multimedia, 212
Transdisciplinary education, 182, 186–189
Trilingualism, 174

V

Virtual field trips, 223
Virtual Lab Solutions, 247, 250
Voyant Tools, 219, 220
Vygotsky's sociocultural theory, 125, 209

W

World Bank, 78, 82, 84, 85

Printed in the United States
by Baker & Taylor Publisher Services